KALEVALA
MYTHOLOGY

FOLKLORE STUDIES IN TRANSLATION
GENERAL EDITOR, DAN BEN-AMOS

KAVLEVALA MYTHOLOGY

Expanded Edition

BY

Juha Y. Pentikäinen

TRANSLATED AND EDITED
BY

Ritva Poom

INDIANA UNIVERSITY PRESS
Bloomington and Indianapolis

The preparation of this volume was made possible in part by a grant from the National Endowment for the Humanities, an independent federal agency. Support for the English-language translation was also obtained from the Finnish Ministry of Education, the Information Centre for Finnish Literature, and the Institute on Western Europe at Columbia University.

This book is a publication of

Indiana University Press
601 North Morton Street
Bloomington, Indiana 47404-3797 USA

http://www.indiana.edu/~iupress

Telephone orders   800-842-6796
Fax orders   812-855-7931
E-mail orders   iuporder@indiana.edu

Translated from *Kalevalan Mytologia*
© 1987 by Gaudeamus
© 1989 by Juha Y. Pentikäinen
Preface and Chapters 11 and 12 © 1999 by Juha Y. Pentikäinen
Translation © 1989, 1999 by Ritva Poom

The paper used in this publication meets the minimum
requirements of American National Standard for Information
Sciences—Permanence of Paper for Printed
Library Materials, ANSI Z39.48-1984.

Manufactured in the United States of America

Library of Congress Cataloging-in-Publication Data

Pentikäinen, Juha.
[Kalevalan mytologia. English]
Kalevala mythology / by Juha Y. Pentikäinen ; translated
and edited by Ritva Poom. — Expanded ed.
p.   cm. — (Folklore studies in translation.)
Includes bibliographical references and index.
ISBN 0-253-33661-9 (cl. : alk. paper). —
0-253-21352-5 (pbk. : alk. paper)
1. Kalevala. 2. Mythology, Finno-Ugrian.
I. Poom, Ritva.   II. Title.   III. Series
PH325.P413   1999
894'.54111—dc21   99-34168

1   2   3   4   5   04   03   02   01   00   99

CONTENTS

FOREWORD

The *Kalevala* has a unique position in world folklore and world literature. Within a relative short period in the modern era it has become the only set of poems from a regional oral tradition, in a language that at the time barely had any writings of its own, that has been incorporated into the world literary canon. Forged into a single epic by Elias Lönnrot (1802–1884), who collected most of the texts, the *Kalevala* has become, first and foremost, a symbol for the nationhood of the Finnish people. Providing a past, either mythological or historical, the *Kalevala* has served as a focus for the formation of the Finnish national identity. For the Finns, who strove to establish their cultural and political independence, the *Kalevala* offered a poetry in a language they could call their own, a set of gods, demigods, or heroes that represented the antiquity of their own nation, and actions that were evocative of the dawn of their nation.

The *Kalevala* began to permeate modern Finnish society with themes, names, signs, and festivals with which people celebrated the traditionality of their newly found and newly formed past. Most specifically the *Kalevala* resonates in Finnish music,[1] art,[2] and drama and literature.[3] Furthermore, the impact of the *Kalevala* has extended beyond the boundaries of Finnish culture. The epic has entered the canon of world literature as a monument to romanticism and the spirit of the Finnish nation. As such it has received the literary treatment reserved for world classics, appearing in numerous translations, multiple editions and adaptations to specialized readership.

Starting with M. A. Castrén's Swedish translation in 1841, the *Kalevala* has appeared continuously in other languages. In addition to major European languages it has also been translated to some major Asian languages such as Chinese and Japanese, over thirty languages in all, among them American, Esperanto, Fulani, and Yiddish.[4] The *Kalevala's* literary impact in America preceded even its translation into English. Shortly after Longfellow published *The Song of Hiawatha* in 1855, Thomas Conrad Porter accused him publicly of plagiarism, arguing that he transferred the *Kalevala* meter and themes to the North American Indians. The literary storm that ensued made the American reading public aware of the epic even before a single line of it appeared in English.[5] Not until 1868 did John Addison Porter publish *Selections from the Kalevala*, translated from the German, and in 1884 Lafcadio Hearn published extracts based on a French translation of the *Kalevala*. The first complete translation was made by John Martin Crawford and published in 1888, the year the American Folklore Society was founded. However, the translation that introduced most of the English reading public to the *Kalevala* appeared in 1907 and was made by William Forsell Kirby. It was to be printed in ten more editions, the latest of which was published in 1985 as part of the hundred and fiftieth anniversary of the epic. Francis Peabody Magoun, Jr., published prose translations of the *Kalevala* and *The Old Kalevala* in 1963 and 1969 respectively, and the most recent poetic translations have been made by Eino Friberg in 1988 and by Keith Bosley in 1989.[6]

In the light of such a prolonged and persistent interest in the *Kalevala* the paucity of English scholarly publications on the epic is surprising. Aside from the most recent celebratory essays in connection with the hundred and fiftieth anniversary of the *Kalevala*,[7] there are in English only a handful of *Kalevala* studies. Among them are general surveys, designed primarily for the foreign reader,[8] or occasionally studies of specific topics such as metrics,[9] formula analysis,[10] performance,[11] and comparative thematics.[12] Missing are examples of the rigorous methodological examinations and reexaminations of the *Kalevala*, its significance and its position in Finnish folklore, literature, language, and culture. While for the non-Finnish reader the *Kalevala* represents "the Finnish national epic," the Finnish folklorists themselves have relentlessly questioned each of the tenets that this epithet manifests, challenging both the national and the generic designations of the *Kalevala*.

Only glimpses into this scholarly tradition are available in English—both translations, one analytical, the other poetic. In his study of Väinämöinen, the central figure in the *Kalevala*, Martti Haavio proposes to view him as a historical figure about whom legends were told. At the historical core he was a sage, a poet, and a shaman. He was the Finnish archetypal "man of words," "master of poetry," and "eternal sage," rather than a forceful chief. In Väinämöinen of the ancient poets join qualities of poetry and spirituality.[13] These songs attributed to and about Väinämöinen have become part of the oral tradition that served as the basis for the composition of the *Kalevala*. The second work is a joint effort by Matti Kuusi, Keith Bosley, and Michael Branch, who published a translation of oral poems that are similar in form and content to those that served Lönnrot in his composition of the Kalevala.[14]

The present volume, a translation of *Kalevalan Mytologia* (1987), is the first comprehensive study of the *Kalevala* that appears in English. Building upon the Finnish illustrious scholarly tradition, Juha Pentikäinen examines the *Kalevala* in analytical self-reflection. In contrast to the Finnish national celebratory attitude toward the *Kalevala*,[15] Finnish folklorists have often approached the epic with a sober scrutiny divorced from romanticism and nationalism. They have sought to uncover the poems that antedated the epic Lönnrot composed, to discover their regional origin, and to discuss their position and function in Finnish peasant society.

In the present study Pentikäinen implicitly and explicitly employs the concept of "mythology" that appears in the book's title in three ways. First, he assumes the *Kalevala* to be the dominant myth that defines modern Finland as independent society; second, he discusses the myth of the epic itself; and third, he analyzes the mythology that is found in the *Kalevala*.

He need not dwell at length upon the position of the *Kalevala* in modern Finnish society; rather, he takes it for granted. All the details that become apparent in Wilson's careful study of *Folklore and Nationalism in Modern Finland* are at the background of Pentikäinen's own research: the incorporation of the *Kalevala* into the school curriculum; its use in the formulation of national ideology and political p—paganda; the celebration of the epic as a national symbol of traditionality, and its subsequent commercialization. Through historical research Pentikäinen examines the cultural construction of the Finnish national ideology and the role of the *Kalevala* has played in it. He points to specific private and public writings of Lönnrot that demonstrate the influence of national-romantic ideology upon him, and his composition of the epic as a direct response to romantic inspiration. Thus Pentikäinen uncovers the circularity of nationalistic reasoning in which a basic instrument for national ideology was in itself fashioned by a similar romantic aspiration.

Elias Lönnrot created the myth of the Finnish national epic under the influence of romantic ideology. He thought that he recovered a lost epic, but as modern Finnish folklorists argue, in all likelihood such an epic never existed, only fragmentary poems did. Moreover, as a result of his own research and that of other scholars, Pentikäinen argues that the singers themselves did not function as performers of epic in their own respective villages. The proliferation of these artists and their singing was in response to Lönnrot's publication of the *Kalevala* and the ensuing increase in demand for them by would-be collectors. Within the context of Finnish folklore studies Pentikäinen addresses two basic issues that concern folklorists and anthropologists everywhere—namely, the effect of their own research upon the cultures they study and the relation of the very process of recording and writing of observed behavior and performed text upon the presentation of culture and folklore.[16] In the case of the *Kalevala* the act of recording transformed the singers and reciters of shamanic poetry, lamentations, and incantations into epic singers and a regional tradition into a heritage of national proportions. The very position of an outsider, an urban collector in a rural district, influenced the formation of the text and its presentation. Lönnrot's wish for a Finnish national epic outweighed the impressions he witnessed and heard.

With other Finnish folklorists Pentikäinen proposes to restore the *Kalevala* to dimensions that conform with its cultural reality, conceiving of it as an epic rooted in shamanic poetry, mythology, cosmology, and symbolism, His comparative analysis demonstrates an affinity between the *Kalevala* symbolic world and Siberian shamanism. This connection relies not just on ancient migrations but also on medieval trade contacts and historical ties that stretched along arctic circles and the silk road.

The transformation of the *Kalevala* from a "national epic" to shamanic poetry enriches its symbolism and establishes for the poem a new position in world literature. Its significance would no longer depend on the romantic national aspirations that propelled it into the attention of literary circles, but would draw upon the cultural symbols and images that are local and universal at one and the same time.

Dan Ben-Amos

Notes

1. John I. Kolehmainen, *Epic of the North: The Story of Finland's Kalevala* (New York Mills, Minnesota: Northwestern Publishing Co., 1973), pp. 263-287; Matti Kuusi and Pertti Anttonen, *Kalevala Lipas* (Helsinki: Suomalaisen Kirjallisuuden Seura, 1985), pp. 204-214. Robert Layton, "The Kalevala and Music," in *Kalevala 1835–1985: The National Epic of Finland* (Helsinki: Helsinki University Library, 1985), pp. 56-59.

2. Kolehmainen, ibid., pp. 288-322; Kuusi and Anttonen, ibid., pp. 215-232; John Boulton Smith, "The *Kalevala* in Finnish Art," in *Kalevala 1835–1985*, pp. 48-55.

3. Kolehmainen, ibid., pp. 218-262; Kuusi and Anttonen, ibid., pp. 189-204; Kai Laitinen, "The *Kalevela* and Finnish Literature," in *Kalevela 1835–1985*, pp. 61-64.

4. Kolehmainen, ibid., pp. 323-350; Kuusi and Anttonen, ibid., pp. 173-184; Rauni Puranen, ed., *The Kalevala Abroad: Translations and Foreign Language Adaptations of the Kalevala* (Helsinki: Suomalaisen Kirjallisuudenseura, 1985).

5. For a history of this literary issue see Ernest J. Moyne, *Hiawatha and Kalevala: A Study of the Relationship between Longfellow's "Indian Edda" and the Finnish Epic*. Folklore Fellows Communications No. 192 (Helsinki: Suomalainen Tiedeakatemia, 1963).

6. Francis Peabody Magoun, Jr., *The Kalevala or Poems of the Kaleva District Compiled by Elias Lönnrot* (Cambridge, Mass.: Harvard University Press, 1963); idem, *The Old Kalevala and Certain Antecedents Complied by Elias Lönnrot* (Cambridge, Mass.: Harvard University Press, 1969); Eino Friberg, trans., *The Kalevala Epic of the Finnish People* (Helsinki: Otava, 1988); Keith Bosley, trans., *The Kalevala: An Epic Poem after Oral Tradition by Elias Lonnrot*. The World's Classics (New York: Oxford University Press, 1989). For information about previous translations into English see George C. Schoolfield, "American Translators of the *Kalevala*," pp. 26-32 in Friberg, op. cit., and in Magoun, 1963, p. 357.

7. M. M. Jocelyne Fernandez-Vest ed., *Kalevala et traditions orales du monde* (Paris: Centre National de la Recherche Scientifique, 1987) [the volume includes articles in English and in French]; Michael Owen Jones, ed. *The World of the Kalevala: Essays in Celebration of the 150 Year Jubilee of the Publication of the Finnish National Epic* (Los Angeles: UCLA Folklore and Mythology Publications, 1987).

8. Bjorn Collinder, "The Kalevala and Its Background," *Arv* 20 (1964):5-112; Kolehmainen *Epic of the North*.

9. Paul Kiparsky, "Metrics and Morphophonemics in the *Kalevala*," in Donald C. Freeman, ed., *Linguistics and Literary Style* (New York: Holt, Rinehart & Winston, 1970), pp. 165-181.

10. Idem, "Oral Poetry: Some Linguistics and Typological Considerations," pp. 94–104 in *Oral Literature and the Formula*, Benjamin A. Stolz and Richard S. Shannon, eds. (Ann Arbor: Center for the Coordination of Ancient and Modern Studies, University of Michigan, 1976).

11. Elsa Enäjärvi-Haavio, "On the Performance of the Finnish Runes," *Folk-Liv* 14–15 (1950–1951): 130–166.

12. Felix J. Oinas, *Studies in Finnic Folklore: Homage to the Kalevala*. Suomalaisen Kirjallisuuden Seuran, No. 387. Indiana University Uralic and Altaic Series, Vol. 147 (1985).

13. Martti Haavio, *Vainamoinen Eternal Sage*. Folklore Fellows Communications, No. 144 (Helsinki: Suomalainen Tiedeakatemia, 1952).

14. *Finnish Folk Poetry: Epic* (Helsinki: Finnish Literature Society, 1977).

15. See William A. Wilson, *Folklore and Nationalism in Modern Finland* (Bloomington: Indiana University Press, 1976).

16. See James Clifford and George E. Marcus, eds. *Writing Culture: The Poetics and Politics of Ethnography* (Berkeley: University of California Press, 1986).

Preface

Why have I, as a scholar of comparative religion and folklore, set out to write *Kalevala Mythology*, a book which first appeared in Finnish in 1987 and 1989, and in English in 1989, and is now being published as a revised paperback edition?

The first reason is my long-held belief, also affirmed by my colleagues, that a book on this topic has long been needed. Since 1972, I have given lectures and seminars about the *Kalevala* and its study at numerous universities abroad, including the University of California at Berkeley, Santa Barbara, and Los Angeles, the Universities of Minnesota (Minneapolis) and Texas (Austin), Indiana University (Bloomington), as well as universities in Rome, Bonn, Edinburgh, London, Grøningen, Cairo, and Budapest. A number of my colleagues and students have urged me to compile my lectures into a book. My warm thanks to them for the initiative which resulted in this work.

The 150th anniversary of the publication of the *Kalevala* in 1985 provided an immense challenge for *Kalevala* scholars. During the festival year I was able to test out, both at home and abroad, the fundamental ideas in my manuscript. As this book evolved, many of my earlier views gained depth or were fundamentally altered. Ideas for further scholarship germinated. As this work proceeded, I became aware of my differences of opinion with regard to numerous aspects of earlier *Kalevala* scholarship.

However, the origins of this book lie deeper than the 1985 anniversary year. As a student of folklore, I was not particularly interested in the *Kalevala*. The prevailing opinion in Finland was that the vocabulary and verses of the *Kalevala* had been thoroughly gleaned, and during the 1960s it was not the favored subject of any field, including literature and folklore.

It was Kalevala Day 1962 which provided the impetus for my folklore interests and proved to be the point of departure for this book as well. As a young student, I had a discussion with the rune singer Marina Takalo of White Sea Karelia, an honorary guest at the Kalevala Festival. Marina viewed this festival as one of the most joyous experiences of her life. As the guest of honor at the Kalevala Festival held at Helsinki University, she had sung "Maailman synty" (The creation of the world). During the course of our discussion, Marina expressed the following thought, which led to our decade of work together: "I'll tell you everything I remember of Karelia. You write down for others what a stranger's life here has been like."

During this time our collaboration became a relationship of reciprocal influence despite the fifty-year difference in our ages and the cultural differences between us, including the fact that Marina could neither read nor write. Thus, for me, Marina Takalo was not a master of the language, informant, tradition bearer, or narrator whose texts I had hungrily been searching for, but rather another individual whose personality, life history, and world view I wished to learn to know. Based upon my field-work experience, I found that the men and women of White Sea

Karelia came to consider themselves rune singers only after the collectors told them they were such.

The rune singers became mythical figures during the period of the *Kalevala* process when the Finnish people, dreaming of their heroic past, were seeking the basis of their national identity in the epic. During this period both Elias Lönnrot, the creator of the epic, and the *Kalevala* itself were mythologized. The *Old Kalevala* was displaced by the *Sole Correct New Kalevala* to such an extent that an edition of the former was not at all available in Finnish during the 1985 celebrations. This was despite the fact that it was actually the publication of the *Old Kalevala* in 1835 which was being celebrated in 1985.

In this book, the influence of Lönnrot as an individual and a scholar on the *Kalevala* will be examined more closely than has previously been done. I will attempt to locate the *Kalevala* along a historical continuum, examining its influence on the history of the Finnish people, an influence which continues to this day.

The title of this book, *Kalevala Mythology*, refers, on the one hand, to Lönnrot's apt perspectives on mythology. On the other hand, it is the approach of comparative religion which is primarily used here in the interpretation of the *Kalevala* and its background. It is hoped that this will open new perspectives for the reader with regard to the epic itself; to Elias Lönnrot, its creator; and to Finnish folklore and its singers, who could neither read nor write. An examination of the *Kalevala* from the perspective of mythology and comparative religion is also relevant in terms of research. It becomes evident that *Kalevala* research in Finland became politicized as part of the nationalistic process. Later, in accordance with the well-known Finnish historical-geographic method, the *Kalevala* came to be viewed as not being genuine folklore and, as a consequence, it was not studied as such. The previous mythological interpretation of folklore also fell under the shadow of Kaarle Krohn's school, although it had already had numerous proponents during the 1700s and 1800s, including Christfrid Ganander, M. A. Castrén, Lönnrot himself, and even Julius Krohn. From this point of view, this book revives the mythological scholarship, overlooked for over a century, and unites it with modern perspectives in the study of comparative religion which is, in itself, an interdisciplinary field.

The *Kalevala* is a cosmogonic epic which relates the elements of Finnish world view: the origins of cosmic order, man, woman, culture, and society. The *Kalevala* is a book of origins and incantations. It describes the Finnish view of the genesis of the world, including its elements and its eschatology. The *Kalevala* is also a book about life and death, offering patterns for life experiences and interpretations. It contains episodes of cult dramas, such as bear rituals and weddings. The essence of the epic lies in the shamanistic world view. Its many heroes are mediators between the reality of this world and the levels of altered consciousness in the upper or nether realms of the universe.

The *Kalevala* is not a homogeneous book. Rather, it contains elements of different historical periods. Comparative study shows parallels with both the Arctic North and Central Asia. Runes with circumpolar or eastern origins appear to be older, generally speaking, than those with apparent contacts to the west. As an entity, however, the *Kalevala* is the result of Lönnrot's own synthesis. This is true even to the extent that the structure and content of the epic were radically altered when Lönnrot's own Weltanschauung changed as a result of new interpretations and of his own life experiences. The *Kalevala* provided not only religious and mythological information, but national symbols as well.

This book is a revised edition of *Kalevala Mythology,* published in 1989, and is similar in numerous respects to *Kalevalan mytologia* (Mythology of the *Kalevala*), published in Finnish in 1987 (Gaudeamus, 2nd ed. 1989). However, it soon became evident that the English-language version would require additional editing and information. This translation and editing was carried out with care and diligent scholarship by Ritva Poom, M.A., who is versed in both folklore and poetry. Without her energy and perseverance, this book would never have been published in English. Collaborating on this translation was a learning experience for both of us. I am deeply grateful to her.

The initiative for this English-language version was sparked during a discussion with Professor Dan Ben-Amos and sponsoring editor Joan Catapano at the Kalevala Symposium at Indiana University in 1985. My thanks to them for their support. Monetary support came from the Finnish Ministry of Education, the Information Centre for Finnish Literature, the Institute on Western Europe at Columbia University, and the Division of Research Programs of the United States Endowment for the Humanities. The generous support of the L. J. Skaggs and Mary C. Skaggs Foundation has made the Folklore Studies in Translation series possible.

Among others, Professor Felix J. Oinas of Indiana University and Professor Börje Vähämäki of the University of Toronto provided helpful comments on the manuscript. Comments on the English-language version were given by Lynn Callaghan, Paul Ahrens, Professor Olavi Arens, Kaarina Kailo, and Anna Makkonen. My heartfelt thanks to them all.

During the course of my work, a number of my students participated in various phases of this project. My thanks to Kari Vesala and Kirsi Norros for their help in editing the text and bibliographical work. Terhi Utriainen and Katja Hyry read the manuscript and helped in compiling the maps and illustrations. Irene Salovainio-Mänttäri and Kari Pentikäinen helped to compile the references and index. Apostolos N. Athanassakis, Santa Barbara, and Arley Hall, Portland, Oregon, have made valuable comments for this text.

I am thankful for the fruitful consultations on this revised edition of *Kalevala Mythology* with Dan Ben-Amos, Joan Catapano, Aili Flint, Ritva Poom, Marja-Leena Rautalin, and William A. (Bert) Wilson. During my teaching period at the University of California, Santa Barbara in 1997, *Kalevala Mythology* was used as a textbook in the graduate course on Shamans and Shamanism, and was commented upon by the following students whom I thank for their cooperation: Martin Ball, Kaija Brandt, Kanaqluq (George Charles), Sean Connors, Mark Kennedy, etc. Colleagues at UCSB whose cooperation in this project is appreciated include Apostolos N. Athanassakis, Professor of Greek at the Department of Classics; Robert A. Erickson, Professor of English; Walter H. Capps, the late founder of the Department of Religious Studies and a Congressman; Richard N. Hecht, Barbara A. Holdrege, Inés M. Talamantez, and Ninian Smart, Professors at the Department of

Religious Studies. All of them have shared their expertise on world epics with me and have made valuable proposals for this revised edition. Meetings with the research group on Oral Epics under the chairmanship of Lauri Honko, e.g. at Turku in 1995, and the sessions at the Nordic Institute of Folklore research group on Sami Folklore in 1993–1997 were also stimulating occasions for the exchange of ideas and led me to further develop concepts in this book.

The revised paperback edition of *Kalevala Mythology* has been written for the general public interested in Finland, its history, culture, literature, and epic. The book is also intended to be used as a university textbook in folklore and literature courses as well as in Finnish, Scandinavian, and religious studies.

The content of the original text has been changed as little as possible. The most recent research on oral epics has been included, particularly Classical Greek, Vedic, and shamanic epic. At the suggestion of numerous readers, I have replaced the former "conclusions" with chapters 11 and 12. They define the place of the *Kalevala* in Finland's history from the point of view of Finnish mythology and mythography. The relationship between these concepts is somewhat problematical, as becomes apparent in the chapters.

I have written these chapters abroad primarily, and discussed them with scholars, students, faculty, and other interested individuals. It has been somewhat easier to understand my own culture in the light of questions posed about the *Kalevala* and Finnishness in other environs and, as a scholar of religions and cultures, in comparisons revealed through the viewpoints of other cultures. My constant companion in the discussion of these ideas has been my wife, Marja Pentikäinen.

I dedicate this book in memory of Kaino Helena Liakka, later Pentikäinen (1910–1996), who as my mother gave me my mother tongue and as my teacher of Finnish language and literature shared with me her enthusiasm for the *Kalevala* and Finnish folklore, and Prof. Matti Kuusi (1914–1998), my first teacher in Folklore at the University of Helsinki. According to Finnish folk wisdom: "We live as long as we are remembered."

Translator's Preface

Translating and editing *Kalevala Mythology* has presented the threefold challenge of rendering ancient Finnish poetry, nineteenth-century texts, and a work of modern scholarship into English. Each of these texts has posed its own unique problems to be solved, including the form and tone of ancient Finnish runes, the style of a nascent literary language, and the intricacies of adapting a scholarly text written for readers in one culture to readers in another.

Existing reference materials were often not adequate, particularly for the archaic language of the runes and for mythological concepts. The project entailed a good deal of transatlantic communication. During this work I was fortunate in having the help of many people. Foremost among them was Professor Juha Pentikäinen, who provided unstinting support throughout our rewarding collaboration. Others included Anna Makkonen, who advised on difficult textual questions; Professor Olavi Arens and Kaarina Kailo, who commented in detail on the translation; Lynn Callaghan and Paul Ahrens, who helped in many ways and gave insightful comments throughout; Professor Elliot Zupnick and Dr. Aili Flint, both of Columbia University; Marja-Leena Rautalin, Director of the Information Centre for Finnish Literature, who was the catalyst for this translation; and Dan Ben-Amos, editor of the Folklore Studies in Translation series. My heartfelt thanks to them all.

The project received generous funding from the Information Centre on Finnish Literature, the Institute on Western Europe at Columbia University, the Finnish Ministry of Education, and the Division of Research Programs of the United States National Endowment for the Humanities.

My gratitude also to my friends and family for their patience and good humor.

Ritva Poom

KALEVALA
MYTHOLOGY

Juha Pentikäinen

CHAPTER

1

A MYTHOLOGICAL VIEW OF THE *KALEVALA*

THE *KALEVALA*: SYNTHESIS OF LÖNNROT'S SCHOLARSHIP AND PRODUCT OF NATIONAL ROMANTICISM

"Here, if anywhere, there is now a pure epic in simple and thus most moving form, an unprecedented treasure. . . . ("Hier sprudelt nun, wenn irgendwo, lauteres epos in einfacher und desto mächtigerer darstellung, ein reichtum unerhörter. . . .")[1] This was Jacob Grimm's evaluation of the *Kalevala* in 1845, and it largely reflected the opinion of his time. At its initial publication in 1835, the *Kalevala* was received enthusiastically, in the prevailing spirit of National Romanticism, as a poetic work "discovered" among the people. Many Finnish enthusiasts, inspired by Romanticism, wished to see the *Kalevala* as an epic which had genuinely existed in the words and consciousness of the people, with Lönnrot's role primarily as its discoverer. The *Kalevala* was considered comparable to the *Niebelungenlied*, the works of Homer, and other celebrated epics. It was to raise the Finns, after centuries of Swedish rule and then living in an autonomous Grand Duchy of Russia, into the ranks of the other "civilized nations."[2]

After its categorization as an epic both abroad and in Finland, the *Kalevala* was long regarded as a document composed of genuine folklore material and, as such, a valid depiction of the Finnish people's past, their thoughts and customs. For many years, scholars examined the epic without distinguishing it from the folklore material on which it was based. This confusion was not due to Elias Lönnrot, who as early as 1835, in his preface to the *Old Kalevala*, had clearly stated his own role in compiling the runes into an epic.* In this preface, Lönnrot stated reservations about decisions he had made and included self-critical appraisals.[3] However, as late as 1883, in laying the foundation for his

*In this translation, the versions of the *Kalevala* published in 1835 and 1849 will be referred to respectively as the *Old Kalevala* and the *New Kalevala*. The word "rune" refers to epical poetry in the trochaic Kalevala meter.

Elias Lönnrot in 1841. Lithograph by J. Knutson. (Finnish National Board of Antiquities)

new interpretation of the origins of the *Kalevala*, the founder of Finnish folkloristics, Julius Krohn, placed particular emphasis on Lönnrot's role in the creation of the epic: "And, in particular, it has been necessary for me to relinquish the idea that all the adventures published in the *Kalevala* have correspondences in runes, at least in that connection with which they appear in the book."[4]

Later research, particularly the seminal textual studies by A. R. Niemi and Väinö Kaukonen, have clarified, verse by verse, the various stages involved in the development of the *Kalevala*.[5] It has been shown that only about two percent of the verses in the epic were actually created by Lönnrot himself. The contents of the *Kalevala* are based primarily on authentic folklore texts as they were sung by rune singers to collectors. The majority of them were, in fact, sung to Lönnrot himself. As a synthesis and adaptation of this material, however, the *Kalevala* is Lönnrot's aesthetic creation.[6] The heated debate over the authenticity and source value of the epic eventually resulted in the rigidly held conclusion that it should be treated as a literary work and as such was subject matter for literary study. At the same time, Lönnrot, as its creator, came to be viewed by the scholarly community primarily as a writer rather than a scholar.[7]

In evaluating Lönnrot's role in the creation of the *Kalevala*, it is necessary to take two aspects of the epic into consideration. The *Kalevala* is, on the one hand, the product of Lönnrot's aesthetic and scholarly work and, on the other, the social mandate of the Romantic Period, a national epic. As Jouko Hautala has noted, a publication of runes in any other than epic form would not have inspired Lönnrot's contemporaries and later generations to the same extent as did the *Kalevala*.[8] The fact that the *Kalevala*, as a publication of runes, does not fulfill the requisites of source criticism which later folklore scholarship, shaped largely by Julius and Kaarle Krohn, was to stipulate is an entirely different matter. From this point of view, the runes on which the *Kalevala* is based, as they were originally preserved, are natural subject matter for research in such fields as folkloristics, comparative religion, and ethnography.

During the early nineteenth century, the boundaries between various disciplines differed considerably from those at present. Within the context of his own time, Lönnrot created the *Kalevala* above all as a scholar of history and language. He was not bound, for example, by the study of folklore in the contemporary, narrow meaning of the term. Rather, in his approach to compiling and interpreting the Finnish epic, Lönnrot could be considered primarily a scholar of comparative mythology. In his time, this emerging discipline included such prominent scholars as Jacob Grimm and Max Müller.

LÖNNROT AS A MYTHOLOGIST

Lönnrot himself emphasized his role as a scholar of mythology, and expressed the hope that his work would bring new perspectives to previous studies. In his introduction to the *Old Kalevala*, he evaluated earlier scholarship: "It is certainly true that Finnish mythology has already been studied to some extent by Lencqvist, Ganander, and Porthan, among others, but without a doubt, it is still subject to great errors, erring in numerous aspects."[9] What was meant by this "mythology," with a tradition of scholarship, to which Lönnrot considered himself related?

In molding the *Kalevala* into a presentation of Finnish mythology, Lönnrot synthesized points of view found in the Finnish scholarship of his time. His preface to the epic includes references to the historic and poetic approach to studying Finnish runes established by Henrik Gabriel Porthan;[10] the historical model for interpreting folklore proposed by Reinhold von Becker,[11] Lönnrot's professor at Turku University; the mythological views of Christfrid Ganander[12] and Christian Lencqvist,[13] among others; and the methods of compiling and organizing runes and motifs delineated by Zachris Topelius the Elder.[14]

Henrik Gabriel Porthan (1739–1804) was a decisive force in creating interest in Finnish folk poetry. Although he was primarily a historian, he took particular interest in Finnish folklore. In his work *De Poesi Fennica* (1766, 1778), he elaborated on the aesthetic value of the runes and their significance for the Finnish language: "At the present time, only a few have aptly and clearly perceived the nature of our poetry in its entirety and then been able to further the well-deserved development of this literary genre. Many of our country's learned men are barely even familiar with the beauty of the poetic meter of our runes."[15]

Porthan's encouragement of the collection and preservation of folklore led to the development of early folklore archives. Porthan himself studied the ritual basis of the charms and came to the rationalistic conclusion, characteristic of a man of the Enlightenment, that these runes were based on ignorance and illiteracy: "No genre of our folk poetry has been more famous or more notorious than the so-called charms or poems of magic, believed in by fools and people blinder than the old crones who put ideas of hidden, wondrous power into other people's heads."[16]

Another study contemporaneous with this one provided a more thorough basis for studying the charms. This was *De Superstitione Veterum Fennorum Theoretica et Practica* (On the theoretical and practical superstition of the ancient Finns) (1782), published as the dissertation of Porthan's student, Christian Erici Lencqvist, but was more accurately the result of research done by his father, Erik Lencqvist (1719–1808). The negative attitude of the Enlightenment toward the practices of folk religion and beliefs related to them is also clearly apparent in this work:

> Thus, to describe the sacred customs of any folk is nothing more than to enumerate trivialities and to twine a long chain of the most foolish tales. It seems hardly worth the effort to embark upon such work. Nevertheless, because all historical knowledge fascinates and because there is hardly anything relating to the ancient customs and institutions of any people from which those interested in ancient matters would not get some aid for their pursuit, I trust that my effort to bring to the light of day the theology and sorcery of the old Finns, even though it is nothing more than ignorant belief in magic, will be welcome to friends of literary culture. For in our time, all civilized peoples have taken a great deal of trouble in portraying their pagan period.[17]

In presenting the charms and myths, Lencqvist examines both customs related to them, which he refers to as superstition, and the beliefs and customs on which they are based, which he refers to as theology or theoretical superstition. A tendency, characteristic of the Enlightenment, to explain these as "faults of the human spirit" predominates in these interpretations. Nevertheless, there is also a noteworthy tendency in Lencqvist's work to clarify that cultural and religious totality of which the runes had been, and to a large extent still were, a significant part.

Christfrid Ganander (1741–1790), a scholar and chaplain of Rantsila parish in North Ostrobothnia, proved a greater influence on Lönnrot's work and views on mythology than either Porthan or Lencqvist. In 1785, Ganander completed his *Mythologia Fennica*, which was published four years later. It contained a significant number of original rune texts organized in the form of a dictionary. *Mythologia Fennica* was a list of concepts concerned with Finnish and Saami religion, history, and dialects. It included explanations in Swedish and Latin as well as quotations in Finnish. As later research has shown, this book, first published in 1789, was an abridged version of Ganander's more extensive work, a Finnish-Swedish dictionary, which remained unpublished until a facsimile edition appeared in 1938–40.[18]

In his *Mythologia Fennica*, Ganander sought to fulfill his stated objective of comparing "the so-called Finnish poems of witchcraft to one another and with the aid of other peoples' mythology."[19] Although he was largely of the same opinion as Porthan and Lencqvist with regard to the primitive fantasies and ignorance on which the runes were based, Ganander did not focus on this in explaining them. Rather, as one who had lived continuously among the Ostrobothnian people and had also collected folklore himself, he attempted to understand the runes by examining beliefs and customs related to them. He referred to the information derived in this manner as "mythology":

> A knowledge of mythology is absolutely essential in order to be able to devote oneself to ancient Finnish poetry, to be able to read our Finnish runes for pleasure and benefit and with appreciation, and to perceive their nobleness, beauty, and attractiveness. Finnish mythology is "clavis poeseos Fennicae." Just as Ovid, Virgil, and Homer can little be understood, or their true significance comprehended, without mythology and a knowledge of Greek and Roman customs, likewise the Finnish runes do not come into their own right without mythology. That is why, in creating this collection of mythology, I have made the Finnish runes available to the public and, for many years, sifted through poetry which has vanished, although some of it may yet exist in the land today. From this I have gathered many hundreds of words as a beautiful supplement to the phraseology of the new Finnish dictionary, which I am even now preparing for publication.[20]

Even by contemporary standards, the scholarly agenda Ganander presented in the preface to *Mythologia Fennica* for the study of Finnish and comparative mythology can be considered quite an appropriate one:

> Finnish mythology, like that of all other peoples, is enveloped in many a dim legend and tale about the ancient gods and goddesses of the land which relate to events in nature and to ordinary matters. In order to explain them, it is best to compare the so-called Finnish poems of witchcraft to each other and with the aid of other peoples' mythology.[21]

When, fifty years later, Lönnrot conceived the idea of presenting the results of his own mythological studies in the form of an epic, he declared Ganander to be his model.[22] There are many similarities between both the scholarly profiles of Ganander and Lönnrot and the results they achieved. For both, mythology was the key to understanding the words of the runes and the essence of the Finnish language. Each compiled a dictionary. Each also considered folklore to be one of the deepest expressions of mythology. However, their concept of the relationship between history and myth clearly differed from today's viewpoint.

In addition to being a collection of Finnish religious beliefs and runes related to them, Ganander's *Mythologia Fennica* is also a compendium of geographical and historical facts. It contains a great number of place names and historical events, such as a description of the "Club War," a peasant uprising in Finland (1596–97); historical figures such as Ilkka, the head of a clan in Ostrobothnia, who died in 1597; and a list of the governors of Ostrobothnia from the 1400s to 1734.

It is fundamental to both Ganander's and Lönnrot's mythological view of folklore that they did not tend to assume that the basis of folklore was paganism or an underdeveloped "theology." This had been a characteristic view of Renaissance scholars, as well as those of the Enlightenment. It is true, however, that Lönnrot sought to compensate by searching for evidence of monotheism in folklore.[23] Nevertheless, for him, the goal of comparative mythological study was to clarify the beliefs and customs of the people as they seemed to be manifested in ancient poetry.

As Lönnrot himself emphasized, Ganander's *Mythologia* served as a model for him, at least during the initial stages when he was formulating the concept of the epic. In considering possible titles for his early work, *Runokokous Väinämöisestä* (A collection of runes about Väinämöinen), Lönnrot seriously considered the title *Suomen kansan mythologia vanhoilla runoilla toimitettu* (The mythology of the Finnish people compiled in ancient runes).[24] Because of its significance in the evolution of the *Kalevala* concept, this work became known as the *Proto-Kalevala*, although it remained unpublished until after Lönnrot's death. The minutes of the Finnish Literature Society dated May 5, 1834, note that Lönnrot had sent them a manuscript of "mythological runes" about Väinämöinen for possible publication.[25]

Thus, even when he was seeking a publisher for the initial manuscript, which did not yet have a title, Lönnrot considered it a mythological work. He also allowed himself the liberty of creating new mythology based on his scholarship. In addition to myths, the epic encompassed folklore and other information which shed light on the pre-Christian religion. From this point of view, the *Kalevala*, as a mythological work, was also the result of Lönnrot's synthesis of the pre-Christian religion of the Finns seen in comparative perspective. While Ganander had sought correspondences in the Semitic traditions and those of antiquity, Lönnrot's search through the comparative mythology of his period was a broader one. For Lönnrot, the *Kalevala* was "mythology" in two regards: it was, on the one hand, a collection of pre-Christian, mythological subject matter, mediated by folklore, and, on the other hand, a synthesis achieved by him as its compiler, the result of his own scholarship. It becomes understandable, therefore, that he was prepared to alter the poems of the *Kalevala* as his own ideas evolved in the light of new comparative scholarship.[26]

Like a dictionary, the *Kalevala* was augmented as new mythological knowledge accrued. Lönnrot also altered it as he gained access to new findings about other cultures through comparative scholarship, which was then flourishing, and incorporated these findings into his own world view. Thus, the *Kalevala* was being continuously augmented, both as poetic subject matter and as a scholarly study. Changes in Lönnrot's point of view were also incorporated into the prefaces of both the *Old* and *New Kalevala*, as well as his other scholarly writings. Just as Lencqvist had previously deliberated the relationship between the two principal deities, Ukko and Väinämöinen,[27] Lönnrot in his preface to the *Old Kalevala* raised a basic question which reflected a crucial issue in his monotheistic interpretation: which of these gods was the principal creator and which the created? In his opinion, one of the errors of Ganander's *Mythologia Fennica* had been that the supreme god, Ukko, was confused with Väinämöinen, who became the main hero of Lönnrot's *Kalevala*.[28]

Lönnrot was both a scholar of mythology and a mythographer who introduced new myths into the then-emerging Finnish nationalism. The various versions of the *Kalevala*, both published and unpublished, provide clues for examining the lively debate which led to the transformation of national history into myths and vice versa. Lönnrot was not a neutral bystander in this debate, and his ideas as manifested in the *Kalevala* led to a great deal of controversy.

FROM MYTHOLOGY TO COMPARATIVE RELIGION

The first written references to Finnish folk religion are the listings of Karelian and Tavastian deities found in Mikael Agricola's preface to his Finnish translation of the *Psalter*, published in 1551. In these lists, both of which contain twelve deities, Agricola briefly characterizes the functions of each deity in verse form. As a consequence, the Lutheran reformer of Finland, Mikael Agricola (1510–1557), is considered to be the father of the study of Finnish religious history.[29]

In the spirit of the Reformation, the propaganda against worshipping these deities was included in the preface to his *Psalter* as part of a dispatch in the vernacular against "paganism." Later scholarship has shown that the Finns never had Olympuses of twelve gods as presented by Agricola.[30] A considerable number of those figures he referred to as gods were not actually gods at all, but local guardian spirits, Christian saints, and names for the deceased. The models for Agricola's lists lay in classical and Germanic mythology and in continental European propaganda against paganism, based on the Reformation.[31] It was characteristic of this movement to translate the basic works of Christianity into native languages. Similar lists of pagan deities had also been published in the prefaces of numerous other translations of the Bible during the same era. It can only be attributed to Agricola's zeal for his mission that, for example, he refers to the Devil as one of the twelve gods worshipped by the Tavastians.

Finnish religious studies remained rather static during the seventeenth century, which is referred to as the Orthodox Period in the history of Lutheran Sweden-Finland. During the eighteenth century, there was a growing interest in folklore at the Turku Academy, which had been founded in 1640 and was the first university in Finland.[32] As a result of this interest, the monolithic interpretation of the nature of folk religion slowly began to change. In 1732, Mathias

Hallenius defended his dissertation, *De Borea-Fennia*. Included in his study were the etymologies of twenty-four Finnish words. Hallenius planned to continue his studies of mythology and stated his intention to "treat the upper, middle, and netherworld deities of our forefathers, their sacred customs, festivities, goddesses, and their handmaidens, their priestesses and the dried straws of papal doctrine and the decayed remains forged into poems in the language of our fathers."[33] Although, unfortunately, this plan was not realized, it was among the first signs of interest in the study of Finnish folk religion.

It was a common, almost obligatory, praxis in dissertations written at the Turku Academy to quote Agricola's lists of deities as a historical source. The students took these lists at face value, quoting them in full or partially, without comment or further interpretation. Critical evaluation of these deities, as well as the information Agricola had provided about them, began only at the end of the eighteenth century. For example, Lencqvist in his dissertation criticized Agricola's interpretations, although he used this material as one of his main sources. In referring to Agricola's list, Lencqvist states: "It includes among the deities of the people of Tavastia and Karelia some who were deities common to all of Finland. Second, it entirely overlooks some significant Finnish deities and mentions others whom it appears doubtful our forefathers worshipped."[34] Lönnrot was also critical of Agricola's tendency to interpret figures appearing in Finnish folklore specifically as "gods." Rather, he considered many of them to be historical heroes. Thus, with some sarcasm, Lönnrot referred to Väinämöinen, who had been listed as one of the deities of Tavastia, making the following assessment, which can be interpreted as a direct evaluation of Agricola's list:

> If, in parts of these poems, Väinämöinen is lowered from his previous stature as a god, then there is certainly nothing I can do about it. I have had to edit them as I received them, without regard to whether Väinämöinen is considered a god or not. We have long since become accustomed to considering him a god of our ancestors, an esteem in which they do not seem to have held him, however, regarding him rather as a powerful hero of great knowledge.[35]

Mathias Alexander Castrén (1813–1852), a colleague of Lönnrot and the founder of the study of the Finno-Ugric languages, was also a noteworthy scholar of comparative mythology. The field trips he made to other Finno-Ugric peoples in northern Eurasia were extremely significant for the development of disciplines concerned with the origins of the Finnish language and culture, including mythology. Castrén used the materials he collected as a basis of comparison for Finnish folk poetry, thus adding an important dimension to the study of comparative mythology as it had been delineated by Ganander. His lectures on Finnish folk religion at Helsinki University were published as *Föreläsningar i finsk mytologi* (Lectures in Finnish mythology) after his early death in 1853. Castrén placed particular emphasis on the value of charms: in his opinion, a collection of charms was "the first mandate of Finnish mythology and its best supplement."[36] This important genre was later neglected by many Finnish scholars. Even Lönnrot excluded a great many texts of charms available to him from the *Kalevala*, although he did later publish them as a unified collection.[37]

During the latter half of the nineteenth century, the way paved to the east by Castrén was followed by numerous explorers, geographers, linguists, and ethnologists, who collected an abundance of material, including ethnographic and religious subject matter, from peoples related to the Finns. Among them were Otto Donner, Heikki Paasonen, K. F. Karjalainen, Toivo Lehtisalo, Artturi Kannisto, and Albert Hämäläinen.[38] As a result of Castrén's influence, the northern Eurasian cultural sphere became a natural focus for the Finnish study of comparative religion, which primarily emphasized Finno-Ugric mythologies. Castrén also expressed an opinion about the then-prevalent debate over historical versus mythological interpretations of the *Kalevala*. His view can be considered accurate even today: "For a mythologist, it is quite the same whether Pohjola or Kalevala existed in reality or not, and how they existed: he clarifies only what a people thought about those places."[39]

To explain the background of the runes, Lönnrot sought evidence in the natural surroundings of their singers and creators, as well as in geographical and historical circumstances. He saw the runes as logical manifestations of how people experienced their surroundings and circumstances. Thus, for Lönnrot, their veracity was found not in objective events, but in people's experiences of them.[40]

During the nineteenth century, there were also adherents of the nature-mythology method of interpretation in Finland. In their view, the Kalevala runes were derived from natural phenomena, such as the opposition of light and darkness, day and night, summer and winter. These were considered the stimuli for poets' flights of imagination. In his essay "Kalevala and Pohjola" (1881), Eliel Aspelin presented a model for this kind of interpretation. His model was supported by Julius Krohn (1835–1888), who became the founder of Finnish folkloristics during the 1880s. Still during Lönnrot's lifetime, Krohn advocated the mythological interpretation of runes and also influenced his son, Kaarle Krohn (1863–1933), in this direction. Although Julius Krohn interpreted the runes mythically, he also strove to situate them in historical time.[41]

The developmental-historical point of view became the early basis for Finnish folklore scholarship. This was initially based on Darwin's theory of evolution[42] and developed side by side with the theretofore dominant interpretation of the *Kalevala* as ancient Finnish history. Later on, diffusion became the main principle of the "Finnish Method," as delineated by Kaarle Krohn. This new field of scholarship, folkloristics, was comparative in approach. According to the "Finnish Method" of folklore research, the prototype of a rune, folk tale, or other folklore was sought by comparing different texts called variants. Each variant was seen as a slightly different version of the prototype, having been altered as the rune or folk tale diffused from one region to another.[43]

As a result of this methodology, foreign equivalents were found for many

Finnish runes, tales, proverbs, and folk customs. It was typically assumed that the Finns, as a relatively young culture, had borrowed these from neighboring peoples during one historical period or another. This Finnish historical-geographic methodology also began to influence *Kalevala* scholarship and resulted in Kaarle Krohn's book *Kalevalan runojen historia* (The history of the Kalevala runes), published in 1903. The book was not concerned with the *Kalevala* as a work, but with the runic poetry on which the epic was based. The primary effect of this methodology on *Kalevala* scholarship was to turn the attention of folklore scholars from the epic itself to the study of the underlying folklore texts alone.

In *Suomalaisten runojen uskonto* (Religion in Finnish runes) (1914), Kaarle Krohn gave a new interpretation to the age of the runic poetry, stating that it had primarily originated during the Christian era. This was in direct contrast to earlier scholars such as Lencqvist, Ganander, and Lönnrot, who had striven to show that the runes manifested the ancient pre-Christian religion of the Finns. In this book Krohn states: "Lastly, doubts have arisen as to the age of the runes themselves, both the epical runes and, in particular, the charms. Do they, even in their origins, predate the Christian Middle Ages, and can they then be used as valid evidence in the study of paganism?"[44]

The study of mythological elements in Finnish folk tradition waned largely as a result of Kaarle Krohn's view that the religion found in Finnish folklore was derived primarily from the Medieval Catholic Period. Krohn stated that "the science of religion," rather than mythology, was the proper field for studying the religious content of the Finnish runes. In his view, this field "focused particular attention on the origins of religion and the clarification of its initial structure." The scholarship based on Krohn's evolutionist view attempted to show that the initial form of Finnish folk religion had been worship of the dead. The original Finnish tradition and the runes had then been augmented by foreign subject matter which had diffused into it.[45]

The scholarly direction initiated by Krohn included a reevaluation of the concept of mythology itself. In his opinion, Castrén had extended Finnish mythology into the religious history of the Finno-Ugric peoples.[46] At the same time another distinguished scholar, Uno (Holmberg) Harva (1882–1949), published an important series of monographs about Finno-Ugric religions following the comparative methodology initiated by Castrén in particular. He became the founder of the study of comparative religion in Finland in the modern sense.[47] The study of folk traditions has played a crucial role in research on comparative religion in Finland. The biased principles advocated by Krohn have been superseded by an attempt to examine pre-Christian, ethnic forms of belief, so-called folk religion or mythology. It has become an interdisciplinary, comparative methodology, with the goal of understanding and explaining the human being, including his or her world view and the experiential world within which folk tradition still plays an important role.

From the point of view of the Finnish study of comparative religion, the mythological approach of Ganander, Lönnrot, Castrén, and others can be viewed as quite modern in its basic tenets. A recent proponent of this approach was Martti Haavio. In his major work, *Suomalainen mytologia* (Finnish mythology) (1967), Haavio followed a dictionary-article format reminiscent of Ganander's *Mythologia Fennica*. However, Haavio's approach included elements of the historical-geographic approach to folklore scholarship. He defined his objective as follows:

> Within the pages of my work, I have attempted to gather examples of ancient human ideas about religion and to group them. I have attempted to show how the concept of deities held by different peoples is uniform in many respects, as are people's feelings of their own vulnerability. I have attempted to bring forth commonly held, very ancient, fundamental beliefs about the origin of existence, "the deepest birth." It is my intention to join the Finnish fragments to that giant mosaic, in places determined by its pattern. How, why, and when these pieces were dispersed to all corners of the earth and what the nearest center is from which they were cast to our land, has not been determined by us in the slightest.[48]

In his specific way, Haavio is a good example of the interplay between the evolutionistic, diffusionistic, and comparative mythological approaches typical of the "Finnish Method." Despite his tendency to see the world of homo religiosus as the force behind religious traditions and to seek phenomenological similarities and differences between religious traditions, Haavio assumes that Finnish tradition is composed of fragments which came to Finland from various parts of the world.

WORLD VIEW AND MYTHOLOGICAL BASIS OF THE *KALEVALA*

Lönnrot's emphasis on mythology becomes manifest in his preface to the *Old Kalevala* (1835), where he discusses the value of his work for understanding the Finnish past: "If these poems would be of any aid to Finnish mythology, . . . then one of my hopes is fulfilled, but there are others as well: from them, I would hope to gain some clarification about the ancient life of our forefathers, and to derive some benefit for the Finnish language and poetic art."[49] Thus, for Lönnrot as a scholar, the *Kalevala* illuminated Finnish mythology, ethnography, language, and literature in the form of an epic. Lönnrot pondered and actively developed his views and interpretations, both while he was compiling the *Old Kalevala* and later, as he broadened and revised it into the *New Kalevala*, completed in 1849. One can follow the development of his thoughts in the various editions of the *Kalevala* and also in his extensive prefaces to both the *Old* and the *New Kalevala*. His articles and studies, including the periodical *Mehiläinen* (The bee), which he himself edited, provide additional insight into the evolution of his thought. Other materials which have been preserved, such as letters and drafts of letters, are also useful for this purpose.

It is appropriate here to consider Lönnrot's multifaceted, often forgotten role and achievements as a scholar. One reason for the limited understanding of Lönnrot to date, as mentioned above, may be that in Finnish scholarship the *Kalevala* fell between literature and folklore. The fact that, even in recent debate, the *Kalevala* has been defined as either a poetic work (Väinö Kaukonen) or a source of original runes (Matti Kuusi) has created confusion about Lönnrot's role. Another and possibly more significant reason for the underevaluation of his scholarly work lies in the overall orientation of the scholarship dealing with the *Kalevala* and the Kalevala runes. At the end of the nineteenth century, the mythological scholarship espoused by Ganander, Castrén, and Lönnrot was superseded by the evolutionistic and diffusionistic currents which then became dominant in Finnish folkloristics. These currents also significantly influenced the study of folk belief in general until the mid-twentieth century. In the light of contemporary Finnish religious scholarship, it is necessary to reevaluate the role of the classical mythological approach in the study of Finnish folk belief.

This study attempts a hermeneutical interpretation of Lönnrot's work as scholar and poet. The epical work he created is viewed from both a human and a comparative perspective. In the following chapters, the role of the *Kalevala*, and the runes on which it is based, will be examined from an interdisciplinary viewpoint, taking into account recent methodological innovations in comparative folkloristics, epical studies and the science of religion. Of primary interest is the world view of the *Kalevala* and the runes.

Whose is the world described in the *Kalevala* and the runes on which it is based? Is it the world of the runes or the myths on which they were based, is it the world of the people or generation who created the runes, sang them, or interpreted them, or, possibly, all of these? And what of Lönnrot himself, to whom, in the final analysis, the copyright to the *Kalevala* actually belongs—how is his world view reflected in the epic? And finally, what of the world view held by the Finns themselves at the beginning of the nineteenth century, when they had become an autonomous Grand Duchy of Russia? What was the role played by the *Kalevala* in Finland's becoming an independent country by 1917, and in Finnish history since that time?

Loosely defined, world view means an understanding of the world in its entirety, including its structures and forces, time, the fundamentals of existence, the interrelationships between the natural and the supernatural, nature, environment, the relationship of people and society to these, and to man himself. It includes concepts of life, fortune, and death, as well as life after death, society, people and government, and the fundamentals of history and culture.[50] In clarifying the world view of the *Kalevala* and its runes, an effort will be made to achieve what Ganander and Lönnrot presented as the aim of their "mythology": an understanding of the world of the Finnish runes, their creators and performers. Because the *Kalevala* came to play such a significant role in Finnish culture and identity, it is also an objective of this book to provide a frame of reference for understanding the world of the Finns in the past as well as the present.

World view is always the experiential aspect of a people. It guides and molds a person's experiences and is also the result and the sum of those experiences. Thus, in studying the *Kalevala* and its runes, one cannot forget the people from whom the runes were derived, their environment, customs and feelings. What, for example, was the reality experienced by the now anonymous poet who created "Väinämöisen Tuonelan-matka" (Väinämöinen's journey to Tuonela)? What were the thoughts of rune singers during various periods as they sang the rune about the creation of the world? Were the runes born of the "people's heart," as was long assumed in the spirit of Romanticism, even among the scholarly circles where the *Kalevala* was being studied? It was, in fact, considered a scholarly breakthrough when Martti Haavio, in his book *Väinämöinen* (1949), established what now appears self-evident, that there was a specific poet behind each rune, although that poet might be anonymous.

It is interesting to study Lönnrot's own world view as well. The roles of scholar, poet, and homo religiosus were complementary in his experiential world. What kind of religiosity did Lönnrot espouse, and was the religion reflected in the runes as significant for him as the aesthetic satisfaction they provided? And what of the experiential world of the Finns in the autonomous Duchy? Having fulfilled the requisite hopes and dreams of nationalists, how, for example, did the *Kalevala*, with its relationship to folk religion, relate to the self-concept of the Finns?

CHAPTER

2

THE GENESIS
OF THE *KALEVALA*

WHOSE WAS THE IDEA FOR A NATIONAL EPIC?

I have endeavored to put these runes into some kind of order, and should then probably give an account of my work. Since, to my knowledge, no one else has attempted this before or even mentioned a word about it, I will first relate how I came upon this idea. While reading previously collected poems, Ganander's in particular, the thought occurred to me that it might be possible to find enough of them about Väinämöinen, Ilmarinen, Lemminkäinen, and other of our memorable ancestors to create even longer tales about them, as the Greeks, Icelanders, and others have done with their ancestors' poems. This idea was reinforced even more in my mind when, in 1826, with the aid of von Becker, Adjunct Professor of History at Turku, I came to write a certain work [M.A. thesis] on Väinämöinen, and in preparing it, I saw that there was no lack of tales about him. In fact it amazed me that Ganander hadn't already done this, but soon I came to understand that he hadn't had enough poems for it. He has published the best passages of the poems he has collected in his *Mythologia Fennica*, but one could hardly get anything complete from them. An early death eliminated Topelius, even had he, with time, been able to devote himself to this work.[1]

This is Lönnrot's view of how the idea of collecting and editing an epic had evolved in his own mind, as presented in the preface to the *Old Kalevala*. In the quotation, Lönnrot acknowledges the influence of comparative models and refers to earlier collections of runes in Finland. He places particular emphasis on those collected by Ganander. Although Lönnrot does state that Reinhold von Becker (1788–1858), his history professor, was his guide, he makes it understood that the idea of compiling a broad, unified epic was his own. He expresses amazement that no one else, including the earlier folklore collectors and publishers Christfrid Ganander and Zachris Topelius the Elder (1781–1831), had set out to realize a comparable idea.

A primary opponent of Lönnrot's observations was Carl Axel Gottlund

The concept of an ancient Finnish epic was first expressed in 1817 by Carl Axel Gottlund. His noteworthy scholarship centered around the Scandinavian "Forest Finns." In the photograph, a memorial to Gottlund stands before the Grue Church in Norwegian forests inhabited by the Finns. There Gottlund is known as the "apostle of the Forest Finns." The question of the "Forest Finns" interested Gottlund so greatly that advocating independence or autonomy for them brought him into conflict in both Sweden and Finland, which belonged to the Russian Empire at that time. (National Board of Antiquities)

(1796–1875), who became a lecturer in Finnish at the University of Helsinki. In 1847 Gottlund, in a bitter tone, wrote an article for *Suomi-lehti* (The Finnish paper) about Lönnrot. He said that Lönnrot had not been truthful in stating that no one else had attempted to combine the poems into an epic. He also criticized the fact that Lönnrot had rewritten the poems, primarily collected from eastern parts of the country, into standard Finnish, which was based on western Finnish dialects. To emphasize his point, Gottlund wrote the article in the Savo dialect of eastern Finland. The following is an excerpt:

We've never demeaned Lönnrot, although there are faults and shabbiness in him (as in us too); we honor him, even if he thinks nothing of us, because we're well acquainted with the difficulty and impossibility of creating something complete and whole in this fashion. Even he himself affirms this and recounts (in the preface to the *Kalevala*—where he is already a bit shameless toward us) that his only reward, thought, or striving is "to get these runes into some kind of order–since (he says), to my knowledge, no one else has attempted this before, or even mentioned a word about it." And actually we would gladly toss this honor to him if, eighteen years before him and the appearance of the *Kalevala*—in our youth, during our talks about these ancient Finnish poems–

Life in Turku during 1814. This watercolor was painted before the Great Turku Fire of 1827, which resulted in the closing of the university at Turku. (C. L. Engel watercolor, Finnish National Board of Antiquities)

we hadn't already declared: "We are so bold as to propose that if we collected these ancient folk poems and created some kind of ordered whole of them, be it then an epic, a drama, or whatever, another Homer, Ossian, or *Niebelungenlied* might be created of them, and through this our Finnishness could yet be celebrated nobly with honor—by the brilliance of its own worth, in its own self-knowledge, and beautified by the knowledge of its own creation—to awaken the wonder of our contemporaries and of those to come.[2]

In the final part of his article, Gottlund cited a text he had written in 1817 for *Svensk Litteratur-Tidning* (The Swedish literary paper), demanding acknowledgment of his own role as the first to propose compiling the runes into an epic, eighteen years before the publication of the *Kalevala*.[3] A reference to this article in Lönnrot's study *De Väinämöinen* shows that Lönnrot indeed was familiar with it.[4] Had he actually made a conscious effort to forget Gottlund's early writings? The competition between the two men is general knowledge and it may, of course, be possible that Lönnrot "actively forgot" Gottlund's article when he wrote his preface to the *Kalevala*. On the other hand, in his preface Lönnrot seems to have been focusing on different issues from those which concerned Gottlund. He was discussing concrete sources and issues involved in developing and realizing an epic and was no longer concerned with the vague romantic dream of creating such a work.[5] However, the debate between Lönnrot and Gottlund does not fully clarify how the concept of a Finnish national epic was born. This question must be examined within the broader context of Finnish and international culture at the beginning of the nineteenth century.

THE CULTURAL ATMOSPHERE IN FINLAND IN THE EARLY NINETEENTH CENTURY

The year 1809 marked a turning point in Finnish history. Finland, which had been a hinterland of the Swedish kingdom since medieval times, now became an autonomous Grand Duchy of Russia. The effects of this change were not perceptible at first. Initially, the old capital, Turku, continued to preserve its central position culturally and economically, although contacts were also being formed to the east. This was quite natural because St. Petersburg, the capital of Russia, had been constructed in 1703 within the area of Ingrian settlement where Balto-Finnic languages were spoken.

However, Turku, along with the Turku Academy, remained the center of Finnish cultural activity and also received cultural influences from continental Europe. There was an extensive library at the Turku Academy, and within the academy's sphere of influence, epics of international reputation such as the *Iliad*, the *Odyssey*, the *Niebelungenlied*, the *Eddas*, the *Song of Roland*, as well as the *Mahābhārata* and the *Ramayana* of India were known and discussed. Around the end of the eighteenth and the beginning of the nineteenth centuries, the literature of continental Europe was also read in Finnish parsonages and among the gentry, who still lived in the Gustavian spirit of the Enlightenment typical of Sweden-Finland at that time.

Following the cultural influences of the Enlightenment, new waves of early Romanticism, such as *The Poems of Ossian*, also reached Finland. It is important to keep in mind that in Porthan's time, interest in Finnish cultural history and the Finnish language was already stirring at the Turku Academy. This interest, which had remained dormant after Agricola's time, revived and diversified. Dissertations about Finnish folklore and ancient religion were written at the Turku Academy and, even before the so-called Period of Turku Romanticism, which lasted from 1810 until the Turku Fire of 1827, activities related to the collection and publication of national culture and folklore were initiated.

Among the leaders of the Turku Romantics, was Adolf Ivar Arwidsson (1791–1858). It is to him that the rallying call of the period is attributed: "Swedes we are not, Russians we can't become, let us then be Finns."[6] During the decade of 1810, Arwidsson was a central figure in the famous "Turku Quartet," a group of nationally oriented Finnish students studying at Uppsala University in Sweden. This group included C. A. Gottlund, Abraham Poppius (1793–1866), and A. J. Sjögren (1794–1855). After Arwidsson returned to Finland, his career there came to an end in 1822, when he was sent to Sweden for political reasons. Meanwhile, another sector of the Finnish intelligentsia gravitated toward the east, including the distinguished scholar of Finno-Ugric languages, A. J. Sjögren, who received the prestigious appointment of Academician at the St. Petersburg Academy.[7]

It was Sjögren who brought the influence of German Romanticism to Turku, including the ideas of J. G. Herder (1744–1803). The following is an example of Sjögren's enthusiastic response to Herder's work: "In Germany, during the years 1778 and 1779, they were bold enough to publish two collections containing folk songs in various languages and from various peoples."[8] Inspired by this German plan to arrange the epics of the world according to countries, periods, languages, and peoples, Sjögren wrote:

> . . . it will be a clarification of them, as the yet-living voice of nations or even that of mankind itself may be heard here and there under varying circumstances, gentle and cruel, joyful and sorrowful, playful and serious, instructing us everywhere. The story of the *Cid*, presented as romances, is as rich in splendid descriptions, noble feelings, and teachings as (dare I say it?) Homer.[9]

This Romantic view that the runes described an aspect of antiquity and that there existed in them "a people's voice" found a positive response among the Finnish intelligentsia who nevertheless spoke Swedish among themselves at that time. The publications of this academic circle, the *Aura-Album* and *Mnemosyne*, served to convey their ideas. J. J. Tengström published an article in *Aura* about obstacles to Finnish literature and culture. In it he gave his views on cultural areas in eastern Finland where the poems could yet be found:

> Those folk songs, traditions, and customs which could give clues or clarify past circumstances have, with the advance of culture, in part perished, in part vanished to the most remote regions of our land, to the backwoods of North Ostrobothnia, Savo, and Karelia, where they, together with many unique characteristics of the Finnish people, are found in their original purity.[10]

Tengström urged that fragments of the ancient period be collected, thereby making it possible to arrive at "the Finnish national character, to become more closely acquainted with both ancient thought and lifestyle." There was also international encouragement to gather these "fragments of antiquity." In 1819, a German-language collection, *Finnische Runen* (Finnish runes), was edited by H. R. von Schröter, who then lived in Uppsala. This work contained nearly two thousand verses, the main body of runes which had been collected by Porthan, Ganander, Gottlund, Arwidsson, and Poppius.[11]

The collecting of epical poetry had already begun, and its significance was being discussed, when Lönnrot, J. L. Runeberg, and J. V. Snellman—three men who were to become the future leaders of Finnish nationalism—all happened by chance to enroll at Turku University in 1822. Also of importance in

Turku at this time was the continental European influence, which came there by way of Uppsala. Despite Finland's new motherland to the east, the ideas developing in Sweden did not go unnoticed in Turku, and vice versa.

In 1827, the Great Turku Fire ruined the academic center of the former Finnish capital. The Turku Academy was officially moved to Helsinki, which was to become the administrative and cultural center of Finland, then an autonomous Grand Duchy of Russia. Turku Romanticism subsequently evolved into Helsinki Romanticism. It was also because of the Turku Fire, which resulted in the closing of the university there, that Lönnrot, temporarily freed from his duties as a student, began his brilliant career as a collector of Finnish folklore.

CREATION OF THE *KALEVALA* IN KAJAANI (1833–35)

Lönnrot's first field trip was carried out in Häme, where he worked as a tutor while the Turku Academy was closed. Later expeditions were supported by grants from the Finnish Literature Society, founded in Helsinki in 1831. Other such trips were integrated into his work as the district physician of Oulu and Kajaani. In 1833, Lönnrot moved permanently to the small township of Kajaani in northeastern Finland. The social and cultural life in the backwoods of Kainuu Province held little interest for him. Rather, it was the proximity of White Sea Karelia which he found inspiring. Annual markets were held in Kajaani. Men from White Sea Karelia often came there and recited their folkloristic repertoires, including epical runes.[12]

On his first expedition, Lönnrot was already interested in collecting runes. He also edited them for publication at inns and resting places during his travels. These plans for publication were first realized in 1829, when *Kantele taikka Suomen kansan vanhoja sekä nykyisiä runoja ja lauluja* (The Kantele, or ancient and present-day runes and songs of the Finnish people) was printed. It contained seventeen previously collected and seven new runes. A. R. Niemi, a scholar of Lönnrot's epical works, states that only three of these runes were published in accordance with the original texts; the rest show traces of editorial deletions and additions.[13] This kind of linguistic and stylistic revision was carried out by Lönnrot throughout all four volumes of the *Kantele* (1829–31), which consisted primarily of charms and lyrics. The fifth volume of this series was completed in 1831, but remained unpublished.[14]

The development in Lönnrot's mind of the plan for an epic can be analyzed on the basis of his correspondence with friends.[15] In May of 1833, he wrote to K. N. Keckman, secretary of the Finnish Literature Society, who had requested him to send the fifth volume of the *Kantele* for publication, that he hoped to come to Helsinki himself to publish the poems. In addition to those runes collected earlier, Lönnrot said that he had "a notebook of beautiful runes from Kajaani about Väinämöinen, Lemminkäinen and other material." Shortly afterward (May 17, 1833), he inquired whether the runes would be published in small booklets or as one volume, because they already seemed to be develop-ing into a collection. Keckman went to Sweden in the meantime, leaving Lönnrot's letters unanswered.

It is noteworthy that Lönnrot was already envisioning publication of the runes in a single book. As a result of Keckman's trip to Sweden, he had the additional time necessary to reorganize his idea of synthesizing the runes into a whole. This plan, which took shape in the summer of 1833, can clearly be interpreted as an early manifestation of the concept which led to publication of the *Kalevala*. It subsequently evolved into the request which Lönnrot sent to Keckman on August 17, 1833:

> How would it be if the Society published anew all the Finnish runes, those which merit it, and assembled them in order, so that what is available about Väinämöinen, Ilmarinen, and others in various places could be joined or pieced together, and lectiones variantes [= differing variants] could be put beneath somewhere or on the final pages?

During this time, Lönnrot planned to edit several miniature epics and envi-sioned a number of epical units centered around heroic figures found in the runes, such as Väinämöinen, Lemminkäinen, Ilmarinen, and Kaukomieli. All of these remained unpublished manuscripts during that period. For example, "Lemminkäinen" (an 825-verse compilation), "Väinämöinen" (1721 lines), and "Naimakansan virsiä" (Wedding verses) (429 lines) were all completed during the fall of 1833.[16] As evidenced by this abundance of preliminary drafts, Lönnrot was in a creative phase. Its primary inspiration may have been the successful collection trip he made during the summer of 1833, when he met two notable rune singers, Ontrei Malinen and Vaassila Kieleväinen.[17] Discus-sions with Kieleväinen about the order of the runes both caused confusion for Lönnrot with regard to his former opinions about the structure of the poem, and also inspired him to arrange the verses he had collected from the singers more freely.

This creative process had significant results. The letters and drafts of letters Lönnrot wrote in Kajaani attest to the intensity of his thought and synthesis there. For example, on December 3, 1833, he wrote to Dr. H. C. Cajander:

> I have about five to six thousand verses of Väinämöinen runes alone, from which you can infer that a sizeable collection will develop. Nevertheless, dur-ing the winter, I plan to slip back into the Archangel [White Sea Karelian] District again, and I'll not cease collecting runes until I get a collection of them which equals half of Homer. In their content, the runes now in my possession are all arranged in a sequence which a certain old man [= Vaassila] in part sang to me and in part related about Väinämöinen in other ways.

It is apparent from this quotation that Lönnrot was already at a new stage in formulating the concept of the epic: he had gathered his earlier drafts into one and compiled them into the 5,052-verse composition *Runokokous*

Väinämöisestä (A collection of runes about Väinämöinen).[18] According to a letter he wrote to Cajander, he had grown more conscious of the Homeric nature of his work during this period. Lönnrot was also actively translating poems from Latin into Finnish. On January 25, 1834, for example, he sent Keckman part of the translation he had completed of the *Odyssey* in hexameter.

Although it was not published until after Lönnrot's death, *A Collection of Runes about Väinämöinen* is considered of such significance as a preliminary work to the *Kalevala* that later scholars referred to it as the *Proto-Kalevala*.[19] Before his plan for publication of this work was realized, Lönnrot managed to embark on a new expedition to White Sea Karelia, where he met Arhippa Perttunen, a renowned rune singer from the village of Latvajärvi. Lönnrot hastened to add Perttunen's runes to his work. The minutes of the Finnish Literature Society dated June 4, 1834, state:

> The Honorable Doctor Lönnrot, who just recently arrived in town [Helsinki] and participated in the meeting, announced that on his new trips to the District of Viena [White Sea Karelia] he had found copious additions to *A Collection of Runes about Väinämöinen*, which he had sent to the Society, and that he was presently compiling a new edition of it. He thought he would be able to complete it by midsummer and he also planned to add variants to it.[20]

Lönnrot worked on this project during the autumn of 1834, also using a previously published collection of runes by Carl Axel Gottlund entitled *Gottlundin pieniä runoja* (Gottlund's small poems) as a source.[21] On November 15, 1834, Lönnrot wrote to his colleague Sabel, the district doctor of Vaasa, for he had heard that Sabel was a supporter of Finnish culture: "I have nearly completed a great *opus* or *epos*, as one could call it, which will contain all that others and I myself are able to collect about ancient Finnish mythological figures. . . . The book will be the same length as Virgil's *Opera Omnia* or Ovid's *Metamorphosis*." On November 28, 1834, Lönnrot related to Doctor Ticklen, another colleague, that he had worked all fall compiling the Finnish runes into one epic poem and its name was now certain: *Kalevala*.

On February 16, 1835, K. N. Keckman received a letter from Lönnrot stating that the runes were complete except for the preface. Several weeks later he expressed his concern over the magnitude of the work: "If I hadn't already sat with these runes so that my backside is right sore, then who knows, I probably wouldn't send them off even yet, because they could well be rewritten and straightened out." Finally, on February 28, 1835, Lönnrot completed the preface to his new poetical work: *Kalevala taikka Vanhoja Karjalan runoja Suomen kansan muinaisista ajoista* (The Kalevala, or old poems from Karelia about the ancient times of the Finnish people). The preface starts out:

> I have at last readied these poems for publication, but unfortunately they still lack a great deal. Hopeful that they will be added to by new collecting, I would by no means have let them out of my hands so prematurely if, in considering the matter from another perspective, I did not fear that I would never com-

plete them. Better plans and endeavors by many have already come to naught in this way.[22]

The conclusion of the preface expresses Lönnrot's ambivalence at the completion of the work:

> The manner in which many others get encouragement for their labor is very different, namely, the hope of achieving a beautiful and complete work. This hope has been entirely lacking in me. I am doubtful even of my ability to edit anything suitable; my doubt about this work has sometimes grown so great that I've been ready to toss the whole bundle into the fire. For I haven't believed in my ability to edit them as I had wanted, and haven't considered it fitting to subject myself, my labor and hard work, to criticism based on a work half finished. Nevertheless, go now, Kalevala poems, even if not quite finished, lest by lingering in my hands a bit longer, the fire makes you more complete![23]

In 1909, the day on which Elias Lönnrot signed the preface to the *Kalevala* (February 28) was officially designated "*Kalevala* Day" in Finland and is celebrated annually.

EARLY RECEPTION OF THE *KALEVALA* ABROAD

Within the framework of nineteenth-century Romanticism, both historical and mythological interpretations were offered for epical folklore. In his compilation of the *Kalevala*, for example, Lönnrot was guided by the historical view he had adopted from Reinhold von Becker.[24] It was, however, the mythological approach which was predominant in continental Europe during this period, and its most prestigious and well-known proponent was Jacob Grimm, the German linguist and scholar of mythology. According to Grimm, fragments of folklore were to be considered remnants of ancient tales about gods and studied as such, within the strictures of mythological scholarship. It was believed that while history was based on actual events, ancient runes were constructed of mythological subject matter, which had formed in and been mediated by the mind of the people.[25]

Grimm's interest in Finnish folklore had apparently begun to develop by 1809, and was based on writings about Finland, including von Schröter's German translations of Finnish folk poetry. He was introduced to the *Kalevala* through M. A. Castrén's Swedish translation of the epic, published in 1841.[26] Castrén's Swedish translation and a French prose version, published in 1854, made possible the wide attention accorded to the *Kalevala* abroad.[27]

Grimm refers to the *Kalevala* in the second edition (1844) of his *German Mythology*, comparing it to Greek and Teutonic myths and fairy tales.[28] In 1845, he gave an enthusiastic lecture about the *Kalevala* at the Berlin Academy of Sciences. This lecture contained information about the Finns, the Finnish language and the content of the *Kalevala*.[29] As a result, a broad interest in the *Kalevala* was awakened in the international scholarly community. Among academic circles of the Romantic Period in continental Europe, it was strongly felt that a new epic had been born.

Because of its recent origins, the *Kalevala* could be studied as a model of how the ancient epics had evolved throughout the world. Grimm also included a comparison of the *Kalevala* epic to ancient Greek, German, and Scandinavian mythologies. In accordance with his mythological perspective, he stated in his lecture that Väinämöinen, Ilmarinen, and Lemminkäinen were clearly deities, although human dimensions were also attributed to them in the runes. According to Grimm, the Sampo, a wondrous object in the *Kalevala* which was the source of bounty, was a talisman comparable to the Holy Grail or the wondrous mill known as the Grotta which in Scandinavian mythology brings good fortune. In the *Kalevala*, therefore, the conflict between the peoples of Väinölä (the Land of Väinö, Väinämöinen) and Pohjola (the Northern Land) would be interpreted as a struggle between the gods over ownership of the Sampo.[30] Thus the ancient mythical battle had historical dimensions in the epics.

In the *Kalevala*, Grimm, as a Romantic, was seeking the expression of a pure epic, "Volkspoesie" or "Urpoesie," in the form of authentic folk poetry. Erich Kunze has shown that Grimm was thereby also attempting to clarify the fundamental nature of his own people.[31] In his attempts to elucidate the German national character, Grimm had also become familiar with Serbian folklore. He compared the *Kalevala* to this material, stating that the Finnish runes were even richer and more ancient. In his enthusiasm, Grimm also praised Lönnrot for his contribution as a rune collector, stating that the *Kalevala* was an example of a theretofore unprecedented rich, pure epic, in simple and powerful form: "And, in particular, I want to call attention to the lively, sensuous feeling for nature, the equivalent of which may be found, perhaps, only in the poetry of India."[32]

Thus, the *Old Kalevala* received more than casual notice abroad: as a result of Grimm's lecture, it was accorded the status of an epic by the world's most prestigious authorities. The Finns were not unaware of this development. Some were joyful, while others sharpened their blades against Lönnrot. As is often the case, public recognition came to the *Kalevala* abroad before it was recognized in its homeland, where opinions were sharply divided as to its significance.

EARLY CRITICISM IN FINLAND

Finnish discussion of the *Old Kalevala* was directed in part at the plan for the epic itself, and in part at how the work had been compiled. There were heated debates over the work and Lönnrot's role in it. At the same time, however, some members of the Finnish intelligentsia accorded the *Kalevala* the status of a national epic. The circle of young enthusiasts which had formed around the Finnish Literature Society showed a particular interest in Lönnrot's work. This organization, founded in 1831, had given Lönnrot monetary support for his work and later published the epic. From 1835 on, the minutes of the society affirm that Lönnrot had created "a magnificent, complete, mythical, national epic, which is a most astonishing discovery."[33]

Lönnrot's self-critical preface to the *Old Kalevala* was overshadowed when, in the enthusiasm of National Romanticism, the epic was received as having been "found" among the people. One of the first to accord it this status was J. L. Runeberg (1804–1877), who later became Finland's national poet. Runeberg's introduction to his Swedish translation of the *Kalevala's* "Kilpakosinta-runo" (Courtship contest rune), published in *Helsingfors Morgonblad* (Helsinki morning paper) in 1835, included the following appreciative statement:

> The editor has not had the opportunity to delve into the other runes of the *Kalevala*, but believes that he can, based upon that at hand, assume with complete certainty that in this poem Finnish literature has received a treasure, which in both flavor and quality, as well as magnitude and even worth, is comparable to both of the most beautiful epic masterpieces of Greek art. All the merits of these works, the grand and self-possessed progress of the presentations and the enduring and sure intent of the images, are found in the Finnish poem as well, and it may perhaps surpass them, insofar as perfection can be surpassed, in the nobility of its depictions of nature and in simple festivity.[34]

In contrast to this adulation, other contemporary intellectuals, such as J. V. Snellman (1806–81), initially reacted to the *Kalevala* disparagingly. Snellman, who was of the Hegelian School of philosophy, assumed that, in order for a people to develop an epic, it was necessary for them to have had a heroic period in their history. As late as 1844, he wrote: "A people such as the Finns cannot have a true epic." Two years later, however, he had decisively altered his opinion: "The fact that the Finns have a national epic, a 'third' true epic on the earth, alongside the *Iliad* and the *Niebelungenlied*, gives reason to assume knowledge not possessed by all peoples."[35] Apparently Snellman's attitude toward the *Kalevala* had been positively influenced by Jacob Grimm's favorable stance toward the work.

During this period, there were many debates over the historical versus the symbolic nature of the *Kalevala*. Its worth as an epic was measured in accordance with these ideas. Its position alongside the Greek epics appeared to be more assured, for example, if the basis for the Kalevala runes was seen as a struggle between gods and demons or good and evil. This was the view advocated by Fabian Collan in 1838.[36] Like his teacher Reinhold von Becker, Lönnrot had adopted the historical viewpoint. He did so despite the fact that the status of the epic might be lowered, as he states in his preface to the *Kalevala*.[37]

The first Professor of Finnish Language at the University of Helsinki, M. A. Castrén, discussed the *Kalevala* in his lectures and writings. Among his criticisms was the order of the poems. Nevertheless, he did accept the *Kalevala* as Finland's national epic. Consciously nationalistic, Castrén made the Kalevala runes internationally known, for example, through his Swedish translation, which was published in 1841. In the preface, he supported the *Kalevala* and referred to those who claimed that the epic was Lönnrot's creation as "turncoats."[38]

For the most part, the *Old Kalevala* was favorably received and accepted as the national epic. However, some of the criticism was harsh. It was based largely on the fact that Lönnrot himself had combined and adapted the runes into a whole. In 1839, A. I. Arwidsson succinctly expressed his opinion: "The Finns have never had an ancient, national epic called the *Kalevala*. Rather, Lönnrot has attempted to join old songs together into a single unity and named the compilation *Kalevala*." That same year Heikki Piponius, with whom Lönnrot corresponded, stated: "There is a great deal which could be objected to in the order of the poems."[39]

However, it was C. A. Gottlund who made the sharpest public statements against the epic. The admiration and enthusiasm accorded Lönnrot and the *Kalevala* roused Gottlund to emotionalism. It amazed him "why that *Kalevala* is constantly spoken about and praised," and he referred to Castrén, D. E. D. Europaeus, and Zacharius Cajander, among others, as "Kalevalaiset" (the Kalevalians) and "Kalevalan palveliat" (the *Kalevala*'s attendants). Lönnrot also received his share of this criticism: "Lönnrot is a fine man, a devoted rune collector, a compiler of old songs; but he is not an exceptional being, nor did he do any extraordinary work for him to be regarded as anything other than that." Gottlund even referred to Lönnrot's efforts at compiling the runes as "blurring them into one."[40]

In his preface to *Runola* (The home of poetry), Gottlund points out that he himself had proposed the idea of joining the runes into one in 1817 and that "it is in this very matter that he [that is, Lönnrot] has completely gone astray and failed, and in a good many respects besides."[41] Despite the fact that Gottlund was so sharply critical without giving many specific examples, Aarne Anttila, Lönnrot's biographer, is not fair to him when he states that Gottlund did not give Lönnrot a single suggestion for change.[42] In 1847, for example, Gottlund wrote in *Suomi-lehti* (The Finnish paper):

[Lönnrot] aspired to make his *Kalevala* the equal of Homer's *Iliad* or *Odyssey*, not only in its deeds but also in its magnitude. This is why it was necessary for him to stretch those Väinämöinen runes to great length and number, to greatly expand them in this way. For this reason, sometimes skillfully, sometimes unskillfully, he poured and stirred into the epic materials quite different in nature and of differing periods, mixing all manner of charms and conjurer's words into it, long incantations to heal snake bites, wounds left by iron, and other ancient prattling, wedding verses, as well as additional superfluous verses. So that repeatedly, even here, every now and then Väinämöinen's, Ilmarinen's, or even someone else's name was also included and he filled the second half of his book abundantly with this.[43]

To support his view, Gottlund cites numerous instances where, in his opinion, runes have been needlessly added to the *Kalevala*. He identifies the last poem as a Christian legend: "In the final one, he also adapted papal songs about the birth and death of the Redeemer—solely based on the fact that they had prattled on about Väinämöinen as well."[44]

FROM THE *OLD* TO THE *NEW KALEVALA*

Although Lönnrot already considered the *Old Kalevala* incomplete when it was being published in 1835, it took almost a decade until he began reediting. Throughout this period, Lönnrot intended to further develop the epic, but his attention became focused on other tasks. The foremost of his projects at the time was collecting material for the publication of a Swedish-Finnish dictionary.[45] However, he also was making preparations for revising the *Kalevala*. He made numerous trips to collect runes in the latter half of the 1830s. He published revised texts of Kalevala runes, along with discussions of them, in his journal *Mehiläinen* (The bee), which he himself edited. He also familiarized himself with epic literature published abroad. The fact that he was editing the *Kanteletar*, a collection of lyrical poems, as well as a publication of charms during this time indicates his continuing interest in publishing folklore. The great amount of folklore then being gathered by other collectors, and their requests that this material be included in the *Kalevala*, provided another reason for Lönnrot to revise the epic. The most ardent of these young collectors was D. E. D. Europaeus (1820–1884), then a young student, who collected a vast amount of folklore in Ingria.[46]

On January 14, 1845, Lönnrot wrote to V. G. Schildt that he was editing the runes Europaeus had collected in order to scatter them throughout the *Kalevala* and the *Kanteletar*. On February 16, 1847, he wrote that he had begun reediting the *Kalevala* and added: "Despite a lack of time, it is necessary for me to do the editorial work because I still consider myself able to do this better than the others, who may have more time for it." Lönnrot was also spurred on by the attention the epic had received internationally.[47] He believed in his task and now had the confidence to treat the material with more daring than previously. During this stage, he consciously worked as a creative poet and not solely as a folklore editor.

Lönnrot reestablished the efficient work rhythm he had had while editing the *Old Kalevala*. On August 3, 1847, he wrote to Rector Matthias Akiander, giving the following description of his method of working and demonstrating his enormous ability to concentrate:

I have been nailed here to the *Kalevala*. I have now been able to gather every-thing relating to the *Kalevala* from the mass of runes sent to me by Europaeus, Polén, Sirén, and others and have arranged it appropriately. You can surmise that I have sweated blood over this more than once. What's left to do now, in addition to this, is to complete the earlier text, and to choose the finest vari-ants, according to my best understanding. I plan to put the variants which I cannot place in the text itself on the respective pages because they always pro-vide new information and are more readily at hand there than at the end of the book, where they were in the first edition. I do not believe that the *Kale-vala* will need any further editing after this, because all such runes now seem to have been collected.

Lönnrot had already requested and received an interleaved copy of the *Kale-vala* from the Finnish Literature Society in 1836, in order to make notes about new variants of the runes. August Ahlqvist (1826–1889), who later became Pro-fessor of Finnish Language and Literature at the University of Helsinki, visited Lönnrot in Kajaani during 1847. He gave a detailed description of how Lönnrot used this interleaved copy:

> Work on the *Kalevala* proceeds in the following manner: he has a board before him, on which the Kalevala runes and their content are ordered sequentially. He reads as long a passage from a collector's book as seems to belong together, and if he doesn't remember where in the epic it belongs, he looks at his board. There he searches through a rune topic index and finds that topic to which the words before him belong. Even the page number is up on the board and the *Kalevala*, now interleaved, is opened to this number. Lönnrot finds the sought-after place and writes the verses in question on the paper oppo-site it.[48]

In a letter dated July 25, 1847, Lönnrot described the pressures of this work:

> Thinking about, searching for, and finding the place where each verse is to be situated in the *Kalevala* takes such an unbelievable amount of time, I can't often do more than 2-3 sheets a day, and I probably couldn't even do that much if I didn't walk to my parents' home in the country every day and write there, for as long as I am at all able to sit. Nevertheless, I have decided that no greater speed can be forced, because it is only by using such an extremely precise method that I can hope to arrange the work most closely approximating its appropriate order. Let the Germans simply publish the previous edition again as it is, if they wish, and let the dictionary be delayed a year.

Lönnrot's reference to the Germans is to the fact that Professor W. Schött of Berlin had begun lecturing about Finnish folklore, and German copies of the *Kalevala* had been requested. Because the first printing had already sold out, the Finnish Literature Society had decided to publish an entirely new edition.[49]

According to Lönnrot's editorial method, whether to add a particular rune variant or verse to the epic was determined both by its epic content and by its relationship to the *Kalevala* narrative. It was possible for Lönnrot to include the wedding runes because the plot of the *Kalevala* was also essentially a recurring wedding drama. However, he did set the runes of lyric sentiment aside to be included in the *Kanteletar*, which he was editing simultaneously. Lönnrot was also planning a separate collection for those charms which were not suitable for the *Kalevala*.[50]

In a draft of a letter written during February 1847, Lönnrot pondered the structure of the *Kalevala* and the criticism it had received. He noted that he had not been able to shape the epic to suit the views of any particular critic, because a hundred others would have had a different opinion. With regard to the general ordering of the runes, Lönnrot stated: "No one doubts that I had to order them in some manner." "Eleven years after having organized these runes, I gladly concede that it was in no way complete enough." Finally he stated that the rune sequence in the *New Kalevala* was simply based on the fact that, in the *Old Kalevala*, all those runes telling of Väinämöinen, Ilmarinen, Pohjola, and Kalevala were joined into one. To a certain extent, this provided a better organized unity than if they had remained individual sequences.

On April 17, 1849, Lönnrot completed the preface to his *New Kalevala*. At the same time, he concluded his life's work as a collector of folk poetry and compiler of the *Kalevala*, although he did still do an abbreviated version of the epic when he retired from his professorship at the University of Helsinki in 1862. Lönnrot's unassuming, self-assertive nature, as well as his historical view of the Kalevala runes, becomes apparent in the first paragraph of this preface:

> This book about the ancient circumstances of our ancestors, their life and situation, appears here in a form much more complete than it was previously (1835). It will probably remain in its present form, because it is unlikely that uncollected runes of this type will be found anymore, since all the localities where there was even the slightest hope of runes being sung have been criss-crossed and searched many times by numerous collectors. Keeping in mind that these will become the oldest singular memories of the Finnish people and language, as long as they continue to exist in the world, an effort has been made to arrange them with all possible care and diligence, and to join them together as best I know how, and to include everything in them which the runes have preserved about the life, customs, and events of that period. There has, however, been a great deal of arbitrariness in arranging them, because not many poems have been found in a single sequence, even from the best singers, and even then they are not of one type. This is why it has, in fact, often been necessary to make the internal claims of the material itself the criteria and, regardless of sequence in the previous edition of the Kalevala occasionally to diverge from that as well. As one would expect, therefore, the work of ordering may not have succeeded to everyone's satisfaction, and without objections still being raised to one thing or another.

CHAPTER
3
THE STRUCTURE OF
THE *KALEVALA*

BASIC CONTENT OF THE EPIC

> If I now knew that the order into which these poems have been arranged was acceptable to others as well, I would stop and not say anything about it. But the matter is such that what one considers appropriate, another sees as unsuitable. It is true that in my opinion the poems flow approximately in the sequence in which they have been arranged here, but perhaps they would flow even better in another. I have paid heed to two things in ordering them: first, what I observed the best singers to pay heed to in the order, and, second, if this was of no help, I have sought the basis of the matter in the poems themselves, and considered them accordingly.[1]

The *Kalevala* was not completed quickly. Lönnrot's understanding of the basic content of the work, as well as the interrelationship of the poems, was altered as the totality of the epic, including the view of antiquity it encompassed, took shape in his mind. In his works which preceded the *Kalevala*, Lönnrot centered the poems around major figures in folklore. At this early stage he constructed portraits of individual heroes. Initially, in the *Old Kalevala*, this material became "mythology," and only afterward did it evolve into the picture of "the ancient times of the Finnish people" which becomes manifest in the outline of the *New Kalevala*. In 1835, Lönnrot still closely adhered to the views and performances of the foremost rune singers. In the *New Kalevala*, however, it is apparent that he himself had already become a self-confident poet. As the body of runes grew, Lönnrot's role evolved from that of compiler to molder, creator, and poet. His view of the runes had also changed.

How had the compilation of the *Kalevala* initially come about? In his revised preface to the *Old Kalevala*, Lönnrot related his view of the unity of the ancient proto-tale and its subsequent multiplicity of versions:

> Building on the original tale, which was by no means as extensive as the present poem, the rune singers wove/created their own threads from generation

29

to generation, set their own wefts; this is even being done today. In singing, good rune singers are little concerned if they don't remember one rune or another word by word, as they heard it from other, previous chanters. Rather, they sing it through the forgotten section as well, perhaps with their own words. And this may well be the reason for these many variants and also, in part, for the present breadth of the poem.[2]

The final compilation can be reduced to the following plot structure: the *New Kalevala* begins with the "Creation Rune" (Poems 1–2), this is followed by the death of Aino (3–5), the forging of the Sampo (6–10), Lemminkäinen's first journey to Pohjola (11–15), Väinämöinen's adventures (16–17), the courtship contest (18–20), the wedding at Pohjola (21–25), Lemminkäinen's second journey to Pohjola (26–30), the tragedy of Kullervo (31–36), Ilmarinen's second journey to Pohjola (37–38), the theft of the Sampo (39–42), the flight from Pohjola (43–44), the struggle over the Sampo (45–49), and the departure of Väinämöinen (50).

As August Annist has shown, the *Kalevala* is balanced and symmetrical in its basic structure.[3] The *New Kalevala* divides naturally into two parts, each containing approximately twenty-five poems: the birth of Väinämöinen and the drama of Aino at the beginning of the epic are symmetrical with Väinämöinen's departure and Marjatta's fate at its conclusion. Within the epic there are four poetic unities which focus on relations between Kalevala and Pohjola. The first two are friendly and peaceful interactions, while the last two depict hostile struggles. Three secondary episodes describing the vicissitudes of Lemminkäinen and Kullervo are interspersed between these four central focal points. These have no bearing as such on the structure of the Sampo plot, around which the *Kalevala* is largely constructed.

When the *New Kalevala* was published, it supplanted the *Old Kalevala*, which had sold out by that time, and came to be considered the only legitimate version of the epic. The *New Kalevala* was seen as the version that had been written down by Lönnrot in its final, tidy form. Thereafter, it came to be considered the common property of the Finnish people and a national cultural monument which has reigned over Finnish culture to such an extent that its content has developed characteristics of canonical meaning. It is typical of such a process that the previous versions of the work and the *Kalevala* process itself have largely been forgotten. During its time, however, the *Old Kalevala* was also considered to be the final version of the epic. It was, in fact, the *Old Kalevala* which was translated into Swedish by Mathias A. Castrén in 1841 and into French by Léouzon Le Duc in 1845. Jacob Grimm also based his well-known essay about the Finnish epic on this version.

A comparison between the *New Kalevala* and the *Old Kalevala* shows that the differences between them are considerable, although both versions begin with the creation of the world and end with Väinämöinen's ruin. Thus, for example, tales about Väinämöinen, Aino, and Joukahainen which were at the end of the *Old Kalevala* are placed at the beginning of the new version. While the *Old Kalevala* began with the shooting of Väinämöinen, in the *New Kalevala* this episode does not occur until Poem 6. The final poems of the *New Kalevala*, 44–49, are a rearrangement of Poems 25–29 in the *Old Kalevala*. However, both versions end with the tale about Marjatta and her son. The most significant additions in content from the *Old Kalevala* to the *New* are the marriage of Lemminkäinen and Kyllikki, and almost the entire tale of Kullervo (*New Kalevala* 11, 34–36). These episodes are almost entirely missing in the *Old Kalevala*. Figure 1 shows how the poems of the *Old Kalevala* were adapted into the *New*.

FIGURE 1.

Redistribution of Content from the *Old Kalevala* to the New Kalevala

Poems of the *Old Kalevala*	Corresponding Poems in the *New Kalevala*	Poems of the *Old Kalevala*	Corresponding Poems in the *New Kalevala*
1	1 & 6	17	26–27
2	7	18	28–30
3	8	19	31–33
4	9	20	37–38
5	10	21	39
6	12	22	40–41
7	13–14	23	42–43
8	15	24	2
9	16	25	45
10	17	26	47–48
11	18	27	49
12	19	28	46
13	20	29	44
14	21	30	3
15	22–24	31	4–5
16	25	32	50

The content summaries prepared by Lönnrot for each version of the *Kalevala* are given side by side in this book, in order that the reader can observe in detail the differences between the two versions of the epic.

The *New Kalevala* replaced the *Old* and was the conclusion of Lönnrot's work in epical creation. However, Lönnrot's *Kalevala* was not the only Finnish effort of its kind. For a century, Finnish folklore scholars have followed the trail blazed by Julius Krohn with regard to questions posed by the individual runes themselves, as opposed to the epical whole. As a result, a number of differing versions of the *Kalevala* have evolved. Some are intended for educational purposes, for example, while others are simply abridged versions or prose editions of the epic. Several are based on the posited original form of the runes, others on alternative variants collected from singers. Among them are Martti Haavio's *Kirjokansi* (The bright dome) (1952) and *Laulupuu* (Songtree) (1952), which are skillful poetical reconstructions of prototypes, based on the runes he considered to be the foundation for the *Kalevala* and the *Kanteletar*. In these works, Haavio, who was both a folklorist and a poet under the pseudonym P.

Mustapää, provides a turbulent vision of the world of ancient Finnish poetry. In contrast to this approach, Matti Kuusi's *Kansanruno—Kalevala* (Folk Poetry—Kalevala) (1976), for use in schools and colleges, is based on original variants of the runes, as is the Finnish-English collection of 148 runes entitled *Finnish Folk Poetry: Epic, An Anthology in Finnish and English* (1977) edited by Kuusi and his British colleagues Keith L. Bosley and Michael Branch.

THE SAMPO RUNES: EPIC HEART OF THE *KALEVALA*

What is the Sampo? This is, without a doubt, the question most pondered in *Kalevala* scholarship, and the one which has most frequently inspired artists to interpret the subject matter of the *Kalevala* runes. The Sampo cycle holds a central place in Lönnrot's *Kalevala*, forming the core of the epic's plot and structure. It is the Sampo poetry that provides the framework for the rest of the poetic subject matter.

The earliest mention of the Sampo is in a rune recorded in 1817 from Maija Turpoinen by Carl Axel Gottlund. The variant given by Turpoinen, a "Forest Finn"[4] from Dalarna in Sweden who spoke the Savo dialect, consisted of only one part of the extensive Sampo poetry, the theft of the Sampo and the casting of it into the sea. "What flew into the sea, brought salt to the sea; what was cast on the land, brought growth to the land. If many of its pieces had reached the land, then grain would have grown with no sowing."[5] It is interesting that Gottlund expressed his idea about a unified Finnish epic in the same year he recorded the fragment from Turpoinen about the theft of the Sampo: "It is quite natural and almost an unconditional prerequisite for a mythical concept that the meaning of the word "Sampo" (or Sammas) itself must remain both mystical and inexplicable; for it is in just this that its exquisiteness lies."[6]

Subsequently, hundreds of versions of the Sampo runes have been collected from Finnish rune areas. Lönnrot first got support for his idea of a unified poetic epic in 1833, when he heard Ontrei Malinen sing a continuous 366-verse version of the Sampo runes.[7] The basic plot of the *Kalevala* actually derives from Arhippa Perttunen's 402-verse "miniature Sampo epic," collected by Lönnrot in 1834.[8] In Perttunen's version, the shooting of Väinämöinen, his drifting on the water, the forging of the Sampo, and its theft follow each other in the same general sequence as they do in Lönnrot's *Old Kalevala*.

The first scholar to study the Sampo runes was A. A. Borenius (1846–1931), who received the impetus for this from the rune singer Ontreini Vassilei, Ontrei Malinen's son. In 1872, while Vassilei was reciting a Sampo rune to Borenius, he interrupted himself and "explained the rune in general terms. It was about the origin of the world; there were preparations for plowing and sowing." In his travel diary, Borenius continues:

The best singers sing the runes about the creation of the world and the Sampo sequence together as one poem. It is inconceivable that the creation of the world would not be part of this rune and happened here by chance. Thus, it is no longer inexplicable why the forging of the Sampo is joined to the rune about creation. If, as I myself believe is indisputable, the Sampo is the sun, then the entire Sampo rune is nothing but a tale about the creation of the world and keeping the creation in force.[9]

The common consensus among folklorists, including Kaarle Krohn, Matti Kuusi, and Martti Haavio, is that the Sampo poetry existed as a continuous epic unity within the folk tradition.[10] There are, however, differences of opinion among the scholars as to the original sequence of the runes and whether, for example, "Kilpakosinta" (The courtship contest) and "Kultaneito" (The golden maiden) are to be included among the original Sampo runes. In his historical-geographic study, expressly named *Sampo-eepos* (The Sampo epic) (1949), Kuusi has given a detailed explanation of the order and the relationships of the Sampo runes as found in various localities. In his opinion, the Sampo epic is composed of five ancient Finnish heroic epics: "Maailmansynty" (The creation of the world), "Sammontaonta" (The forging of the Sampo), "Sammonryöstö" (The theft of the Sampo), "Kilpakosinta" (The courtship contest), and "Kultaneito" (The golden maiden).[11] Haavio concurred with this theory, although he believed that "The Courtship Contest" and "The Golden Maiden" had been added to the Sampo cycle by chance.[12] In Kuusi's opinion, the Sampo epic consists of four "acts." In the first, the Lapp shoots Väinämöinen, who drifts to Pohjola; in the second, the elements of the cosmos are created; in the third, the Sampo is forged; and the fourth consists of the theft of the Sampo and the battle which ensues over it.[13]

The rune about the creation of the world describes how Väinämöinen, wounded by an arrow, comes to drift on the sea and eventually reaches the shores of Pohjola. There the Old Crone of Pohjola, Louhi, finds him and takes him into her care. In the *Kalevala*, Lönnrot has combined this material with that of "The Courtship Contest" and made Joukahainen, who is avenging a former defeat, the one to wound Väinämöinen. However, in most variants of the rune, such as those sung by Ontrei Malinen[14] and Arhippa Perttunen,[15] the marksman is "the slant-eyed Lapp," whose motives are given no further explanation.

Basing his argument primarily on stylistic analysis, Kuusi maintains[16] that there are two runes of two different periods united in the Finnish poem "The Creation of the World." In his view, the first part of the rune, including Väinämöinen's drifting on the sea and the creation of the sea bottom, is related to older cosmogonic poetry, while the conclusion, in which Väinämöinen floats to the shores of Pohjola, reflects a more recent stylistic period in which the mythical hero has become completely human and deplores his fate:

A man heard weeping
a hero howling
The weeping is not a woman's weeping
nor is the weeping a child's weeping
this is Väinämöinen's weeping
Untamoinen's wailing"
(Sung by Arhippa Perttunen to Elias Lönnrot, 1834)[17]

Väinämöinen's drifting to Pohjola serves as an introduction to the forging of the Sampo. In his monumental analysis of the Sampo (1932), Professor of Finnish E. N. Setälä showed that two parallel versions of its forging exist in folk poetry. According to one version, the Sampo is forged as a price for Väinämöinen's escape from Pohjola, and according to the other, the forging of the Sampo is once again a task related to "The Courtship Contest." In this latter version, the prize for completion of the task is the Maiden of Pohjola.[18] In Lönnrot's Kalevala, these two versions have been united. Väinämöinen is able to leave Pohjola after promising Louhi that he will get Ilmarinen to forge the Sampo. Upon reaching home, he tells Ilmarinen of the Mistress of Pohjola's promise to give her daughter to the one who forges the Sampo. Ilmarinen departs, forges the Sampo, and obtains his wife.[19] Matti Kuusi also stresses the possibility that a "second Sampo" was forged and places the forging of the Sampo after the theft of the initial one.[20] In this, he concurs with the theory presented by Setälä, that two Sampos had actually been created. "When you forge the new Sampo, decorate the spectrum lid," Louhi demands of Väinämöinen in Arhippa Perttunen's variant of the rune.[21]

The rune about the theft of the Sampo tells how Väinämöinen and Ilmarinen sail to Pohjola to get the Sampo. Among those helping them is Iku-Tiera or Jompainen. When he unified the Kalevala, Lönnrot shifted this helping role to Lemminkäinen. During this journey, Väinämöinen lulls the people of Pohjola to sleep with his music, and his men are then able to take the Sampo into their boat. However, their premature celebration wakens the men of Pohjola and, under the leadership of Louhi, they take up violent pursuit.[22] The sea chase and the depiction of the battle which follows constitute the climax of both the Sampo runes and, above all, the Kalevala. There are, however, differing interpretations of how the Sampo sequence ends. Among the rune singers, for example, Ontrei Malinen maintained that the Sampo sank into the sea, while in Arhippa Perttunen's version, the Sampo breaks into pieces. Its cover remains with Louhi, and Väinämöinen collects the pieces which have drifted ashore.

Although the Sampo runes follow basically the same sequence in Lönnrot's New Kalevala as they do in the versions sung by Malinen and Perttunen, they are not in succession. Lönnrot has scattered them throughout various sections of the epic. As a consequence, the Sampo runes appear to bind together the rest of the Kalevala material. The Kalevala begins with the creation of the world and Väinämöinen's drifting on the sea. However, the next Sampo episode, about Väinämöinen's drifting toward Pohjola, does not appear in the *New Kalevala* until Poem 7. It is followed by "The Forging of the Sampo" in Poem 10, "The Courtship Contest" in Poem 18, and "The Golden Maiden" in Poem 27. The "Theft of the Sampo" is found toward the end of the epic, in Poems 39, 42, and 43. In the *New Kalevala*, the Sampo runes are placed within the framework of a war between the people of Kalevala from the south and the people of Pohjola from the north. This struggle is presented as the primary motive for individual actions.

THE LEMMIKÄINEN SERIES

There may be some in Finland who have not even heard of Lemminkäinen, and others who care little, even if they do hear. We too would let Lemminkäinen sleep his sleep of a thousand years and longer if at times nature didn't draw our minds away from the present; sometimes we are drawn back to recall the origins of past life, and at other times into the future, to inquire about the directions life is to take. Thus, even as we progress along our life's hectic course, we embrace the opportunity to meet light-hearted Lemminkäinen alive. And, as a result of this journey, we hope at least to discover whether our present situation has changed greatly from ancient times and become civilized, in order that, without hesitation, we might stand abreast of those past times and demonstrate that we have succeeded in what is fundamental to all being, activity, and life—to improve bit by bit, to become more beautiful and civilized.[23]

Lemminkäinen is among the most captivating heroes in the *Kalevala*. Thus, in 1985, the year marking the 150th anniversary of the epic, it was Lemminkäinen who was made famous by Keith Bosley of the British Isles, in his translation of *Kalevala* poetry entitled *Wanton Loverboy*.[24] The Lemminkäinen poems were already of interest to Lönnrot when he first began arranging the poems about the *Kalevala* heroes. He had, in fact, completed a miniature epic about Lemminkäinen in 1833, but it remained unpublished.[25] This poem contained the marrow of the Lemminkäinen runes based on Lönnrot's familiarity with them up to that point. However, the overlapping names of characters in the rune variants preoccupied Lönnrot. In his introduction to *Lisiä vanhaan Kalevalaan* (Supplement to the *Old Kalevala*), which was published posthumously by A. R. Niemi, Lönnrot clearly stated his dilemma: "The poems about Lemminkäinen and Kullervo, as well as those about Lemminkäinen and Joukahainen, are greatly confused with each other. At times it is indeed unclear which belongs to which, and likewise with those about Väinämöinen and Ilmarinen or Lemminkäinen."[26]

In his preface to the *New Kalevala*, Lönnrot remarked on the variation in names found in the runes: "Runes obtained from different singers and different localities vary not only in their sequence but often in the personal names used in them. One sings of Väinämöinen what another does of Ilmarinen, and a third of Lemminkäinen; one sings of Lemminkäinen what another does of Kullervo or Joukahainen, as in the case of Kullervo's journey to collect taxes, for example, which in other runes is made by Tuiretuinen, Tuurikkinen, Lemminkäinen or vanha Väinon poika [old Väinämöinen's son]."[27]

As Lönnrot progressed in his revisions toward the final version of the *Kalevala*, the solution he adopted was to make Lemminkäinen the third major heroic figure of the epic, in addition to Väinämöinen and Ilmarinen. Thus Lemminkäinen's adventures span the entirety of the epic. In the *New Kalevala*, he is at the center of the stage three times: first in Poems 11–15; again in Poems 26–30, when he is a central figure at the wedding of Pohjola; and in Poem 39, when he joins Väinämöinen and Ilmarinen as the third hand in the Sampo journey. As a consequence, he is present when the Sampo is stolen and at the final battle over it. It was in this manner that Lönnrot greatly expanded the plots found in the rune texts to create an abundance of action and motifs for his favorite figure.

Scholars have presented somewhat divergent opinions as to the basic structure of "Lemminkäisen virsi" (The Lemminkäinen rune). In Matti Kuusi's opinion, it is a poem about a journey and tells of Lemminkäinen's departure "to his brothers-in-law in Luontola, his sisters in Väinölä." Lemminkäinen is warned of the dangers of the journey, but he overcomes them, arrives at his destination, drinks the snake mead served to him, and kills the one who served it.[28] Martti Haavio[29] has reconstructed a five-act version of the poem with the following plot development: a festivity is organized at Päivölä to which all capable of attending are invited, except for Lemminkäinen. Lemminkäinen hears the sounds of celebration and decides to go as an uninvited guest, although his mother warns him of three deadly perils looming on the journey. Using his powers as a sage, Lemminkäinen overcomes these perils. The first is a grave full of hot stones, the second a snake with many eyes, and the third an iron-beaked bird, an eagle, on a burning, rocky islet–all subject matter which recurs in shamanistic tradition.

Having surmounted the dangers, Lemminkäinen arrives at Päivölä, where he is insulted, first by being served beer with snakes swimming in it and then by being seated in the doorway. He demands a seat at the back of the room, a place of honor. In the battle which ensues with the Master of Päivölä, .either with weapons or with words, Lemminkäinen eventually emerges victorious to sit at the place meant for a sage. At issue here is a chanting competition between shamans, in which animals are sent by turns to attack the opponent. Next Lemminkäinen chants those attending the feast "to glimmmer as gold, to shine as silver," but he leaves one unsung, the old man of Ulappala. In retribution for this oversight, the old man kills Lemminkäinen, dismembers his body, and casts it into the River of Tuonela. At home, Lemminkäinen's mother infers her son's demise from omens and departs for Päivölä. Despite the dangers, she reaches her destination and, by threatening the murderer, learns her son's fate. She makes herself a large rake, with which she succeeds in dragging her son's remains out of the water. She then joins them into one and brings her son back to life. According to Arhippa Perttunen, "a woman previously married" rakes Lemminkäinen's body parts out of the River of Tuonela and brings him to life by means of an ointment of words, that is, with the aid of charms. Thus Lemminkäinen's mother also has shamanistic attributes.

Lemminkäinen is a many-faceted character in Finnish folk poetry as well. On the journey to the festivities at Päivölä, which Lönnrot locates in Pohjola, Lemminkäinen's role is that of a shaman. With the Master of Pohjola as his opponent, he also participates in a chanting competition, as do Väinämöinen and Joukahainen, and, like Väinämöinen, he also makes a journey to Tuonela. In both Finnish folk poetry and the *Kalevala*, the figure of Lemminkäinen has taken its dimensions from many heroes.

In the figure of Lemminkäinen, the shamanistic sage and the man of great power are united in an impetuous Viking hero. Lönnrot made Lemminkäinen into one of the main figures in his *Kalevala* by combining characters from various versions of the rune under the one name. His Lemminkäinen evolved into a Finnish peasant hero, a skilled chanter, a high-spirited rogue, a Finnish Don Juan.[30] On the other hand, he is also a tragic hero with an almost Oedipal relationship to his mother. In his preface to the *Old Kalevala*, Lönnrot evaluates the hero in the following manner, comparing him with Väinämöinen and Ilmarinen:

> Lemminkäinen was of a different sort, wanton, young, arrogant, boastful of his power and knowledge, short-sighted with regard to the future, though even valiant and a hero. The courtship tasks designated for him at Pohjola cannot, in truth, be clarified, for on another occasion exactly the same tasks are even given to Ilmarinen. I have chosen runes in which it is possible to make a slight distinction between them.[31]

Based on Lönnrot's extensive article about Lemminkäinen in *The Bee*,[32] it is possible to examine the role of Lemminkäinen in Lönnrot's world view. In this article, Lönnrot created a historical figure of Lemminkäinen. He presented the historical concept of a war chieftain named Kaleva, who "was capable of leading the largest Finnish force of his times to those lands." Among those closest to him was Lemminkäinen. Lönnrot considered Lemminkäinen to be the son of the renowned war chieftain Lempi. Lemminkäinen was lulled to sleep by his mother's lullabies after the death of her husband, thus the name "Lieto Lemminkäinen" (Light-hearted Lemminkäinen). In Lönnrot's opinion, the character Kaukomieli was related to Lemminkäinen as well, because he desired to make distant journeys.

Particularly interesting is Lönnrot's opinion that the presentation of chants, "laulaminen" (singing, chanting), was a skill in which Lemminkäinen excelled. This signified a command of incantations about origins, as shaman-

Lemminkäinen, the eternal seeker in the Finnish epic, is a figure parallel to the wandering Odysseus. This international myth has been depicted in a multiplicity of ways, both in the visual arts and in folklore. On this vase, from the third century B.C., Odysseus is pictured among sirens. (*The Mythology of All Races.* 1916)

A mid-fifteenth century fresco, restored on the walls of the church at Korppo in southwestern Finland. Beside the Tree of Life is a ship bearing the same number of passengers as depicted on the Greek vase in photo above. (Finnish National Board of Antiquities)

ism. For Lönnrot, the provincial doctor, Lemminkäinen was above all an ancient healer, his colleague. Lönnrot gives a detailed description of how Lemminkäinen was trained in shamanistic skills at home by his mother:

> All such knowledge was understood as chanting at that time, and Lemminkäinen's mother was very well versed in all this. Through her, as time passed, the boy was also able to increase his skill and power in these matters. Thus he, like other sages, always had with him a pouch full of various objects from a journey which were needed in addition to charms for different purposes. The materials carried in these purses were those most often used in everyday life or those which were otherwise needed. Thus, evidently, in addition to flint, fish hooks, and other smaller implements, there were animal hairs, bird feathers, and other such things in Lemminkäinen's pouch. As a consequence, no matter where he was, Lemminkäinen needed only to gather those hairs or feathers, fish fins, human bones or hair, tree bark, substances indicating water and fire, etc. from his pouch and then, by chanting, even a bird, fish, human, tree, water, fire, or other things came alive from them. In addition to this knowledge, Lemminkäinen had many other skills and learning. He shod his own horse, constructed boats and skis, sowed land, and went into the forests as an archer.[33]

Thus, in Lönnrot's early writings, there existed a view of Lemminkäinen which has largely been overlooked in later study of the *Kalevala*. In addition to being a warrior and a Don Juan, he was the prototype of a shaman who, by his knowledge, attained the level of "wise old" Väinämöinen. On the other hand, a classical model for Lemminkäinen's journeys also exists in Homer's *Odyssey*. As one who perpetually longs for distant lands, Lemminkäinen in his aimless wanderings and shamanistic journeys is kin to such other seekers and adventurers as Odysseus.

THE KULLERVO TRAGEDY: AN EPICAL DRAMA

One of the greatest changes from the *Old* to the *New Kalevala* centers around the figure of Kullervo. The story of Kullervo, related in a single poem of the *Old Kalevala*, was broadened into an epical drama by Lönnrot in the *New Kalevala*. Poem 19 of the *Old Kalevala* tells of the ill-fated Kullervo from Kalevala, who is sold to Ilmarinen as a slave at a young age. He fails at all the tasks assigned him and becomes a shepherd. When he finds a stone in his noonday bread, put there as a trick by Ilmarinen's wife, a struggle ensues between them. Ilmarinen's wife, who was formerly the Maiden of Pohjola, beseeches the god Ukko to have Kullervo die in battle. Kullervo, for his part, asks that diseases destroy her. Ilmarinen's wife dies, Kullervo goes off to war, and, for this phase of the epic, his role is over in the plot of the *Old Kalevala*.

During the 1830s and 1840s, however, Lönnrot received a good number of runes about Kullervo, primarily collected from southern Karelia and Ingria. As a result, he had a great deal of new information available. The arrangement of these runes, and their place in the *Kalevala*, subsequently preoccupied him for a long while. In his revised preface to the *Old Kalevala*, published posthumously, Lönnrot states: "The Kullervo runes were particularly confused. First, a number of variants relate that his parents had been killed by Untamo—while he himself, yet unborn, was taken into captivity inside his mother's womb. Still others tell of his bidding farewell to his parents, and others describe his departing for war."[34]

It was not easy for Lönnrot to weave the character of Kullervo, found in the runes from the southern regions, into the plot of the *Kalevala*, which was otherwise based primarily on White Sea Karelian elements. Nevertheless, he considered the Kullervo poetry so significant that he sought a place for it. In the end, the Kullervo runes were preserved almost as a unified epic sequence. Thus Poems 31–36 of the *New Kalevala*, which focus on Kullervo, interrupt the narrative, which is otherwise largely constructed around the Sampo. Its point of unity with the epic as a whole is that Kullervo becomes Ilmarinen's slave. Ilmarinen, in turn, has married the Maiden of Pohjola, whom he received as a reward for forging the Sampo. When she is killed as a result of Kullervo's act of revenge, the plot continues with Ilmarinen's attempt to forge a maiden of gold.

There are parallels to the opening of the Kullervo poems in stories about mythical heroes found throughout world mythology, who are born under abnormal circumstances and often become gods. In a feud between brothers, Untamo destroys Kalervo's folk so completely that only one pregnant wife is left alive. Captured by Untamo's forces, she gives birth to a son, Kullervo, who vows revenge while still in his cradle. Untamo attempts to slay Kullervo, who nevertheless grows to manhood and brings ruination to all the tasks he undertakes. He is sold to Ilmarinen as a slave. This aspect of the poetry reflects the actuality of the feudalism and serfdom which reigned south of the Gulf of Finland. It had a powerful impact on the folk poetry of Estonia and Ingria, in which these harsh circumstances manifested themselves in songs strongly critical of society, such as the "Song of the Estonian Serf."[35]

Having been sent to herd sheep, the slave Kullervo finds a stone in the bread that Ilmarinen's wife has baked for him. In cutting it, he ruins his knife, the only memento he has left of his kin. Using shamanistic powers, he drives the herd into a swamp and sends bears to tear Ilmarinen's wife to pieces. Upon learning his old mother is still alive, Kullervo goes in search of her. On his journey, he comes across a young girl whom he seduces. The young pair soon discover they are siblings. Having broken an incest taboo, the sister drowns herself in a waterfall, finding "refuge and mercy in death," according to the poem.[36] At issue here is the Oedipal theme of forbidden sexual contact which leads to suicide.

Kullervo rushes home and tells his mother what has happened. She con-

Numerous bold visions of the *Kalevala* were created by foreign artists. Pictured above is Louis Sparre's vision of the climax of the Kullervo poem, in which Kullervo abducts his sister. During the 1800s, Sparre, a count of Italian-Swedish descent, traveled to Karelia with Akseli Gallén-Kallela and Emil Wickström, among others. (Atheneum Museum, Helsinki)

vinces him not to commit suicide and urges him to hide. Kullervo then goes to war, slays Untamo's forces, and returns to his desolate home. His family has died while he was away. He finds only an old black dog, which accompanies him into the forest. Kullervo comes to the spot where he had seduced his sister, throws down his sword, and casts himself on it to his death.[37] The death wish characteristic of Kullervo's spirit is fulfilled by his suicide.

In 1853, Fredrik Cygnaeus (1807–1881) published his study of the tragic subject matter in the *Kalevala*. He argued that the deepest cause of Kullervo's misfortune lay in the fact that nature had made him a hero, but fate had subjugated him to slavery.[38] The primary topic of this poem is the fatalism characteristic of the Finnish world view. It has been easy for Finnish men to identify with the figure of Kullervo. According to Kalle Achté, a Finnish psychiatrist, the role model for men in Finnish culture is a superman who advances inexorably toward his fate, which may even be suicide. Men feel they are not supposed to show their emotions. They are not permitted to cry or to show weakness.[39] Kullervo's tragic fate may also be re-

The *Kalevala* experienced a renaissance at the end of the nineteenth century, when numerous prominent artists focused on it in the spirit of nationalism. These included the figures depicted in Akseli Gallén-Kallela's renowned *Symposium,* dated 1894. *From left to right:* Gallén-Kallela himself, with the composers Jean Sibelius and Robert Kajanus (b. 1856). *Symposium* was painted two years after Sibelius had composed his famous *Kullervo Symphony.* (Finnish National Board of Antiquities)

garded as a model for heroic suicide—a common phenomenon in Finland, particularly during difficult times such as the period of Russian oppression at the turn of the twentieth century.

The tragedy of Kullervo proved to be a subject deeply felt and portrayed by Finnish writers (Aleksis Kivi), poets (Eino Leino), visual artists (Akseli Gallén-Kallela), and composers (Jean Sibelius). In fact, it is clear that Kullervo's fame, both in Finland and abroad, is based primarily on the art he has inspired, rather than on his role in the *Kalevala* itself. Particularly noteworthy in this regard is the symphonic poem *Kullervo,* which was completed early in the 1890s by Sibelius, then a young composer. At its première in 1892, it was conducted by the composer himself. The symphony proved to be Sibelius's breakthrough and initiated a new era in the history of Finnish music. Oskar Merikanto, a renowned Finnish composer and critic, wrote: "Sibelius takes us to completely new territories, unknown tonalities, he brings before our eyes the most beautiful pearls of our national epic; he caresses our ears with Finnish tunes, which we know to be ours, although we've never heard them expressed this way before. . . ."[40]

Sibelius himself was greatly inspired by the folk songs he collected from the Ingrian rune singer Larin Paraske. The Finnish musicologist Erik Tawaststjerna has shown that Sibelius's use of these folk songs in his symphony was the first time folk melodies had been adapted into Finnish classical music. The meeting between Sibelius and Paraske took place in Porvoo, during November of 1891. This was a time of intense creativity for Sibelius, when *Kullervo* was coming to fruition.[41] His traveling companion, Yrjö Hirn, gave the following description of Sibelius's journey to meet the renowned folk singer:

> I was on a journey with Jean Sibelius from Loviisa to Porvoo by way of Hämeenlinna. My traveling companion, five years older than I, was then developing the plans which would lead to the symphonic poem *Kullervo*, completed and performed the following year. He greatly desired to hear how the Karelian rune sounded when sung by an authentic singer, and I was certainly happy to be able to witness this meeting of the new and old. I don't dare state my thoughts about how much it may have meant for the master's compositions on *Kalevala* themes that he was able to hear Paraske at that time. I only remember his carefully following the song and noting down the course and rhythm of the melody.[42]

How deeply Sibelius entered into his subject matter becomes apparent from his letters to his fiancée, Aino Järnefelt. Depicting Kullervo's relationship with his sister in the composition was particularly difficult for Sibelius. During the final stage, he worked intensively night and day, revealing to his fiancée that he was almost at the brink of suicide. This work was so painful for him that, after its prèmiere in 1892, he forbade its performance until after his death in 1957. Thus the great work, which climaxed in the destruction of Kullervo's sister, could not be performed again until the Sibelius Festival in 1958.[43]

AINO: A FEMALE METAMORPHOSIS

Aino is one of the central female figures of the *Kalevala*. She is more Lönnrot's creation than a figure found in oral poetry. Specific poetry about "Aino" does not exist as such in Finnish runes. In fact, it was only in the *New Kalevala* that Lönnrot found a name for this female figure who was needed at the beginning of the epic. In the *Old Kalevala*, Aino is still Joukahainen's nameless sister. In the *New Kalevala*, she has become one of the main female figures. The "Aino Poem," as compiled by Lönnrot, is noticeably longer and more enigmatic than the variants on which it is based. It

Väinämöinen and Aino (1861), India ink drawing by R. V. Ekman. (Atheneum Museum, Helsinki)

is joined to the rune about angling the Maiden of Vellamo and together with it forms a separate dialogue of death and sexuality.

After failing to rebuff the old suitor, Väinämöinen, in Lönnrot's *Kalevala*, Aino leaves home and wanders through the forest to a lakeshore. She does not violently destroy herself by throwing herself into the water; rather, she wishes to join the water maidens who swim freely and happily in the lake. The rune describes Aino's disrobing with particular detail: item by item of clothing and piece by piece of jewelry, she casts off her tokens of culture and status. Her death combines the desire for freedom and separation with a bitter desire for revenge. Her self-drowning is a clear message to those who remain behind, and she herself inscribes her metamorphosis by listing the various elements of the lake with which she becomes identified. Through her death, Aino becomes part of nature.

> She cast her blouse upon the willow
> Her skirt upon the aspen,
> Her stockings upon the bare ground,
> Her shoes upon the stone in the stream,
> Her beads upon the sandy shore,
> Her rings upon the gravel.
> A rock bright upon the waves,
> Akin to gold it shone:

She sought to swim to the rock,
Wished to flee to the boulder.

And having reached there
To settle herself then
Upon the bright rock,
The gleaming boulder,
The rock rang into the water,
The boulder fled to the bottom,
The Maiden upon the rock,
Aino on the edge of the boulder.

Water is a central element in the *Kalevala*, and in this poem it is a primary symbol of the feminine consciousness, as well: the maidens swim in the water; the tears of Aino's mother metamorphose into streams.

The poem about Aino can also be analyzed from the viewpoint of psychoanalytic theories which interpret still water as an expression of motherhood and womanliness.[44] In this interpretation, Aino's diving into the water could alternatively be reversed and seen as a rising from the water and a rebirth. It is both a giver of birth and a reference to death, for water bears life, which flows with it from the body. The fact that Väinämöinen succeeds in snaring Aino, who has metamorphosed into a wondrous fish, supports the view of her rebirth, which is also embodied in the Finnish folk religion.

But why does Aino yield to becoming the sage's booty when it was specifically to escape him that she entered the realm of death? Her metamorphosis into a fish, which symbolizes fertility and womanhood, can perhaps be interpreted psychoanalytically as a girl's changing into a woman. Aino knew immediately that Väinämöinen was not the right man for her, that the old man would not be able to satisfy the woman waking within her, and that he really wanted a servant girl, someone to sweep his floors. Väinämöinen does not, in fact, recognize his bride when he encounters her as a fish (i.e., a woman, surrounded by the moist, feminine element) but rather prepares to slice the fish for his meal. Aino's mocking answer: "Oh, oh, you poor old dim-witted Väinämöinen / You no longer recognized the wet maiden of Vellamo / The only child in the glade!"[45] With these words she points out to Väinämöinen that he did not, in fact, recognize the girl's womanhood, and thus would never have been able to satisfy it.

For Aino, therefore, death meant becoming one with the Other. As such, it offered greater sexual fulfillment than the life which would have awaited her. Arctic cultures offer parallel concepts, in accordance with which it was acceptable for a girl to kill herself rather than take an old or otherwise undesirable groom. It was believed that she would achieve a better and more desirable suitor in death.[46] Western literature also offers abundant examples of the theme that true love is possible only in death, for life is filled with obstacles. The most famous of these may be the French tale of Tristan and Isolde. Aino does not, however, appear again as a bride but as a water maiden, whose death can be considered the fulfillment of her womanhood.

A young girl's metamorphosis as a result of her being pursued by an ardent old suitor is a central theme in the mythology of antiquity, as well. The girl seldom changes back into her former being. The metamorphosis is a radical change, and a change is also always a sign of something, a message, a manifestation and a parting. Death is metamorphosis par excellence, and in this way Aino, who has changed into a fish, demonstrates conclusively to Väinämöinen the impossibility of their union, the gap which reigns between them. The fact that Aino, having changed into a fish, speaks and makes herself understood to a living person, however, demonstrates that the boundary between life and death can be crossed over and is not final. The Kalevala runes are filled with figures who experience death, figures who have been beyond the boundary and returned. There are also numerous instances of communication between the living and the dead. In some variants of the Aino rune, the dead girl herself responds to her mother's plea that she return to the realm of the living, and Kullervo's dead mother also speaks to him from beyond the grave. This topic frequently occurs in the *Kalevala*.

Having lost Aino, Väinämöinen is advised by his mother to go court the Maiden of Pohjola. Pohjola is the simultaneously frightening and alluring "land of women," to which each hero of the *Kalevala* journeys in turn to seek a wife. It is a territory of both womanhood and death. Overcoming this challenge provides a certain initiatory test for a man.

THE WEDDING DRAMA OF THE KALEVALA: HEROIC ATTEMPTS AT COURTSHIP

In addition to epical runes, all versions of the *Kalevala* contain a great deal of ritual poetry. On his earliest journeys to White Sea Karelia, Lönnrot found many wedding runes, and in 1833 he edited them into a collection entitled *Naimakansan virsiä* (Wedding poems). Over the years, he incorporated sections of the wedding runes into the various versions of the *Kalevala* in such a manner that the epic became largely a wedding play and a courtship drama. The *Kalevala* came to be centered around the wooing attempts of its main heroes, particularly the aging Väinämöinen, who remained unsuccessful in all his efforts.

Along with the battle over the Sampo, the struggle over the Maiden of Pohjola can be considered another focal point of the epic. Väinämöinen, whose "solitary birth" forms the opening episode of the *Kalevala*, sets out early in the epic to court a young maiden, Aino. Unsuccessful in this, he sets his sights in vain on the Maiden of Pohjola. This proves futile, and the end result of his egoism is that the Sampo, which was forged by Ilmarinen, is eventually lost to Pohjola. At the end of the epic, having failed in all his efforts at courtship, Väinämöinen leaves the stage after having been found guilty of fathering an illegitimate child. Ilmarinen and Lemminkäinen were more successful in their courtship efforts.

The plot of the *Kalevala* changes course in Poems 19 and 20, when the epic focuses on the wedding at Pohjola, which is a celebration of the marriage of Ilmarinen and the Maiden of Pohjola. The preparations for the wedding, feasting, drinking, and singing drama, continue for six poems (20-25). From the wedding, the narrative turns to the fortunes of Lemminkäinen, who arrives at Pohjola as an uninvited guest. The basic content of the wedding at Pohjola consists of the wedding runes, which Lönnrot and his companions first collected from the women of White Sea Karelia. At Karelian weddings, ritual singing included both a lead singer and a female chorus and simultaneously served a dramatic purpose.[47] Lönnrot carefully preserved this pattern when editing the original runes into the *Kalevala*. These wedding runes form a section of ritual songs found at the center of the epic plot.

In his preface to *The Supplement to the Old Kalevala*, Lönnrot discussed the role of the wedding runes in the epic:

The Pohjola wedding runes are the characteristic wedding songs in Karelia even now. It would be difficult and even impossible to separate the original words from those added later. . . . The wedding songs, and those about giving over the bride, were greatly augmented by those I received later. They were certainly not all originally sung in this context. Nevertheless, good singers did add them here, and for this reason, in one way or another, we have fully included what is found in the *Kanteletar* as well.[48]

In constructing the episodes of the wedding at Pohjola for the *Kalevala*, Lönnrot's dilemma was an abundance rather than a dearth of material. He included these episodes within the structure of the mythical runes and made the wedding, farewell, and welcoming songs part of the epic poem. In this way, the ritual poetry of the Karelian wedding ceremony became part of the epic. In these poems of the *Kalevala*, the central heroes, Väinämöinen, Ilmarinen, and Lemminkäinen, competed with each other in courtship and celebrated the wedding. Lönnrot also included a significant portion of these wedding verses in the *Kanteletar*. This poetry, sung by women, also served to soften the masculine nature of the epic and briefly diverted it from the tumult of battle by focusing on the everyday course of life and ritual in a White Sea Karelian village.

The *Kalevala* is, in fact, very much a wedding drama. At various stages, its epic content is structured around the courtship drama of the "unhappy suitor," Väinämöinen, and his unsuccessful efforts at wooing. It is worth noting here that Lönnrot himself married only in 1849, at the age of forty-seven.[49] This was the same year the *New Kalevala* was published. Sagely, he left future generations only to speculate about the extent to which he himself may have identified with Väinämöinen.

Scholars have contended that Väinämöinen's human fallibility and incompetence appear ill suited for the figure of an old sage.[50] This has been deemed a characteristic of recent rune degeneration. Kaarle Krohn was of the opinion that the oldest runes came from western Finland. According to his hypothesis, the once-perfect heroic runes degenerated when they were diffused to peripheral areas such as White Sea Karelia. Krohn wondered at Väinämöinen's sensitivity, stating: "He has become a lamenter only by dint of the White Sea Karelian singers who, as wandering singer-minstrels in far-off places, have adapted their own laments here."[51] Thus Krohn considered the old hero's liking for young women quite a recent development in runic poetry. He also noted that, in the transition from the *Old* to the *New Kalevala*, Väinämöinen's role changes from that of a Don Juan figure to one of increasing complexity. Ilmarinen, on the other hand, is characterized by Krohn as a passionless lover.

Many critics of the *Kalevala* have contended that it contains too much wedding poetry.[52] However, Lönnrot defended the central role of the wedding runes in the epic. He based these arguments on his view of the historical past of the ancient Finns. Lönnrot argued that the *Kalevala* was also a depiction of their customs, stating:

And I do not intend to spend much time dwelling on what aspect of these poems would serve to explain ancient customs. I could, indeed, provide a number of examples of this, were there time to reflect. The *Old Kalevala* Poem XIII. 116. shows how the folk of ancient times would have prepared their food on hot stones and by throwing water on these. In numerous other passages, we would find that parents were held in honor, even if Lemminkäinen, in manly fervor, deviated a bit from his mother's wish. Similarly, we see that during those times, it was customary to think up conditional tasks for suitors. But many people may be of the opinion that there has been too much discussion of these courtship matters and that the entire book could simply be adapted to the new style of fiction or tales (novels). And if that is how it is, then so be it, but let us also remember that our ancestors did not have today's complicated affairs and matters to discuss. Courtship plans, warfare, catching fish and game from the forest were the most memorable events in their solitary life. And that is why these matters are so often related in the poetry.[53]

In Lönnrot's mind, the *Kalevala* was also an ethnographic work and should therefore give an authentic description of the ancient Finnish lifestyle, including its daily activities and festivities.

LÖNNROT'S SYNOPSIS OF THE *OLD KALEVALA*

The *Old Kalevala*, composed of thirty-two runes, was first published in two parts during the years 1835–36. It is a poem of broad scope based on folklore, "Lönnrot's epic." The basic structure corresponds to the structure of Lönnrot's earlier work *Runokokous Väinämöisestä* (A collection of poems about Väinämöinen), which became known as the *Alku-Kalevala* (Proto-Kalevala) and to which he then added new subject matter. The *Proto-Kalevala* was constructed around the Sampo sequence, as was the epic itself.

The version of the *Kalevala* most commonly available today is often referred to as the *New Kalevala*. The Finnish Literature Society has published twenty-four editions of this version, the first in 1849. In constructing it, Lönnrot added newly found material and placed particular emphasis on symmetry and authenticity in uniting the runes and the subject matter. In addition to the epic itself, this version contains a prelude by Lönnrot as well as a glossary of names and uncommon words and a listing of charms.

Poem 1. The singer makes ready and begins to relate how Väinämöinen, having lain in his mother's womb for thirty summers and winters, is born into the world. He then obtains a horse and sets out to ride. A Lapp, who bears a grudge against him for some reason, is watching to kill him. He sees Väinämöinen riding on the surface of the sea and shoots his arrow at him. Firing a second and even a third, he fells the horse from beneath Väinämöinen. As a consequence Väinämöinen, swimming about the waters, creates reefs, islands, crags, and lake-bottom hollows for fish. An eagle searching for a nesting place discovers Väinämöinen on the sea and lays eggs on his knee. When his knees move, the eggs roll into the sea and break on the reefs. Thereupon Väinämöinen creates the earth and the sky, the stars, moon, and sun from the fragments of the eggs.

Poem 2. The wind carries Väinämöinen to the shores of Pohjola. There he weeps and laments at being in a strange place and not knowing how he will ever reach his homeland. The Mistress of Pohjola hears him weeping, gets a boat from the shore, and rows over to him. She takes Väinämöinen to Pohjola. There she gives him food and drink and finally asks why he is weeping. Väinämöinen says that he longs for his homeland. The Mistress of Pohjola promises to send him home if he will first forge her a Sampo. In addition, she will give him her daughter as payment. Väinämöinen says he does not know how to forge, but promises to send Ilmarinen to perform this task when he reaches home. Thus he gets a horse from the Mistress of Pohjola and leaves.

Poem 3. On his way, Väinämöinen meets the Maiden of Pohjola sitting on the rainbow and beautifully dressed. He asks her to be his wife. The maiden smartly replies that she will consider him as a husband if he will draw an egg into an imperceptible knot and split a horsehair with a dull knife. These tasks completed, Väinämöinen renews his request. The girl, still acting smartly, demands that he build a boat out of spindle fragments. She promises to come when this is completed if in hewing his ax does not touch a stone. Väinämöinen sets about building the boat and accidentally strikes his knee. He leaves to find a blood stancher; he goes to two places in vain but finds one in the third.

Poem 4. Väinämöinen gets up from his sleigh and enters the cabin. A vessel is brought to catch the flowing blood, at least some of it. The old man is taken aback at the amount of blood and would begin his conjury, but he cannot remember the origin of iron. Väinämöinen relates this to him, and the old man begins to recite other charms. With these he halts the flow of blood, ties the veins, puts ointment made by his son on the wound, and wraps it with a bandage. Having been freed from his pain, Väinämöinen recovers to feel better than he did before and publicly thanks the God of heaven who has helped him in this way.

Poem 5. Väinämöinen departs for home; by chanting he conjures up an immense fir tree on his journey, with the moon and the Great Bear on its crown. When he arrives home, Ilmarinen asks him why he is distressed. Väinämöinen says there is a beautiful maiden in Pohjola and he urges Ilmarinen to go court her. This makes Ilmarinen suspect that Väinämöinen has promised him to Pohjola, and he refuses to depart. Väinämöinen then bids him to come look at the strange fir. He goes with Väinämöinen, comes to the spot, and rises to get the moon and the Great Bear from the crown. Väinämöinen chants up a great wind which takes Ilmarinen to Pohjola on the fir. There they have heard that he is a smith, and he is set to forging a Sampo. He builds a smithy, gets the fires blazing, and forges the Sampo. When the Sampo is completed, the Mistress of Pohjola stores it in a stone hill. Ilmarinen himself, not having won the maiden, leaves Pohjola for home and tells Väinämöinen that he has forged a Sampo.

Poem 6. Lemminkäinen sets out to court the Maiden of Pohjola. His mother forbids him to go, fearing her son's death at the hands of the Pohjola sages. While brushing his hair, Lemminkäinen throws the brush from his hand, saying that when he is murdered, the brush will run blood. He then gathers his stores and leaves on his journey. He comes to a village, drives from house to house, and requests in vain at two places for someone to unharness his horse. He is unsuccessful and drives to the Pohjola courtyard. He hears singing in the main room and slips inside. They marvel at who this stranger may be, for not even the dogs bark at him. Lemminkäinen says that this is not what he has come for and begins to chant. Thus he chants all the men out of the room except for one blind old man, whom he leaves unsung. The old man asks why he did not chant to him as well. Lemminkäinen says he will have nothing to do with one so despicable. Infuriated, the old man sets out for the River of Tuonela to await Lemminkäinen.

Poem 7. Lemminkäinen asks the Mistress of Pohjola for the girl as his wife, and he is given the task of skiing down an elk behind the demon's grasslands. He prepares new skis and departs for the forest, boasting that there is nothing he cannot attain on his skis. The Demon, having heard the boasting, makes an elk which Lemminkäinen sets out for in such a way that his skis break apart after a few firm starting kicks. Then, in the manner of a huntsman, he tries for his prey with charms and prayers to the guardian spirits of the forest, and this finally succeeds. He then repeats his request to the Mistress of Pohjola and is given the new task of bridling the Demon's horse. He bridles it and requests the girl for the third time. Then he is given the task of shooting a swan on the River of Tuonela in one attempt. He goes to the River of Tuonela and is killed by the old man who was watching for him there. In addition, this son of Tuonela chops him into five pieces with his sword.

Poem 8. At home Lemminkäinen's mother is already complaining that he is taking so long in his courting. Blood is seen streaming from the hairbrush. This makes the mother anxious, and she sets out for Pohjola to find out about her son. At first the Mistress of Pohjola conceals the truth, but finally she reveals it. She says she set him skiing after elk, bridling horses, and shooting birds. The mother goes to search for her son along these paths. She searches and searches but does not find him. She comes to a road and asks whether it knows anything of Lemminkäinen. The road conjectures that he has ended up in the Demon's domain; however, he is not found there. She sees the moon, asks the moon. The moon thinks he may have drowned in Pohjola's pond. He is not found there either. She then finally asks the sun, who says he has probably been killed at the River of Tuonela. In order that she might drag the river, the mother prays to the sun to put Tuonela to sleep for that time. By dragging she recovers Lemminkäinen piece by piece. From these fragments she brings him to life again, making the boy even a bit better than he previously was.

Poem 9. In building his boat, Väinämöinen finds that he lacks three charms in his construction tales. He goes to obtain them. First he searches in other places; when he does not find them, he even goes to Tuonela. On the shore of the River of Tuonela, he calls for a boat to take him across. The response is that he cannot get a boat until he states his reason for coming to Tuonela. Väinämöinen says that Tuoni (Death), iron, fire, water have brought him to Tuonela; they do not believe him or bring the boat. Finally he gives the true reason as well. He's come to obtain charms from Tuonela. A boat is brought; he is transported across the river, given food and drink and a place to sleep. But while he is asleep, nets are set up in the river to prevent his return. As a result, Väinämöinen must change himself into something else, become smaller so that he can swim through the meshes of the net. In this way he escapes Tuoni's nets, but he gets no charms from there.

Poem 10. Väinämöinen is still in need of the charms and thinks he can get them from Antero Vipunen. But the journey there is particularly difficult: one leg is over needle points, one is over sword tips, and one is over ax blades. He must go nevertheless. For the journey, he has Ilmarinen make him iron footwear, a coat of mail, and an iron cowlstaff. And so he sets out, pattering along; he comes to Vipunen, who has long since died and lies in the ground. On that spot there grows a great forest of various trees. Väinämöinen clears the forest and plunges the cowlstaff into Vipunen's mouth. Vipunen easily chews off the malleable iron on the cowlstaff, but he cannot bite through the steel at its core. Thus having made Vipunen's mouth into a very large opening,

Väinämöinen goes into it, and from there into the stomach. Once there he begins to forge, causing Vipunen great pain and suffering in his belly. Not knowing or surmising what may be the cause, Vipunen tries to rid himself of it by charms. However, Väinämöinen does not budge and says he will not leave until he gets to hear the charms. Then Vipunen begins to chant, and when Väinämöinen has heard charms enough, he returns to his boat.

Poem 11. Väinämöinen sets off after the Maiden of Pohjola. He sails on the sea, coming to a point on a headland where Ilmarinen's sister, the maiden Annikka, is washing her clothes. At first she wonders who he might be. When he nears she recognizes him to be Väinämöinen. She asks him where he is journeying. Väinämöinen lies about where he is going. But the Maiden does not believe the lies and threatens to overturn the boat. Väinämöinen finally tells the truth: he is on his way to court the Maiden of Pohjola. The Maiden rushes home and tells her brother that there is a danger that someone else may get the Maiden of Pohjola. Hearing this, the smith acts quickly. He bathes, rinses, dresses, harnesses the stallion, and departs for Pohjola. And so they come to Pohjola, Väinämöinen on the water with his sail, Ilmarinen along the shore with his horse. The dog at Pohjola then begins to bark. They go and look, recognizing the strangers to be suitors. The Mistress of Pohjola advises her daughter to marry Väinämöinen, but the daughter prefers Ilmarinen.

Poem 12. Having entered the large common room at Pohjola, Ilmarinen asks for the Maiden as his wife. As previously happened with Lemminkäinen, he is assigned three tasks: to plow a snake-filled field, to bridle forest beasts, and to catch a huge man-eating pike from the River of Tuonela. He successfully accomplishes all these tasks, comes back, and asks for the girl once more. Now granting her, the Mistress of Pohjola marvels and wonders how Ilmarinen knew the Maiden was growing up in Pohjola. Ilmarinen replies that there were good reports about the father, the mother, and the girl herself, and from this he knew. The Mistress of Pohjola says that it is indeed difficult to conceal a girl. Väinämöinen, having returned home from Pohjola, warns everyone about courting a maiden in competition with Ilmarinen.

Poem 13. Preparations are underway for a wedding at Pohjola. First an immense ox is slaughtered, and the brewing of beer is begun. The beer is brewed, but it does not ferment. The brewer considers how to get it to ferment; he tries in numerous ways but is not successful. Then finally he gets honey brought by a bee from beyond nine seas, and with this the beer is fermented. The beer rises, ferments to great strength, threatens to break the hoops of the vessel if a chanter is not brought at once. Chanters are sought to resolve the crisis, but no competent one is found. The beer continues to overflow. Finally the invitations to the feast at Pohjola are sent out with a warning to invite everyone, even old Väinämöinen. Only Lemminkäinen is not to be invited. The slave departs on the journey and invites the folk according to these orders.

Poem 14. The folk gather for the wedding at Pohjola, the son-in-law in their midst. The son-in-law's horse is taken care of, and he himself is brought into the large common room, which looks a bit odd so beautifully cleaned. After the son-in-law has entered, his mother-in-law looks at him more carefully in the light of a candle and praises him as handsome. The beer is brought forth and then encounters its legitimate chanter in Väinämöinen. Väinämöinen demands that Ilmarinen join in. Ilmarinen says that, being a visitor, he is reluctant to do so and urges Väinämöinen to chant alone. Thus Väinämöinen chants and wishes those at Pohjola good fortune in the future as well. Having drunk and sung, all the folk are fed the Mistress of Pohjola's abundant food.

Poem 15. The bride is finally gotten ready and bequeathed to Ilmarinen. Her mother reminds her once more that she is in fact leaving home forever. Very distressed over this, the bride says all her former hopes were that she would marry, but now she's come to feel differently. Her mother consoles her, saying she has found a very enterprising husband, a good provider. She then instructs her daughter how to conduct herself in her new environs and cautions the bridegroom not to lead her astray or treat her badly. The bride, at her departure, thanks the household and bids them farewell. Saying farewell, Ilmarinen snatches his sleigh and departs from Pohjola. Already on the road, the bride, still distressed, wishes she were anywhere but in the groom's sleigh. Consoling her, Ilmarinen tells her not to worry, her future home will be a good one.

Poem 16. Ilmarinen and his bride arrive home. His mother meets them joyfully and asks her son whether the trip was a healthy and a happy one. She asks the bride in, saying she has long been awaited. She looks the bride over and praises her beauty; she gives the folk abundant food and drink. Starting to chant, old Väinämöinen begins to extol the bridegroom and the bride, praises the mistress and master of the house, the "patvaska,"[54] the "saaja nainen,"[55] and all the folk invited.

Poem 17. Lemminkäinen hears that the folk are arriving at the Pohjola festivities. He is offended that he himself was not invited. He nevertheless prepares to depart from home. His mother forbids him to leave, for there are many deaths on the journey, much to fear if her son reaches his destination. First he must watch out for a fiery eagle; if he survives this, he may happen into a fiery grave. And he must escape a nest of vipers. He could be killed by wolves and bear in Pohjola's courtyard and his skull placed on a stake. Paying little heed, Lemminkäinen sets out as he had planned, having received much advice and warning from his mother, as you might suppose. He wanders about, escapes the deaths, arrives at Pohjola. The Mistress of Pohjola says it is unfortunate that he did not come later; the drinks are not yet prepared nor the food cooked. Lemminkäinen asks why he was not invited to the wedding and demands food and drink. A stale, spoiled drink is brought to him, which he drinks only after he has fished out the refuse and creatures. He asks for something better. The Master of Pohjola tolerates Lemminkäinen's haughtiness no longer and tries to slay him by chanting magic. When this proves futile, he challenges him to a duel with swords.

They go outside and begin to fight with measured swords. Lemminkäinen knocks off the other's head with his first blow. He then chants the entire Pohjola family asunder, except for the Mistress, who, more accomplished even than he, chants up new folk to take revenge on Lemminkäinen.

Poem 18. Lemminkäinen comes home from Pohjola. His mother asks why he is distressed: was he insulted in a drinking bout, jeered at by women, or even shamed with horses? Lemminkäinen tells his mother to find him some provisions; swords are being sharpened for his head in Pohjola. Why are they being sharpened? his mother asks. Lemminkäinen answers that he has slain a man in Pohjola and asks where to hide. The mother faults her son; all hiding places are dangerous, he will find death everywhere. But when he finally swears that he will no longer go to war, she advises him to flee to an island nine seas beyond. Departing, Lemminkäinen sails to his destination, and asks permission to haul his boat ashore. Having gotten permission, he does so, then departs for the island villages and lives there daringly with the girls. One morning, once again on his way to see the girls, he sees men readying weapons to kill him. He wants to leave, but when he arrives at the shore he finds that his boat has been burned. He builds a new boat and leaves the island. This is greatly lamented by the maidens. Having sailed out, he leaves his boat on a reef where it weeps, sobbing that it is no longer taken to war. Lemminkäinen forbids it to weep, and promises to go to war immediately. He gets Teuri as his second and departs. Cold comes from the northern sea, sent there by the Mistress of Pohjola, and freezes Lemminkäinen's boat. This was Cold itself, but somehow, by the use of charms, Lemminkäinen gets free and leaves to go inland, abandoning his boat. There, in his distress, he recalls how far he is from home.

Poem 19. A boy named Kullervo is born in Kalevala and as a small child is quickly sold to ¨ narinen as a slave. No matter what task he is assigned, he fails at them all and does the household harm. While rocking a baby, he kills the child and even burns the cradle; when felling a clearing, he bewitches the land so that a forest will never grow on it, nor a kernel of grain; when set to building a fence, he builds one which nobody can get over; when rowing, he rows the boat asunder; when beating fish into a seine, he beats the net and the fish together into sand. Finally he is put to tending a herd. The Mistress prepares a repast for the shepherd, lets out the herd, and recites the usual charms to protect the herd, for an abundance of milk, against peril, etc. Later, in the countryside, looking at his repast, the herder finds a stone in his bread. He believes the Mistress has played this joke and considers how to pay her back. Thus he scatters the cows into the forest and in the evening drives home bears. He plays his horn as he nears home. The Mistress goes out to milk, and when first looking at her herd, she is overjoyed at its beauty. When she comes closer the bears attack her and tear wounds into her. The Mistress prays to Ukko for the son of Kaleva to be destroyed in war, while the son of Kaleva, for his part, prays to Ukko for the Mistress to be killed by plagues. Kullervo departs from Ilmarinen's home and goes to war.

Poem 20. Having mourned his wife for some time, Ilmarinen finally begins to forge another out of gold and silver. His work is not successful, for instead of a maiden, the fire initially yields a sword and then a stallion. Only on the third try does he get a maiden, and even she needs a mouth, eyes, and other essentials. These added, he puts her beside him for the night, but finds her to be quite unsuitable. He then thrusts her to Väinämöinen who, having lain beside her for the night, feels cold in the morning and warns everyone against wishing for a woman of gold or silver. But Ilmarinen himself sets out for the younger daughter of Pohjola, whom he does not obtain, however. When he arrives home in a bad state of mind, Väinämöinen asks him news of the Mistress of Pohjola. Ilmarinen describes life at Pohjola as good and carefree thanks to the Sampo.

Poem 21. Väinämöinen urges Ilmarinen to accompany him to demand the Sampo from Pohjola. Ilmarinen thinks it is better for the Sampo to remain in Pohjola than to go demand it. He nevertheless agrees to go. First he forges a sword for Väinämöinen, and he is then ready for the journey. Ilmarinen would prefer to go by land, Väinämöinen by boat. While thinking about the trip they hear a boat weeping. Väinämöinen asks why it weeps. The boat responds that it is rotting, always resting on its bow. Väinämöinen gets the boat into the water and people into the boat. They row past many headlands and are seen by Lemminkäinen. Lemminkäinen gives a shout from the shore and begs to go along on the journey. He is then taken into the boat.

Poem 22. Väinämöinen draws away from the headland; he comes to a rapid, and the boat gets caught on a pike's shoulders. He hauls the pike into his boat with his sword, chops it apart, and begins to build a kantele of the bones. When it is finished, he invites his fellow travelers to play it. When their playing produces no joyful music, he takes the kantele farther off. But there is no player farther off either. Then old Väinämöinen himself begins to play. Joyful music comes forth. There is no living creature in the forest, no bird in the air, no fish in the water which does not hasten to hear him. Even the spirits of the water, air, and forest listen with joy to the kantele playing. Finally everyone there bursts into tears, and Väinämöinen himself weeps so that large tears roll from his eyes onto the ground. From the ground the tears run into the sea, where they become beautiful pearls.

Poem 23. Väinämöinen, Ilmarinen, and Lemminkäinen come to Pohjola. The Mistress of Pohjola asks what their purpose is: To share the Sampo, answers Väinämöinen. The Mistress of Pohjola says the Sampo is not to be shared. Väinämöinen uses sleep needles to lull the folk of Pohjola to sleep. They go to get the Sampo from the stone hill. Väinämöinen chants the gates of the fortress into motion, and Ilmarinen opens them. Lemminkäinen plows the Sampo free, and the three men then carry it to the boat. With the Sampo in the boat, Väinämöinen leaves the shore and, at Lemminkäinen's urging, he finally begins to chant some distance off. A crane, frightened by the song, screeches in a loud voice and wakens Pohjola from its sleep. The Mistress of Pohjola goes to look at the Sampo and sees that it is gone. She immediately conjures up a great wind to overturn Väinämöinen and she would, in fact, have sunk the boat if Lemminkäinen had not steadied its sides. Thus Lemminkäinen, watching from the mast, sees the boat from Pohjola approaching and overtaking them. Frightened, Väinämöinen creates a reef to obstruct the boat from Pohjola. The boat breaks asunder, but the Mistress of Pohjola approaches Väinämöinen's boat in the form of a bird, taking all her men with her. A battle then ensues in which Väinämöinen cuts off her wings and talons with an oar. Only one pinkie is left, and with this the Mistress of Pohjola lifts up the Sampo and it falls into the water, where it shatters. The wind drives the pieces of the Sampo every which way, providing bounty for many a spot. The Mistress of Pohjola is able to get the lid back to Pohjola.

Poem 24. Having found fragments of the Sampo on the shore, Väinämöinen gives them to Sampsa Pellervoinen, ordering him to sow the fields. Sampsa sows and plows the land. Many kinds of trees rise up from the plowed land, but no oak rises. Finally even an oak tree grows, spreading its branches up to the heavens so that not even the sun is visible any longer. Thus it becomes necessary to fell the newly grown tree once again, but it is difficult to get someone to fell it. Then a tiny man rises from the sea. He takes his ax and does indeed fell the tree. Väinämöinen then sows some seeds of fog onto the land and hopes for good luck with the crop. The Mistress of Pohjola threatens to destroy his entire crop, to send many different disasters to Väinämöinen's fields. Väinämöinen, for his part, tries threats to no avail, and hopes that his Finland will be fortunate once again.

Poem 25. The Mistress of Pohjola exposes herself to the wind and becomes pregnant. When her time approaches, she heats up the sauna, recites old crone's charms, and gives birth to nine sons, all of them evil and murderous. She then sends them to Väinämöinen's region to burden the people there with diseases. Suddenly all the folk in Väinämöinen's territory fall ill, but by using standard remedies, he drives off the disasters. He exorcizes the pains into Pain Mountain and finally, with the help of ointments, gets his ailing people back to health again.

Poem 26. The Mistress of Pohjola seizes the sun and the moon from the heavens. In order to find out what is preventing these orbs from shining, Väinämöinen and Ilmarinen rise into the heavens. They strike fire for light and fire pierces down from the heavens. Even they themselves go searching for fire. They learn that after doing great damage, fire has gone into Lake Alue and been swallowed there by a fish. They ready a seine and go fishing on the lake. With much work and great difficulty, they finally catch the fish which swallowed fire. They cut it open. Fire is freed and burns many lands and even injures Smith Ilmarinen. But the smith is cured by recounting the usual charms for fire.

Poem 27. However, the moon and the sun remain concealed, and Väinämöinen orders Ilmarinen to forge new ones. When completed, they are raised into the heavens. But they give no light. Väinämöinen decides to set out for Pohjola. Upon arriving there, he asks, "Where is the moon, where is the sun?" They're said to be in the mountain and cannot be gotten from there. Then Väinämöinen challenges the sons of Pohjola to a test of swords. Having defeated them all, he goes to the mountain but cannot open the lock. He departs again, and asks Ilmarinen to forge keys. Ilmarinen steps into the smithy and begins to forge. The Mistress of Pohjola comes to the window of the smithy in the form of a bird: "What are you forging?" "A neck ring for the Mistress of Pohjola." The Mistress of Pohjola flies home, anxious to save her neck by any means whatever. She must let the moon and sun out of the mountain. Once again she flies to Ilmarinen to bring word that she has already freed the moon and the sun from the mountain. Ilmarinen sees that this is true and tells Väinämöinen to come look. Seeing the moon and the sun in their former places, Väinämöinen gives his old friends a heartfelt greeting.

Poem 28. Väinämöinen is preparing to slay a bear. He comes to its den and fells it. Making music, he takes the bear home. The folk at home hear the music and hasten to the courtyard to receive the spoils. Bruin is then welcomed from the lane to the courtyard, from the courtyard into the room, and then is settled on a stool on the floor. After the bear is skinned, it is put into a kettle and its meat is cooked for the funeral feast. It is then ladled from the kettle into bowls, and all the folk of Tapio are invited as guests. In celebrating the feast, Väinämöinen relates how the bear was slain. After the folk have eaten, drunk, sung, and carried on other doings, the bear skull is taken to a tree, and in the end Väinämöinen hopes there will be other such joys in the future for these environs.

Poem 29. Because he is in good spirits, Väinämöinen would gladly play the kantele, but it is still sleeping at the bottom of the sea. He gets an iron rake and begins to rake the sea, but does not find the lost instrument. On the way home he hears a birch weeping. Asked why it weeps, the birch responds that it is lamenting evil days and willingly relates everything. Väinämöinen forbids it to weep, for its cares will yet become joys. He makes a kantele right there, gets nails from the oak and strings from the hair of a singing girl. Then he sits down to play the new kantele, and there is no one who is not moved by his playing.

Poem 30. Väinämöinen and Joukahainen meet on a road. Joukahainen, considering himself superior, will not yield the way and begins to relate all manner of things so that the other will also recognize his superiority. Finally, as Joukahainen is recounting the initial creation of the world, Väinämöinen also relates his knowledge, having himself participated in those works. Not about to give up, Joukahainen threatens to overcome Väinämöinen by chanting. This angers Väinämöinen, and he chants Joukahainen up to his armpits in the earth. In desperation, Joukahainen begs Väinämöinen to free him, promising first other things and finally his only sister as a ransom. Väinämöinen saves Joukahainen, who goes home weeping, and tells his mother that he has promised his sister to Väinämöinen. But there is nothing to weep about, for the mother has already long wished for Väinämöinen to be her son-in-law.

Poem 31. In the forest Väinämöinen meets Joukahainen's sister, who is making a bath whisk. He warns the girl that from now on she should desire only him. The girl goes home crying; she tells her mother that in the forest someone from Kalevala came and told her to grow up to be his alone. The mother forbids her daughter to be upset and tells her to go to the storehouse and there dress in her finest clothes. The girl goes into the courtyard, out of her mother's sight. There she weeps copious tears. When the mother asks why she continues to weep, she responds that she would rather go to the bottom of the sea than to old Väinämöinen. And so the girl disappears into the sea. Now it is the mother's turn to weep; she weeps so greatly that three broad rivers form of her tears. The girl gets caught on Väinämöinen's hook in the form of a fish while he is angling. At first Väinämöinen thinks this is strange indeed; finally he takes it to be a salmon. He takes his knife and begins to slice it up; then the fish splashes out of his hands into the sea and rejoices in letting him know. Väinämöinen asks it to come back once again; it does not. Then Väinämöinen greatly regrets that he hadn't brains enough to hold onto the girl he'd long yearned for. Even in a dream he has, the girl is depicted as unobtainable.

Poem 32. Marjatta, having long been a maiden at home, goes to tend the herd, eats an odd berry, and from this berry she bears a son. A priest is brought to baptize the child; the priest asks who could serve to judge the fatherless boy. They get old Väinämöinen; he condemns the boy to be taken into a swamp. The two-week-old child opens its mouth and babbles that it has been unfairly judged. This angers Väinämöinen, who chants himself away from the land of the living, leaving the kantele as the only remembrance of himself.

LÖNNROT'S SYNOPSIS OF THE *NEW KALEVALA*

Poem 1. Prelude. The Maiden of the Air descends into the sea, where she is impregnated by the wind and the water to become the Mother of Waters. A scaup builds its nest on her knee and lays eggs in it. The eggs roll out of the nest and break into pieces; the fragments form the earth, sky, sun, moon, and clouds. The Mother of Waters creates headlands, bays, and other shores, deep and shallow places in the sea. Väinämöinen is born of the Mother of Waters and floats on the waves for a long time until he finally comes to the shore.

Poem 2. Väinämöinen comes to a treeless country and sets Sampsa Pellervoinen to sowing trees. At first the oak will not sprout, but after being sown again it rises and overshadows the entire earth, its leaves hiding both the sun and the moon. A tiny man rises from the sea and fells the oak; the moon and sun are visible once again. Birds sing in the trees; grasses, flowers, and berries grow on the earth; only barley does not yet grow. Väinämöinen finds some barley-corns in the sand on the shore, fells a clearing, and leaves one birch growing on which the birds can sit. The eagle, delighted that a tree has been left standing for its sake, strikes a fire for Väinämöinen with which he is able to burn his clearing. Väinämöinen sows the barley, prays for its growth, and hopes for good fortune in the future as well.

Poem 3. Väinämöinen's knowledge grows, and he becomes famous. Joukahainen sets out to overcome him in knowledge and, when he does not win, challenges him to a sword duel. This angers Väinämöinen, and he chants Joukahainen into a swamp. Joukahainen is greatly distressed in the swamp and finally promises his sister to Väinämöinen as a wife. Väinämöinen is appeased by this and lets him out of the swamp. Joukahainen goes home distressed and tells his mother how unfortunate his journey has been. His mother rejoices when she hears that she will get Väinämöinen as a son-in-law, but the daughter grows sorrowful and begins to weep.

Poem 4. Väinämöinen meets Joukahainen's sister preparing a bath whisk and requests her for his wife. The girl runs home crying and tells her mother what has happened. The mother forbids her to weep, telling her to be more joyful and to dress in fine clothes. The daughter continues her weeping, saying she does not want to marry an age-old man. In her sorrow, she gets lost in a wildwood while walking, comes to the shore of a strange lake, goes to wash herself, and drowns in the water. The mother weeps night and day for her lost daughter.

Poem 5. Väinämöinen goes to fish for Joukahainen's sister in the lake and catches her on his hook in the form of a strange fish. He tries to cut her into pieces, but the fish escapes from his hands into the sea and there reveals who she is. In vain Väinämöinen tries with words and tackle to get the fish back again. He returns home with a heavy heart and is advised by his dead mother to go court the Maiden of Pohjola.

Poem 6. Joukahainen bears hatred against Väinämöinen and lies in wait for him on his journey to Pohjola. He sees him riding across the lake and shoots at him, but hits only his horse. Väinämöinen falls into the water; a strong wind bears him out to sea and Joukahainen rejoices, thinking that Väinämöinen has now chanted his last verses.

Poem 7. Väinämöinen floats on the open sea many days; the eagle spies him and, still grateful that Väinämöinen had left a birch standing for it in his burnt clearing, takes Väinämöinen on its back and carries him to the shores of Pohjola. There the Mistress of Pohjola accompanies him to her home and receives him well. But Väinämöinen longs for his own country, and the Mistress of Pohjola promises not only to send him there, but even to give him her daughter as a wife if he will forge a Sampo. Väinämöinen promises that upon reaching home he will send Smith Ilmarinen to forge the Sampo and is given both the Mistress of Pohjola's sleigh and her horse for his journey home.

Poem 8. During his journey Väinämöinen sees the beautifully dressed

Maiden of Pohjola and asks her to be his wife. The Maiden finally promises Väinämöinen her consent if he can build a boat from the fragments of a spindle shaft and move it into the water without touching it in any way. Väinämöinen begins to build, strikes a great wound into his knee with his ax, and cannot stanch the flow of blood. He goes in search of a sage knowledgeable about stanching blood and finds an old man who promises to do this.

Poem 9. Väinämöinen tells the old man the origin of iron. The old man reviles the iron and recounts the charms for stanching blood. The flow of blood is halted. The old man sets his son to making ointment, dresses and binds the wound; Väinämöinen is healed, and he thanks God for the help he has received.

Poem 10. Väinämöinen comes home and urges Ilmarinen to go court the Maiden of Pohjola, who can be won by forging a Sampo. Ilmarinen refuses ever to go to Pohjola. As a result, Väinämöinen must use other magic to set him on the journey against his will. Ilmarinen comes to Pohjola; he is well received and is put to forging the Sampo. Ilmarinen forges the Sampo, and the Mistress of Pohjola takes it to Pohjola's stone hill. Ilmarinen requests the Maiden as payment for his work but the Maiden makes up excuses, saying she cannot leave home yet. Ilmarinen gets a boat, returns home, and tells Väinämöinen he has already forged the Sampo.

Poem 11. Lemminkäinen goes to court a maiden among the great clans of Saari. At first the island maidens make fun of him, but they soon come to know him even too well. But there is one, Kyllikki, who is the real reason he has come, and whom he cannot persuade amicably. He finally seizes her by force, tosses her into his sleigh, and leaves on a journey. Kyllikki weeps and is especially reproachful of Lemminkäinen's taste for war. Lemminkäinen promises never to go to war if Kyllikki will promise never to run about the village and both swear to uphold their promises. Lemminkäinen's mother is overjoyed with her young daughter-in-law.

Poem 12. Kyllikki forgets her oath and goes to the village. This greatly angers Lemminkäinen; he immediately decides to desert her and go court the Maiden of Pohjola. His mother tries by every means to dissuade her son from going, saying he will meet his death there. Lemminkäinen, who is brushing his hair, angrily throws the brush from his hand, declaring that if blood flows from him, it will flow from the brush as well. He makes preparations, departs for the journey, comes to Pohjola, and chants all the men out of Pohjola's large common room. There is only one, a malicious cowherd, to whom he does not chant.

Poem 13. Lemminkäinen asks the Mistress of Pohjola for her daughter. She assigns him his first task, that of skiing down the Hiisi elk. With arrogant defiance, Lemminkäinen leaves to hunt the elk, but to his displeasure he soon learns that defiance will not get him the elk.

Poem 14. By asking appropriately with a huntsman's ordinary charms and prayers, Lemminkäinen finally attains the elk and takes it to Pohjola. The second task assigned him is to bridle the fiery-mouthed Hiisi gelding, which he bridles and drives to Pohjola. His third task is to shoot a swan on the River of Tuonela. Lemminkäinen comes to the River of Tuonela; there the cowherd he scorned awaits him, slays him, and casts him into the rapids. In addition, the son of Tuonela cuts his body into pieces.

Poem 15. In a few days blood begins to drip from the brush in Lemminkäinen's home. From this, his mother immediately surmises her son's death. She hastens to Pohjola and asks the Mistress of Pohjola what has become of Lemminkäinen. The Mistress of Pohjola finally tells her what tasks she had assigned him, and the sun gives her exact information about Lemminkäinen's death. Lemminkäinen's mother goes to the Tuonela rapids, a long rake in her hand. She rakes the water until she gathers all the pieces of her son's body. She joins them together and, with the aid of charms and ointments, restores Lemminkäinen to his former self. Once revived, Lemminkäinen relates how he was slain at the River of Tuonela and leaves for home with his mother.

Poem 16. Väinämöinen sends Sampsa Pellervoinen in search of wood for boat building. He hews a boat of it but lacks three magic words. When he cannot obtain the words elsewhere, he goes to Tuonela, where they would like to keep him. However, using his powers, Väinämöinen escapes from Tuonela and, on his return, warns that no one should go there of his own free will. He describes the terribly wretched and horrifying conditions in which the evil people there live.

Poem 17. Väinämöinen goes to obtain the magic words from Antero Vipunen and wakens him from his long sleep beneath the earth. Vipunen swallows Väinämöinen, and Väinämöinen begins to torment him greatly in his stomach. Vipunen tries many a charm, spell, conjury, and threat to get Väinämöinen out of his stomach, but he threatens not to leave before he gets the necessary boat-building words from Vipunen. Vipunen chants forth all his knowledge to Väinämöinen, who then leaves Vipunen's stomach, returns to his boat building, and finishes his boat.

Poem 18. Väinämöinen sails to court the Maiden of Pohjola in his new boat. Ilmarinen's sister sees, calls him to shore, learns of his journey, and hurries to inform her brother that the bride he earned long ago is in danger of being lost to him. Ilmarinen makes preparations and, on his horse, he also hastens to Pohjola along the shore. The Mistress of Pohjola, seeing the suitors coming, advises her daughter to choose Väinämöinen. But the daughter promises to go to Ilmarinen, forger of the Sampo, and tells Väinämöinen, who is the first to come inside, that she does not want him.

Poem 19. Ilmarinen comes to the large common room at Pohjola, requests the daughter, and is assigned perilous tasks. With the Maiden of Pohjola advising him, he succeeds in completing these tasks. First, he plows a field of snakes; second, he captures the bear of Tuonela and the wolf of Manala; third, he captures a huge, terrible pike from the River of Tuonela. The Mistress of Pohjola promises and betroths her daughter to Ilmarinen. Väinämöinen returns from Pohjola in low spirits and forbids everyone to embark on a courtship contest against someone younger than they.

Poem 20. A huge, enormous ox is slaughtered in Pohjola for the wedding. Beer is brewed and foods prepared. Messengers are sent to invite folk to the wedding. Only Lemminkäinen is left uninvited.

Poem 21. The bridegroom and his party are received in Pohjola. The guests are given abundant food and drink. Väinämöinen praises and chants to the household.

Poem 22. The bride is prepared for her departure and reminded of her past life and of that to come. She grows sorrowful. Laments are sung for the bride. The bride weeps. The bride is consoled.

Poem 23. The bride is instructed and advised how to conduct herself in her husband's house. An old vagrant crone recounts the stages of her life as a girl, in marriage, and finally separated from her husband.

Poem 24. The bridegroom is advised how he should behave toward his bride and is admonished not to treat her badly. An old beggar man tells how he once brought his wife into accord. With tears in her eyes, the bride recalls that she is now leaving her beloved birthplace for the rest of her days and bids farewell to all. Ilmarinen snatches the bride into his sleigh, leaves on his journey, and reaches his home on the evening of the third day.

Poem 25. The groom, the bride, and their entourage are received at Ilmarinen's home. They are given abundant food and drink. Väinämöinen praises and chants to the master and mistress of the house, the bride's attendant, and the rest of the wedding folk. On the way home from the wedding, Väinämöinen's sleigh breaks down; he fixes it and drives home.

Poem 26. Lemminkäinen, angered that he was not invited to the wedding, nevertheless decides to go to Pohjola despite his mother's warnings and the many deaths which will imperil him on the journey. He departs on the journey and, by his knowledge, succeeds in passing through all the perilous places.

Poem 27. Lemminkäinen comes to Pohjola and behaves arrogantly in many ways. The Master of Pohjola is angered and, when he is unable to gain victory over Lemminkäinen in conjury, demands a duel. During the duel, Lemminkäinen cuts off the Master of Pohjola's head, and to avenge this, the Mistress of Pohjola gathers an army against him.

Poem 28. Lemminkäinen quickly flees from Pohjola, comes home, and asks his mother where he can go to conceal himself from the people of Pohjola, who he says are coming as a great band to wage war against him, one man alone. His mother scolds him for going to Pohjola; at first she recommends one, then another dangerous hiding place. Finally she advises him to go to an island beyond many seas, where his father also once lived peacefully during years of great war.

Poem 29. Lemminkäinen departs to sail across the lake and arrives safely at the island. He lives too daringly with the girls and other women on the island. This angers the men, and they decide to kill him. Lemminkäinen swiftly flees and leaves the island to his own great sorrow and that of the island maidens. A great storm wrecks Lemminkäinen's boat on the sea; he escapes by swimming ashore. He obtains a new boat and with it sails to his native shores. He sees his former home burnt and all the environs deserted. He begins to weep and lament, especially because he believes his mother has been killed. However, his mother is alive and lives in a new spot in the backwoods, where, to his great joy, Lemminkäinen finds her. His mother relates how the forces of Pohjola came and burned the buildings. Lemminkäinen promises to build new, even better buildings, and to have revenge on Pohjola. He tells his mother about his merry life on the island while he was in hiding.

Poem 30. With his former fellow warrior Tiera, Lemminkäinen goes to wage war against Pohjola. The Mistress of Pohjola sends severe cold against them which freezes their boat in the sea and would slowly have frozen the heroes as well if Lemminkäinen hadn't been able to restrain it with his powerful charms and spells. Lemminkäinen and his companion get to shore across the ice; they wander the backwoods for a long time in a sorry state until they finally make their way home.

Poem 31. Untamo wages war against his brother Kalervo; he fells Kalervo and his forces so that only one pregnant woman remains alive of the entire clan. He takes the woman with him, and a son, Kullervo, is born to her in Untamola. Already in his cradle he plans revenge against Untamo, and Untamo tries in several ways to kill him but is unsuccessful. As he grows up, Kullervo ruins all the work he undertakes, and in torment, Untamo sells him to Ilmarinen as a slave.

Poem 32. Ilmarinen's wife sets Kullervo to herding and malevolently bakes a stone into his noonday bread. After reciting bear charms, she lets the herd out to pasture.

Poem 33. While herding, Kullervo takes the bread from his sack in the afternoon, begins to cut, and completely ruins his knife. This weighs on his heart all the more because the knife was the only memento he had left of his family. He plans revenge on the Mistress, drives the herd into a swamp, and gathers a drove of wolves and bears which he drives home in the evening. When the Mistress goes to milk them, she is torn apart and killed by the wild beasts.

Poem 34. Kullervo flees from Ilmarinen's home, wanders dejectedly through the forest, and learns from an old woman that his father, mother, brother, and sister are still alive. Advised by the old woman, he finds them along the border of Lapland. Kullervo's mother relates how she thought Kullervo had been lost long ago and also how her elder daughter had been lost while gathering berries.

Poem 35. Kullervo attempts various work for his parents, but because he is of no help to them, his father sends him on a journey to pay export tax. On Kullervo's return journey after the taxes have been paid, unbeknownst to him, he meets his own sister who was lost while berrying. He tempts and seduces her. Afterward, when their kinship is revealed, Kullervo's sister casts herself into a river. Kullervo hurries home, relates the terrible tale of his sister's suicide to his mother, and then ponders doing away with himself as well. His mother persuades him not to kill himself and urges him to go to some hiding place and raise his spirits. But Kullervo decides that, before all else, he will go get revenge on Untamo.

Poem 36. Kullervo prepares for war and says farewell to his home. There no one but his mother cares about him, where he is going, or whether he will live or die. He comes to Untamola, strikes everything to the ground, and sets fire to the buildings. He returns home and finds the house deserted and no one alive there but an old black dog which accompanies him into the forest to hunt for food. On his forest journey, when he comes to the spot where he seduced his sister, he ends his sorrow with his own sword.

Poem 37. Ilmarinen long mourns for his dead wife. Then, with great labor and effort, he forges himself a new wife out of gold and silver. He sleeps a night beside his bride of gold and in the morning feels the side he had turned toward her to be very cold. He abandons his golden bride to Väinämöinen, who does not care to have her and tells Ilmarinen to forge the gold for other purposes or to send her to other lands where they desire gold.

Poem 38. Ilmarinen goes to Pohjola to court his former wife's younger sister. There the response is insulting words. Ilmarinen grows angry, steals the maiden, and leaves for home. On the journey even the maiden insults Ilmarinen and angers him so greatly that Ilmarinen finally chants her into a seagull. He returns home and tells Väinämöinen about the carefree life lived in Pohjola now that they have the Sampo, and also tells him how his courtship journey went.

Poem 39. Väinämöinen urges Ilmarinen to go get the Sampo with him from Pohjola. Ilmarinen agrees to the idea, and the heroes depart in a boat. Lemminkäinen spies them on their journey and, on hearing where they are headed, offers himself as the third man. They gladly take him.

Poem 40. The Sampo travelers come to a rapids where the boat gets caught on a huge pike's back. The pike is killed; its front part is hauled into the boat, cooked, and eaten. Väinämöinen makes a kantele out of the pike's jaws. Many try to play it but do not know how.

Poem 41. Väinämöinen plays the kantele, and all living creatures, whether of the air, the earth, or the sea, hasten to gather and hear the music. All hearts are so moved by the playing that tears well up in their eyes. Large tears even fall from Väinämöinen's eyes, drop to the ground, and roll into the water, where they become beautiful blue pearls.

Poem 42. The heroes arrive at Pohjola, and Väinämöinen announces that they have come to share the Sampo: if they cannot get half by good will, they will take all by force. The Mistress of Pohjola will not give it willingly or be forced to do so. She gathers the forces of Pohjola in opposition. Väinämöinen takes the kantele, begins to play, and lulls all the forces of Pohjola to sleep with his music. He then goes in search of the Sampo with his companions.

They get it out of the stone mountain and take it to their boat. With the Sampo in their boat, they leave Pohjola and travel happily toward home. On the third day, the Mistress of Pohjola wakes from her sleep and, seeing the Sampo gone, prepares a thick fog, a great wind, and other troubles to stop those who took the Sampo until she can catch up to them. During the storm Väinämöinen's new kantele is lost to the sea.

Poem 43. The Mistress of Pohjola prepares her warship and goes in pursuit of those who took the Sampo. When she reaches them, a battle ensues between Pohjola and Kalevala on the sea and is won by the latter. However, the Mistress of Pohjola succeeeds in getting the Sampo from the boat into the lake, where it shatters into pieces. The larger pieces sink into the water to become the sea's riches; the smaller ones are driven ashore by waves. Väinämöinen is pleased by this and hopes to gain good fortune from the land even from them. The Mistress of Pohjola threatens to use all her might and destroy Kalevala, a threat to which Väinämöinen pays no mind. Greatly distressed over the destruction of her power, the Mistress of Pohjola returns to Pohjola with nothing but the cover of the Sampo. Väinämöinen carefully gathers the fragments of the Sampo from the shore and plants them, hoping for eternal good fortune.

Poem 44. Väinämöinen leaves home in search of his kantele, lost in the lake, but he cannot find it. He then makes a completely new kantele from a birch, which he again plays, enchanting all nature's creatures.

Poem 45. The Mistress of Pohjola sends a terrible pestilence to Kalevala. Väinämöinen heals the folk with powerful charms and ointments.

Poem 46. The Mistress of Pohjola conjures up a bear to destroy the Kalevala herds. Väinämöinen slays the bear and, according to custom, a great feast is held in Kalevala. Väinämöinen sings, plays his kantele, and hopes that life in Kalevala will be this joyful in the future as well.

Poem 47. The moon and the sun descend to hear Väinämöinen's music. The Mistress of Pohjola seizes them, hides them inside a mountain, and even steals the fire from the homes of Kalevala. Ukko, the Supreme God, is taken aback at the darkness in the sky and casts fire for a new moon and sun. The fire falls to the ground, and Väinämöinen, along with Ilmarinen, goes in search of it. The Maiden of the Air tells them that the fire has fallen into Lake Alue and been swallowed there by a fish. Väinämöinen and Ilmarinen try to capture the fish with a seine of bast, but they do not succeed.

Poem 48. A net of linen is prepared. The heroes then set off and catch the fish, which has swallowed the fire. The fire is found in the fish's belly but suddenly springs up and burns Ilmarinen's cheeks and hands badly. The fire advances to the forest, burns many lands, and continues ever onward until it is finally captured and taken to the dark homes of Kalevala. Ilmarinen recovers from his burns.

Poem 49. Ilmarinen forges a new moon and sun but cannot get them to shine. Väinämöinen learns by divination that the moon and sun are in Pohjola inside a mountain. He goes to Pohjola, battles with the folk of

Pohjola, and is victorious. He goes to search for the moon and the sun inside the mountain but cannot get inside. He returns home for implements with which he can tear open the mountain. As Ilmarinen is forging them, the Mistress of Pohjola begins to fear for her own well-being and lets the moon and the sun out of the mountain. Seeing the moon and the sun in the heavens, Väinämöinen greets them, hoping that they will always travel beautifully and send the land good fortune.

Poem 50. The virgin Marjatta swallows a lingonberry; as a result, she gives birth to a boy. The boy disappears and is finally found in a swamp. An old man is brought to baptize him. But the old man will not baptize the fatherless child before it is studied and decided whether the child will be allowed to live. Väinämöinen comes to study the matter and decrees that the peculiar boy be put to death. But the two-week-old child accuses him of an unjust sentence. Ukko baptizes the boy King of Karelia. This angers Väinämöinen and he leaves, prophesying that he will be needed again to make a new Sampo, kantele, and light for the people. He leaves for a land between the earth and the sky, where he may yet be, but he leaves his kantele and great songs behind as a legacy for the people.

AN EPIC OF CHARMS

In addition to the objections about wedding runes, many were disturbed by the number of charms included in the *Kalevala*.[56] Particularly during the period of Romantic enthusiasm, Finnish interpreters were disposed to see the epic as the ancient past of the Finns, a battle between two peoples. As a result, the mythological basis of the *Kalevala* and the ancient runes, as well as the religious rites associated with this material, long went unnoticed in Finland, despite the fact that, in creating the epic, Lönnrot himself had borne these aspects in mind. Nor is it a coincidence that scholars abroad were the first to call attention to the ritual aspects of the epical work. There are so many charms in the *Kalevala* that as early as 1892 the Italian scholar Domenico Comparetti referred to it as "an epic of charms." Comparetti's contribution to *Kalevala* scholarship lay in the fact that he stated that the charms were a significant aspect of the *Kalevala* runes because "they tell of the life of the people and relate this to its religious past, its remembrances and ideals."[57]

While the Finns were still interpreting the *Kalevala* as a depiction of the Finnish past, the relationship of the runes to other epics throughout the world was becoming apparent to comparative scholars abroad. It was at this point that the charms assumed a key role. The shamanic sage was seen as a conjurer, and the primary significance of the rune singer and even rune singing itself became shamanistic conjury. Likewise, Comparetti also correctly noted that "synnyt" (charms about origins) played a central role in the epic and that the sage transmitting them was actually relating the origins of such phenomena as sickness.[58] In the ancient religion of the Finns it was believed, for instance, that an explanation of the origin of an illness would serve as a cure.

Lönnrot had actually pondered a similar set of questions, and for this reason he eventually decided to include a great many charms in the epic. In the preface to the *Old Kalevala*, he divides the ancient runes into the following two categories:

> With regard to the Finnish runes, it may already have been written that in sum they are of two different kinds, narrative tales and charms. And it may also have been noted somewhere that in the beginning, even charms were nothing more than narrative runes which, in accordance with the circumstances, began to be altered into something else.[59]

Despite the criticism he received, Lönnrot added a considerable number of charms in the transition from the *Old* to the *New Kalevala*. In his opinion, they had originally been epic "rune tales" and were therefore a significant aspect of ancient Finnish folklore and mythology; like wedding runes, they could be considered authentic descriptions of ancient Finnish life.[60] The inclusion of ritual poetry, such as wedding runes and charms, in the *Kalevala* once again concurred with Lönnrot's ethnographic point of view.

CHAPTER

4

ELIAS LÖNNROT: THE INDIVIDUAL AND THE NATIONAL MYTH

ELIAS LÖNNROT'S LIFE

Lönnrot's private life and personality are often overshadowed by the enormity of his lifework and the *Kalevala* process. During his relatively long lifespan (1802–1884), Lönnrot had time to be involved in numerous additional activities. For a long while, *Kalevala* romanticism obscured the true nature of his contribution to the creation of the Finnish national epic and his life as an individual, and he evolved into a national mythical hero.

Lönnrot was born on April 9, 1802, in a tenant farmer's cottage in the southern Finnish parish of Sammatti, the son of a poor tailor. His intense desire for knowledge spurred him on to scholarship despite financial difficulties. Lönnrot came to the Turku Academy in 1822 by way of the Tammisaari Elementary School, the Turku Cathedral School, and the secondary school at Porvoo. In 1827 he became a candidate for a doctoral degree, and thereafter he continued his studies in Helsinki, where the Turku Academy was moved after the Turku Fire of 1827. In 1832, he received a doctorate in medicine and began his career as a medical doctor.[1]

Among the subjects studied by Lönnrot at the Turku Academy were the classical languages Latin, Greek, and Hebrew, as well as Russian. He also received grades for Greek literature, rhetoric, mathematics, general history, Eastern literature, physics, theoretical and applied philosophy, chemistry, natural history, and the history of literature. One must bear in mind, however, that the boundaries between disciplines were not yet sharply delineated at that time. The theses Lönnrot wrote for his master's degree and his doctorate were entitled, respectively, *Väinämöisestä, muinaissuomalaisten jumalasta* (On Väinämöinen, a god of the ancient Finns) and *Suomalaisten taianomaisesta lääketaidosta* (On magic in Finnish medicine).[2] The titles clearly indicate Lönnrot's interest in folklore. His folklore collecting journeys began in 1828, when he served as a tutor in the family of Professor J. A. Törngren at Laukko,

As the *Kalevala* was gaining renown, mythical lore developed about its creator and his childhood. Finnish schoolchildren learned of an Elias Lönnrot who sat in a tree reading and forgot to eat. In his *Finland framstäldt i teckningar* (Finland presented in pictures) (1845) Zachris Topelius published this idyllic landscape depicting the tenant farmer's cottage in Sammatti where Lönnrot was born. (J. Knutson, Finnish National Board of Antiquities)

in Häme Province. He became a great friend of the family and corresponded with Mrs. Anna and Miss Eva Törngren as long as they lived.

In 1832, Lönnrot became an assistant to the district physician in Oulu, and in 1833 he himself became the district physician in the small, remote town of Kajaani. Although Lönnrot was the only doctor in northeastern Finland at this time, his medical work did not take up all his time and energy except during major epidemics. The folk were not accustomed to trusting a doctor, and Lönnrot's duties in Kajaani were primarily those of an inspector. He carried out his inspection trips with great care. The travel inherent in his work also provided him with good opportunities to collect folklore throughout his district.[3] Lönnrot's routine reports to the medical authorities as district physician provide detailed accounts of health conditions in northeastern Finland. In Kajaani, his medical work also included the translation of numerous health-care manuals into Finnish and the compilation of *Suomalaisen talonpojan kotilääkäri* (The Finnish farmer's family doctor) (1839), a book about home health care based upon a Swedish model.

At the beginning of his career, Kajaani was a difficult environment for the young doctor. Epidemics raged in the small town, and its spiritual atmosphere did not seem to provide him with nourishment. Before he was able to adjust to Kajaani, Lönnrot experienced a severe crisis. On February 2, 1833, he wrote to his friend J. F. Elfwing in Helsinki:

> I would prefer a thousand times over to be there or in any choleric city what- ever than here, during these times. Well, the devil take it, I looked cholera in the eye in Helsinki and elsewhere during the fall of 1831, but neither that nor any other plague can be compared to the epidemics, hunger, and distress here. I am beginning to believe that I was born under the most unlucky star in all the vast firmament when, right at the beginning of my practice, I've ended up in such infernal circumstances, as indeed I have. . . . I've time for nothing but writing prescriptions and, with Mrs. Hammarlund, imploring Jesus for help.

At the end of February, Lönnrot himself fell seriously ill with typhus. A rumor of his death even reached Helsinki.[4] Upon hearing it, Lönnrot, who had already recovered, wrote jestingly to another friend, J. E. A. Wirzen: "If I can believe the Finnish proverb 'Illness brings fame to the wealthy, but the poor never attain fame, not even in death,' then I should at least be a millionaire, for this proverb to remain true." In the beginning of June 1833, his friend Elfwing re- ceived the following letter: "Faith gives you life, but if I don't succeed in build- ing faith on a firmer foundation than now, then, devil take it, sooner or later I'll leave the entire field of medicine. A farmer at least wants to get his seed from the field; I'll persevere as a doctor as long as necessary to pay those debts which accrued in studying this skill."

Insights into Lönnrot's feelings in Kajaani have been preserved in his abun- dant correspondence from that time. This material clearly shows that his main interests were not in his career as a medical doctor. He had apparently sought this economically secure medical position in order to pay the debts he had ac- quired while studying and to care for his parents, who lived with him in Kajaani until the end of their days. On May 19, 1833, Lönnrot wrote to a friend: "The only thing I can undertake, lest I grow numb as a bear in its cave, is to write to my friends of past times. And that's what I do quite often to renew myself. Life here is extremely monotonous, if no note is taken of the changing of the seasons with which God the Father brings joy to his children on earth." Based on this early correspondence, it can be asked whether Lönnrot's interest in folklore was in part a flight from the difficulties of the Kajaani period and his feelings of futility about practicing medicine. He surely must have felt some- what torn between his medical career and his folklore interests.

During the 1840s, Lönnrot was on leave from his medical duties for a num- ber of years. He had been entrusted by the Finnish Literature Society with the task of compiling a Finnish-Swedish dictionary, to contain the entire vocab- ulary of the Finnish language. It also was during this period that he began his linguistic field work with Castrén. Combined with his other tasks, the editing of the dictionary proved to be laborious. For Lönnrot, who had even worked on the *Kalevala* in two stages, first in the early 1830s and then in the late 1840s, this dictionary became his longest project, lasting four decades. The first volume, which included over two hundred thousand words, was finally published in 1867 and the second in 1880, when Lönnrot was seventy-eight years old.[5]

Lönnrot held his position as district physician for twenty years (1833–1853), until he became Professor of Finnish Language and Literature at Helsinki University after the death of Professor Castrén, who first held this chair. In 1848, Lönnrot held the first series of lectures ever given in the Finnish language at the University of Helsinki. He retired from his professorship in 1862 at the age of sixty, and thereafter dedicated himself to working on the dictionary. His other noteworthy role was as chairman of the Finnish Hymnal Committee. His contribution to the hymnal, which was published after his death, was greater than that of any of the other contributors.[6]

Lönnrot was a man of many activities who also found time to edit the Finnish-language journal *The Bee* in Kajaani. During the 1840s, he founded *Suomi-aikakauskirja* (The Finnish review) and served as editor-in-chief of a Swedish literary periodical. In the 1850s, he published *Oulun Wiikko-Sanomat* (The Oulu weekly).[7]

During his lifetime, Lönnrot became part of the rising national *Kalevala* cult. The *Kalevala* came to have its own role in Finland and abroad. Lönnrot, its creator, stepped into the background and went on to other tasks. At the same time, the cult created a mythical figure of Lönnrot, depicting him as the poor, unassuming Elias of Paikkari cottage. It is often difficult to distinguish Lönnrot's true personality from the narratives about him. Many-faceted scholarship and a powerful motivation for work were combined in his personality. Unassumingly self-assertive, Lönnrot generally avoided public controversies and competitive situations. On November 1, 1847, for example, he wrote the following with regard to the newly established chair in Finnish language and literature to which he was aspiring: "Should something come of that, then only if von Becker and Castrén do not seek it."

Unlike many Romantics in Finland during that time, Lönnrot was not given to slogans and patriotic platforms. Although he was captivated by the Romantic idea of an epic, he maintained a down-to-earth attitude while actualizing it. In the preface to the *Old Kalevala*, he wrote the following characteristic statement:

> There are both those persons who hold our ancient runes in great esteem, and those for whom they haven't the slightest worth. I would not want the runes to be disparaged, or to be unequivocally celebrated, either. They are by no means equal to those of the Greeks and Romans, but it is quite sufficient if they at least demonstrate that our ancestors were not unenlightened, even in their spiritual efforts, and that the runes do demonstrate.[8]

Less is known about Lönnrot's personal problems and worries. In Kajaani he cared for his parents and his medical practice ensured their economic security. Lönnrot married relatively late, at the age of forty-seven. Tragically, his children died young. So it is understandable that he made out his final will to the Sammatti School of Domestic Arts for Girls, in remembrance of his lost daughters.[9]

THE THREE BASIC PARAMETERS OF LÖNNROT'S WORLD VIEW

Based on Lönnrot's life history, activities, and voluminous literary production, it is possible to distinguish at least three different dimensions to his world view, although these were joined into an almost seamless whole in his personality. As Hannes Sihvo has shown, the rationalism of the Enlightenment, the Lutheran faith, and an enthusiasm for folk poetry characteristic of Romanticism influenced Lönnrot's world view throughout his life.[10]

As a child, Lönnrot was already imbued with the Christian world view of Lutheranism. Toward the end of the 1830s, this tradition became more deeply personal for him and led to the development of his quiet faith. Christianity, as represented by the Finnish Evangelical Lutheran Church, predominated among his friends and his circle of acquaintances, which also included clergymen.[11]

No doubt Lönnrot's religiosity was influenced by the cholera epidemic in Kajaani during the 1830s, when he saw many around him die prematurely without being able to help them in spite of his office as their physician. In May of 1838, Lönnrot openly described his personal feelings to his friend J. F. Cajan, who had recently experienced a religious awakening: "Thus I, like many others, have had my period of doubt. But now I am already partially over it and hope, with God's mercy, to overcome it altogether. Indeed, the world gives us no peace and even if it did so, that peace is only the appearance of peace. Are we able to build a house on the ice, which will but last the winter?" In accordance with his moderate stance, however, Lönnrot gave his friend the following advice at the conclusion of the letter: "Nevertheless, do not part from the companionship of those on earth, but merely from that which offends, as from all evil. The fool says: Do not go to sea, but a wise man prepares his boat and makes use of the sea."

During crises in his own life, Lönnrot sought God's guidance. This was the situation on Whitsuntide in 1839, for example, when the boat following his overturned on the way to church and his brother's son and a servant girl perished. In a draft of his letter to Sexton Bisi, whose sister Beata drowned in the accident, Lönnrot openly described his religious feelings and views with regard to "the merits of life" and "God's mercy":

> I can hardly even bear my own sorrow, let alone console you, but I know that God can and I hope that he wishes to console you there as well as us here. I have also implored Mr. Saxa to console you, with what power he has. Although your sorrow is indeed great, mine is even greater still, because of both

Beata and my brother's son. And my nephew Kalle's mother causes the greatest concern. Before Christmas, she lost her husband and now, so soon after, she has lost her oldest son, for whom there was fine hope. But because we have no knowledge of the days to come, we must believe that God, who knows all, gathered them at a time well suited for Him. And for the most part I've tried to console myself that, during her lifetime, Beata looked after the salvation of her soul and lived in such a manner that we all remember her with gratitude and a sense of loss. My brother's son was still of the age (16 years old) that even if his faith may yet have been weaker, I nevertheless hope that, based on his merits, God our Redeemer, in His mercy, also took him there, to where we hope He may someday help us as well.

Upon his retirement in the 1860s, Lönnrot moved to Sammatti and often preached in the local Lutheran church there. The hymns he was then preparing clearly attest to the depth of his religious devotion. During the last twenty years of his life, as chairman of the Finnish Hymnal Committee, Lönnrot made a huge contribution to this work. To his great disappointment, this hymnal was not adopted by the Church. When it was finally accepted, after Lönnrot's death, his contribution proved to be greater than that of anyone else. It included 17 hymns written by Lönnrot, 64 translated by him into Finnish and 194 to which he had made basic revisions.[12]

The influence of the Enlightenment and of Romanticism is clearly apparent in Lönnrot's earliest hymns. Their quiet style and clarity, as well as their emphasis on comprehensibility and their submissive attitude toward life, including the didactic and moralizing tone typical of many of them, are characteristic of the Enlightenment. The emphasis on experiencing the presence of the Deity through nature which is found in these hymns has been attributed to the influence of Romanticism, e.g., the "Summer Hymn," for example, which Lönnrot adapted from Psalm 65. The poetry of Lönnrot's hymns has been praised for the freshness of its artistic expression and for the fact that Lönnrot, in accordance with his task, attempted to balance the use of Finnish dialects in them.[13] Thus, Lönnrot also included a noteworthy amount of eastern Finnish vocabulary in the hymnal.

For Lönnrot, Christianity was not so much experiential as a "way of life." Lönnrot as an individual was a reasonable man who advocated a self-possessed, virtuous life. He was a prime example of compliance to the Protestant work ethic. As becomes apparent from letters and drafts of letters which have survived, Lönnrot believed that spirituality should play a significant role in a person's life. Spirituality did not, however, exempt an individual from taking care of societal obligations.

Another characteristic of Lönnrot's Christianity was tolerance for the opinions of others, including both Christian and non-Christian religiosity. He could not abide narrow moralism or restrictive norms. His attitude toward other religions was quite moderate. In a June 1836 issue of *The Bee*, Lönnrot responded to an allegation that the Turks were godless pagans by stating that they too believed in one sole god, although their manner of believing was slightly different from that of the Christians. This tolerant attitude, inherent in Lönnrot's Christianity, was in clear harmony with his personality. During his life, Lönnrot systematically avoided arguments, preferring to step aside himself. This was not done with the bitterness of martyrdom. Rather, it was softened by a sense of humor and optimism. The same attitude also helped him persevere throughout the difficulties of his medical practice and rune-collecting journeys.

As a result of his medical studies, Lönnrot adopted the rationalistic mode of thought then prevalent in scientific circles. His reports throughout the various stages of his medical practice, as in *Suomalaisen talonpojan kotilääkäri* (The Finnish farmer's family doctor) (1839), reflect the attitude and thinking of a scientist who based his opinions directly on the empirical model of cause and effect. Lönnrot was also able to systematize his research material, as becomes apparent from the preliminary charts and statistics he prepared for his dictionary. Exactitude and systematization were apparent throughout his work in creating the *Kalevala*.

Later scholarship has proved untenable many of the theories put forth by Lönnrot with regard to the historical nature of the *Kalevala*, as well as the monotheism of the ancient Finnish religion. Nevertheless, these ideas demonstrate the scientific and rationalistic mode of thought which characterized his world view. In accordance with the scholarship and theories of his time, Lönnrot obviously wanted to see the world as a logically consistent field of phenomena. The tolerance characteristic of his Christianity made this entirely possible. In the spirit of the Enlightenment, the attitude of the scientific community toward Christianity at that time was mild and tolerant. At the beginning of the nineteenth century, the western scientific community did not yet oppose or even question the basic doctrines of the Christian faith.

During his years as a student, Lönnrot was greatly influenced by the spirit of Romanticism at the Turku Academy. The concept of the great past of the ancient Finns was fostered there. However, Lönnrot's attitude toward National Romanticism did differ from that of many of his contemporaries. It was primarily expressed in practical, hard work and not in fanaticism or programmatic declarations.

In addition to compiling collections of folklore, Lönnrot's National Romanticism was channeled into activities for the general enlightenment of the people. These included *The Finnish Farmer's Family Doctor* and dictionaries. Along with providing the people with important practical and spiritual knowledge, Lönnrot also considered it necessary to enlighten them about their own past. This was his primary justification for publishing the *Kalevala*. Thus, Lönnrot's moderate stance with regard to Finnish identity did not signify a lack of enthusiasm for National Romanticism. Rather, it indicated his realistic view of the societal conditions which then prevailed. Lönnrot's enthusiasm was also channeled into the Kalevala runes themselves. He even taught himself to play the kantele and to sing old runes.[14]

In his article "Laulusta" (On song) published in *The Bee* in February 1839, Lönnrot expressed his enthusiasm for the eloquent, aesthetic nature of song, stating that singing was a natural way for all peoples to express "an emotion of the heart." He was also able to create poems about himself in the trochaic meter, later referred to as the Kalevala meter. An example of Lönnrot's enthusiasm for Kalevala folk song is demonstrated in a letter he wrote to his friend Appelgren in November 1833. In it, he gives poetic form to his feelings about the field work he was doing at that time:

> Walking in Kuhmo
> In church at Kianta
> And even yet farther
> Across the violent borders
> Of Vuokkiniemi Parish
> In the finest place of song
> In the mighty land of Russia
> Where my sack grew full
> Bringing runes when I returned
> Written down in villages
> Found in houses
> Chanted in boats
> To be put down on paper
> Some telling of Old Väinämöinen
> A verse about his great works
> Some about young Joukahainen
> Plotting with his bow
> With fair Kaukomieli
> The light-hearted boy, Lemminkäinen's,
> Unceasing tasks
> Or of Smith Ilmarinen's
> The eternal forger's
> Autumnal coals
>
> Winters not long past
> Of his feats in the smithy.

LÖNNROT'S COMPROMISE:
"PAGANISM" VERSUS FINNISH LUTHERANISM

One significant issue is the relationship between the world of the runes and the reality Lönnrot observed on his expeditions. It is apparent from his correspondence and travel journals that he witnessed numerous circumstances where runes were performed in ritual context. For example, he attended the Ascension Day Festival at Ritvala, which included a runic drama.[15] He also attended a feast to celebrate the slaying of a bear, as well as many traditional Karelian wedding ceremonies,[16] and made an arduous journey to Kola Lapland to witness Saami shamanic rituals.[17] Clearly, there was abundant evidence that runes could indeed be utilized for other than purely aesthetic experiences.

In addition to funerals, the occasions which brought the people of White Sea Karelian villages together included a girl's leaving for another village to be married and the departure of the men on their annual peddling journeys. Particularly poignant was that moment when a young man, after casting of lots, was designated to leave for twenty-five years of service in the Russian army. These were occasions for traditional lamenting. This photograph was taken by the ethnographer and ethnomusicologist A. O. Väisänen in 1915. (A. O. Väisänen, Archives of the National Museum of Finland)

It was, however, their aesthetic aspect which Lönnrot primarily valued. This was also one way to solve the problem created by the conflict between the reality expressed in the runes and the living religious tradition. Lönnrot considered the "ancient paganism" of the runes acceptable. To him, the beliefs manifested in them were an expression of the "dead religion" of the ancient Finns as opposed to the "living" religion of nineteenth-century Finland. Lönnrot consciously compiled the *Kalevala* to be the epic of a staunchly Lutheran people. Lutheranism had traditionally taken a completely negative view of the folk religion. For centuries, the Finnish clergy had considered the runes part of the pagan religion. Some revivalists did, in fact, accuse Lönnrot of encouraging paganism by collecting and publishing folklore.[18]

Despite his staunch Lutheranism, however, Lönnrot did not consider the inclusion of charms to be problematic in creating the *Kalevala*. In his opinion, they depicted the superstitions of the ancient Finns and not the religious views of contemporaries.[19] Because of the historical gulf he envisioned between the reality expressed in the runes and those who sang them, Lönnrot was able to achieve a balance between these, at least in his own mind.

The functions of the runes had, in fact, already been greatly secularized by Lönnrot's time. Their ritual uses in conjunction with hunting, sowing, and other activities had decisively diminished. Rune singing had become largely a leisure-time activity. Increasingly, the singers were beginning to view the religious content and significance of the runes from a Christian perspective. Thus, for many singers, the myths and beliefs embodied in the runes were no longer an organic part of their own world view. For example, Castrén called attention to the fact that Arhippa Perttunen, one of Lönnrot's most important informants, often interpreted the runes from a Christian point of view. After meeting Perttunen in 1838, Castrén stated that the singer even considered shamanism a sinful and "godless thing."[20]

In accordance with his rationalistic world view, Lönnrot interpreted the Kalevala poems from the perspective of historical time. As a consequence, he considered such heroes as Väinämöinen, Ilmarinen, and Lemminkäinen to be purely historical figures. He saw them as great Finnish heroes, among whose few negative attributes were their superstition and paganism. In his opinion, however, this paganism was not of the worst kind. In accordance with Lönnrot's belief that the primordial religion of the ancient Finns had been monotheistic, he considered it a credit to them that they had believed in a single, supreme deity, Ukko. According to this view, the ancient Finnish religion had already been amenable to "knowledge of one sole god," which the Christian religion had then provided.[21] Thus, Lönnrot interpreted the ancient religion of the Finns, as it was depicted in the *Kalevala*, to be a kind of "good" paganism, an aspect of the distant, pre-Christian past. The heroes of the *Kalevala*, as skilled in magic as they may have been, were not seen by him as related to the harsh reality of the folk healing practices he witnessed daily in his role as the Kajaani district doctor. Lönnrot was not interested in the "living use" of folklore, but rather in obtaining a rational narrative which could then be joined into an intelligent plot about the historical Kalevala.

Although Lönnrot valued the Karelian men who sang runes for him, and as a nationalist held the character of the Finnish and Karelian people in esteem, he also had another, more rationalistic view of the contemporary folk. For him, folk healers were incompetent competitors to the medical profession, continuously resorted to by ignorant and superstitious people. His dismal observations of the abject living conditions and health of the people living in the Kajaani region, as well as what he considered their drunkenness, uncleanliness and laziness, no doubt lent credence to his view that they were uncivilized. He seldom saw actual counterparts to Väinämöinen, Lemminkäinen, or Ilmarinen, the lofty heroes he envisioned in the *Kalevala*.

It is therefore understandable that Lönnrot considered himself primarily an enlightener of the people and, in his mind, vaguely imagined a valiant, proud past for the Finnish people as it was depicted in the *Kalevala*. As a consequence of this attitude, however, he was limited in his ability to gain deeper insight into the world view concealed in the Kalevala runes themselves, which still influenced the experiential reality of people contemporary with him.

LÖNNROT'S VIEW OF MAN:
THE RATIONAL VERSUS THE EMOTIONAL

It has been shown that rationalism, in the spirit of the Enlightenment, was part of Lönnrot's world view. He considered normatively approved conduct and self-controlled experience to be the basis of physical and psychological well-being. A peaceful, balanced emotionalism and a harmonious, self-possessed demeanor were characteristic of his personality. Lönnrot's impassioned description of the trend toward religious ecstasy in the Kajaani region and his interpretation of powerful emotions as illness indicate that emphasis on rational thought, as opposed to emotional experience, was a basis of his world view and not merely an aspect of his personality. In accordance with this rational mode of thought, he interpreted ecstatic religious experiences as "some kind of psychological illness."[22]

Lönnrot's negative view of emotionalism is clearly reflected in the article "Vimmoista" (On manias) which was published in *The Bee* and in *The Finnish Farmer's Family Doctor* in 1839:

> Emotions affect even the body, for the spirit and the body are united in such a manner that neither endures anything alone. Rest, hope, satisfaction, and moderate joy keep a person healthy, and sometimes even cure an ill one. But excessive joy and happiness are dangerous, as are excessive sorrow, care, and even depression. If someone is severely subject to a sudden emotion, that person's clothes and laces must immediately be carefully eased off, and fresh air let into the room by opening the door and the windows. He or she should be given cold water to drink and, in the most severe cases, even veins should be opened and an enema applied. Even more important, the patient must avoid sudden changes of emotion, and whenever possible, sorrows and cares must be dispelled from the mind. The patient must not burden him- or herself with cares, but rather have faith and hope that everything in God's command is for the patient's good, although this may not always be comprehended. All ill people, but particularly those giving birth to children, the weak, the sickly, and those with a sensitive nature, require such spiritual rest.[23]

The therapeutic directives given by Lönnrot are clear: the experience of intense emotion or excitement should be avoided. One should accept even difficult life circumstances, in which trust in God has a balancing effect. A person remains physically and psychologically well if his mind is calm. Strong emotions and negative behavior must be avoided.

The significance for Lönnrot of this rationalistic view of man is also clearly

White Sea Karelian girls. White Sea women were accustomed to taking charge of matters in their villages. All the men were gone from some villages during winter as a result of their trade as peddlers. Strong women, who had to make decisions for their families because their husbands were away, were also found among the White Sea rune singers. (A. O. Väisänen, Archives of the National Museum of Finland)

apparent in the explanations he gives for practices in folk religion. In explaining the healing practices related to a Saami shaman's trance, for example, he proceeds from empirically observable events and causalities. If a sage did, in fact, succeed in obtaining information about an illness, Lönnrot did not believe it had actually been obtained from a spiritual being or from the dead. As a rationalist, he assumed that the sage had received the information from someone who had previously been with the patient or, circuitously, from the patient him- or herself.[24] It was Lönnrot's assumption that events in the world were based on a rational order, and he did not initially seek supernatural explanations for them. He placed more emphasis on the cognitive than the experiential aspect of religion. In his view, ultimately it was the acknowledgment of one sole God at the moment of death which determined the state of the soul and ensured salvation. In Lönnrot's view, only God could intervene in those matters which people sometimes tried to solve by means of sorcery or magic. In 1836, he made the following statement in *The Bee* with regard to love charms:

Often the parents were so concerned about their female children that, immediately on their birth, they began performing love charms. No one need even mention that all such acts for the sake of girls' good fortune in marriage are empty, senseless sorcery, all the worse if it is thought something can be won by them without the aid of God. The best "lempi" (luck in love) for girls is ensured if they are virtuous in their deportment, cleanly in life, and skillful and diligent in their work.[25]

LÖNNROT'S ATTITUDE TOWARD RELIGIOUS REVIVALISM

It was natural for Lönnrot and the *Kalevala* to become the symbols of the national awakening in Finland. This period of mythologizing coincided with the religious revivalist movements which were then attracting people throughout the country. At the same time as Lönnrot was moving about the Savo-Karelian villages to collect folk poetry, northern Karelia and northern Savo were being influenced by two powerful religious movements of this kind.

In northern Savo, revivalism was bolstered in the 1790s by an ecstatic religious awakening which took place in the township of Lapinlahti. At its initial stages, this movement, which was known as the "heränneet" or the "körttiläiset"[26] in Finnish, was led by Juhana Lustig (Puustijärvi), who had moved there from the Tornio River Valley. He was considered an enlightened, broad-minded lay leader. During the 1820s, however, the leadership of this movement was taken over by the famous peasant leader Paavo Ruotsalainen (1777–1852), who had already participated in the meetings of the movement from the 1790s onward. Under his leadership, this revivalist movement entered a new phase. Ecstatic elements reappeared, and its identity became more rigidly dogmatic. In northern Karelia, there was another revivalist group centered around the chaplain of Liperi, Henrik Renqvist. In his sermons, Renqvist strictly emphasized the value of Christian morality and the ritual of knee-praying.[27]

These two competing movements were spreading rapidly among the peasant populations of Savo, Karelia, and Kainuu, where Lönnrot traveled as the district physician and as a folklore collector. Lönnrot personally encountered revivalists in Kajaani. His attitude toward this kind of religious activity seems to have been quite negative. This aversion is apparent, for example, in a series of articles entitled "Nykysistä ajoista" (On present times) which he published in *The Bee* during 1836. In his report, he strongly advocated the standpoint of the Lutheran clergy, criticizing the revivalists for their isolation and zealousness in a kind of "pietistic" Christianity he disliked:

> To be pious here, it used to be sufficient to attend communion and the parish catechetical meetings, to read your primer and catechism book, the hymnal, and the Holy Bible, and, subsequently, to try to adhere to these in your life, but now they are nothing. In order to become a Christian, you must separate yourself from other people, even your father, mother, brothers, and sisters,

In his travel accounts, Väisänen describes the departure ceremony for the men taken into the Russian army (Väisänen 1915, 4-5): During these days, there was so much sadness in the villages that the usual gossip about the relationships of young people was forgotten: lamenting took its place. The day after next a group of young men was to leave Ruva for Kouta to cast lots. (*Note*: All the young men made the trip; no one knew in advance who was to be chosen.) At the time of departure, no one was safe–every mother, girlfriend, etc., thought that her son or beloved would take the path of sorrow. "How to bear this grief?" was the predominant question in the mind of many a mother, young bride, and betrothed. At the moment of parting, this sorrow burst forth in laments. The young men held back their tears until the farewells. But then, in hugging those closest to them and saying, "Please bless us," sorrow also wrenched tears out of them. When the fathers and brothers of the young men stepped into the boats, those departing had to part from the embrace. Simultaneously, a wailing lament issued from the group of women, and one mother lamented lying prone on the ground. Then the church bells began to chime, echoing the chaotic sentiment in the air. A few moments later, a shot rang from the departing boats. The lamentation then subsided and the group dispersed, leaving them to their "paths of grief." Laments sounded on those shores from which the boats had departed. In the picture, a mother-in-law embraces a young bride whose husband has departed. (A. O. Väisänen, Archives of the National Museum of Finland)

scarcely talk, eat, and repose with them. You must dress in Pietist clothing, even cast off your urgent work, and harp on Zion's verses throughout the nights, read *Huutavan ääni* (The calling voice) or other such books.

Religious revivalism also became influential among student circles at the University of Helsinki during the 1840s and 1850s, when Lönnrot was a professor there. It both attracted and repelled people and was a divisive influence on the Finnish intelligentsia. For example, the clergyman and poet Lauri Stenbäck became deeply involved in the revivalist circles, while J. L. Runeberg, the national poet of Finland, became a strong opponent of the movement.[28] Lönnrot was reluctant to take a strong position and did not participate in revivalist meetings. Like the official Lutheran Church, which maintained a policy of noninvolvement in revivalist issues, Lönnrot personally tried to remain above these arguments. However, he may well have been irritated by the peasant coarseness and vehemence of Ruotsalainen and his supporters.

Thus, in his attitudes toward the religiosity of others, Lönnrot was a moderate man who remained aloof from the overzealousness of the revivalists throughout his life. This was in spite of the fact that his daughters had connections with the Evangelical movement in Sammatti.[29] Lönnrot disliked any kind of extremism, including the revivalists as well as Karelian lamenters and Saami chanters. Another conflict between him and the revivalists resulted from their negative attitude toward folklore and the *Kalevala*. The revivalists considered folklore sinful.

The Finnish national awakening had been spurred on by the *Kalevala*. It initially found support among the young intellectual circles, whereas religious revivalism was of peasant origins. At first these two movements followed distinctly separate paths. It was not until the end of the nineteenth century, during a period of great pressure from Russia, that the nationalistic movements inspired by Lönnrot's epic and the revivalist movements in Finland united their efforts. From that time on, the revivalist movements also began to focus on patriotic nationalism and eventually became an important element in both the young independent republic and its Evangelical Lutheran Church.[30]

CHAPTER
5

THE SOURCES OF ANCIENT
FINNISH RUNES

TEMPORAL STRATA IN RUNIC POETRY

The origins and the cultural context of the epical poetry on which the *Kalevala* is based have been the subject of heated debate in Finnish folklore research up to the present day. In examining what the runes tell us about the Finnish world view, it becomes apparent that their content and the expression of this content in poetic form are two separate issues. Thus, for example, the religious concepts contained in the runes can be much older than their verse form.[1] Poetic form is particularly bound to the textual norms of language and culture and is therefore more difficult to transfer across linguistic boundaries than content. It was easier for the plot and motifs on which the runes were based to be transferred from one culture to another through contacts between peoples.

Elements of various layers of culture are often intermingled within the same genre. Thus, for example, the Catholic Middle Ages left its mark on many Finnish charms, whereas numerous mythical incantations contain aspects which seem to greatly predate the Middle Ages.[2] It is therefore impossible to view the runes as solely a product of the imagination of eighteenth- and nineteenth-century Karelian folksingers. In fact, many of the elements preserved in this poetic form are so archaic that they are not found in the prose tradition which was recorded at the same time. Lönnrot observed the fact that runes change. In the preface to the *Old Kalevala* he states:

> The reader may ask whether our ancestors sang these songs in any particular sequence or individually. It appears to me that these poems, as things happen as well, appeared individually. The poems about Väinämöinen, Ilmarinen, and Lemminkäinen must be the compositions not of one person, but of many. One person related one thing into memory and another something else, whatever that person had seen or heard. Nowadays, I rarely come across a rune which has been preserved down to our time in exactly its original wording. He who knows how easy it is for many a peasant to create a poem, if he or she wants to sing about some familiar subject matter, will soon discover that not even

the best memory can preserve, word for word, what is heard from another in long runes. Rather, it is the subject matter everyone remembers more easily. And passage by passage, if the person remembers most of them, he or she relates them from the poem to another as well, forgetting some, altering others. Gradually, even the poetic subject matter itself can be altered from its original character, so that it is then related quite differently. This may, in part, already have happened, at least with regard to proper names. As the Christian doctrine spread in the land, often Jesus, Saint Peter, Ruotus (Herod), Judas, etc., were substituted for ancient heroes, and for the women, the Virgin Mother Mary.[3]

In preliterate cultures, information which was sacred or important was often transferred to new generations in the form of narrative poetry. Under these circumstances, poetic form served as a technical aid to memory, whereby particular details came to be repeated more precisely than in prose narratives. Living poetry which exists as oral tradition is not, of course, preserved as such, but is disposed to change, facilitated by various s cultural and individual factors. A rune may be handed down from one generation to the next, but each generation treats it in accordance with its own conceptual world.

In most instances, the "world" of the rune can be delineated through comparative study of text variants. Using this method, in addition to being compared to each other, runes are examined in the light of other folklore and all possible scholarship available about the culture being studied. Based on analysis of style and content, for example, runes have been categorized in the following manner:[4] mythical runes, which tell about acts of creation in primordial times and about the origins of the world and its phenomena; shamanistic runes, which have as their primary heroes sages and conjurers who govern ecstatic techniques and contacts with the other realm; adventure runes, which focus on courtship and the plundering journeys of their heroes as primary subject matter; and fantasy runes, which include fairy-tale figures and animals. Part of Finnish poetry also derives from Christian saints' legends. In addition to epics and charms, runic poetry in the Kalevala meter also includes lyric elements. Among the most recent subgenres of this runic poetry are medieval ballads, and historical poems about wars and historical figures such as kings, dukes, and war chieftains.

The study of the historical background of the runes in the *Kalevala* is complicated by the fact that the same rune may have been incorporated into the epic several times.[5] Furthermore, there may also be competing poetic versions of the same subject matter. Runic poetry in the Kalevala meter also reflects the breach created when Finland and Karelia were gradually, and almost simultaneously, absorbed into different spheres of Christianity. Most of Finland was absorbed into the Roman Catholic Church by way of continental Europe, while Karelia was absorbed from the east by the Orthodox Church with its Byzantine origins. As a consequence, the respective influences of Western and Eastern Christianity are important in the study of Finnish cultural history. From the eleventh century on, competitive Christian versions of mythical and shamanistic poetry developed. Some of these runes may also be the products of Christian missionary propaganda, consciously meant to replace a particular pre-Christian cultural hero or shaman with a Christian saint or even Christ himself. Thus, for example, the rune about Väinämöinen's boat journey became "Jumalan pojan laivaretki" (The boat journey of God's son). Based on its content and style, "Väinämöisen tuomio" (Väinämöinen's judgment), the final episode of the *Kalevala*, was attributed to the late Christian Middle Ages by Lönnrot, who himself pondered the age of the Kalevala runes. On March 30, 1851, Léouzon Le Duc, the French translator of the *Kalevala*, received the following letter from him:

> There is no longer any precise historical certainty as to the general age of the Kalevala runes. Even their average age must be left primarily to the vagaries of supposition.–However, I would consider the oldest to be the cosmogonic runes and the Sampo runes as well as those about Väinämöinen and Joukahainen, then the runes about Lemminkäinen and Kullervo, followed by the courtship and wedding runes and the most recent, "Väinämöinen's Judgment," which is hardly more than five hundred years old.

In structuring the *Kalevala*, Lönnrot did, in fact, keep in mind the hypothetical age of the runes in addition to the unity of the plot. The *Kalevala* begins with the creation of the cosmos and ends with "Väinämöinen's Judgment." In Lönnrot's view, then, the rune of most recent origins became the final one in the entire epic.

The problem of dating folk traditions and defining their origins has been a central focus of the "Finnish" or "historical-geographic" method. The basic principles of this method were introduced to the comparative study of folklore by Kaarle Krohn. Based on this methodology, the variants of the runes are grouped chronologically and geographically to distinguish older elements from more recent ones. As a result of these analytic techniques, some runes prove to be older than others. Using this methodology, Matti Kuusi in his book *Kalevalaista kertomarunoutta* (Kalevala narrative poetry) concluded that there were four periods in the development of runic poetry in the Kalevala meter. The oldest of these was the Proto-Finnic Era, dating from 500 B.C. to A.D. 500. This was followed by the Early Kalevala, the Middle Kalevala, and the Late Kalevala periods.[6]

Kuusi is of the opinion that in general the structure of runic poetry progressed from simpler to more complicated forms. According to the temporal divisions he has outlined, the origins of the Kalevala meter derive from the time between the Proto-Finnic Era and the Early Kalevala Period. He believes that the Kalevala meter developed during the Proto-Finnic Era when the Finns were settling in Finland. This was followed by the Early Kalevala Period from A.D. 500 to the Christianizing of Finland. The Middle Kalevala stratum of poetry begins with the Crusades in the twelfth century, when Finland came into the cultural sphere of the Christian Church. The Late Kalevala stratum begins with the Reformation and the birth of the Finnish literary language in the sixteenth century.[7]

Kuusi's approach is a modification of the historical-geographic method. It includes five complementary aspects: motif analysis or the study of content; structural analysis; functional analysis; stylistic analysis; and redaction analysis. Kuusi particularly emphasizes the importance of style as the indicator of the age of a rune. He stresses the use of a special technique of "hearing" the material, which utilizes a scholar's expertise in differentiating the temporal layers of these runes on the basis of stylistic nuances. While this approach is based on scholarship, Kuusi holds that even the early singers themselves were aware of these differences in age and style. In his opinion, for example, "there is no doubt that a select twelfth-century community could immediately have distinguished which of our ancient runes was modern at that time, which was aging a bit, and which was very ancient in style."[8]

Although preliterate Finnish runic poetry was recorded primarily during the past two centuries, it can provide insight into much earlier times. Kuusi believes that the oldest of the runes date from prehistory.[9] The *Kalevala* scholar Väinö Kaukonen argues that a renaissance of the runes took place just before they were collected. In Kaukonen's opinion, therefore, Lönnrot's collection work was done at precisely the right time.[10]

THE ORIGINS OF BALTO-FINNIC RUNE SINGING

Stylistically, the most significant features of the so-called Kalevala runes are trochaic meter, alliteration, and parallelism, which also indicate their age. Runes in the so-called Kalevala meter are known only to Balto-Finnic peoples, i.e., Finns, Karelians, Ingrians, Ludes, Veps, Votes, Livonians, and Estonians. For example, the Saami, whose linguistic connection to the Finns is posited to have been severed during the early Proto-Finnic Era, do not sing runes in the Kalevala meter.[11] Rune singing in this meter is therefore estimated to be 2,500 to 3,000 years old at most.[12] The poetic meter then formed became the pattern according to which both religious and historical traditions were created and transmitted.

In studying Balto-Finnic runes, it is interesting to compare this genre to the traditions of geographically distant peoples related to the Baltic Finns and to the traditions of neighboring cultures. Among the questions which can be asked are the following: Have the runes of the Balto-Finnic peoples preserved aspects common to Finno-Ugric folklore? Do they perhaps relate something about the cultural contacts of the Proto-Finns? Where might these runes have originated?

During recent years, scholarship in numerous fields has yielded findings which together have broken down the old traditional concept of a relatively isolated community of Finno-Ugrians living somewhere in eastern Russia at approximately 3000 B.C. It was believed that this group later diverged linguistically, resulting in the Finno-Ugric groups presently known.[13] Based on contemporary scholarship, particularly comparative linguistics and archeology,[14] it has become possible to examine more thoroughly the contacts which the Finno-Ugric peoples had with other cultures. The Finno-Ugrians, along with the Samoyed, belong to the Uralic language group. The relationship of this linguistic family to a number of other Asian languages is an interesting, still unanswered, question. It appears, however, that the Uralic peoples only gradually became differentiated from each other. They were primarily nomadic and migrated long distances annually, adapting to their environs in various ways.

Ecological and archeological studies have shown that the Uralic peoples adapted rather early to three different kinds of environments. The Arctic tundra region was settled by the northernmost groups, whose descendants include the Saami, the Zyryans, and various Samoyed peoples. However, the majority of the peoples related to the Finns settled in the sub-Arctic environment of coniferous forests. The westernmost of these peoples became the Baltic Finns who, having combined hunting and fishing economies, crossed over huge forest areas, eventually settling the Finnish peninsula and the area to the east and south of the Gulf of Finland. The Hungarians settled on the steppes. Although these groups gradually became differentiated from one another and dwelled in regions far apart, various contacts continued to exist among them, as well as with other peoples. Archeological findings, including burial sites, give abundant evidence of complex trade relationships.[15] These mutual contacts with other cultures have made it rather difficult to extract the common core of the ancient proto-culture. It is possible, however, to approach it by linguistic research and, as will be shown, by studying other primary cultural phenomena.

The long-held theory that Finland was settled relatively recently, approximately at the birth of Christ, by way of either Estonia or the Isthmus of Karelia, has proved untenable in the light of present-day scholarship.[16] This theory may have been influenced by the erroneous hypothesis that the Finns already had a pattern of fixed settlement when they first arrived in Finland. The same concept also dominates the theory that the original home of the Finnish peoples was in the area around the bend of the Volga River. The influence of the agrarian way of life has been overestimated in studies of the early histories of Finno-Ugric peoples. It is unlikely that agriculture would have been of such significance to the Finnish tribes during their early stages that a group would have remained settled in an area primarily for the purpose of cultivating it.

In Arctic and sub-Arctic areas, it is much more common to combine various modes of sustenance, thus eliminating the risks posed by the environment. To a certain extent, migration remains inherent to this way of life even after the group has settled a particular area. Because natural resources are scarce, livelihood is usually derived from numerous sources. In the past, it was natural for such peoples to be strongly involved in trade. Rather than remaining isolated communities, they preferred contacts with other peoples who lived within their ecological sphere as well as outside it. This was also the way of life of the Finno-Ugric peoples.

The hypothesis that pre-Christian Finland was uninhabited is negated by the fact that there exists a uniform series of archeological findings in Finland dating from approximately 7000 B.C. A stone ax and a spearhead unearthed at Paltamo in Kainuu date from 7000 B.C. and are attributed to the early phase of the Suomusjärvi culture, thought to have lasted approximately 3,000 years.[17]

Who the people then occupying the Finnish peninsula were, is still an unanswered question. Based on current scholarship, it is hypothesized that there was a considerable amount, perhaps even a predominance, of Uralic content in the Suomusjärvi culture. The historian Eino Jutikkala has written about this interdisciplinary puzzle:

> The people of the mysterious Suomusjärvi culture may also have left a trace of themselves, in the form of shamanism, on the world of beliefs depicted in the Kalevala runes. And because there was never a complete break in settlement, and the populace never died out to the point of having no descendants, there should yet live, in Finnish genes as well, traces of the legacy of these people from nine thousand years ago. It can be assumed that the genetic tradition of both the Suomusjärvi culture and the Finno-Ugric immigrants was eastern.[18]

According to the archeologist C.-F. Meinander, it is impossible to point to any specific time period when the peninsula would have become Fennicized. Rather, it is a question of a long process which included numerous stages and was marked by the gradual differentiation of various cultures in the coniferous and mixed forest belt of northeastern Europe.[19] In the opinion of both Finnish and Soviet archeologists, the Comb Ceramic culture which originated in the Balto-Finnic area about 3000 B.C., may indicate the arrival of a new wave of Finnic peoples to northeastern Europe. From 3000 B.C. onwards, there are numerous correspondences found in archeological remains of northeastern Europe throughout the area between Finland and Central Russia.[20]

In the opinion of the linguist Mikko Korhonen, the Uralic language would have been spoken in the area between the Volga and the Ural Mountains, perhaps even on the eastern side of the Urals.[21] However, this does not negate the possibility that early migrations may have brought some Uralic-speaking cultures to the eastern Baltic before the dispersal of linguistic unity. The development of these languages was a gradual process during the course of which people living at great distances from each other became linguistically differentiated.

Korhonen concisely states that, based on present knowledge, the Proto-Uralic language evolved into the Proto-Finno-Ugric and Proto-Samoyed languages during the period 6000–4000 B.C. Following this, the Finno-Ugric proto-language evolved from 4000–2000 B.C., the Volga-Finnic at approximately 1500 B.C., and the early Finnic-Saami proto-language at 1000 B.C. In Korhonen's opinion, "It appears that before the dispersal of its language, during the final stage of its history, the Proto-Finno-Ugric group inhabited an extensive area between the East Baltic and the Urals. It may be that the westernmost of these

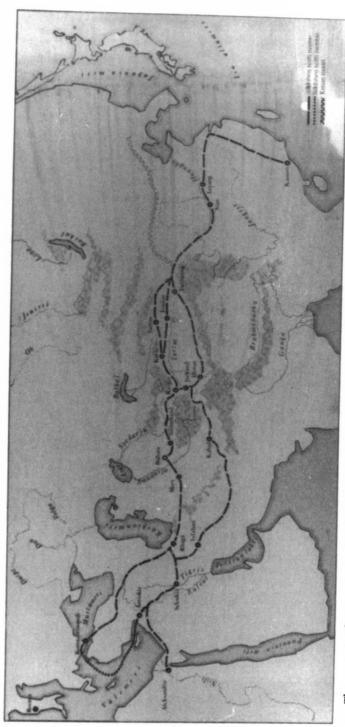

The most significant ancient cultural route extending from Europe to the Far East was the Silk Road. It led from the Mediterranean via the Black and Caspian seas and through the cantons of China to the shores of the Pacific. Numerous myths found in the *Kalevala* were also told along this route.

groups had already come to Finland at that time, roughly estimated at 4000 B.C."[22]

Because rune singing in its archaic trochaic form is known only to Balto-Finnic peoples, it must, of necessity, have developed after the period of the Finnish-Saami proto-language. It was developed by peoples who then spoke a common proto-language known as Proto-Finnic. There are, however, numerous Slavic and Germanic loan words in Proto-Finnic, which is an indication of the lively contacts this proto-culture had with other peoples. In addition to loan words and other linguistic indicators, archeological findings provide further assistance for fixing these cultures in a specific time period. Contacts with various Aryan or Indo-European cultures may have continued without interruption for up to five thousand years and this fact must also be taken into account in studying folklore. Therefore, a commonality of cultural elements does not necessarily derive from the intense interaction during Viking times, as has been assumed by Martti Haavio and other scholars until recently.[23] Rather, this may be a question of a common cultural fabric encompassing thousands of years, the manifestations of which may be found in Finnish runes as well as Old Norse and Icelandic sagas.

Soon after the archeological findings of C. - F. Meinander and Jorma Koivulehto's philological studies,[24] which led to a similar hypothesis, even Matti Kuusi was prepared to reexamine his delineation of stylistic periods for the Kalevala runes. In 1981 he stated: "It appears that the Finnish-Estonian-Karelian Early Kalevala stratum of Baltic influence, and the Middle Kalevala stylistic period which followed it—the stratum found in Finland and Karelia of Germanic influence—were not clearly successive developmental periods as was previously supposed."[25] The new findings did, however, support his view that Karelian influence played an important role in the development of Kalevala poetry. In Kuusi's opinion, the Eastern Proto-Finnic Veps-Izhors-Eastern White Sea element became estranged from the Kalevala poetry, whereas the western group brought folk poetry with it to Karelia, where it later had its golden age.

The content of the runes may, however, be much older than rune singing itself. In the comparative study of folklore, loans have often been sought and, when correspondences were found, it was generally assumed that the Finns had borrowed epical materials from elsewhere and subsequently incorporated them into their runic poetry. Perhaps largely as a result of the so-called Finnish or historical-geographic method, in which the concept of borrowing is inherent, the runes were not thought to contain a great deal of independent subject matter. Rather, the debate focused on whether they were derived from the east or the west. The origins of the runes cannot, however, be attributed to either the east or the west. Rather, it is a question of either eastern or western cultural influences being absorbed into the style, form, and meter of the ancient poetry. From this point of view, Kuusi's conjecture regarding the "westernness" of the runes is particularly controversial. In this study, an effort is made to find parallels to the motifs of the runic poetry based upon broader comparative analysis.

ANCIENT CULTURAL CONTACTS ALONG THE SILK ROAD

It has been shown that rune singing is a Balto-Finnic cultural phenomenon. But what of the contents of the runes? Do the motifs have a Balto-Finnic origin or are they even more ancient? According to current opinion, the Baltic Finns may have adapted many myths, which they had initially heard as prose, into poetic form.[26] It has been posited that many of these myths were adapted into their world view as well. A related question is what portion of the ancient motifs found in the Finnish runes is native to the Finns and how much has been borrowed from neighboring peoples.

Of course, tradition does not migrate without contacts between peoples. Trade and cultural exchange has been a significant aspect of those bonds which Finno-Ugric cultures have had with other peoples. In order to answer these questions, it is therefore of crucial importance to delineate the areas used by the Finno-Ugric groups, as well as where they traveled and migrated during various periods of their history. It is also necessary to determine which contacts were the primary channels for innovation.

Recent archeological, ethnographic, and linguistic findings shed considerable light on these issues. Of particular interest in this regard is the influence of the ancient Central Asian herding peoples on Finno-Ugric cultures. A joint Finnish-Soviet scientific symposium held in 1985 entitled "Traces of the Central Asian Culture in the North" resulted in a reevaluation of contemporary research in this area. One central issue which emerged was the pervasive influence of the Silk Road in mediating these cultural contacts.

Herodotus (485–425 B.C.), among others, told of a Silk Road which began at the mouth of the River Don and extended through the territories of numerous peoples, including the Sarmatians and the Scythians. An even earlier source exists in the form of a book written by Aristeas in the decade 630 B.C.[27] At approximately 1000 B.C., a herding culture, well suited to arid conditions, developed along the Silk Road. This area then became inhabited by numerous high cultures, including the Scythians (800-300 B.C.), whose territory extended from Lake Baikal to the Volga River. The Scythian Period was followed by those of the Sarmatians and the Huns (300 B.C.-A.D. 400). This was followed by the period of the ancient Turks (A.D. 400-900), characterized by numerous Byzantine cultural influences. These migrations had a significant influence on Europe. As a result of trade along the Silk Road, numerous cultural innovations from the peoples of the steppes became known in Europe, including trousers.[28]

In their recent research, Soviet archeologists have found burial remains to be a primary source of information about the Scythian culture. V. A. Gorodtsov and K. A. Smirnov, among others, have called attention to traces of Scythian culture near those regions of the Volga, Oka, and Kama rivers where it is hypothesized that Finno-Ugric peoples also lived during the final millennium B.C. Indications of three Finno-Ugric cultures characterized by a particular textile ceramic have been found in the area. Based on this evidence, it has been conjectured that, from the sixth to the second centuries B.C., the Finno-Ugric peoples moving about the areas surrounding the tributaries of the Volga River had extensive contacts with cultures of the steppes and the Silk Road.[29]

Archeological findings support the hypothesis that Central Asian influences might have come to northern Karelia—ancient Bjarmia—by way of the Viena River and Perm, which was located near the upper course of the Volga River. C.-F. Meinander has studied belt trimmings found at six Finnish burial sites and confirmed their relationship to corresponding finds in the vicinity of the Kama River, a tributary of the Volga. Among the artifacts found in Finnish graves, the belt trimming found at the Huittinen burial site in Satakunta is an artifact which clearly derives from Central Asia. On the basis of these findings, it is possible to say that Finland, in particular, played a central role in trade with the Kama region.[30]

Also well known are the so-called shaman's plates found in the municipality of Saarijärvi in central Finland, as well as the Åland Islands, at burial sites dating from the seventh to the fifth centuries B.C. The primary motif of these shaman's plates is a bird with outspread wings. Although interpretation of the religious content of these plates is problematic, based on them, C.-F. Meinander and the Soviet archeologist Y. A. Ryabinin[31] have concluded that a water route existed from White Sea Karelia to the Volga and Oka rivers. Ryabinin concludes:

> Having accepted this fact, one can suppose that the appearance in Finland of the previously mentioned "shaman's plates" reflects the existence of close contacts between the Finns from the Kama River who had advanced to Lake Ladoga, and tribes living in Finland. It is worth mentioning that, according to archival materials, similar cult figures were found in the southeastern area of Lake Ladoga.[32]

This water route mediated contacts between the peoples living in the Arctic taiga, the sub-arctic forests, and the steppe areas. Many cultural products were exchanged between cultures and new ones created along this route. It has been hypothesized that there existed an ancient, influential Permian-Tshudic culture along this water course which may have played a central role in mediating and preserving cultural traditions. Interestingly enough, this ancient cultural route seems to coincide with the areas where rune singing was a primary cultural institution. Present studies show that Central Asian elements are manifest in the epical motifs of the Finnish runes.

The majority of the pictographs are found at the confluence of water routes in eastern Finland. An elk, the primary subject matter of the pictographs, is depicted here; in the lower right hand corner there is a human being. This pictograph is from Uittamonsalmi at Ristiina. (Finnish National Board of Antiquities)

The subject matter of the pictograph field at Astuvansalmi, approximately sixty square meters in area, forms a series which can be read through the day as the sun's rays strike the picture field. These pictures have been painted on during the interim, as is also apparent in this photograph. The primary subject matter is an elk. It has been posited that the female figure to the left is a shaman. However, this may in fact symbolize the mythical, totemistic primordial mother, whose relationship to the elk is described in Finnish and Karelian Folklore. (Finnish National Board of Antiquities)

AN EPIC ON THE BOULDERS?

Often the study of folklore alone cannot solve the question of the age of a particular rune. The interdisciplinary support of other fields, such as philology, archeology, or anthropology, is needed. Thus, for example, an etymological treatment would take into account the vocabulary common to ancient runes as well as Uralic and neighboring languages. In dating a particular phenomenon, archeology may utilize more precise methods and techniques than comparative linguistics, folkloristics or mythology, for example. If similar epical motifs are found in words, names, archeological findings, and runes, it may be possible to draw conclusions about the period as a whole.

One must be cautious, however, about making generalizations based solely on a particular detail. An expert in a single discipline should be critical of information which does not fully satisfy the requisites of his or her particular field. An example of erroneous results achieved in this manner is the conclusions drawn by some Finnish archeologists in directly comparing archeological findings to specific verses of the *Kalevala*.

Dr. Jorma Leppäaho gave a description of the *Kalevala* world view based on archeological findings, making noteworthy observations about the Bronze and Iron ages, the periods about which the Kalevala runes undoubtedly tell. He also related a particular line of the *Kalevala*, "karhu karjui naulan piessä" (the bear roared atop a nail), to the spear tip adorning the royal grave of the Swedish royal Mendel family. However, he did not notice that this particular verse of the *Kalevala* had not been derived from authentic folk poetry, but had been added by Lönnrot.[33] As C.-F. Meinander has shown, Leppäaho erred despite his awareness that the *Kalevala* was an epic compiled by Lönnrot, and that its value for scholarship is more akin to that of an aesthetic essay than authentic folklore material.[34]

At times a specialist in one field becomes enthusiastic about findings in another, although these findings may in fact be dealt with more cautiously by those who made the discoveries and are aware of the methodological pitfalls of their own fields. In 1983, the Finnish ethnologist Niilo Valonen completed a study in which Finnish runes were examined with the aid of ancient art found on boulders.[35] The basis of his study was the White Sea Karelian petroglyphs found at Lake Onega and at the mouth of the Uiku River. These had been published by the Soviet archeologist W. J. Raudonikas. The Uiku River flows into the White Sea, and its field of 190 petroglyphs is at the mouth of the river. These have been dated from 2500-1000 B.C., the end of the Stone Age, while those at Lake Onega are attributed to the Neolithic Stone Age. In his study, Valonen argues that these petroglyphs can be interpreted directly, based on particular variants of Finnish-Karelian folk runes.

It was Valonen's aim to relate runic poetry to this Karelian art and to interpret its mythology based on astrological information derived from the movements of the stars in the northern sky. He analyzed rune variants in detail, attributing words and motifs derived from them to the field of petroglyphs and, in addition, to the star-filled northern sky. Valonen's basic tenet was that those who created the petroglyphs considered the epic runes to be star tales.[36] This interpretation is akin to that of E. N. Setälä and Jouko Hautala who, in part, supported an astrological interpretation of folklore.[37] Valonen also refers to the totemistic origins of the petroglyphs and, from this point of view, explains many zoomorphic concepts found in the runes—bears (osmos), swans (joukahainens), etc.—to be manifestations of early beliefs about the relationship between men and animals and their celestial counterparts.

A detailed criticism can be made of Valonen's interpretation. From a folkloristic point of view, it is unlikely that runes were being sung in the Kalevala meter at the time this art was being created. This, then, invalidates Valonen's basic premise that the petroglyphs were specifically composed to concur with the runes verse by verse. The runic texts on which the folkloristic part of Valonen's analysis is based were also recorded quite a distance from the boulders at Lake Onega and the Uiku River where the petroglyphs were found. The divergence in time between the creation of the carvings and the recording of the folkloric texts during the nineteenth century A.D. amounts to thousands of years. In spite of this criticism, however, it does seem possible to agree with Valonen's basic assumption that a bit of Karelian mythical history is indeed depicted on boulders at the Uiku River and on the shores of Lake Onega.

From the point of view of Finnish mythology and folklore, this art on the boulders does, in fact, offer new material for interdisciplinary analysis. During recent years, pictographs have been discovered at about fifty locations in eastern Finland. Archeologists have dated these paintings, done in red clay, from the end of the fourth millennium B.C. to the final centuries B.C. Thus the initial stages of the tradition would have been in the Stone Age, while its final stages lay in the Iron Age. Elk and human beings are the primary subject matter of the pictographs. Boats are also depicted almost as frequently. The most uniform of the Finnish painting fields is Astuvansalmi at Ristiina in southern Savo, where there are over sixty different pictures.[38]

In examining these images, it is necessary to pay particular attention to the whole, rather than to individual motifs. Furthermore, it is necessary to remember that a field of images was generally not created at one time; rather, the same boulder was repainted over the course of many generations, a period of hundreds and thousands of years. Old images have often been painted over or augmented. Therefore the art, like the runes, represents a tradition which has its own continuity, and there is no reason to attribute a precise date to any rune based on it. On the other hand, it is probable that runes were sung at the same time as the most recent images on the boulders in eastern Finland were being carved and painted, and these runes may even have dealt with the same subject matter. It is, in fact, equally possible that their common basis was more that of a vision, narrated orally as a tale, or acted as some kind of ritual or drama, or sung as a myth, in connection with a particular ceremony, for example. Most assuredly, this art is the manifestation of the particular world view found in its images and bound to time and space. An effort to explain the origins of this material naturally utilizes comparative methods to seek correspondences and meanings from other cultures in which the art and mythology on which it is based may perhaps be more fully represented. Thus, there is reason to search for parallels to them in, for example, the mythology of the Uralic peoples as well as other groups in northern Eurasia.

CHAPTER

6

THE CONTRIBUTION
OF THE RUNE SINGERS

WHITE SEA KARELIA, FOCUS OF EARLY
FOLKLORE COLLECTORS

At the beginning of the nineteenth century, Viena or White Sea Karelia became the object of National Romantic dreams, as the source of Finnish folklore in general and of runic poetry in particular. A primary reason for this was the rune texts collected by the physician Zachris Topelius the Elder on his journeys to vaccinate the populace. From 1820 on, when Topelius lay paralyzed in his home in Central Ostrobothnia, he also recorded runes from wandering Karelian peddlers. He published his collection in five volumes entitled *Suomen kansan vanhoja runoja ynnä myös nykyisempiä lauluja* (Ancient runes and more recent songs of the Finnish people) (1822–31). In his preface to the second volume, Topelius clearly describes the state of rune singing as he had experienced it during the 1820s: "Today, those old rune songs have entirely disappeared from the shores of the Gulf of Bothnia. They are chanted only in the eastern extremes of Finland, and excellently only in a few parishes in northwest Russia–it is only there that the origins of the Finnish people are found in their purity and worth." In the introduction to his fifth volume, Topelius stated:

> One sole country nook, and even that is outside the Finnish border, or a few parishes in the White Sea District, particularly the parish of Vuokkiniemi, still preserve the old customs and tales of the ancient heroic folk with faithfulness and purity. There Väinämöinen's voice still chants, there the kantele and Sampo still play, and from there, also, I've gotten my best runes, albeit with much travail. Perhaps there would be hope of additional material from there; nevertheless I must end my work. If God grants age enough, these and other supplements can appear in the future.

Reinhold von Becker, who was Lönnrot's teacher and had a great influence on him, also encouraged folklore enthusiasts to go to White Sea Karelia. In *Turun Wiikko-Sanomat* (The Turku weekly news), von Becker set forth a plan for collecting folklore which directly indicated that the runes should be sought in distant Karelia and in Ostrobothnia:

> The only information which the Finnish people still have about Väinämöinen is found in ancient runes. In Savo, Karelia, and North Ostrobothnia, such runes are still honored in accordance with their worth. It is true that remarkable and wondrous things are often sung about in them. Many old Finnish customs and wisdoms are treated in them, and the Finnish language is so nicely adapted into song in harmony with its own nature that the beauty and richness of the language, as well as its clarity, are best discerned and experienced in these runes. The esteem in which they have been held, even by scholars abroad, is apparent in the fact that the German Doctor von Schröter translated numerous Finnish runes into German while he was in Sweden and published them last year. Thus it would be a shame if the Finns themselves did not know enough to honor these runes.[1]

Jacob Fellman, parson at Utsjoki Parish and a scholar of the Saami, had journeyed to the rune villages of White Sea Karelia before Lönnrot. In 1829, while he was primarily making observations about the Saami, he also wrote down the following description of the "rune territory," which he may in fact have edited somewhat after the *Kalevala* was published:

> Here in the highlands, particularly in Vuokki and Vuokkiniemi, there live on the lips of the people countless tales and runes about the heroic deeds, views, and beliefs of their forefathers. As the sky was beautiful and bright, I long observed the border region of Finland and Russia on the ridge of the highlands (from Maanselkä), that home of song, as my driver talked extensively about the heroic, bloody deeds of the inhabitants on both sides of the border in ancient times during ongoing border wars against each other. This classic land of the Finnish muse, beginning with Puolanka, forms an ever-verdant region of variously shaped hillocks, and between them are curving, peaceful lakes surrounded by beautiful deciduous trees. In nearing the border of the former empire, which is formed by the ridge of this upland, these hillocks are visible, surrounded by rivers and brooks bordered with small willow, spruce, bird cherry, and birch trees. On either side of the ridge, in the far distance, broad bodies of water are visible, joined into waterways, and on their shores solitary old villages, whose inhabitants, bewitched by the rapturous landscape, care little about the good of this world, and live in memories of how, in the echo of the kantele left here at the gates of Pohjola by their forefather, Väinämöinen, they glorified in song the deeds of their gods, heroes, and fathers, as well as the heroic feats of their brothers or, in this rune composition, they have given expression to their joy and sorrow.[2]

Lönnrot followed Topelius's and von Becker's guidelines precisely in seeking out and eventually collecting runes. In the preface to the *New Kalevala*, he in fact thanks them, stating that "without these two men the Kalevala runes might yet remain hidden as they were before." Lönnrot then presents his opinion of the area where the runes were found:

The best and richest home of runes is definitely Vuokkiniemi Parish in the White Sea or Archangel District. Proceeding eastward from here, to Lakes Jysky and Paana, or north to Lakes Tuoppa and Pääjärvi, the runes deteriorate. They are better preserved to the south, first in Repola and Himola in the Olonets districts and then crossing that border to Finland, at Ilomantsi, Suojärvi, Suistamo, Impilahti, Sortavala, and along the western shores of Lake Ladoga to Ingria where, even recently, some Kalevala runes are yet remembered, albeit imperfectly.[3]

Because the area where runes were to be found had been delineated by so influential a source as Lönnrot, later collectors were prevented from seeking them outside the boundaries he defined. As a consequence, numerous rune singers living in other areas were to remain entirely undiscovered.

THE CONTRIBUTIONS OF ONTREI MALINEN AND VAASSILA KIELEVÄINEN

On April 29, 1828, Lönnrot departed on his first folklore-collecting journey, which was to last four months. A detailed diary exists of this journey, *Vaeltaja eli muistelmia jalkamatkalta Hämeestä, Savosta ja Karjalasta* (The wanderer, or memories of a journey on foot to Häme, Savo, and Karelia). Lönnrot traveled from Häme to Karelia through Savo. This journey yielded almost three hundred rune or charm texts. Of these, nearly a third were chanted by Juhana Kainulainen, a North Karelian churchkeeper from Huumovaara in Kesälahti. Meeting Kainulainen was the high point of Lönnrot's journey, and he describes it in a lively manner in his travel diary. Among the materials he recorded from Kainulainen were variants of the "Courtship" and "Lemminkäinen" runes which proved significant for later versions of the *Kalevala*. The majority of the runes sung by Kainulainen were incantations, including charms sung in connection with hunting.[4]

On his first journey, Lönnrot also planned to go to White Sea Karelia, but his funds did not suffice. This plan was again not realized on his second journey (1831), made while he was on vacation from his medical studies and which was supported financially by the newly established Finnish Literature Society. However, Lönnrot did go to White Sea Karelia on his third journey, although he was not able to spend more than five days there.[5] Lönnrot's fourth rune-collecting journey (1833) is considered the decisive one for his discovery of the *Kalevala* concept. After numerous attempts, he finally succeeded in going to White Sea Karelia, where he planned to meet with Arhippa Perttunen, the well-known rune singer from Latvajärvi. Because Arhippa was not at home, Lönnrot went to the neighboring village of Vuonninen, where he met Ontrei Malinen and Vaassila Kieleväinen. His travel diary gives the following description of this famous meeting:

At Tsenaniemi I was advised to make a digression to Miina's house in Vuonninen, which was some distance upward from the shore, the furthermost house on the left. This house was said to be the best constructed and wealthier than the rest. It is true that the sons of the house were said to be a bit wild or intent (or whatever the word "jyry" [forceful, robust] actually means?), but otherwise they appeared to be honorable men. The most able singer, Ontrei, was said to dwell a brief distance from there, as did the other great singer, Vaassila. Thus I went to Miina's house, where I met both fellows just mentioned. . . . The next day, in the morning, I had Ontrei chant. I would greatly have liked him to remain with me in the afternoon as well; but he was indispensable to drawing the seine, so he could not stay. I wished him a good catch and made an agreement with him beforehand that, if they caught the allotted amount of fish, he would promise to sing all the next day; and he agreed to this. The catch was not as abundant as I had hoped; nevertheless, the next day it was possible to write down numerous runes as dictated by him. But in the evening, since Ontrei had gone to draw the seine, I went to Vaassila's, who lived on the other side of the narrow sound. This Vaassila, who was primarily familiar with charms, was an old fellow. At any rate, his memory had become so enfeebled during recent years that he no longer knew what he had known before. Nevertheless, he did relate a number of things about Väinämöinen and numerous other mythological beings which I hadn't known previously. And when it happened that he had forgotten something which I already knew, I asked him about it more precisely. Then he remembered it again and, in this manner, I came to know all of Väinämöinen's heroic deeds in a single sequence, and in accordance with this, then, I have ordered those runes about Väinämöinen which are known.[6]

Because of his fishing duties, Ontrei Malinen did not have time to sing his entire repertoire of runes to Lönnrot. This makes the discovery of the 366-verse Sampo cycle, sung as one poetic unity, all the more remarkable. Under more opportune circumstances for collecting, Malinen could have provided even more runes. Later collectors did in fact collect an abundance of them from him and even more from his relatives. Among these singers were Ontrei's son Jyrki and Anni Lehtonen, the well-known rune singer and lamenter discovered by Samuli Paulaharju.[7]

Because Malinen had left to take care of his obligations, Lönnrot went to speak with another old man named Vaassila Kieleväinen. According to Lönnrot, Vaassila had forgotten a good number of his runes. Nevertheless, it was in talking with him that the idea of uniting the fragments into a whole occurred to Lönnrot and eventually resulted in a 157-verse poetic sequence. Lönnrot inspired Vaassila to recall the Väinämöinen runes as a single sequence, which, however, differed from that sung by Ontrei Malinen.[8] The collector's intuition bridged what the rune singer did not recall, and the runes were ordered in a sequence approved of by both the collector and the singer.

In his synthesis, Vaassila unified the following runes: "The Maiden of Vellamo," "Forging the Golden Maiden," "The Creation of the Universe," "The

Forging of the Sampo," "The Theft of the Sampo," and "The Courtship Contest." It is clear that, out of Malinen's songs and Vaassila's synthesis, Lönnrot
created "Runokokous Väinämöisestä" (A collection of poetry about Väinämöinen), also known as the *Proto-Kalevala*, and eventually the sequence of the
Old Kalevala as well. Vaassila Kieleväinen's significance to Lönnrot is also veri-
fied by that which Lönnrot related to Runeberg soon after returning from his
journey. Runeberg in turn related Lönnrot's tidings to J. Grott: "You see, he
met an old man who had, in part, preserved in his memory the order and plot
of a narrative tale about Väinämöinen, although he no longer remembered the
runes word by word."[9] In examining Vaassila's verses more closely, Lönnrot also
decided to augment them with other poetic units.

MYTHICIZING THE RUNE SINGERS

Urged by Zachris Topelius the Elder and others, Lönnrot went in search of
White Sea Karelian men and women who remembered runes. From the material he collected, he created the *Kalevala*. Once the *Kalevala* had been completed, the White Sea Karelian singers who preserved the epic songs became
mythologized. This process of mythicizing, with its own characteristics, can be
examined through the notes and diaries of folklore collectors.[10]
    The *Kalevala* canonized the concept of a golden age of Finnish rune singing.
It was believed that this golden age had existed a generation or two before
Lönnrot's journeys to collect folklore. His field notes lent support to the idea
that singers had always derived their runes from master teachers much more
proficient than they.[11] This is partly true. In passing from one generation to
another, runes generally do deteriorate. On the other hand, the Romantic idea
of a golden age of ancient runes, now irrevocably past, is clearly attributable
to the *Kalevala* process. It was believed that the ancient epic had once been
alive, then decayed, and now existed only here and there, preserved by the
best singers.
    Such epical works as the *Niebelungenlied*, the *Songs of Ossian*, and Homer's
works, in particular, provided an international model for this mythologizing
process. An important stage in the birth of any epic is the phase during which
orally preserved tradition becomes literature. When runes, songs, and tales become a national epic, they also take on new life. At its creation, an epic is often
interpreted as the sacred history of a people. It is the source of their identity
and strength and serves to transform both the creation of new myths and the
passage of history. This has also been true of the *Kalevala*.
    The rune singers themselves were mythologized in the same manner. Based
on the model of Homer, the prototypes of Ontrei Malinen, Arhippa Perttunen,
Vaassila Kieleväinen, and others came alive. The rune singers were described;
their likenesses painted, cast in bronze, and poured from gypsum. Karelian
enthusiasts went to the White Sea Karelian wilderness in search of them. When

The most noteworthy of the rune singers encountered by Lönnrot was Arhippa Perttunen of Latvajärvi. His rune tradition has survived to this day among members of the Perttunen family in White Sea Karelia. No photograph exists of Arhippa. Before the 150th-year anniversary of the publication of the *Kalevala*, his grave was exhumed and Soviet experts constructed a bust resembling him, which is exhibited in the Petrozavodsk Museum. (Finnish Literature Society)

At the turn of the century, Arhippa's son, Miihkali Perttunen, was venerated as a blind rune singer and a mythical hero. Karelian enthusiasts sought him out for the experience of encountering a Homeric hero of the Kalevala tradition. (Finnish Literature Society)

the song festival tradition was established at the end of the nineteenth century, rune singers began to travel from festival to festival, earning money by singing old traditional material. It was the renowned woman singer Larin Paraske, in particular, who awakened in the public the image of the poor rune singer who sang and created runes to earn her living.[12]

Initially, not much attention was paid to the individual personalities of the rune singers. They remained nameless: "an old rower, "Hotto," "a White Sea Karelian woman." Often it was the women's names, in particular, which remained unrecorded. Accounts were given only of the singers who remembered the most material. The prototype of the rune singer became an old man from White Sea Karelia who knew how to sing the longest versions of the runes. The Perttunen family is one example of this mythologizing process. Arhippa Perttunen of Latvajärvi became the most renowned of the White Sea Karelian rune singers discovered by Lönnrot. In April 1834, Lönnrot spent two days with him and wrote down forty-two runes, which included over four thousand verses. In his diary, he wrote enthusiastically:

> At Latvajärvi, in Vuokkiniemi, Arhippa, the old fellow of the house, now in his eighties, spoke, and from him I gathered as much as I could, wrote for two days straight about such times as the following: "Oh," he said, "when I went with my dad to the seine at Lapukka, we had as a day laborer a certain man from Lapukka, also a fine singer but not equal to my dad. All through the nights they sang without stopping, and without repeating a thing. They used to chat then. And I, just a little fellow, sat beside them at the seine, listening to and learning what I even began to remember as well. But a great deal is lost from my memory. If my dad were alive now, you wouldn't write down his songs in two weeks. Singers like that are no longer born in the land, and all those old songs, they're disappearing among the folk. Today's folk cast away those beautiful old runes and fashion their own, mostly about pranks between boys and girls, which I would be ashamed to have come from my mouth."[13]

Without a doubt, the discovery of Arhippa Perttunen was crucial to the creation of the *Kalevala*. Despite Arhippa's pessimistic prediction, his son Arhippaini Miihkali became a well-known rune singer. Miihkali's home was visited by many sojourners to Karelia, and as a blind old man, he received a pension from the Finnish Literature Society.[14] Miihkali's son, Pekko Perttunen, was also esteemed by his community as a well-known sage and an expert in charms. It has thus been possible to record the rune tradition of the Perttunen family from numerous descendants, both those who continued to live in White Sea Karelia and those who immigrated to Finland.

As late as 1962, I still had the opportunity to meet one of them, Mikko Perttunen (b. 1882). His grandfather's brother had been Arhippaini Miihkali. Mikko recalled, as a ten-year-old boy, having come on old Miihkali fishing: "Miihkali Perttunen was a keen fisherman. That summer he always drew the net, fished alone. He left the seine on a cord at the opposite shore. A boy circled around in a boat and then they pulled the seine out, Miihkali and the boys of the family. When he was younger, he was a hard worker, though he was blind."

Lönnrot's visit to Arhippa has been incorporated into the mythical history of the Perttunen family. This tradition has been passed down through the family, and it has been altered by succeeding generations. As Mikko recounted it, "Once, even that professor, Elias Lönnrot, was here for two days. Arhippa said that he sang two thousand songs without having anything written down, all from memory. He had a good memory. He could even just make up a rune."

From approximately 1910 on, Mikko Perttunen lived in Finland, first as a pack peddler, then as a wandering merchant, and finally as a village shopkeeper following the White Sea Karelian way of life. He gladly recalled the White Sea Karelian times and customs, weddings, healers, and hunters. Mikko's runes were few in comparison with those of Arhippa and Miihkali. Nevertheless, during the 1960s he was still able to transmit lullabies and nursery rhymes sung by the Perttunen clan.

It is typical of this mythologizing process that there was much more interest in finding good prototypes of singers than in the material they actually sang. For example, Miihkali Perttunen, whose songs were considerably fewer in number than those of his father, Arhippa Perttunen, became a mythical figure during his own lifetime. For Finnish enthusiasts the figure of this poor, blind rune singer has become the embodiment of a true preserver of the Homeric tradition.[15] Prototypical rune singers such as Iivana Onoila and Petri Shemeikka came alive in the same fashion, modeled on heroic figures, as they traveled from festival to festival. The mythical rune singer was typically a gray-bearded, masculine figure, a kantele maker and player like Väinämöinen. The fact that each generation thought it had found the "last rune singers" has played a significant part in this mythologizing process. As a result, collection work has had the aura of preserving the last, disappearing elements of a tradition.

Before *Kalevala* romanticism, no halo was accorded to the rune singers. They were considered ordinary people of flesh and blood, although certain people in the community were considered more knowledgeable about old runes than others. In the 1980s, however, over 150 years after publication of the *Kalevala*, it appears that this is indeed the final generation of singers to have learned the runes orally. The remainder of this chapter will focus on three of these singers: Marina Takalo (b. 1890) and Mari Remsu (b. 1893) of White Sea Karelia and the Estonian-IngrianValpuri Vohta (b. 1887), each of whom I worked with during the 1960s.[16]

HOW DOES ONE BECOME A RUNE SINGER?

With regard to the definition of rune singer, one may ask: Who actually is a rune singer? How does one become a rune singer? Customarily, individuals who were the source of epical runes in the trochaic Kalevala meter were called rune singers. Neither the quality nor quantity of the runes sung was the determining factor. The criterion was simply whether they had sung or recited rune material to a collector. From this it can be inferred that a rune singer is the product of field work.

For example, Juhana Kainulainen would never have become conscious of being a rune singer if he had not been discovered and urged to sing by Elias Lönnrot. Many a rune singer has been created merely as the result of a collaborative effort with a collector. It is true that the singers were people with good memories. Nevertheless, they usually became defined as rune singers only after having been discovered by a collector. In Finland, White Sea Karelia, Olonets, and Ingria, rune singing as an institution was not a primary or a secondary occupation. Only some female singers and lamenters at weddings and funerals were exceptions. They were paid either in money, food, or clothing for their songs, which were sung in a ritual context. However, this was never their daily work. Runes were sung along with other work or on request, often with remuneration from the collectors.

The most noteworthy achievements with regard to quantity of runes have been attributed to those singers with whom a particular scholar or nonprofessional collector has been able to develop a long-term, reciprocal relationship. Among the best examples of such collaborative work are the runes collected by Pastor A. Neovius and other collectors from Larin Paraske. Another example is Samuli Paulaharju's extensive collection of Anni Lehtonen's runes, laments, and charms.[17] Marina Takalo's traditional material was collected in much the same manner as a result of my work with her during the 1960s. It showed that a deep reciprocal relationship between a scholar and singer is possible only with the trust which comes after a number of years of friendship.[18] Collecting most of the runes in the thirty-three-volume *Suomen Kansan Vanhat Runot* (Ancient poems of the Finnish people) was, however, not based on such long-term reciprocal relationships. In most cases, these volumes contain only those fragments of the singers' repertoires which they sang to the collectors. Only the runes best remembered by the singers at a particular moment would ordinarily have been related to a collector, who was a stranger to them. It can be assumed that the singers' deepest feelings and experiences were not revealed under such circumstances and, as a consequence, their full repertoires were not recorded.

The fact that so many runes have been collected during brief encounters between singers and collectors indicates that this oral tradition was valued by the people themselves. Another reason is that epic runes were not subject to the same taboos, personal fears, or strong emotions as, for example, subjective lyric poetry, personal laments, or narratives about religious experiences might have been. Most runes could be sung to any interested stranger in search of them.

On his expeditions, Lönnrot carried an edition of the *Kalevala* with him.[19] He and his companions used it to formulate questions for the singers. Thus, although a rune might not have been complete when it was written down by the first collector, it might have been possible for another Karelian enthusiast

Marina Takalo on the shores of the Oulanka River. Taimi Pitkanen, who took the photograph, related that on a trip to the Kiuta rapids made by the senior citizens of Kuusamo, Marina sat on the embankment overlooking the Kiuta Waterfall. The bus was leaving when it was noticed that she was missing from the group. Someone went back to get her. She was sitting on a rock dampened by the spray of the waterfall–the Oulanka River flowed to Oulanka, where she had originally come from, and where she always felt her true home to be.

to return a few years later and obtain the sought-after rune in its entirety. Often, the singer had retrieved this material from memory during the intervening period. When a rune was transferred in this manner, seemingly "complete" from the singer to the collector's notebook, the misleading notion developed that it had always existed as such in the singer's memory. This misconception hampered text-oriented scholarship for a long time.

In field work with rune singers lasting over long periods of time, it has been observed that runes are often retrieved from the deepest layer of memory and were impressed on the singer's mind early in childhood. Often they were passed from one person to another across several generations. The traditional Karelian dwelling provided an excellent setting for the preservation of clan and family culture. In the architecture of the Karelian home, the common room and chambers, as well as the accommodations for the herd, were joined. These were shared by members of the extended family, as well as servants, and included members of all generations then alive. Thus representatives of several generations lived beneath the same roof. It was characteristic of the division of labor within the extended family that the transmission of culture was carried out by members of the oldest generation living in the house. The elders taught and reared the children. It was they who cared for the young, rocked them to sleep, amused them with tales. They worked about the house doing handiwork, needlework, and carpentry and mending nets. As these tasks were carried out, oral traditions were also being transmitted across several generations. Thus, for example, Marina Takalo learned her runes from her father's aunt, Olonja Nikitin, who later drowned on a fishing expedition in 1898 when Marina was less than eight years old. Marina gave the following description:

> I don't know where Olonja Nikitin had gotten those songs. I never thought of asking. Probably she heard them from the old folks. She wove and patched nets and seines, made and mended them during winters, that's the only handiwork she did. She was an outdoor worker, even a reindeer herder, but no good at women's handiwork. Summers, she was off at Lake Kouta fishing. I listened, we played on the floor and listened. Oddly, they've stayed in my head. Never thought then that they'd be needed. But then I began living here, passing time with the children sometimes, rowing the children, and I sang them. Now they come as from my fingertip, those songs. While I was growing up, my late aunt was a fine support for the family. As she sang, I learned, and now I sing to the children. In May [1959], my grandson was three years old. As I sing, he sings the song word for word. When my mouth moves, his is already moving. Then he says: "You sing me those, Grandma." The other older children aren't even interested.[20]

Children are known for their ability to learn oral tradition very quickly and for having good memories. As a result of our patient work together, the "Olonja songs," learned in early childhood, reemerged from Marina Takalo's memory when she was seventy or eighty years old. This was despite the fact that almost no one else in Oulanka or during Marina's immigrant period in Finland knew these songs, and presentations of them were therefore rare. During our working sessions together, I suggested folklore topics, and Marina called the material to mind. Sometimes it took several years before a rune became complete and met with her approval. Then she would remember it with astonishing accuracy, compared with earlier variants of the rune as sung by others in the same area. This accurate recall took place despite the fact that Marina had definitely not heard those songs anywhere during the interim, or otherwise had access to them. Because she could neither read or write, she had refined her capacity for oral learning and memory. Psychological studies of memory also seem to support the old adage: "What one learns in youth, one knows in old age."

Marina Takalo was tradition-oriented. She was familiar with all the cultural genres in White Sea Karelia. Her repertoire of runes was also quite extensive. The epic runes she had learned from her father's aunt, Olonja Nikitin, formed a special category in her repertoire. She considered ritual poetry, such as charms and wedding runes also known by other women, to be distinctly separate from these narrative songs. "They've been learned from generation to generation, those wedding verses and betrothal songs, all of them. The one who created them, he really was a songsmith. We who now hear them have no problem singing those created before, but the one who forged them, now there was a smith." With regard to lullabies, Marina stated: "Yes, you can even make them up yourself, if you get the knack of it."

It was during the latter part of her life that Marina became an active rune singer. Although she had assuredly learned her runes when very young, they had remained passive knowledge until her later years. Other evacuees from Kuusamo recalled having heard Marina relate fairy tales on the evacuation journey in 1944. Runes were not yet mentioned in this connection. Marina first appeared in public as a rune singer at the Kuusamo "Kalevala Festival" in 1956.

In her old age, Marina became both a rune singer and a conscious poet who wished to cross the threshold of literacy by means of poems. Through the poems she herself created, she felt that she had attained the level of those poets who wrote down their work. In addition to runes in the Kalevala meter, Marina was familiar with numerous more recent folk songs, including the ballad "Kävelin lahden rantoa" (I walked the shore of the bay). She kept this rune strictly separate from the Kalevala runes sung by the older people. In singing the rune for the first time in 1960, she affirmed: "These runes were sung when I was a girl. This one was usually sung by the young, not the old. It was considered a sinful poem." In 1962 she added four new verses to the song. In response to Professor Pertti Virtaranta's question "Where did you hear this?" Marina gave the following reply:

Well, I don't know myself, I must have heard it as a girl at home. My brother, the late Hilippä, probably sang it. I hadn't sung it for ten, maybe twenty years, then it came to mind when I sang for Juha Pentikäinen. Isn't it a beautiful song? Many are amazed when I sing it, that it's so beautiful. And others remark, too, by what miracle does she unearth them? They just come to mind. If you get hold of the beginning, then it continues.

In singing the epical rune "Lunastettavan neito" (The maiden to be ransomed), she stated: "If I remember the beginning, it goes on as if pulled by a cord."

Mari Remsu (b. 1893), from the village of Tollonjoki in Vuokkiniemi, was three years younger than Marina Takalo. Mari's life story is similar to Marina's in numerous respects. Like Marina, she fled from White Sea Karelia to Finland in 1920 and lived in Kemi from 1924 to 1948. There the two singers knew each other, if not as experts in White Sea culture then at least as immigrants who shared the fate of Karelian refugees. During the 1940s, Mari lived in Martinniemi under the same roof as Marina. A thin cardboard wall separated them. In reference to socializing with Marina, Mari said: "We seldom visited each other, although there was only a wall between us. I was in her home a

The rune singer Mari Remsu of Vuokkiniemi in White Sea Karelia, who spent the latter part of her life in Sweden. (Johannes Runeberg)

few times. We'd meet by chance in the washing room. We weren't very good friends." In response to my question, "Did you hear that Marina remembered and sang those Karelian runes?" she answered: "There was no singing then at all." Did she tell fairy tales? "We weren't together enough for her to have told anything. There was little storytelling; there wasn't such a custom." Marina's remarks about Mari were similar. For both of them during this time, Karelian folklore still remained latent.

In 1948, at the age of fifty-five, Mari Remsu emigrated to Sweden. It was there that Professor Pertti Virtaranta discovered her. He considered her, along with Domna Huovinen, to be one of the best lamenters from White Sea Karelia. I met Mari for the first time in western Sweden in 1966 and continued my field work with her on her visits to Finland. Like Marina Takalo, Mari was an extremely versatile singer, a lamenter, and a narrator of fairy tales and stories, and she was particularly knowledgeable about religious tradition.

Mari had learned laments from her mother, Varvana, born in Vuokkiniemi circa 1864. Varvana did not sing old runes, however. Mari learned her runes as a child from her father's mother, Muarie. As with Marina Takalo, this learning had taken place across a generation. Muarie had sung while weaving and setting nets. "Grandmother sang to us. I took the most from her. When she did handiwork, set nets and seines, she was always singing. When she'd take a net-mending needle in her hand, she'd say: 'The needle said to sing, the eyes of the net to play.' With that she began to sing, and some of them even stayed in my head."

Mari's grandmother was ninety-five years old when she died. At that time, Mari, who was still young, had lived in the same large common room with her for a long time. Mari attributed narrative runes, such as the song about felling the great oak, to her grandmother. While living in White Sea Karelia, Mari had joined a chorus of wedding singers. She was able to give detailed accounts of White Sea Karelian wedding practices and sang runes related to them. She was particularly adept at laments, which were an obligatory part of wedding rituals.

How did Mari Remsu come to remember the old folk tradition? "When I was old, I left work, was quite idle, so that I no longer had anything to do. When Virtaranta came [1951], I still didn't remember. They were all forgotten, but then I kept thinking about them, and some came to mind." In the cases of both Marina Takalo and Mari Remsu, the influence of a sympathetic and encouraging outsider was needed to inspire recollection. During this process of recollection, both of these women became conscious rune singers.

Valpuri Vohta (b. 1887) was born in Kallivieri, in Estonian Ingria. She was a Lutheran, whereas both Takalo and Remsu were Russian Orthodox. However, there were both Orthodox and Lutherans living in her native village in Ingria. Among the genres Vohta learned from Russian Orthodox women were laments. Dr. Elsa Enäjärvi-Haavio was the first to interview Valpuri Vohta in 1936. Two years later, Lauri Laiho (later Simonsuuri) met her, and in 1940 Aili Laiho (Simonsuuri) also met her. Since the Second World War, Vohta has lived in Sweden, where Lauri Honko and Kari Laukkanen also interviewed her. I met her for the first time in 1965, in Fagersta, Sweden.

Vohta was a systematic, thorough narrator who in 1966 could still well remember what she had sung or related to Haavio or the Simonsuuri couple thirty years earlier. Of particular significance was her detailed description of wedding practices.

As a rune singer, Vohta specialized in ritual poetry. She could sing the wedding runes and laments of the Orthodox people in spite of the fact that she herself was Lutheran. She was also inspired to create her own poems during the 1920s and '30s. The poems were created under circumstances political in nature and related to the brief period of Estonian independence between World Wars I and II. Vohta participated as a leader in the Estonian Women's Society, the activities of which included organizing festivals for visitors from Finland. "I made up the poems then, depending on where the guests were from." With regard to creating the poems, Vohta stated: "You know, I'm the kind of person who wants to sing. When I couldn't sleep at night, I made up

The Ingrian rune singer Valpuri Vohta, from the village of Kallivieri in Estonian Ingria, met with Finnish folklorists during the period of Estonian independence in the 1920s and '30s. She spent the latter part of her life in Sweden as a refugee from Estonia. (Finnish Language Archives, Helsinki University; photograph by Helmi Virtaranta)

poems. They're about things that happened at that time. My own life brought the verses. The verses were like the life which had been lived." In response to my question "When did you learn your first songs?" Vohta responded: "At my sister's wedding; there were two years between us when she got married. I sang my first song at her wedding: Like a little chick I grew, I rose a young maid, beside five brothers, a flower among six bells. Made them up out of my own head. This is from my inner being." Vohta said she had still sung the rune "Helise heliä metsä" (Chime bright forest) on her son's birthday in Sweden during the 1960s.

In addition to ritual runes, Vohta enjoyed singing lyrics of sentiment: "Early died my mother, early my honorable elder, left me like a skylark on a stone, a gull on a heath. The hare left three, my mother one. The hare left them to run, my mother, me, to weep." Her usual concluding line was: "That was long, that serf girl's hymn, and here it ends." The singing was done while sitting beside the canal in summer. The girls sang to themselves, sat and sang: "Sweet sisters, girls, sweet apples. What work worries the girls, what makes the birds mourn?"

Valpuri Vohta consciously preserved oral tradition throughout her life. Hers was the role of singer and lamenter at Ingrian weddings. She also grew up in a community where tradition was valued, and became an active tradition bearer during her youth in the 1920s. She continued to preserve Ingrian culture as an exile in Sweden until her death. For Vohta, the role of rune singer was an activity specifically related to rituals and festivities. She was glad to perform runes when they were needed, in order to celebrate rituals related to childhood and youth, such as weddings. She later performed them at cultural and political gatherings and finally, as an ethnic tradition, in Sweden, at the festivities of Ingrian, Estonian, and Finnish immigrants, as well as those of her own family.

THE SIGNIFICANCE OF THE RUNES FOR THE SINGERS

> And look, we created the songs:
> they're part of us
> they're the children of sorrow and joy
> and of the night and sun.
> They hasten the March wind's way
> to the drinking bout of the gods
> We, the poor, adorned them
> to resound in gold.
> P. Mustapää, *Unohdetut runoilijat*
> (The forgotten poets)[21]

In studying the runes, it is important to remember that the worlds of those who created them and those who sing them are not necessarily the same. The singers' unique life experiences become manifest in how they sing and interpret their repertoires. The world of the unknown, typically anonymous poet who created the rune remains a question, whereas the world of the singer can be approached by interviews.

There is often a close reciprocal relationship between the scholar or collector of folk tradition and the rune singer. Each singer is a unique individual, and no two have exactly the same repertoire. Nevertheless, the three rune singers mentioned above have a great deal in common. Marina Takalo, Mari Remsu, and Valpuri Vohta were all refugees who had fled to Finland or Sweden from their original communities. Of them, Vohta had already consciously been a tradition bearer in Ingrian Estonia, her native region. She actively participated in Estonian cultural work and also fostered contact with Finnish women's groups. The White Sea Karelian singers, Mari Remsu and Marina Takalo, became active in their roles as conscious bearers of tradition only during the 1950s, when they had reached the age of sixty. These singers were all strong women who made the decisions in their families. For them, tradition was a channel into which they poured their tribulations and which also gave them esteem in the eyes of the community. Marina Takalo once said: "I'm no longer trampled like a doormat." Mari Remsu did not like to be asked the origins of her runes, for she felt the poems to be her own. Each of these singers was also a creator of tradition and aware of her own abilities. They were self-assured, stern women with broad life experiences who were guided by their heritage. They had not, however, defined themselves as rune singers before others began to refer to them as such.

In each case, during the singer's youth, a person two or three generations older had lived with her under the same roof. From this person she had learned the custom of singing runes while tending to everyday tasks. This person had also served as a role model for other aspects of her life. The runes learned early in childhood remained in the deepest layer of memory and were recalled only in the latter stages of these women's lives. Collaborative work with a folklore collector was decisive during that phase when they began to grow conscious of the value of the tradition they remembered.

Thus, the men and women of White Sea Karelia, Olonets, and Ingria identified themselves as rune singers only when collectors made them aware of this. They were ordinary people, whose time was primarily taken up with daily tasks. Lönnrot, for example, experienced difficulty in trying to draw the rune experts away from their everyday tasks. This was also the case in 1828 with Juhana Kainulainen, Lönnrot's primary singer. Ontrei Malinen hastened back to his nets when he extricated himself from Lönnrot. Later collectors of tradition have had the same experience, although tape recorders have proved useful in saving both the singers' and the collectors' time.

Early rune collection focused primarily on texts. Only later did interest in the meanings and functions of the runes develop. Such information was often given quite spontaneously. Thus, for example, Jyrkini Iivana, who belonged to the Malinen clan, said to Kaarle Krohn in Vuonninen: "During spring and fall sowing, first sowing words were sung, then the song about the forging of the Sampo and its theft, and the pursuit of the Mistress of Pohjola. The conclusion describes how Väinämöinen cast out the Mistress of Pohjola by sending her into the cold."[22] Such information is a veritable lodestone for folklore scholars. Presumably, eighteenth- and nineteenth-century rune singers knew more about the significance of traditions and the circumstances of performance than is found in the materials which were collected. At that time, the collectors did not question the focus or significance of the runes; nor was there scholarly emphasis on this at the time.

Lönnrot did not leave extensive source notes in the records he kept about the singers he interviewed. However, his diaries, which included travel observations and descriptions of the occurrence and demise of folk song, are much more fruitful. In his periodical *The Bee*, Lönnrot presented the rune "Anni, the Water Bearer." In a footnote to it he gave his view of the differences between runes, making an important distinction between men's and women's songs. "Anni, the Water Bearer" is included among the latter. Distinct from these are the Karelian songs, the so-called runes or "songs about ancient heroes and their deeds, which the (old) womenfolk don't remember at all."[23]

Runes of origins and other "loihtoluvut" (charm runes) are common to the traditions of both men and women. However, there are also different categories among these, as Lönnrot affirms: "Herding charms, milking and cowshed charms, and tales are the old women's, while the men's are forest, seine, and soldier's charms and ones about rowing into rapids. Charms against disease are also common to both." In the same article, Lönnrot compares runes from Karelia, Tavastia, and Estonia and gives his view of how the runes migrated.[24]

Incomplete contextual information does not necessarily signify a lack of imagination on the collector's part or an ignorance about the significance and function of the runes on the part of the singer. It may well have been the current state of the rune-singing tradition as it existed at that time. In their final stage, runes were preserved individually for their own worth, without ritual context. In 1962, for example, Mikko Perttunen, a descendant of the Perttunen clan, sang Lemminkäinen runes and lullabies about the slaying of the great ox without knowing their ritual basis. Marina Takalo sang "The Creation of the World" without knowledge of the cosmic association posited for this rune. Mari Remsu altered the context of "The Creator's Hymn" from Christmas to Easter.

In my interviews with rune singers such as Valpuri Vohta, Mari Remsu, and Marina Takalo during the 1960s and '70s, it was repeatedly observed that runes often lived on even though their previous meanings had been forgotten. Through systematic work with the generation of rune singers still alive at that time, it was possible to study the meaning of the runes in relationship to the singers' other knowledge of tradition. Likewise, it was possible to observe how the singers themselves differentiated between runes and other traditional genres. Vohta, Remsu, and Takalo were multifaceted experts in the folklore of their communities. They were able to name and identify numerous genres of tradition, even noting shades of difference between them, such as the fact that a subjective lament, "luajittelu," was a specific kind of lament, a deep channel of expression for a person's own life, experiences, and feelings. Ancient runic poetry did not serve this function. It remained the same in content, even when its function had changed. The rune singers did, however, have a tendency to explain the runes in terms of their own lives. Thus, for example, the historical "Song about the Stolen Maiden" had personal significance for Marina Takalo. It reminded her of her daughter, whom she had left in White Sea Karelia during the 1922 Karelian uprising. Marina had experienced a great deal of guilt over this until, forty-three years later, in 1965, she learned that her daughter was still alive.

In the past, runes served a variety of functions as compared to their more recent role. These included their inherent worth as a tradition to be transmitted from one generation to the next. The origins of the Finnish word "runo" (rune, poem) refer to a sage, and "laulaminen" (singing, chanting) signifies a special technique which played a role in shamanistic sessions. Numerous ancient runes appear to have played such a role. During the nineteenth century, many singers still recalled the ritual context of the runes. During later phases of tradition, however, runes came to be valued for their own sake, that of preserving the rare, disappearing genre in question.

Rune singing was also significant for cultural identity and was a way of transmitting feelings for a tradition within an alien culture. All her life, Valpuri Vohta was a conscious bearer of cultural traditions which reminded her, as well as other Estonian and Ingrian emigrants, about the golden period of Estonian independence between World Wars I and II. The emigrants from White Sea Karelia, Mari Remsu and Marina Takalo, initially preserved the tradition without being aware of its cultural significance. Unbeknownst to each other, they became active rune singers during the 1950s. For both women, rune singing meant the fostering of Karelian culture in their new homelands.

In some respects, Marina Takalo can be characterized as a marginal individual, having suffered from the oppression caused by her numerous minority identities and the feelings of neglect caused by being a stranger. In 1962 she stated the primary goal of her collaboration with me to be the creation of a book about Karelian culture: "I'll tell you everything I remember of Karelia. You write down for others what a stranger's life here has been like." Marina didn't find a permanent home in Finland. She moved thirty-four times during her lifetime and lived in very difficult circumstances. The first time she lived under her own roof was in 1956, at the age of sixty-six. Throughout her life, she held an alien passport, the use of which caused considerable difficulties for one who could neither read nor write. In other ways, as well, Marina belonged to a minority. She was Orthodox in religion, but belonged to the persecuted Old Believers (Staroviero), although she became estranged from them later in life. Marina was a homeless wanderer who intended to return to Karelia all her life. She said of her songs, as she did of her icons: "They're old Karelian tradition."

Runes were presented in many different ways, of course, in order to express the state of mind of the singer, to preserve the sacred prehistory of a nation, tribe, or clan, or as the religious content of healing dramas, bear slayings, or festivities related to the life cycle and seasonal rotation. As such ritual contexts slowly waned, the runes continued to live for several generations, divorced from these contexts. Their significance, derived from a past idyllic period experienced religiously, then became decisive. With the waning of rune singing and the increase in literacy, the preservation of runes probably fell to just a few individuals. It is indeed possible that during this time the runes were linked to form more unified, epic wholes. It is quite likely that this stage in epic poetry occurred late and near White Sea Karelia, where the epic was first sought, and that the runes which were found there became the core of the epic Elias Lönnrot created.

THE RIGHTS AND OBLIGATIONS OF A RUNE SINGER

What were the rights and obligations of the rune singer with regard to the transmission of runes? This question concerns the influence an individual may have on the formation and transmission of culture. The issue is recent because, even in this century, the views of many folklorists were governed by nineteenth-century Romantic concepts of a folk who collectively created their traditions. Romantic thinking claims the runes existed as isolated entities and that the task of the rune collector such as Lönnrot was merely to copy and compile the epic from the people.

The Finnish historical-geographic school created an image of rune singers as mere mediators and disseminators of culture, from whom collectors gathered ready-made folklore. This theory was significantly altered by Martti Haavio in his article "Kansanrunouden sepittäjät ja esittäjät" (The creators and performers of folklore) (1949). There Haavio presented Mateli Kuivalatar, a woman from Ilomantsi who had been a source of runes for Lönnrot, as a poet with her own individual repertoire. Haavio argued that each rune had been created by a "poeta anonymus" and wrote: "A creative, individualistic rune is something entirely different from the chance adaptation of an already existing rune suited to the needs of a particular social group. Rune singers complied with the laws of epic approved by their social group."[25]

In stressing the significance of the principles governing folk singing, Haavio concurs with the "epical laws" of folk traditions presented by the Dane Axel Olrik in 1908. In Olrik's opinion, all narrative tradition conforms to rules which transcend time and are independent of culture. He argued that national distinctions were merely differences in dialects. He stated: "We call those principles laws because they place restrictions on the creation of oral tradition which are different from and more stringent than those of other literature."[26] A similar question has also been asked in reference to folk tales. However, the American folklorist Alan Dundes criticizes how, in searching for laws, scholars often overlook the people who are actually the tradition bearers. He asks: "Are they themselves aware of the structural models on which their tales are based?"[27]

Claude Lévi-Strauss argues that narrators are not aware of the formulaic aspect of tradition.

> Although the possibility cannot be discounted that the speakers who create and transmit myths may become aware of their structure and mode of operation, this cannot occur as a normal thing, but only partially and intermittently. In the particular example we are dealing with here—their affinity for mythological narratives—it is doubtful, to say in the least, that the natives of Central Brazil, over and above the fact that they are fascinated by mythological stories, understand the systems of interactions to which we reduce them.[28]

The Soviet scholar Vladimir Propp also argues that narrators do not perceive the structural principles which govern their creations.[29] However, Dundes states: "Storytellers in some sense do 'know' the structural patterns which underlie their narratives." Albert Lord, who studied Balkan epic poetry, holds that oral tradition—meaning in this case narrative poetry—is orally learned, created and transmitted. Lord considers each singer a poet who creates his or her repertoire in relation to the circumstances of performance. Thus, in his view, the epic singer is not primarily one who bears tradition, but rather a creative poet. In singing, he or she is both the creator and performer of the rune. Lord holds that the same song differs for individual singers and during various stages of an individual singer's life. He also emphasizes that, although all singers use traditional material in formulating their repertoires, they do not use it in the same way. The singer's speed is dependent on familiarity with the techniques of composition and style in his or her culture. Lord's observations are based on his studies of Yugoslavian epic.[30]

How does this relate to runic poetry? It should be noted that almost none of the rune singers could read or write. This is also true in Finland, a country with almost 100 percent literacy, where the rune singers who preserved the tradition through the 1960s and '70s were largely part of the rare minority in that country who were illiterate. On the other hand, singers who could read and write often relied on literary sources such as the *Kalevala* in their composition and modified their versions according to literary patterns. Presumably, trochaic meter as well as the style, form, and content related to it have been decisive aids in preserving this genre of tradition in memory. Singers make some effort to memorize each rune word for word from one generation to the next. This is made possible by techniques of rune compilation, poetic meter, alliteration, parallelism, and the generic norms of structure, language, style, and content. Familiarity with these techniques may also make it possible for some rune singers to create epic units in poetic form based on their own life experience. During her last years, Marina Takalo orally created poetry in the Kalevala meter, using symbols resembling those of fairy tales. However, she did not classify those creations as ancient Karelian runes. In her poem "I Made a Flower Bed" (1965) Takalo gives an account of her relationship to her own children:

I Made a Flower Bed

I made a bench, planted flowers,
the flowers grew beautiful and fair.
I took a basket,
put the flowers in the basket,
I went walking with the flowers.
A flower fell from the basket,
the gate swung shut,
I stretched, tried to catch the flower, couldn't,
yearning, I longed, weeping, searched many years.

The leaf flew, the flower lived.
I got into the sledge,
the sledge moved on rubber wheels,
I went in search of the flower.
But a flower came toward me,
It was that flower,
but the flower had dried,
its leaves were yellowed,
but it was the same flower
which fell from my basket.[31]

Marina's interpretation of her poem sheds light on the feelings it contains about her daughter, who had remained in Karelia in 1922 and with whom she was reunited in 1965:

When I created children, I created a flower bed, planted flowers. The flowers grew, the children grew. I gathered the flowers in a basket, went walking. A flower fell, one flower, and the gate swang shut, the border was closed, one flower was left outside the border. That's what's in it [the poem]. Right? I search, crying; yearning. I longed for her. A flower flew, a letter came, the flower was alive. I got into the car. That's the 'korja' [sledge], isn't it? I got into the sledge. The sledge traveled on rubber wheels. I went in search of the flower. I met the flower, when I met my daughter, but she had faded, the leaves yellowed, the flowers faded. She was old.(1182)[32]

Fundamental to runic poetry is a special technique of compilation which governs the composition of the unknown but popular poet who orally creates the rune. This technique was also familiar to those rune singers whose task was to preserve tradition by remembering it. During the 1960s and '70s, it was characteristic of the last rune singers to reproduce their runes and even create new ones. At least in the case of Marina Takalo, this was done consciously. Because of her familiarity with the generic norms of style, form, and content within the tradition, she was able to recall old poetic entities and also to create new ones. Rune singing followed a knowledge of the laws of tradition, and deviations from these laws were not accepted in rune singing in the same manner as they were, for example, in laments and other traditional genres which encouraged a more spontaneous mode of presentation. It was necessary to try to preserve the rune in its original form. This relates, in part, to the question of survival of the tradition during a period when rune singing was no longer widely known and shared by the society as a whole. In Finland after World War II, the rune singers had almost no societal controls on their runic traditions. Nevertheless, as a result of the strict norms inherent in this genre, for decades the poetry which was composed by the singers themselves based on these techniques, was reminiscent of the runes collected from White Sea Karelia a hundred years earlier. The rune singer governed this generic code so adeptly that he or she was able to create new content based on it.

From this point of view, rune singing was an act of creation, in addition to being an act of transmission or preservation. This was the point of view stated by Lönnrot in his preface to the *New Kalevala*. There he outlined the important distinction between vertical (from one generation to the next) and horizontal (within a society) transmission of culture:

> As to the authenticity of the runes, the matter is as follows: At festivities and other social gatherings, someone hears a new song and tries to commit it to memory. Then on another occasion, while singing it to new listeners, he recalls the subject matter more precisely than its word-by-word narration in every detail. Those parts he does not remember in precisely their original words, he relates in his own, in places even more pleasingly, perhaps, than they were before. And if some less significant passage is left out, it can be replaced by another from the singer's own head. The second and third persons who hear it then proceed to sing it in their own way, and the song changes, as it is wont to, more in particular words and details than in subject matter. Parallel to this kind of versified story, however, there exists another, which better preserves it in its ancient words and connectives, namely, a child's learning from its parents from generation to generation.[33]

Lönnrot made the following evaluation of the *Kalevala* and his role as its creator:

> The order in which rune singers themselves sing their runes cannot be completely disregarded, although I do not attribute great worth to it, because they vary a great deal among themselves in this. This divergence, the frequent difference in the the order of the runes for different singers, and the fact–as recording the same runes from different singers proved–that for the most part they sang two songs or even more in some kind of order, it didn't matter which, strengthened my previous opinion that all such runes could perhaps be joined together. I could not maintain one singer's order to be more authentic than another's; I simply explained the sequence to be derived from a person's innate desire to arrange his knowledge in some kind of order, and divergences among the singers as the result of differences in their natures. Finally, when not a single singer could any longer rival me in knowledge of the runes, I felt myself to have the same right which, according to their conviction, most singers bestow on themselves, namely, to be able to order the runes as they are best suited to be joined together, or, in the words of a rune:
>
> > I conjured myself into a conjurer
> > a singer came of me.
> > That is: I considered myself as good
> > a singer as they.[34]

Lönnrot's knowledge of the generic norms for poetic work was also significant in the compilation of the *Kalevala*. Lönnrot knew these rules, but it was necessary for him to learn not to be continuously aware of them and to enter into the spirit of his new role:

Although I myself am weak in poetic work and therefore seldom touch it, in reading others' works over time, I have nevertheless wondered why one of them is beautiful, and another unpleasant to the ear. In thinking about the reason, I have observed that in the former, rules of poetry have been followed, while in the latter, the poems have been constructed contrary to them, those rules which touch on fitting together words, though nothing about the narration of subject matter or anything else pertaining to poetic scholarship need be mentioned. And even if it isn't to everyone's liking, let us remember that different localities may also have their different requirements for poetry. I have but followed what is demanded of poetry here and on the Russian side of the border. Let no one think that I am writing the following as a primer for anyone. That has not been my intent—and besides, nature makes a better poet than scholarship.

> Nature makes the singer,
> Imparts the ardor
> To the brave poet,
> How to order a song.
> It would be well if I could but show what
> runes are esteemed in our country.[35]

This honest statement is a self-evident testimony by Lönnrot about his role in the creation of the *Kalevala*. He wanted to be a "natural" poet, not dependent on theory. At the conclusion of his work on the *Kalevala*, Lönnrot felt that he had been successful in creating an epical work as a "natural" poet. Just as the Homeric epics had been transmitted by the oral poets of antiquity, Lönnrot felt that he had accomplished his task in harmonizing the role of the rune singer with that of the natural poet which he aspired to be. Because a good natural poet had been able to internalize the rules, the poems came naturally. In the same way as individual deviations and modifications were permitted in traditional performances, Lönnrot, as compiler of the epic, felt that he had the right to attempt his own version based on his taste and his knowledge of the techniques of generic patterns used in composing runic poetry.

THE REGION OF EPICAL RUNE SINGING

Lönnrot was unique among the creators of epics in that he left his entire body of work, with records of all its sources as well as its printed and unprinted phases, for the evaluation of his contemporaries and succeeding generations. His travel notes, diaries, and letters, and the various editions of the *Kalevala* and the revisions they were subject to, are in the Lönnrotiana Collection of the Finnish Literature Society and available to the public. In his preface to the *Old Kalevala*, Lönnrot reported his sources, simultaneously disclosing the geographical area where epical poetry was sung in the trochaic Kalevala meter:

Above all, I consider it an obligation to explain how these runes have been obtained. Many of them have already been published, perhaps even less complete, in the works of the late Lencqvist, Ganander, Porthan, and Topelius, but a much greater number are previously unknown. I have collected these over time from Finnish and Russian Karelia, and even a few from the Kajaani region. In addition, some were sent to me from elsewhere. The areas where these runes have primarily been collected are Kitee, Kesälahti, Tohmajärvi, Ilomantsi, and Pielinen in Finnish Karelia, the parishes of Vuokkiniemi, Paanajärvi, and Repola in Russia, and the parishes of Kuhmo and Kianta in Kajaani. I haven't gotten anything worth mentioning from the other places I've been to for this purpose. In 1828 I collected them from the places mentioned above in Finnish Karelia, in 1831 and in 1832 from Repola, and in the years following from Kuhmo and Kianta. Having myself been transferred to Kajaani, I have gone to the Russian parishes four times, a number of weeks each time.[36]

When the *Kalevala* was published, it was noted that Lönnrot had not used all the rune sources available to him verbatim. As a response to his critics, Lönnrot wrote the following remarks which, however, remained an unpublished supplement to his preface to the *Old Kalevala*: "Do not reproach me if all the different kinds of poems which have previously been included in the works of Lencqvist, Porthan, Ganander, and others have not been included here as such, for 'many of them are not worth singing from the back of a boat' as a man from Lonkka aptly said in Vuokkiniemi."[37]

During the fifteen-year period between publication of the *Old* and *New Kalevala*, the collecting of folklore continued briskly.[38] The *Old Kalevala* was based primarily on the voices of old men from White Sea and, in general, North Karelia. In his *New Kalevala*, Lönnrot was also able to include the runes collected by Europaeus and his companions from areas in the south, including Olonets, Border, and South Karelia, and Ingria. Much of this new material had been gathered from female singers.

As a result of Lönnrot's hypothesis, as stated above, this particular area became canonized as the "cradle of rune singing," and it was here that many of the runes were collected. It is possible to demonstrate noteworthy differences between various rune-singing areas. North Karelia, White Sea Karelia, and Olonets are areas of masculine rune singing and, in particular, of epic runes. Orthodox South Karelia, the Karelian Isthmus, Ingria, and Estonia are centers of women's lyric poetry where less epic material has been found than in the north. The ancient poetry of western Finland was noticeably influenced by medieval Catholic poetry and Scandinavian ballads. This area has also been the source of a great many proverbs in the Kalevala meter. The eighteenth-century runic poetry collections are derived primarily from Ostrobothnia, Savo, and Kainuu, where less runic poetry was later recorded, with the exception of a rich store of charms and incantations.

In reference to his own observations about collecting, Lönnrot made his well-known statement about the final stage in the development of runic poetry, which concluded with the period of Bjarmian dominance in White

Sea Karelia. He stated his romantic viewpoint in the preface to the *New Kalevala*:

> There have also been numerous suppositions as to the time and place of the genesis of these songs. More apt than the rest seems to be the one which views them as having been created during the period of Bjarmian dominance on the southwest shore of the White Sea or in the areas of those great lakes, Voiko, Onega, and Ladoga, which lie like an arc on the Onega Bay, the White Sea on one side and the Gulf of Finland on the other. That segment of Finns in Russian Karelia among whom these runes have survived throughout the centuries appear to be directly descended from the old, wealthy, powerful, and famous Bjarmian people. More than other Finns, they still have a certain outward, traditional culture derived from the past, curious vestiges of some kind of communal life, a special enthusiasm for all trade which rejects every difficulty and obstacle, agility in both bodily movements and presence of mind in their endeavors, all of which, together with their present dwelling places, their memory for poetry, the words of Swedish origin found in their language, the unique ornaments of their womenfolk, and so forth, is best explained by taking into consideration ancient Bjarmian times. In bodily agility, in their almost visible quickness of mind and desire to trade, the Ostrobothnians and Karelians of Finland are most closely akin to them and the latter, together with the Ingrians, in recalling poetry as well.[39]

Previously, Lönnrot steadfastly held the opinion that rune singing had achieved its zenith during the period when he was doing his collection work. Several centuries earlier, there had been fewer runes, and with the publication of the *Kalevala*, the song tradition would decrease. Thus he refers to "the feared disappearance of the ancient runes" in the preface to the *New Kalevala*:

> Based on the fact that ancient runes and their singers have been held in esteem until present times in Russian Karelia, one might conclude that singers are not forgetting their runes, but rather have improved and beautified them into their present form in numerous variants. Several centuries ago, these might not have been found in such abundance, although certainly, even at that time, they were all sprouting and expanding. They are again beginning to wane, rather than increase with new supplements, because whoever wants can now obtain them as a complete book, and in a fuller version than anyone's individual memory could sustain. Thus the worth of singing from memory will disappear and, its worth lost, even singing itself will disappear.[40]

In Lönnrot's mind, oral folklore evolved in the same manner as the various dialects of a language which lose their local characteristics when a written language has been established. Lönnrot believed that runic poetry would gradually wane when it had been written down and published as the *Kalevala*.

Lönnrot's hypothesis that rune singing flowered, renaissance-like, in White Sea Karelia at the turn of the eighteenth and nineteenth centuries has subsequently found support among other scholars. These include Väinö Kaukonen who, for example, compares the fame achieved by traditional Karelian runic poetry to the discovery of bylini, the ancient Russian heroic poems. This Russian genre was discovered in the northern Ural Mountains and later in the northwestern Russian areas surrounding Lake Onega. Kaukonen calls attention to the preservation of archaic cultural traditions in the proximity of this linguistic border and strongly emphasizes similarities in the development of the high cultures of both Karelia and Russia: "At the territorial boundary between the Karelian and Russian languages, approximately one thousand years ago, there developed a multifaceted, unique culture, which had as one of its central features folk art and, of particular significance here, folklore in all its breadth."[41]

In speaking about the late flowering of runic poetry, Lönnrot, like Kaukonen, may have been correct, since the linking of runes into such longer epic unities as the Sampo or Lemminkäinen cycles, as was done by some singers, is a recent phenomenon. Previously, runes had usually been sung individually in various contexts. For example, as the use of runes in ritual context waned, they clustered in the memories of talented singers and became linked into sequences. At this stage, runic tradition became the property of a particular family. It is probable that such clans as the Malinen and Perttunen families became famous for their singing during a creative period of this kind. Of the later singers, Larin Paraske, Anni Lehtonen, and Marina Takalo were among the singers who actively shaped and reproduced parts of their own poetic repertoires. Able singers with good memories joined runes together consecutively which were otherwise usually presented individually. In the case of such central figures as Väinämöinen, Ilmarinen, Lemminkäinen, and Kullervo, this linking together of runes resulted in unified narrative poems about single individuals. Having observed this, Lönnrot also began to construct miniature epics using a technique which eventually culminated in the *Kalevala*.

It is worthy of note that the last of the Slavic bylini tradition was also preserved in a nearby cultural area.[42] This parallel existence of broad, narrative poetic units in largely the same geographic region inhabited by two peoples of differing linguistic and cultural heritage cannot be a coincidence. Environmental circumstances have been posited as the reason for this phenomenon by Lauri Honko (1985). According to this hypothesis, the same environment created common needs and produced a similar tendency in both cultures to construct broad, narrative, epic poems.[43] It is unlikely, however, that an evolution of this kind is solely the result of physical surroundings. It is much more likely that, for some historical reason, two groups which were conservative and also very creative settled in the border areas of northwestern Russia. Among them, ancient tradition, in addition to preserving its vitality, also demonstrated the capacity for renewal.

The attention of these peoples focused on preserving their cultural traditions, particularly during periods when they were threatened as an ethnic, political, or religious minority. The wilderness of northwestern Russia, behind the great uncleared Veps and Karelian forests, offered a retreat for groups of people persecuted during various periods of Russian history who had no recourse in the more densely inhabited areas. Thus a tribe of Karelians, somewhat divergent from other Baltic Finns, and a settlement of Slavic origin which had been established there were found side by side having a reciprocal influence on each other. This no doubt also occurred in White Sea Karelia, where both ancient Karelian runes and Russian bylini have been found in the same area. At present, rune singing is disappearing in the Balto-Finnic areas. Its last remnants are found among minority cultures surviving within the dominant culture, in such areas as Tver and Novgorod Karelia, as well as White Sea Karelia in the Soviet Union.

In Finland during the 1980s only a few Karelian emigrants are still alive who learned the runes orally during childhood and preserved them by memory without writing them down. Because most of them are Russian Orthodox, there is reason to consider the impact this religious identity has had on preserving culture. In addition to being a divergent religion, Russian or Greek Orthodox, in Finland this has also meant divergence from the dominant culture, which is Evangelical Lutheran (approx. 90% of the population). The religious issue, however, is further complicated by the fact that several sects exist within the Russian Orthodox Church. Among the most significant is the Old Believer sect, a conservative group which differs from the others in a number of everyday customs, norms, and rituals, as well as religious world view.

THE WHITE SEA KARELIA OF THE OLD BELIEVERS, CRADLE OF THE *KALEVALA*

The first collectors of folklore and dialects in northernmost White Sea Karelia, such as Mathias Alexander Castrén and Elias Lönnrot, had the opportunity to visit the Holy Island and the Skiitta monasteries of the Old Believers in Kiestinki. Lönnrot's travel diary gives a detailed account of these monasteries, which were destroyed in the middle of the nineteenth century. However, Lönnrot did not understand the inhabitants of the monasteries or their religion. His description of circumstances there is quite negative. Lönnrot was disappointed that the monasteries did not live up to his expectations: "I spent only one night here, in a building which looked more like a thieves' nest than a monastery."[44] In the village of Vaara in Kiestinki, Lönnrot spent a night in the home of the lay leader, Homa. The importance of the Old Believers, particularly in northernmost White Sea Karelia, is also reflected in the fact that Lönnrot depicted the religious situation in White Sea Karelia in his journal:

> In these regions, as far as I know, there are three religions, none of which deem it appropriate to eat from the same dishes. The true "Papinviero" [the group which followed the Orthodox priest], which is also called "Miero" [the world] and its followers "Mierolainens" [the worldly], is exceedingly small in number and uniformly diminishing. In contrast, the Tuhkanen sect is expanding rapidly. Its priest, and the propagator of this sect, is said to live in the village of Karkalahti, on the seacoast between Kieretti and Kemi. Since his

district is exceedingly large, it has been necessary for him to hire various priests who go to his smallest districts in order to baptize children, conduct marriages, bury the dead, and carry out other functions. It is said that he himself journeys through his extensive province about once a year and takes care of whatever is necessary. Thus, he, as well as his subordinate priests, must be driven about and fed by the Tuhkanen villages during their travels. I really don't know whether they get any salary other than what people give of their finery; this need not be, because nothing is said about it. What a strain on the province if it is also necessary to pay them, because a true, legitimate priest must be paid what he decrees for all the clerical functions which these (Tuhkanens) require of their priests, although they do nothing more for them than take care of the matter in secrecy. I have often asked Tuhkanens how their religion differs from that of the Mierolainens but have not yet gotten any clarification of this. They themselves don't even seem to know. They merely say that the priest sprinkles water with different fingers than God decreed, and some even mention that he who prays in the manner of an Orthodox priest should be cursed.[45]

As he progressed northward, Lönnrot continually encountered Old Believers. His affinity for smoking tobacco was not tolerated in most of their homes. If the master of the house did permit it, the women left the room. However, as the district doctor, Lönnrot considered it positive that the Old Believers had a great respect for cleanliness and cited their habit of eating from separate bowls as well as their taboos with regard to hygiene.[46]

In 1839, Castrén went to the village of Vaara in Kiestinki, where there lived only Old Believers. He could not get food at a certain house because there were no utensils for those of other religions. Castrén then posed the following question for the villagers: Was it a greater sin to force a fellow human being to starve than to taint a wooden dish? An old man then solemnly gave Castrén food, although he had to eat out of a stone dish and not a wooden one.[47] In the latter case, impurity would have permeated the dish so deeply that not even washing would have cleansed it, whereas they believed a stone dish could be cleansed by rubbing it with water and sand.

Lönnrot's and Castrén's journeys took place during a period when northern White Sea Karelia was primarily settled by Old Believers. Even after the monasteries had been destroyed, the Old Believers found strong support in the districts of Kemi and Kola in northwestern Russia. According to the statistics, there were approximately twenty-five thousand Old Believers still living in these areas in 1863. Similarly, the sect had considerable support in southern Onega and in the neighboring areas on the Finnish side, up to Savo and northern Karelia. However, statistics often err with regard to the number of Old Believers because, fearing persecution, many concealed their religion.[48]

"Old Believers" is the common name given to sects derived from the original Russian Orthodox monks and their followers who came to be persecuted in Russia during the middle of the seventeenth century because of their opposition to the liturgical reform carried out by Patriarch Nikon. They were also called

Raskolniks which, in Russian, means sectarians or turncoats. The Old Believers should not, however, be considered merely a religious sect which originated in the seventeenth century, but rather a Russian Orthodox sect which retained the oldest teachings and rituals of the Eastern Church under circumstances of liturgical reform. This persecuted group also further disintegrated into various sects. A major distinction can be made between those sects with priests (popovtsy) and those without (bezpopovtsy). The former also used clergy in their services, the latter used only laymen.[49]

The Old Believers were persecuted by both the Russian government and the official Russian Orthodox Church. For this reason, from the middle of the seventeenth century on, they moved to the most remote geographical regions of the country and established monasteries to support theological scholarship and liturgy. At various times, the monasteries came into armed conflict with the government. Such a battle ensued, for example, in the Solovetski Monastery at White Sea, which sided with the Old Believers. The monastery was subdued in 1676. Despite this, the opposition of the monks was not broken. They captured the Paleostrov Monastery and defended it. Ultimately, 2,700 people burned themselves to death when they realized the destruction of the monastery was imminent. Enclaves of hermits then formed in distant parts of Karelia, including Saari (Holy Island) and Skiitta, which Lönnrot visited.[50]

When the monasteries were destroyed, the monks withdrew to wilderness areas and lived among the local people. Their influence greatly increased during this period in northern White Sea Karelia, and a tradition developed whereby wealthier houses maintained a hermit's house or "kelja" in the forest. In it lived a "worshipper of God" or "biegloi," a hermit or monk who prayed for the people of the household. The household, in turn, took care of the daily needs of the hermit or monk. This practice was also known on the Finnish side of the border, where the Old Believers expanded their influence as a consequence of their being persecuted in Russia. There was also an Old Believers' monastery at Lake Tava in Kuusamo, where the last monks died only after the Second World War. Similarly, there were monasteries on the Finnish side of the border, in North Savo and Karelia, where they escaped the persecution of the Russian czar and the Church.

The religion of the Old Believers has been relatively little studied and, as a result of the above-mentioned persecution, there is scant hope for precise statistical information about its geographical distribution thus far.[51] In twentieth-century Finland, this religion has been assimilated into the Finnish Orthodox Church. Even today, however, it is possible to find aspects of behavior and world view characteristic of Old Believers in the local traditions of such Orthodox areas as Kainuu, North Karelia, and Savo.

In Czarist Russia, the pressures on the movement were not eased until the end of the nineteenth century. The Old Believers were officially granted religious freedom in 1905. It has been estimated that before the Russian Revolution and the First World War, there were from three to fifteen million Old Believers in Russia. Beyond these statistics, however, their numbers in the Soviet Union are impossible to estimate, because of the position taken by the Soviet government toward religions after the Revolution.[52]

According to the Soviet ethnographer Ludmila Kuzmina (1983), there were approximately two million Old Believers in the Soviet Union in 1912, including numerous communities in Siberia. At present, the leader of the church lives in Moscow and serves simultaneously as the Bishop of White Russia. Over one hundred thousand Old Believers, approximately ten to twenty percent of the population, live in the vicinity of Lake Baikal. It is characteristic of the Soviet Old Believers that their large families focus attention on old customs, particularly in eating, dress, and rituals. In the Soviet Union, Old Believers still observe numerous ancient taboos with regard to food. Furthermore, according to Kuzmina, they have preserved their oral traditions to a greater extent than other cultural groups living in the same area. This is also true of ancient taboos with regard to dress, including the wife's cap, and religious customs, such as wedding rituals. Characteristically, the religious identity of the Old Believers, including customs in food and dress, begins to manifest itself when they reach the age of thirty to thirty-five. The religious tradition has, in fact, been preserved primarily among the older members of the group, those over sixty.[53]

As a result of centuries of continuous persecution, the Raskolniks wandered repeatedly from one area to another. Thus the Old Believers in the Soviet Union have moved to many remote areas of the country such as Baikal, Siberia, and Karelia. From the Soviet Union, many of them have moved on to Manchuria, China, Hong Kong, Brazil, Uruguay, and the United States. In fact, since the 1960s, a community of approximately five thousand Old Believers belonging to the priestless sect has lived near Woodburn, Oregon. It has preserved its linguistic and cultural tradition, including its ancient wedding ritual. Religious ceremonies are conducted in Old Slavonic. The younger generation, however, has been under great pressure to acculturate into mainstream America. For this reason, in 1968, approximately six hundred members of this group continued their migration to the Nikolaevsk settlement in Alaska and also to areas of Alberta in Canada. There, like the Hutterites, they have established their own economically viable institutions in order to support their own schools and other institutions.[54]

The Old Believers say: "Life is a difficult rite." They have striven to preserve their religious traditions in the Slavic language and view folklore and culture as part of that tradition. The wedding customs of the Old Believers in Oregon are reminiscent of White Sea wedding rituals, which were led by female lamenters. It also appears that what kept alive the last of the runic poetry in northern White Sea Karelia, as well as the priestless wedding and burial rituals, is derived from the religion of the Old Believers.

Lönnrot observed prejudices among the Old Believers as well as rules about the separation of bowls, which he shunned.[55] He did not perceive that it was, in fact, the Old Believers who, as part of their religious customs, were also the last to preserve the rune-singing tradition in many areas. Undoubtedly, religious isolation and differentiation encouraged the preservation of oral traditions

The Russian Orthodox population in Kainuu and northern Karelia were characteristically Old Believers, and manifestations of this ascetic religiosity can still be found in their culture today. To celebrate the 150th anniversary of the publication of the *Kalevala* in 1985, an Orthodox mass was organized on Kalmosaari Island in Suomussalmi to commemorate the rune singers Domna and Hilippä Huovinen. This is the most western White Sea Karelian settlement, located on the Finnish side of the border between Finland and the Soviet Union. The ceremony was attended by numerous members of the Huovinen family, who still carry on traditional activities, including rune singing and playing the kantele. (Juha Pentikäinen)

among the sect. If they experienced difficulties in maintaining their identity, they preferred to move to another area rather than adapt, and the exodus of the Old Believers continues to this day. When they experience pressures to acculturate or direct persecution, they move on to a new location in order to be able to practice their ancient traditions and religious customs. This is also the basis for their most recent moves to the United States and Canada.

Studies have shown that women preserved the religion of the Old Believers longer than did men. One reason the men among the White Sea Karelian Old Believers ceased to heed their ancient norms was their occupation. The peddler's trade required them to travel from house to house throughout Finland, particularly in Finnish- and Swedish-speaking areas of southern and western Finland. It was not easy for a peddler of the Old Believer faith to adhere to rituals which required, for instance, carrying his own food vessel, eating separately from his own dish, and adhering to complicated daily rules. This is also a reason why women were the last to preserve the White Sea Karelian rune-singing tradition. During the nineteenth century, many of the singers were men, while in the twentieth century they were primarily women.

Folklore collectors' notes do not generally give specific information as to whether or not a singer was an Old Believer. Rather, this religion was mentioned only when it created difficulties for the collector's living arrangements or other circumstances. Most of the rune singers encountered during the second half of the twentieth century were raised in homes of Old Believers and were, at least in world view, still Old Believers, even while living in Finland. Among the last generation of singers encountered during the 1960s and 1970s were many who had the religious tradition of the Old Believers in their family or societal histories. Marina Takalo is an example of a rune singer whose religious beliefs corresponded primarily to this world view.

From her childhood on, Marina belonged to the Tuhkanen sect. However, her connections with it were severed when, on a fishing trip during her youth, she drank water from the cup of another sect, the Mierolainens, and, as a consequence, lost her status as an Old Believer. During the latter stages of her life, Marina's world view even shifted toward Lutheran teachings. Nevertheless, she remained Russian Orthodox until the end of her life. Her norms were those of the Old Believers, although she did broaden her religious views and rejected numerous aspects of the Old Believers' faith such as separation of bowls and their norms of dress.[56]

Another norm of the Old Believers which Marina questioned was whether rune singing was blasphemy. At that time, she came to the conclusion that singing most runes was not blasphemous because they spoke of God and good things. In contrast, she considered laments, as well as the runes through which a person expresses feelings of bitterness and rebellion against the Creator, to be blasphemous. Of the genres Marina was familiar with, she included charms and joiks in the category of blasphemy. The singing of game songs was sinful, as were play and dance in general.

Marina believed that blasphemy in runes was an ambiguous question and had to be judged individually for each rune. Thus, for example, because there is a bird in the rune about the creation of the world, she considered it God's rune and held that the bird signified the Holy Ghost. On the other hand, "Lunastettavan neidon runo" (The rune of the maiden to be ransomed) was considered blasphemous, because the girl was trying to pay back her father and mother for not saving her. "One shouldn't take revenge, no matter what evil another does!" Her father, Iivana Nikitin, didn't tolerate the children singing runes learned from Olonja. As Marina said: "There in Karelia they said that songs would be blasphemy. They were always saying that they shouldn't be sung. At our place, Father was angry about everything. That's why I didn't dare sing them along with my late aunt [Olonja Nikitin]. As a girl, I never sang within my father's and mother's hearing; only when I was alone."[57]

It is an interesting paradox that Iivana Nikitin entirely forbade rune singing at home, despite the fact that he himself was not an Old Believer but rather a Mierolainen, and he occasionally even hummed a rune himself. Olonja Nikitin, Marina's father's aunt, was a member of the Tuhkanen sect, but she sang runes in spite of this. In fact, Marina admired her broad-mindedness. The close emotional ties between the grandparents' generation and the grandchildren is also apparent from the following comment which Marina made about "The Rune of the Maiden to Be Ransomed": "Partly it is that the old grandfather was the most beloved; neither the father nor the mother ransomed her, but the old man ransomed her, the old grandfather."

The institution of the extended family created a reciprocal relationship between the oldest and youngest generations in the White Sea Karelian community, which also served to preserve the conservative rune-singing culture as part of people's daily life. The role of this tradition was supported by the religion of the Old Believers, which emphasized adherence to tradition. When a tradition was fused into a mental landscape fundamentally religious in nature, its preservation came to be experienced as a sacred obligation. Thus, before it waned as a tradition, rune singing was evolving toward a religious function similar to that which it had previously had, although the singers themselves may not have been aware of this.

CHAPTER

7

COSMIC DRAMA

EVOLUTION OF THE CREATION RUNE

How was the *Kalevala* created? In order to answer this question, let us examine the structure of one rune which appears to have been central to all versions of the epic. Like the first books of the Bible and many other mythological texts, each version of the *Kalevala* begins with the creation of the world. Its point of departure is a complex of Finnish runes about the creation of the cosmos.

The most well known variants of the Finnish creation rune are undoubtedly those published by Lönnrot in his *Kalevala*. Lönnrot's versions of the poem are also the result of a lengthy process of maturation and revision. Its evolution from those initial verses of the Sampo sequence[1] which he heard Ontrei Malinen sing in September 1833 to the multiverse epic sequence which opens the *New Kalevala* is a very long one. From Malinen, Lönnrot obtained a 366-verse version of the Sampo sequence. Previous to singing this for Lönnrot, in 1825 Malinen had also sung it for A. J. Sjögren, the well-known linguist and ethnographer, who later became an Academician in St. Petersburg. At that time, Malinen's version of the Sampo sequence had been 321 verses in length. Sjögren was aware that he had discovered a cosmic rune and named it "Maailman alku munasta" (The birth of the world from an egg).[2]

In Malinen's version of the rune, "The Creation of the World" precedes "Väinämöinen's Journey to Pohjola," "The Forging of the Sampo," "The Theft of the Sampo," and "The Courtship Contest." Its main elements are as follows:

> A slant-eyed Lapp held a week-long grudge against old Väinämöinen. . . . He shot three arrows; the first two missed, but the third one reached its destination, the blue elk. . . . Väinämöinen fell into the water for seven years, and plowed the sea bottom. . . . Where the land lies against the land, there he blessed the places for casting nets, dug the fish-filled lake-bottom. Where he stepped upon the sea, there he cast rocky islets, raised rock reefs. Ships were sunk upon them, merchants' heads were lost. . . . The goose, bird of the air, flew in search of a place to nest. Väinämöinen raised his knee from the sea as a green hillock. The goose made a nest on Väinämöinen's knee, and laid six eggs, the seventh one of iron. As the bird brooded her eggs, Väinämöinen felt his knee grow warm and moved it. At this point, the eggs rolled into the sea. Väinämöinen said:

The birth of the cosmos from an egg as illustrated by the Estonian artist Harald Eelma. (*Kalevala*, Eesti-Raamat, 1985; illustrated by Harald Eelma)

What's in the bottom half of the egg, that's the bottom mother earth.
What's in the upper half of the egg, that's the upper sky.
What's brown in the egg, that's to shine as the sun.
What's white in the egg, that's to gleam as the moon.
What's bits of bone in the egg, that's to be stars in the sky. . . .

This was the approximate version of the rune included by Lönnrot in "Väinämöinen" (1833),[3] the miniature epic poem he edited again the following fall into the version which came to be known as the *Proto-Kalevala*. It is true that this precursor to the *Kalevala* began somewhat clumsily with Väinämöinen's fishing trip. The words of creation are found in verses 139-198. As Lönnrot continued to meet new rune singers, including Arhippa Perttunen from Latvajärvi, he was ardently developing his Homeric idea of ordering the runes into one whole.

When the Sampo sequence became the epic core of the poem, the "Creation Rune" became its introduction and the beginning of the *Kalevala*. In the *Old Kalevala*, the version of the "Creation Rune" used by Lönnrot closely followed

In the *Old Kalevala*, it is Väinämöinen who initiates the events of creation. Pencil and India ink drawing by R. V. Ekman (1858), "Kotka munii Väinämöisen polvelle" (The eagle laid an egg on Väinämöinen's knee). (R. V. Ekman, Atheneum Museum)

the singing tradition of White Sea Karelia. An examination of the *Kalevala*'s stages shows that completion of the rune was a lengthy process, despite the fact that its position in the epic was clear to Lönnrot from the beginning. In 1839, during the transitional period between the *Old Kalevala* and the *New*, Lönnrot reevaluated the content of the "Creation Rune," and at the same time international scholarship provided him valuable clues as to the direction the structure of the rune might take. In his article "Alkuluomisesta" (On the original creation), which was published in December 1839 in *The Bee*, Lönnrot also included the "Creation Rune" as he envisioned its content at that time:

> Wise old Väinämöinen
> traveled six years from here,
> followed seven summers,
> wafted eight years,
> on the sea,
> on the open high seas,
> before him liquid water,
> behind him blue sky.
>
> There the man read the sea,
> the hero studied the waves;

where his head rose,
there he ordered islands;
where he turned his hand,
there he named a cape;
where his foot stepped,
there pike were provided;
when he went near the land,
there he built beaches;
rested his head upon the ground,
there a bay was prepared;
turned his side upon the ground,
there a smooth shore;
his feet turned on the ground,
there a salmon weir.
Thus swimming farther,
he stood on the sea,
created crags on the open sea,
raised secret reefs,
on which ships sank,
merchants' heads were lost.

The eagle rose from the northeast,
along the spruce sprig to the sky,
the eagle wasn't the largest,
or the smallest:
one wing brushed the sky,
the other touched the water.
Its eyes shot fire,
its mouth spewed lightning.

Flying, soaring,
looking, turning;
flew the east, flew the west,
flew all the sky winds,
finally flew to the northwest
reached the farthest north,
seeking a nesting place,
pondering a land to settle.

Then old Väinämöinen,
in the middle of the sea,
when he saw the eagle coming,
the bird gliding down,
thought the sun was shining,
the sweet one beaming.

Thus he raised his knee from the sea,
thrust it as a nest for the eagle,
a hay-covered hummock,
a dried straw sod.

That eagle, wretched bird,
saw the hummock on the sea;
"Fresh turf would be there,
if I made my nest there."

It flew, it soared,
landed on the knee,
kneaded a nest of hay,
gathered dry grass:
thus laid six eggs,
a golden egg the seventh.

It kneaded, it brooded,
warmed up the knee:
from this old Väinämöinen
felt his knee grow hot,
his limb warm.
He jerked his knee,
moved his limb,
the eggs rolled into the water,
into the waves of the sea.

Old Väinämöinen said:
"Poor eagle, mean bird!
The eggs already rolled into the water,
cracked upon the sea boulders."

He looked, he turned,
the eggs had already changed:
the lower half of the egg became
the lower mother earth:
the upper half of the egg became
the upper heavens:
what was brown in the egg,
that came to shine as the sun;
what was white in the egg,
that came to gleam as the moon;
the other bits of the egg,
they came to be stars in the sky.

Of this the sun was born to us,
of this the new moon gleamed,
of this sky could come,
and the great earth endure,
from the eagle's six eggs,
from the seven newborn ones.

In this version, Väinämöinen still was a sovereign deity of creation. In the beginning, the wounded hero fell into the primordial sea. There he plowed the waters, created the crags, and raised boulders. As the eagle brooded its eggs on his knee, Väinämöinen uttered the cosmic creation words. In this version of the poem, published in 1839, Lönnrot still followed the plot of the *Old Kalevala*, although his thoughts were already elsewhere, as will subsequently be discussed. Ten years later, in the *New Kalevala*, this poem was quite different.

AND IN THE BEGINNING THERE WAS WOMAN: THE FEMALE ORIGINS OF THE COSMOS

The epic now began with a woman, Ilmatar, the Maiden of the Air, whom the wind and water had impregnated. In this version, it was she, lying on the waves, who performed the primary acts of creation.

> So I heard it said,
> knew that verses were created:
> solitary the nights come to us
> solitary the days dawn;
> solitary Väinämöinen was born,
> the ancient singer emerged,
> from the slender bearer,
> from the mother, Ilmatar.
>
> There was a maiden, daughter of the air,
> a slender, fair nymph.
> Long she kept her purity,
> throughout the ages her virginity,
> on the broad yards of the air,
> on the level farmyards.
> Her time grew dreary,
> her life grew strange,
> being ever alone,
> living as a maiden,
> on the long farmyards of the air,
> on the empty farmyards.
>
> Now she's come down lower,
> settled upon the waves,
> upon the broad sea,
> upon the vast ocean.
> There came a great wind gust,
> from the east angry weather. . . .
> (Poem 1, The *New Kalevala*)

In her travail the maiden, impregnated by the wind and water, implores the supreme god, Ukko, for help.

A new dimension in this version of the poem was the fact that in the acts of creation, Ukko superseded Väinämöinen. What Lönnrot quotes here is a charm commonly used during childbirth. "Ukko, the supreme god, the sup-

The climax of the Creation as depicted in S. A. Keinänen's paintings (Finnish National Board of Antiquities): Väinämöiner's mother Ilmator gives birth to him as an old man:

> Thus the mother of waters,
> Mother of waters, maiden of the air
> Raised her knee from the sea
> Her shoulder blade from the wave.
> As a place for the duck to nest.

> Väinämöinen rose from here
> His feet on two heaths
> On the back of the island,
> On the treeless headland.

porter of all air" is the "Deus Otiosus" of Finnish folk belief. He is also the god of thunder. His name is often used in charms. By including Ukko in the creation drama, Lönnrot made him the sovereign of all the cosmos. It is also possible that Ukko, as the god of air and thunder, may even have been the father of Ilmatar. In that case Lönnrot had, in fact, constructed a version of the poem which included the frequently found mythological theme of primordial incest between two deities who were father and daughter.

The redhead duck laid its eggs on the knee of the Maiden of the Air. From them, the cosmos was created without the use of any special creation words. Likewise, the islands and capes were created without the aid of Väinämöinen, who remained in the womb of the female creator.

Already the islands were ordered,
crags created in the sea,
the sky's pillars set,
lands and continents sung into being,
patterns written into the stones,
lines drawn into the boulders.
Väinämöinen is not yet born,
the eternal singer has not appeared.
Steadfast old Väinämöinen
wandered about his mother's womb
three score summers,
the same number of winters as well,
on those gentle waters,
on the foggy waves.

He pondered, he thought,
how to be, how to live,
in his dark recess,
in the narrow abode,
where he never saw the moon
or spied the sun.
There he spoke his word,
made this utterance.

"Moon, free me, sun, let me out,
Great Bear, ever guide
the man out of strange doors,
alien gates,
from this small nest,
from cramped dwellings!
See the traveler to earth,
to the air the human child,
to view the moon in the sky,
to wonder at the sun,
to learn of the Great Bear,
to scan the stars!"

When the moon did not free him
or the sun release him,
he thought his time strange,
grew impatient with his life:
moved the fortress gate
with his ring finger,
slid the bony lock
with his left toe;
came by his nails from the threshold,
by his knees out of the passage gate.[4]

In the *New Kalevala*, Lönnrot had finally completed a myth complex which synthesized the content of numerous rune texts and was augmented by his own ideas. The variants of the "Creation Rune" sung by Malinen and Perttunen were but a small part of this. Väinämöinen had clearly been relegated to the background with regard to the events of creation, and he had also been over-shadowed by Ukko. Väinämöinen was no longer the primary creator: he now had a smaller role. Instead of creating all the universe, he merely shaped things like the bottom of the sea. He was no longer the main god, but rather func-tioned as a culture hero. Despite all these changes, however, the initial poem of the *Kalevala* remained a tale about Väinämöinen's birth. The deity of creation had, however, been lowered to earth from his celestial role. He was now born of a woman:

That's how Väinämöinen was born,
proud poet of the race,
from a slim bearer,
from the mother Ilmatar.

Why did Lönnrot make so radical a change and shift the honor of creation from Väinämöinen, who represented the masculine power of the "eternal heroes" in Finnish folklore, to Ilmatar, who was almost unknown in the authentic folklore? Although Ilmatar remains undefined, she represents the feminine principle of creation.

There are stories about the creation of the world or an island which do not contain Väinämöinen or another masculine deity of creation. They are particu-larly characteristic of southern poetry areas, such as Estonia and Ingria. In 1960, Marina Takalo sang the following version of the Creation Rune "Pääskynen on päivälintu" (The swallow is a day bird) for me:

The swallow is a day bird,
the night bird is the bat,
the swallow flew a summer day,
a dark fall night as well,
searched for land to lie on,
a field to nest on,
a thicket for its eggs,

it found no land to lie on,
nor a field to nest on,
nor a thicket for its eggs.
It flew to a high hill,
to a high peak,
even saw a ship sailing,
a red-mast sailing.
It flew to the ship's gangway,
came down on the ship's bow,
cast its tiny copper nest,
laid its tiny golden egg,
God created a great wind,
sent it from the west,
tipped the ship's bow,
turned the ship on its side,
into the black mud of the sea,
into the dense sand of the sea.
From this there grew an island,
there grew a hillock,
there grew a maiden on the hillock.[5]

The rune continues. In addition to relating the birth of an island and the creation of the first human being—"in the beginning there was woman"—this rune is also about the courtship contest for the Island Maiden. The victor is Death itself: "Nurmituoma [Nurmituoma ("Turf Thomas") is an expression meaning death in Finnish] took the maiden into his sleigh." Marina was unaware that she was singing the "Creation Rune." She did not believe that the world could have been created from an egg. Rather, as a baptized Old Believer, she held that "God created it." For her "The Swallow Is a Day Bird" was a "beautiful song about God's bird" with no cosmic connection to the events of creation. She did not consider singing this song blasphemous or sinful.[6] In 1828, however, Jacob Fellman was given another reply by an anonymous man in White Sea Karelia: "Well, good brother, we have the same belief as you. The eagle flew from the north, set an egg on Väinämöinen's knee, and created the world from it. And that's what you believe too."[7] Bearing these White Sea Karelian concepts in mind, we will examine more closely both the "Creation Rune" of the *Kalevala* and the general background of the numerous versions of the Finnish creation rune. What was Lönnrot's purpose in creating and reconstructing the cosmic drama in the *Kalevala* as found in its final form in the epic?

THE INFLUENCE OF THE EPIC OF INDIA

What in fact are the origins of Ilmatar, the Maiden of the Air, who in the *New Kalevala* usurps Väinämöinen's role as regulator of cosmic events? How did Lönnrot decide on so radical a departure from the *Old Kalevala*, one which also happens to undermine somewhat the otherwise balanced structure of the poem? Lönnrot's own writings from the marginal period between the *Old* (1835) and the *New Kalevala* (1849), particularly those in the issues of *The Bee* published during 1839 help to answer this question. Seeing parallels for the Finnish creation rune in other mythologies, Lönnrot took the perspective of comparative mythology–a new field of scholarship which was only beginning to develop internationally at that time. During this period, he apparently incorporated this new approach into the epic he was creating:

> Both published and unpublished variants of this rune about the initial creation of the world exist. Some have a goose, scaup, or whistling duck in place of the eagle, and it is sung that the eagle or another of those birds lays only two or three eggs. Or they tell of the eagle's having come from Turja or Lapland and made its nest of gold or copper. When the eggs roll into the water and break, in some variants it is Väinämöinen who decides if the yolk is transformed into the moon and the white into the sun, whereas in other versions, the bird says the transforming words. Which of these variants would be better than the others, that we won't even begin to examine now. Rather, we will encourage others to ponder whether or not this tale about the original creation might have some connection to the Indian creation story.[8]

At this time, Lönnrot was developing the "Creation Rune" in his role as a scholar of comparative mythology. The translations of sacred Indian texts, which were then becoming better known throughout continental Europe, provided the impetus for his new insights. In them Lönnrot discovered parallels to Finnish mythology which caused him to view the origins of the Finnish epic in a new way:

> Early on, all the peoples in the world have their story about the original creation, namely, the creation of the earth and the world, the appearance of people and other beings, both animate and inanimate, etc. All of them are in agreement that before the creation of the earth nothing existed but some formless emptiness or a mixture of substances which was similar throughout, and one place in it was not distinct from another. In their sacred books, the Indians of Asia relate that this original being initially began to think of its own accord. From this, it took the form of an egg and from the egg developed the creator of the universe, the God Brahma, who placed the upper half of the egg as the heavens, the lower part as the earth. From its insides, he created the air and the sea. In the middle of the sea there rose a mainland, and around it appeared iron walls. From the mainland came the substance for all kinds of beings which, however, had no spirit before the creator imparted that as well.[9]

As an example, the story of creation in the *Kalevala* is reminiscent of the one found in the *Satapathabrāhmana*. In the latter, the world was initially water. The waters yearned: "How might we be conceived?" From the internal warmth created by their thought, a golden egg was born, and it floated about for a year. From it was born a man, Prajāpati, who broke the golden egg. After a year, he attempted to speak and said "bhūh," whereupon the earth was created;

"bhuvah," whereupon the atmosphere was created; and finally "svah," from which the heavens were created.[10]

In India, as in Finland, water is the initial element. In both cases the cosmic elements are created from an egg as a result of the creator's words. The Indian influence on Lönnrot's version is clear. From this point of view, it becomes apparent that Ilmatar is kin to the well-known Indian goddess Brahma. Inspired by these parallels to Indian mythology which he had discovered, Lönnrot was prepared to transform the opening drama of the *Kalevala* to coincide with the pattern of Hindu mythology.

THE BIRTH OF MAN IN INFINITY

In the creation hymn of the *Rgveda* (ca. 1200 B.C.), original chaos is symbolized by water. The impetus for the initial creation is presented as an abstract desire to create. From this power, the original One is initially formed as Being and then separates into masculine desire (above) and feminine energy (below).

> For in the beginning there was nothing, there was neither air nor heaven beyond. What was there then? Where? In whose charge? Was there measureless, deep water? There was no death then, nor deathlessness, no signs of day or night. That One breathed, of its own power, without wind. There was not yet anything but that One. In the beginning darkness was hidden in darkness, undifferentiated, all this was water. That which came into being was shrouded in emptiness, the One was born of the warmth of its own desire. In the beginning desire came over it, that was the first seed of thought. The sages, searching their hearts with wisdom, then found the bond of being in non-being. Their bond was extended across, did there exist an "above" or "below"? Impregnators and powers existed, there was energy below and desire above. Who can say for sure? Who here can say, whence those were produced, whence this creation? Even the gods were born only after this creation. Who then can say whence it evolved? He, from whom this creation has evolved, whether he initiated it or did not—he who is the surveyor of this in highest heaven, he alone knows, or perhaps even he knows not.[11]

In 1839, while pondering Indian material which paralleled that of the "Creation Rune" in the *Kalevala*, Lönnrot wrote: "Here that unformed primordial being would have separated into water and Väinämöinen, and the concept would be depicted by an eagle. Likewise, then, in their tale as in ours, the upper half of the egg becomes the heavens, the lower half, the earth; for them the inside becomes the air and the sea; for us, the moon and the sun."[12] To support his viewpoint, Lönnrot presented his theory about the etymology of the word "Väinämöinen." He derives it from "vein emoinen," meaning mother of waters, guardian spirit of the water.

Perhaps, initially, the discussion in this entire creation tale may not have been about Väinämöinen, but rather about "Vein emonen" [Mother of Waters]. "Emo, emäntä, emonen" [Mother, Mistress of the House] was the general term for that from which each substance derives its sustenance, solidity, strength, etc. Thus "Vein emonen" [Mother of Waters] need not necessarily be understood as a particular "naisjumala" [female goddess] in the water, but generally as "veden ylläpitäjä" [one who sustains the water], "veden omituinen voima eli juuri" [the water's unique power or root]. The word is clear Finnish and has a clear meaning; however, it appears that because of closeness in sound, it would have become confused with Väinämöinen's name.[13]

Thus, according to Lönnrot's etymology, even Väinämöinen derives from the secret power of feminine creation–he is shown to be a hero whose name has a feminine root. Ultimately, Väinämöinen is defined as the impersonal, unique element of power in water. According to Lönnrot's article as well as contemporary comparative mythology and Freudian analysis, water is the manifestation of female sexuality. Could Ilmatar, then, be considered the offspring of Ukko, the masculine god of air and thunder, and of Väinämöinen, defined as "vein emonen," the feminine element of water? In this case, Väinämöinen, born of Ilmatar, turns out to be her reincarnation.

In Indian religious philosophy, the original unity was not a deity but a complex central principle expressed in the concept of Brahman, which governed the universe and its basic order. It exists and will exist eternally from one era of the world to the next. Like humans, gods are born and vanish into the reality governed by this principle, which at its most fundamental signifies the eternal, cyclical journey from birth and from one reincarnation to another. In Hinduism, for example, salvation means liberation from this circular rotation and entails the unification of the human soul, Ātmán, with the soul of the cosmos, Brahman. In Buddhism, it is the quenching of the thirst for life in Nirvāna. Thus, the world view of Indian philosophy is cyclical. The beginning of existence is of interest in itself, but the rhythm of creation extends from one phase of the world to the next. The elements of the universe are created, destroyed, and created anew. Indeed, the Vedic verses depict Time (Kāla) as the fundamental god:

Time travels, a seven-reined horse, hundred-eyed, ancient, with many-seeds— wise seers rise to time, all beings are within its wheel. Seven wheels take that time, seven hubs, eternity as the axle—it, time, encompasses all these beings, travels as the foremost of the gods. It has created all beings and will also last beyond all beings, it is their father and, at the same time, son. There is no higher light. Time once gave birth to the heavens, time also gave birth to the lands, that which is and which will be, exists as a result of time. Time created the earth, the sun glows in time, all existence is in time, the eye sees in time. In time, the mind; in time, the breath; in time, the name gathered; with the advance of time all these beings rejoice. In time there is power, in time the highest, in time Brahman gathered. Time is the master of all, he is Prajapāti's father. This world is of his consequence, his birth—his founding. Time, having become Brahman, bears Paramesthin within itself. Time gave birth to beings, in the beginning time created Prajapāti, from time was born the unique kaśyapa, and the world's initial warmth."[14]

The issue of time or timelessness is also a characteristic of the "Creation Poem" in the *New Kalevala*. Väinämöinen is born alone, after Ilmatar has borne him in her womb "seven hundred years, nine eternal nights." The birth itself does not take long, but the hero floats "seven years, eight," before he stops at a "nameless headland." In this regard, as well, Ilmatar is related to Brahman and Väinämöinen is kin to Paramesthin, the first human: "In solitude do the nights come to us, in solitude do the days dawn to us, in solitude Väinämöinen was born—of the mother, Ilmatar. In *The Bee*, Lönnrot pondered this question and finally comes to the following conclusion: "If we wished to further extend these conjectures, then we could also call to mind that the six eagle eggs in our tale might well depict the six days in which God created the world, and the seventh golden egg, that day of rest which followed. But we had better end our conjectures here."[15] Ultimately, the scholar of comparative mythology was once again superseded by a Christian poet who placed primary emphasis on the story of creation canonized in Genesis.

This was written in 1839, during the transition period between the two *Kalevalas*. In the *Old Kalevala*, Lönnrot based the "Creation Rune" on the popular variants presented by his best singers, Ontrei Malinen and Arhippa Perttunen. In the *New Kalevala*, however, a myth from Indian Aryan Vedic poetry appeared in its stead. In the *Old Kalevala*, Lönnrot let Väinämöinen create the cosmos. In the *New Kalevala*, the creator became an impersonal, primordial force based on Indian mythology, the feminine Ilmatar, who is kin to the Indian goddess Brahma. However, Ilmatar's origin lay in the initial relationship between air (Ukko) and water (Väinämöinen), whom desire united into the principle of timelessness known as Brahman in Hindu philosophy.

FINNISH COSMOLOGY: SYNTHESIS OF MYTHS FROM THE ARCTIC AND THE SILK ROAD

The initial poem of the *Kalevala* is a cosmogonic myth in which two very ancient creation myths are united. The myth of the world egg is found primarily in the south and is widely known in the mythologies of the eastern Mediterranean, India, Japan, the islands of the Pacific, and Peru, while the diver myth is more northern in origin. It is found in eastern Europe, in north and Central Asia, and among the American Indians.[16]

According to Matti Kuusi, the essence of the creation runes collected from the Estonians, Ingrians, and Karelians can be stated as follows: "The bird of the air (an eagle?) flies over the sea in search of a place to nest and, having found (a hummock), it lays either one egg or three. A gust of wind rolls these eggs into the sea and from them are created (the earth and the sky, as well as?) the sun to shine, the moon to gleam and the stars in the sky."[17]

There is no mention of Väinämöinen in the version of the "Creation Rune" sung in Estonia and Ingria. In the White Sea Karelian variants, however, Väinämöinen holds a central place. The poem opens with his birth and his arrival on the sea after he has been shot by a "slant-eyed Lapp." Also joined to Väinämöinen's drifting on the sea is the myth about the formation of the sea bottom:

> Where he fell against the earth,
> there he blessed the sweep of the seines,
> dug lake bottom hollows for fish;
> where he stopped on the sea,
> there he fixed heights,
> raised reefs. . . .[18]

As Väinämöinen drifts on the sea, a scaup flies overhead searching for a nesting place and finds it on his knee. As the duck broods its eggs, Väinämöinen's knee grows warm, and when he moves it, the eggs roll into the sea and disappear. It is at this point that Väinämöinen utters his words of creation.

The plowing of the sea in this manner is also Balto-Finnic subject matter. The Estonians, for example, tell of two people, Bebelus and Babelus, who together divided the sky and measured lands from the sea. Matti Kuusi has shown that this theme is related to the myths of paleo-Arctic, circumpolar cultures. It is familiar to the Eskimos, the North American Indians, and several northern Eurasian peoples.[19] In constructing the "Creation Poem," Lönnrot emulated the White Sea Karelian singers, who were familiar with the unified version of the egg and diver myths described above.

The founder of Finnish folklore scholarship, Julius Krohn, affirmed the diver myth to be Finno-Ugric in origin.[20] Kaarle Krohn also came to the conclusion that the rune "Pääskynen on päivälintu" (The swallow is a day bird) was created by Estonian girls as a swing song.[21] In Martti Haavio's opinion, it was created in the same region as the "Creation Rune," the maritime environment of southern Finland.[22] Matti Kuusi had accepted the theory of "wandering" inherent in the Finnish historical-geographic school when he stated that "a tale about a hero who floats in the primordial sea and about his creating whirlpools and isles in the sea has, in its basic configurations, 'wandered' unchanged from the shores of the Indian and Pacific oceans to the shores of the Baltic, through areas for whose inhabitants 'sea' and 'rocky isle' were but distant, legendary concepts."[23] The maritime elements of the runes do not necessarily support Kuusi's hypothesis. The maritime ecological environment is part of the Baltic area as well. It can also be argued that the eye cannot see the opposite shore of the Baltic Sea.

Another question relates to the view of diffusion inherent in the Finnish method: Was it in fact the runes or the peoples which wandered? In the study of rune variants and redactions per se, the so-called Finnish method has gone astray in its emphasis on diffusion to the exclusion of other factors. This has led to numerous erroneous conclusions about the origins and migration routes of the runes themselves. When runes were studied as such, the scope was too narrow. The subject matter for a phenomenological, comparative study should, in fact, be international cosmogony in a broader perspective.

This is also the case with regard to the Finnish "Creation Rune." At least three sources can be discerned in its variants. The dualistic diver myth is derived from Arctic culture; the God-king and his opponent are derived from the high cultures of the Near East, as Martti Haavio has shown;[24] and the area of the world where the myth of the world egg is found extends from the shores of the Baltic, across Central Asia, to the islands of the Pacific. Doubtless, it may even have been told along the Silk Road. In any case, this myth is familiar to numerous cultures on the steppes of Central Asia, as well as herding and trading peoples who traveled the Silk Road. It is most probable that the Balto-Finnic peoples adopted this material through contacts along the Silk Road. When he used Indian mythology as his literary source in constructing the final version of the first poem in the *Kalevala*, Lönnrot was progressing along much the same lines as the Finnish runic folklore he was adapting into his epic work. The egg myth was, roughly speaking, derived from the same source as Finnic oral poetry: a Central Eurasian myth about the creation of the universe from the components of an egg.

THE FINALE OF THE EPIC: VÄINÄMÖINEN'S ORDEAL

Early in the process of creating the *Kalevala*, Lönnrot decided that the rune "Väinämöisen tuomio" (Väinämöinen's judgment) would become the climax of the epic. He had first heard this rune sung by Ontrei Malinen as synopsized below:

> A son is born to Marjatta, the youngest child in a family. The father of the child is the naughty Tuurituinen boy. They do not know what to name the boy. Virokannas, the priest, is called on to perform the baptism, and a judge is called on to decide what to do with the foundling. The judge, old Väinämöinen, states: "Take the boy to the swamp, strike him on the head with wood!" The two-week-old boy begins to speak and condemns his judge. The clergyman baptizes the child as King of Metsola [the Forest] and guardian of Rahasaari [Money Island]. Väinämöinen grows angry and ashamed. He chants himself a copper boat, in which he descends "down the rapids, down the course of the whirlpool, turning the rudder."[25]

The Judgment of Väinämöinen" is a unique rune in Finnish folklore. It has been recorded primarily in northern Karelian provinces. Singers have also speculated about the ending of the poem, and they have had differing opinions

Väinämöinen's departure is the finale of the *Kalevala*. Pictured is Herald Eelma's vision of this—the old sage leaves his kantele behind. (*Kalevala*, Eesti-Raamat, 1985; illustration by Herald Eelma)

about Väinämöinen's fate. According to Ontrei Malinen, Väinämöinen "disappeared for all time." Martiska Karjalainen related that Väinämöinen left "for the lower earth mother, the lower heavens."[26] In 1836, Outokka, a woman from Venehjärvi, told Cajan that "fire seethed in the water" at the mouth of the whirlpool.[27] This is why Cajan associated it with the undercurrent known as "the Maelström." In 1894, a blind woman from Venehjärvi named Hoto wondered if it was true that Väinämöinen had been hurled into the whirlpool and whether he was still there.[28] In 1872, Ohvo Homani of Vuonninen told Borenius, "It's there our Väinämöinen's gone." "Although it's said he'll yet come, that he yet lives."[29] This view encompasses the concept that Väinämöinen is among those messiahs who return, one of the deities who never die.

The recorded variants of the rune differ a bit in their details. Lönnrot has added the subject matter of Marjatta and the lingonberry to the rune, while the boy judged by Väinämöinen is most frequently interpreted to be the child Jesus. Here the child's speech is long and detailed. It cites two specific crimes which stain Väinämöinen's character: "You borrowed your mother's child / To save your own head" and "Lured young maidens / Beneath the deep waves." Different specific accusations are found in other variants. In most of them, the child accuses Väinämöinen of incest: "For you seduced your own mother; on the sea rocks on the shore."[30]

There are two parts to the rune "Väinämöinen's Judgment": (1) the threat to cast out the child when its father refuses to speak up and give him a name, which is followed by the child judging his father. Väinämöinen is declared to be the father; and (2) acknowledgment of the accusation and Väinämöinen's de-

parture, resignation, and death. Many other runes also tell of child abandonment. Lönnrot has joined this motif to the mythical, voluntary departure of
the old sage, which is characteristic of Arctic culture.

Lönnrot situated the poem about Marjatta's son at the end of the *Old Kalevala*. In this version, Marjatta bears a son whom the pastor, Virokannas, comes
to baptize. The judge is the sage Väinämöinen, who orders the child killed.
The boy points out the injustice of Väinämöinen's verdict and is baptized.
Väinämöinen is angered and disappears from the cosmos.

> Chanted for the last time,
> chanted a copper boat,
> chanted an iron-bottomed craft,
> glided down the rapids,
> in a brass boat,
> in a copper craft,
> to the upper reaches of the earth,
> to the lower reaches of the heavens.
> Went there with his craft,
> disappeared with his boat,
> he left the kantele behind,
> an eternal joy for Finland,
> grand songs for his children.[31]

Thus the cosmic drama ends with Väinämöinen's departure. The Finnish people are left the child and the kantele as symbols of the Christian faith and hope
for the future of their own culture. Lönnrot put this poem in the same place
in the *New Kalevala*, although that version was somewhat augmented. He interpreted the rune as signifying the victory of Christianity over paganism.[32] It
was an appropriate conclusion for that period of antiquity which Lönnrot saw
the *Kalevala* primarily as depicting. The child was Marjatta's (St. Mary's) son,
thus providing a link with the birth of Christ. Based on his work with the rune
"Luojan Virsi" (The Messiah), Lönnrot interpreted the fundamental theme of
the rune to be the birth of Christ.

Lönnrot's hypothesis that this rune was derived from the transitional period
between paganism and Christianity can be seen as quite apt. There exists no
other rune in ancient Finnish poetry which would have been as well suited
for describing the end of the "pagan" era in Finnish history and the transition
to Christianity. The basic theme of "Väinämöinen's Judgment" can be fixed in
historical time: abandonment was decreed to be a criminal act during the missionary period of Christianity and the ordeal became a part of medieval legal
processes. The poem is related to the early missionary period of Christianity,
at the end of the medieval period.[33]

The Christian religion had decreed the abandonment of a child to be a criminal act. Väinämöinen judges Marjatta's son, who is Christ. This is the marrow
of the cosmogonic drama developed by Lönnrot, which is the finale of the entire epic. Thus "Väinämöinen's Judgment" is a mythical rune. Its basic subject

matter can be fixed in historical time: abandonment was decreed to be a criminal act during the missionary period of Christianity, and the ordeal or judgment of God was a common medieval legal process. A similar ordeal, such as a trial by water, blood, or the bearing of irons, was undoubtedly also used in ancient Finnish legal processes, and is described in folk legends.

A COSMOGONIC EPIC

Myths are central to the religions of the world. They are usually held sacred in their cultures and considered true explanations of the origins of the cosmos as well as events related to the genesis of culture. They relate in detail how the world, humans, the animal kingdom, and central elements of culture were created, thus establishing a world order. They are often incorporated into the present by means of rituals. In myths, religions have offered provocatively different answers to people's questions of "why." Finnish mythical runes describe the actions of early gods and culture heroes. They depict the origins of the world and its various phenomena and explain why things now are as they are. Some myths were part of a drama on which specific rituals were based. The relationship of preliterate, mythical runes to rituals became obscured as these runes were passed down through generations of singers. The mythical tales of the Proto-Finns have been absorbed into and united with the subject matter of later poetry, as well as other modes of presentation.

The oldest elements of Finnish runic poetry are tales about the bird of the air, from whose egg the heavens, earth, sun, moon, and stars were born; a gigantic figure which milled the sea bottom into shoals and lake bottoms into fish hollows; the first spark and how it was freed from the pike's belly; the Great Oak; the birth of the bear and elk; the journey of the first shaman to Tuonela, etc. This tradition was also being supplemented with new myths which, for example, told of the origin of iron, the carving of the boat, and the creation of the five-stringed kantele. All these narratives found a place in the *Kalevala*, which has been characterized as a mythical epic of "origins." In its fundamental structure, the *Kalevala* strives to be a cosmogonic epic.

It is not by chance that the *Kalevala* begins with the creation of the world and ends with the destruction of the deity, Väinämöinen. Lönnrot was already pondering the question on December 3, 1833: "Väinämöinen's end is extraordinary. As confused and incomplete as this rune is, it is nevertheless apparent that it signifies the coming of Christianity and that the boy himself is probably the Redeemer and Marjatta is the Virgin Mary."[34] In this manner, Lönnrot formed a structure which also corresponded to the linear world view of Christianity. Like the Bible, the *Kalevala* begins with the creation of the cosmos. At its conclusion, Väinämöinen departs into the vortex of a whirlpool. The *Kalevala* presents a unified interpretation of the history of the world, depicting it from creation to the destruction of the god.

Pekka Ervast (1875-1934) was so greatly enthused by the *Kalevala* as a sacred work that, based on ideas drawn from theosophy, anthroposophy, and the *Kalevala*, he formed a concept of the ancient religion of the Finns. Ervast's teachings are followed to this day by a religious group called the Ruusuristi (Rosicrucians). (Finnish National Board of Antiquities)

In his plot structure, Lönnrot avoided depicting the end of the world, the Christian eschatological climax, by ending the epic with the rune discussed above. The ending of the *Kalevala* depicts the victory of the Christian faith over the pre-Christian religion of the ancient Finns. As a consequence, the epic was given a Christian veneer despite the fact that its myths are derived from ancient pagan religion. The end result was that the pre-Christian myths in the *Kalevala* were arranged according to the Christian linear concept of time and history. In the Christian world view, there is one sole world and everyone lives but once. Time is seen as the segment of a line with a beginning and an end point. God creates the world, but then withdraws to appear again during the eschatological events which end the world. However, the world view of those rune singers who did not believe in the destruction of Väinämöinen was in direct conflict with the linearity of the *Kalevala*. The structure of the epic as it was constructed by Lönnrot was fundamentally western and Christian, while the world view of the rune singers was cyclic.

THE *KALEVALA* AS A SACRED BOOK

The *Kalevala* has played a central role in the Anthroposophical Society founded by Rudolf Steiner, which was derived from the Theosophical movement. On April 9, 1912, Steiner lectured on national epics in Helsinki, focusing in particular on the *Kalevala*. He repeated the basic tenets of this speech on November 9, 1914, at the outbreak of the First World War. From that point on, as Hans Fromm has shown, the *Kalevala* has been included in the body of mystical, exegetic texts by the Anthroposophists.[35]

The spiritual science of Anthroposophism is based on the premise that through the ages the course of history has distorted ancient archetypes. It is believed, however, that insight achieved through training can reveal those original concepts again. According to Steiner, "Spiritual science makes fully comprehensible that which is most sacred in this people [the Finns] and which is revived anew when people become familiar with the *Kalevala*. The *Kalevala* will then come alive throughout the cultured world." In Steiner's opinion, the three heroes of the *Kalevala* at the conclusion of the Sampo journey express three component levels of the soul: Väinämöinen, the soul of feeling; Ilmarinen, the soul of intelligence; and Lemminkäinen, the soul of knowledge. Lemminkäinen's opponent, the old man of Ulappala, symbolizes a mocking, critical earthly intellect.[36] An example of the enthusiasm such ideas inspired toward the *Kalevala* is given below in verses from Kersti Bergroth's poem "Väinämöisen paluu" (The return of Väinämöinen). This poem was published in "Antroposofilehti" (The Anthroposophical paper) in February 1931.

> Can one not yet distinguish the voice,
> The distant voice of our future hero,
> The call of Väinämöinen's kantele?
> Presentiment ever promised
> The coming of a new prince,
> Proud, unique, beloved of our time
>
> Is he, perhaps, already near,
> The secret hero of our time,
> The unknown hero?

Like Steiner, the well-known Finnish Anthroposophical writer Pekka Ervast also wished to revive the *Kalevala*. Having left the Theosophical and Anthroposophical societies, Ervast founded the Ruusuristi (Rosicrucian; "Rosenkreutz" in German) organization. His view of the *Kalevala* is stated in his book *Kalevalan avain* (Key to the *Kalevala*), published in 1916. In criticizing the Finnish *Kalevala* scholarship produced by the historical-geographic school, Ervast states: "Nothing has been lost, for nothing has yet even been discovered. Even scholarly accomplishments are not yet at an end. Further observations and discoveries will be made which will refute current conclusions. But what of them!

The real worth of the *Kalevala* lies elsewhere. Its true worth is in its own secret content."[37] According to Ervast, this "secret content" is to be found by approaching the *Kalevala* as a sacred text:

> If the *Kalevala* had existed as such during pagan times, in what esteem would the Finnish folk have held it? Would not the folk have seen themselves reflected therein, seen the best of their efforts, their most eternal selves? Would not the folk have sought consolation and advice from the *Kalevala* for their mind, joy for their heart, peace for their consciences? Undoubtedly. The *Kalevala* would have been a Bible for them, a sacred book. And if it would have been so then, why couldn't we take the same position now? Why couldn't we approach the *Kalevala* now as a sacred book?[38]

According to Ervast, the suitors in the Sampo sequence represent divine evolutionary forces which were attempting to cultivate the human soul. Väinämöinen represents will, Ilmarinen intelligence, and Lemminkäinen feeling. The Sampo is "that secret wisdom which mankind's original sages brought with them from elsewhere."[39] According to this interpretation, the struggle over the Sampo is a striving for knowledge and power, or the possession of "true magic." Ervast saw no conflict between the *Kalevala* and Christianity. Like Steiner, he saw both as part of mankind's spiritual development.

> Väinämöinen's return to the Finnish people has meant the revival of old memories, the forging of a new Sampo, etc. The formal task has already been partially completed [the collecting of the *Kalevala*]. It is now the task of the Finnish people to bring the ancient Väinämöinen spirit and wisdom to life again and to assimilate it into the consciousness educated and enlightened by the present-day Christian faith.[40]

On the anniversary of the *Kalevala* in 1985, the Anthroposophists' interpretation of the epic was represented by newly completed translations and numerous *Kalevala* seminars, including some held in continental Europe. There was also a theatrical adaptation of the *Kalevala* presented at the Bomba House in northern Karelia at Nurmes. From the Anthroposophical view, the *Kalevala* is regarded as a sacred book of universal, all-encompassing import.[41]

CHAPTER
8

WORLD VIEW
OF THE *KALEVALA*

MYTHICAL AND HISTORICAL TIME

There is always a difference between reality as depicted in runes and the reality of the singers. Thus, for example, although firearms have long been used to slay bears, in runes this is always described as being done with a bow and arrow. Apparently encouraged by such observations, Lönnrot set out to depict the ethnography of the ancient Finnish way of life. The customs and practices sung of in the runes, which often seemed poorly suited to the present, were perhaps more relevant to the earlier period envisioned by Lönnrot as he was creating the *Kalevala*. The crucial difference between historical and mythical interpretation is related to the comprehension of time. Historical time is linear, continuous, and without return, while mythical time is cyclical and repetitive. It encompasses and unites two temporal dimensions: original time and the present.[1]

A myth is a covenant of the world order. It is invoked to establish rules of conduct, social institutions, moral codes, and systems of norms as well as to ensure the efficacy of religious ritual and the sanctity of the cult. The proper environment for myth is ritual. Ritual presentation of myth is an affirmation of the world order. By imitation of events illustrative of the sacred, the world is prevented from falling into chaos. For a religious person and his or her social community, the events related in myths are sacred and true. A myth is part of an accepted, internalized world view. According to this interpretation, history is concerned with profane time, which myth actually destroys and replaces with sacred time. Thus many myths can be characterized as "sacred history."[2]

In order to endure the stress of historical events, a person may turn to mythical time, holding as actual and true only that for which a prototype exists in the events of the vast beginning. By means of these models of the vast beginning and the concepts which are brought into the present through the aid of ritual, narrative, or symbol, a person acquires both knowledge and a strategy for action. In this way, everyday events are translated into the language of myth and transferred into mythical time, which replaces profane time. Myths are of a more durable nature than their ritual enactments. The thinking process inherent in a particular myth may survive for a long period, divorced from actual religious function. Words and appellations may, at times, preserve religious content dating back thousands of years.

This is also of relevance to runic poetry. In the Kalevala runes, Väinämöinen, Ilmarinen, and Lemminkäinen have many roles. They appear as mythical gods of creation and culture heroes, as well as prototypes of the first shamans, healers, and sages. Information which has survived about the ritual use of folklore indicates that, despite general secularization of the function of the runes and their diminished significance in ritual contexts, mythical time, as described in the runes, was still a powerful experiential factor during the nineteenth century. This was particularly true for specialists in folk religion, such as healers and sages.

On a general level, Lönnrot was able to sharply distinguish between the world of the runes, along with the traditions which might be related to them, and living religion. Considering his own cognitive balance and the social pressure exerted on him by his contemporaries, this was quite natural. Lönnrot found it necessary to establish the legitimacy and cultural appropriateness of the Kalevala for both himself and others. His solution was to create a unified time span which encompassed, first, the mythical prehistory of the ancient Finns (expressed by the Kalevala), followed by the historical period which began with the coming of the Christian religion at the end of the epic. This was a conscious decision made by Lönnrot. He finally opted for the historical interpretation in spite of his awareness that runes often depicted the mythical time which became manifest in ritual drama.

WHERE ARE THE KALEVALA HEATHS?

In addition to the concept of time, it was also necessary for Lönnrot to define the spatial parameters of the epic. What is the background of the concept "Kalevala"? After a great deal of thought, Lönnrot gave the epic a title. Why was Kalevala specifically decided on? In his preface to the Old Kalevala, Lönnrot gave the following explanation for his decision:

> Although it is no longer possible to get any clarification about them, I nevertheless believe that Kaleva is much older than Väinämöinen, Ilmarinen, and the other heroes named. I would say, therefore, that perhaps he was the one who first led the Finns to these regions. And because the places where his descendants settled appear to have been referred to by the name Kalevala [Kaleva's Region], which may have been the common designation for such specific locations as Väinölä [Väinö's Region] Ilma [Sky], Utuniemi [Misty Headland], Terhensaari [Fog Island], Suomela [Finland], Kautoniemi [Kauto Headland],

Päivilä [the Sun's Region] Vuojela [Gotland], Luotola [Rocky Island], Jumalisten [the Region of the Gods], and so on, I have therefore titled this collection of poems *Kalevala* as well. A title it had to be given, and in accordance with this explanation, most of the action took place in Kalevala.[3]

Lönnrot considered Kalevala to be a historical place, one which was simultaneously shrouded in prehistoric mythology. However, not until the dictionary he completed as an old man in 1880 did he explicitly state that the word "Kalevala" in fact had two meanings: "1. The home of the sons of Kaleva, the land of the people of Kaleva. 2. The Finnish national epic." In this same work, Lönnrot defined Kaleva as the father of the giants. He defined Kalevainen as a descendant of Kaleva and one of the Kaleva people, which also included Kalevan poika (Kaleva's son) and Kalevatar (Kaleva's daughter).[4] This mythical depiction of the genealogy of the Kaleva people was augmented and continued to grow more historical in nature from the *Old Kalevala* to the *New*, as the material of Europaeus and other rune collectors became available to Lönnrot. The central figure in these runes was Kullervo, who was closely related to the Estonian tradition of the gigantic Kalevipoeg (son of Kalev). Folklore about Kalevipoeg was found on the southern shores of the Gulf of Finland and was largely a prose tradition. It was later compiled into the Estonian epic *Kalevipoeg*.[5]

Thus Kalevala, its people and heaths, were part of Lönnrot's mytho-historical vision of Finnish prehistory. Without this vision, the *Kalevala*, in its entirety, would not have come into existence. In his preface to the *Old Kalevala*, Lönnrot gave the following assessment of this subject matter:

The people to which Väinämöinen, Ilmarinen, and Lemminkäinen belong, I have named the people of Kaleva. But lest I be criticized for having erred in this designation, since many consider the name Kaleva to be nearly equivalent to Hiisi [Demon] and Lempo [Devil], let me perhaps state my idea more clearly. It appears to me that Kaleva, of whom we know nothing at present, was the most ancient Finnish hero. It may have been he who first settled permanently on the Finnish peninsula and whose kin then diffused throughout the land. The places where Väinämöinen and the others lived are often called Kalevala. Elsewhere, there is mention of Kaleva's heaths, burnt-over clearings, wells, dogs, cuckoos, and so on. Thus, for example, in an old Karelian song, a girl asks her suitor: "Did you go to Kalevala?" Suitor: "Yes, I went to Kalevala." Girl: "Did Kaleva's dogs bark on the Kalevala heaths?" Suitor: "They did bark, indeed, etc." Girl: "Did the cuckoos call on Kaleva's well-road (burnt-over clearings)?" Suitor: "They did call, indeed, etc." Girls: "Did Kaleva's maidens look out the windows of Kalevala?" Suitor: "They did look, indeed, etc." And because Kalevala is mentioned in connection with such charming matters as the courtship conversations between girls and boys, I would not consider it equivalent to Hiitola [the dwelling place of the demon] or Lempo. For when does one hear such things about those, Manala [the Netherworld] or Tuonela [the Realm of Death]?[6]

It is apparent that Lönnrot did not consider Kalevala to be a mythical place like Tuonela, Manala, or Hiitola. For him, it was a geographic location. Although shrouded in myths, Kalevala was a significant aspect of ancient Finnish prehistory as Lönnrot envisioned it. In their courtship conversations, its heroes were as red-blooded and human as young men and maidens. And it is these figures Lönnrot basically describes in the *Kalevala*, constructing the entire plot of the epic around a series of courtship dramas. Lönnrot believed that Kalevala, ancient Finland, had been located in Southwestern Finland, somewhere in the southwestern part of the country. In the initial twelve pages of Cajan's "History of Finland," which he published in *The Bee* as an introduction to pre–nineteenth century Finnish history, he basically relates that the *Kalevala* text is the section which describes Finland's prehistory.[7]

As a scholar of the Finnish language and a colleague of M. A. Castrén, Lönnrot had adopted the view that the origins of the Finns lay in the Ural Mountain region. In his Finnish history, he stated:

> Here, several thousand kilometers to the east-southeast of present day Fin-
> land, in the western regions of Asia, between the Ural and the Himalaya
> mountains, on the upper courses and tributaries of the Ob and Syr rivers, they
> would have had their extensive traditional dwelling areas, under the name of
> the Hun peoples, whose descendants, or at least kinfolk, were the future
> Huns, Hungarians, and Finns. Shortly before the birth of the Redeemer, the
> Finns separated and moved northward, coerced by the Scythians and other
> peoples. After this, they lived for some time on the western side of the Ural
> Mountains, on the tributaries of the Volga and the Kama rivers, moving west
> and north from there until, at the end of the fourth century after the birth
> of the Redeemer, they appear to have reached their present areas of settle-
> ment.[8]

In Lönnrot's opinion, when the Finns reached Finland, they initially divided into two peoples, the Finns and the Lapps, who "even have a great divergence in their present day language, customs and life." With time, the Finns split again, into the Tavastians and the Karelians. Of these, "the Tavastians traveled and lived to the west, the Karelians to the east of each other." According to Lönnrot, the Lapps moved ever northward as these groups diffused throughout Finland.[9]

Lönnrot dates the origins of runic poetry to the period when "the Karelians had already separated from the Tavastians but nevertheless still dwelled in smaller areas, not as diffused as they are at the present time." According to him, the deeds of noted historical figures such as Väinämöinen and Ilmarinen which are described in the runes would have taken place in the areas where the Karelians and Tavastians slowly began to settle when they reached Finland, and also gradually diffused westward across the country. Lönnrot described the initial stages of this diffusion:

The Tavastians settled to the west of the Kymi River and Lake Päijänne, along the Gulf of Finland and the Gulf of Bothnia up to the borders of Ostrobothnia, whereas the Karelians occupied the eastern half of the country, spreading from there to Ostrobothnia under the name Kainulainen. From there, they expanded to the other side of the Tornio River, that is, to Sweden, on the western side of the Gulf of Bothnia. There, however, they were again thwarted by the Swedes, namely, those Finns who had not been assimilated by the Swedes to such an extent that they eventually even forgot their kin name. Several hundred years later, the land between the Tavastians and the Karelians was still primarily desolate, or occupied by migrating Lapps.[10]

Scholars who have adopted Lönnrot's historical viewpoint since that time have measured their prowess by advocating either the westernness or easternness of the *Kalevala*. Clearly, there are runes with western origins in Finnish folk poetry such as "The Death of Elina" and the Ritvala Whitsuntide verses, but many more of them seem to have originated in the east.

In the final analysis, the Kalevala heaths are mythical places mirrored in Lönnrot's imagination. As envisaged by him, they belong to the great past of the ancient Finns, when the sons of Kaleva were in Finland battling the northern folk of Pohjola. It has not been possible to locate them anywhere on the Gulf of Bothnia, the Gulf of Finland, or Lake Ladoga, in White Sea Karelia, or on the islands of the Baltic Sea, although historical *Kalevala* scholarship has attempted to do so for a century and a half.[11]

For Lönnrot, it was important to provide the *Kalevala* with a physical location in order to maintain the consistency of his historical interpretation. Another question is why the location of the runes has remained so important a question in Finland: On the one hand, the reason may lie in the methodology of the so-called Finnish or historical-geographic approach to the study of folklore. On the other hand, however, it is also an issue which concerns the self-identity of the scholars themselves.[12] They have frequently not been objective in their hypotheses about where the Kalevala heaths were located. During some periods, the predominant tendency has been to see the roots of the national epic in the east, and during other periods, the tendency has been to see its roots in the west. Scholars' views on this issue have often been influenced by where their own roots lie, and it has not always sufficed that the *Kalevala* originated in Finland or among Finnish-speaking peoples.

GODS OR HUMANS?

Another question related to that of the Kalevala heaths and present throughout the *Kalevala* is: Who were the heroes of the *Kalevala*? Were they gods or humans? This question intrigued Lönnrot, and he already discussed it in the preface to the *Old Kalevala*. Who were Väinämöinen, Ilmarinen, and Lemminkäinen, the folk of Kalevala and the sons of Kaleva?

In folk legends today even Kaleva's sons have two kinds of reputation. Some consider them evil giants, others refer to them as Väinämöinen, Ilmarinen, Lemminkäinen, Joukahainen, Kihavanskoinen, Liekkiö, Kullervo and so on, of whom nothing particularly bad is said, if we exclude Kullervo, the last named, who was even banished from his home for that reason. . . . In any case, it is always said that there were twelve of them. Now, whether Väinämöinen was a first-generation son of Kaleva or of some succeeding generation, that we cannot judge. However, I would think he was of some latter generation, for as a first-generation son, he and Ilmarinen would have been brothers. This does not seem to have been the case, although in places Väinämöinen does refer to Ilmarinen as his brother and a child of his mother. In the same manner, even Lemminkäinen would become Väinämöinen's brother, but the latter never calls him that, referring to him now and then only as his greatest friend. Even if they are of a later generation, there are grounds for their being called Kaleva's sons; the Jews are still called the children of Abraham and Israel. From this it would also be understandable how Kullervo, who is specifically called Kaleva's son (that is, descendant), could be sold to Ilmarinen, another son of Kaleva. I can also mention that I have heard some people identify Antero Vipunen with Kaleva himself, as is even stated in one rune.[13]

During this phase, Lönnrot was still writing an epical work on Finnish "mythology," based on Ganander's model. His problem lay in the fact that he found few epical runes about the supreme deities he hypothesized. He eventually concluded that Väinämöinen, as a central figure, had overshadowed the others.

I suppose people sing about Väinämöinen what was sung in the name of others long ago, for who could prevent it? What is attributed to him with regard to the creation of the world, moon, sun, and stars may in the past have been told of some other deity, and when even the names of these deities were forgotten, everything was attributed to Väinämöinen. Why have Antero Vipunen, Kaleva, and the supreme deity, Ukko, been left almost entirely unpoetized . . . ?[14]

A comparison between the *Old Kalevala* and the *New* shows that, in his depiction of ancient pre-Christian Finnish history, Lönnrot strove to delete Christian subject matter from the runes. He also made the deities increasingly more human. A number of divine acts, including Väinämöinen's role as creator, were eliminated. Lemminkäinen became a womanizer, a Finnish Don Juan, and the figure of Ilmarinen was also given more human dimensions. Correspondingly, the Mistress of Pohjola and her daughter, who became Ilmarinen's ill-fated wife, as well as Aino and Marjatta, figures created by Lönnrot from various runes, were brought down to earth. In the *New Kalevala*, Kullervo became so human a figure that it was easy for Finnish readers to identify with him.

AN ANCIENT FINNISH OLYMPUS OR THE
KINGDOM OF ONE GOD?

In his preface to the *Old Kalevala*, Lönnrot makes a strong statement: "It is always said that there were twelve of them." Following in the footsteps of Agricola, Lönnrot resolutely sought an ancient Olympus which was to include twelve names as did the tribes of Israel, the pantheons of the Romans, Greeks, Germans, and Scandinavians and Agricola's twelve deities of Tavastia and Karelia. Although the rune texts gave him no basis for assuming that the Finnish heroes were all brothers, as were the sons of Jacob, he nevertheless believed there should be twelve of them. For this reason, he also included Kihavanskoinen and Liekkiö, although they were never mentioned in the runes. He himself placed Antero Vipunen, the long-dead shaman to whom Väinämöinen went for advice, on a par with Kaleva, the primordial progenitor. Lönnrot did, in fact, find an ancient Finnish Olympus (as well as a hierarchical, genealogical structure to support it) because he wished to find it. He actively sought evidence for the concept that one deity, higher than the rest, was present in this Olympus. Based on his scholarship, Lönnrot came to the conclusion that Ukko was to be the supreme deity, whereas Väinämöinen was to be a historical hero:

If, in these runes, Väinämöinen has sometimes been lowered from his former stature as a deity, there is of course nothing I can do about it. I have had to publish them as I received them, without regard to whether Väinämöinen is considered a god or not. From time immemorial, we have been accustomed to considering him a god of our forefathers, an esteem in which they do not seem to have held him, viewing him, rather, as a powerful, very wise hero. Often he himself prays to the supreme deity, Ukko, for help, and thus acknowledges with his own lips who was the god. Even without divinity, Väinämöinen has name and honor, and it may be better for anyone to be a high-minded peasant than a bad lord, better a wise human being than a wooden god. And even now, if the folk in those regions where the memory of Väinämöinen best lives are asked who Väinämöinen was, they immediately respond as follows: "He was a memorable hero, among the first of our forefathers, and a famed singer." Whereas if you ask them whom they consider to be their gods, most often they respond that it is Ukko, who created the heavens and the earth, that they pray to. And I don't doubt that, before the Christian doctrine, our forefathers had knowledge of one sole "jumala" [god] who was sometimes served using his present name, sometimes using the name Ukko or "Luoja" [Creator], and I don't consider it a great stupidity on their part if they were not so clever in searching out a great pantheon of gods for themselves, like some other ancient peoples.

In these runes, Väinämöinen is primarily referred to as earnest, wise, forward looking, seeking good for future generations, a great sage, all-powerful in song and music, and a hero of Finland. Other than this, he is always referred to as old, although his age alone may not have impeded him so greatly in his courtings.[15]

Not everyone was prepared to agree with this radical view that Väinämöinen was a historical hero and not a deity, and that it was Ukko who was the supreme deity. As a consequence, Lönnrot was forced to reexamine his assertions. A few years later, in the introduction to "Supplement to the *Old Kalevala*," he wrote: "Regrettably, it has been necessary for me to make statements about Väinämöinen which do not raise his former stature, but rather lower it. He has been considered the supreme deity of the Finnish people since time immemorial, but in these runes it is often stated that, in a difficult situation, he sought aid from Ukko the creator."[16]

As has previously been shown, the *Kalevala* was Lönnrot's own "mythology." It was augmented as the scholar's own knowledge increased and his world view changed. Once again, references to this evolution are found in the articles he wrote during the period between the two editions of the *Kalevala*. In January of 1836, Lönnrot published an article entitled "Muinelmia" (Antiquities) in his periodical *The Bee*. In it he discussed the concept of primitive monotheism, which he adopted after having broadly familiarized himself with the religio-historical and cultural scholarship of his time. He adopted a theory quite compatible with the Christian world view. According to this interpretation, mankind originally had knowledge of one god, but this knowledge had been lost by numerous peoples, including the ancient Finns.[17]

In Lönnrot's opinion, the primordial religion of the Finns had been monotheistic. After becoming polytheistic, however, they had gradually regained their lost knowledge. Evidence to support Lönnrot's theory about Ukko's position lay in concepts related to thunder and lightning. Ukko was described as the deity of the celestial sphere, the god of thunder (ukkonen), the god of air and the one who supported the bright dome of the world. Because Lönnrot was well aware that there was more than one deity referred to in Finnish mythology, it was necessary for him to expand this monotheistic system into a hierarchy of deities and cultural heroes. Because the Supreme Deity had not had the time to create everything himself, concepts of lesser deities had developed. Thus Lönnrot, like Agricola, envisaged a Finnish Olympus, which included a great number of lesser deities: Tapio (forest spirit), Ahti (water spirit), Lempi (erotic love), and Hiisi (demon), Tuoni and Kalma (concepts for death), Mielikki (female forest ruler), the Ogresses, Otava (the Big Dipper, the Great Bear in Finnish mythology), and goddesses of Nature, the Moon, the Sun, the Wind, Summer, the South, and the Netherworld. It is worthy of note that this Olympus included many female deities.[18]

According to Lönnrot, the highest deity in the Finnish Olympus was Ukko. Even at this early stage, Lönnrot considered Kaleva, Väinämöinen, Ilmarinen, Lemminkäinen, and Joukahainen to be clearly differentiated from deities and wrote: "Sometimes, perhaps, they are considered to be on the level of a deity; for us they are but valiant heroes of the ancient Finns."[19] As a proponent of the proto-monotheistic theory, Lönnrot also incorporated it into his view of ancient Finnish mythology, which explains Ukko's rise in stature and Väinämöinen's loss of stature from the *Old Kalevala* to the *New*. The hierarchy of the other deities was also structured in relationship to Ukko:

> Leaving aside here what we have said about Kaleva and his sons, we ask how has Ilmarinen come to be considered the god of wind, air, and even lightning? It is hardly possible to find a single instance in the runes which would give even the slightest support for this idea. It appears that, because of his name, he was made god of wind and air, and as a result of his forging, even of fire. The latter may also be derived from the fact that he once cast lightning in the sky with Väinämöinen. He is not this way in the runes, however. Wind was prayed for only from Ukko, who was ruler of the wind as well as all else, and it was Ilmarinen, more than the others, who suffered from the winds when returning from Pohjola. What of it that in forging the Sampo he got the winds blowing; that matter can well be explained in another way. There is no need to make him god of the winds because of it. And if he had been the god of the air, then Väinämöinen could hardly have forced him to Pohjola in the air against his will, and it was Väinämöinen, not Ilmarinen, who did the conjuring against the Old Crone of the North when she threatened to set the rains, sleet, and cold to ruin what the Sampo had set growing.[20]

In Lönnrot's mind, Ilmarinen was a human figure:

> According to the runes, Ilmarinen was nothing more than a splendid iron-, copper-, silver-, and goldsmith. Other than that, whenever encountered, he was an earnest, grave, and honest man, energetic in his work, seldom having contact with others. And it is indeed an honor to him that he need no longer be embellished as a wind god.[21]

In Lönnrot's opinion, religions could be ranked on the basis of their knowledge of one sole god. The highest form of religion was Christianity. Lönnrot interpreted the ancient religion of the Finns to be a kind of "good paganism," which had had a childlike presentiment of the existence of one sole deity. The coming of the Christian religion completed this evolution in Finnish religion, and is specifically referred to in the final poem of the *Kalevala*. Lönnrot expressly wished to see the main figures in the *Kalevala* as historical. The epic did not extol a living, pagan religion. At most, it depicted the Finns' shift to Christianity which, according to this interpretation, had already occurred at the confluence of prehistory and history.

THE ORIGIN AND BASIS OF CULTURE

In the *Kalevala*, a complex of myths explains substantial elements of the Finnish economic and social order as well as Finnish culture. The background of this complex is, of course, runic poetry, which can be linked to the more ancient life and culture of the Uralic, Finno-Ugric, or Proto-Finnic peoples during various stages of their history. Mythic and ritual tradition related to hunting and agrarian cultures is particularly stratified. But myths cannot be dated by simply stating that the oldest strata are derived from hunting and fishing culture, and the later strata solely from agrarian culture. Rather, it is quite probable that the forefathers of the Finns practiced a mixed economy, as is characteristic of cultures in the Arctic and sub-Arctic which seek to minimize the risks inherent in their environment by utilizing diverse means of livelihood. For the Finns, such a combined economy incorporated hunting, fishing, keeping small herds, and trade, as well as slash-and-burn agriculture. For a long period, they were either partially or entirely mobile, nomadic or seminomadic, and occupied relatively broad areas covered by the yearly migration of herds.

Elk and bear mythology clearly derives from hunting culture, whereas the runes about sowing, as well as those about the creation of barley and beer found at the beginning of the *Kalevala* (Poem 2), are myths derived from agrarian culture. "The Origin of Iron," "The Hewing of the Boat," "The Origin of the Kantele," and "The Great Ox" are examples of the mythology of a technologically more advanced culture. The rune about the Great Ox, which in the *New Kalevala* is found in the section describing the wedding at Pohjola, is reminiscent of the rune about the Great Oak. In Matti Kuusi's opinion, "The Great Ox" was created to be sung either at the initial or final celebrations of the season (planting-harvesting).[22] Its origins may lie in the Mithraism of Persia and Byzantium. Karelian performances of this rite took place until World War II at the Mantsi Island Ox Festival on Lake Ladoga.

The rune about the origin of fire is a cult myth. When those aspects of it derived from the Christian period are eliminated, we are left with the pan-Arctic fire myth. The oldest theme found in this rune concerns spark-bearing animals, which in the case of the Finns are fish. According to this myth, a spark of fire jumps from the Maiden of the Air and falls into the water to be swallowed by fish. Subsequently, Väinämöinen and Ilmarinen go fishing for the pike which has swallowed the fire. This myth portrayed the lighting of the first fire, and it was used in numerous rituals along with ancient techniques of friction for starting a fire.[23]

The Sampo cycle is of particular interest as a myth about the origin of culture. Although the Sampo is frequently mentioned in the runes, it is never specifically described. However, it seems to connote thriving and prosperity.[24] Folk singers' interpretations of the Sampo have varied, and in some cases they have not had a specific image of what it meant. Arhippa Perttunen interpreted the Sampo as a mill; Maija Turpoinen interpreted it as an eagle; the singers at Ilomantsi saw it as a boat.[25] Perhaps its meaning for folk singers is best approximated by examining what little information has survived about use of the Sampo runes in ritual. Jyrkini Iivana, of the Malinen family, made the following statement to Kaarle Krohn in 1881: "During spring and autumn sowing, first the sowing words were sung, then the song about the forging and theft of the Sampo, as well as the chase by the Mistress of Pohjola. The ending showed how Väinämöinen did away with the Mistress of Pohjola by sending her out into the cold."[26]

A closer examination of the final verses of "The Theft of the Sampo," as sung by Ontrei Malinen in 1825 and 1833, clearly indicates that the rune was actually sung in rituals to aid the growth of grain:

(When Väinämöinen proposes to the Mistress of Pohjola, who is pursuing him and his men, that they share the Sampo, she responds:)

"I'll not share the Sampo,
inspect the bright dome."
Thus old Väinämöinen
sifted mist with a sifter,
shifted across the fog,
himself said these words:
"Hither plowing, hither sowing,
hither all kinds of grain,
hither moons, hither suns,
to wretched Ostrobothnia,
to Finland's vast spaces."

(The Mistress of Pohjola drowns the Sampo in order to enrich the sea.)

Said the Mistress of Pohjola:
"I'll try a bit of magic
on your plowing, sowing:
rain down ice of iron,
of steel let it fall."
Said old Väinämöinen:
"Let ice of iron fall,
of steel be cast down,
at the end of Pohjola's lane,
on the shoulders of Saviharju [Clay Hill]."[27]

Kuusi argues that it may be possible to interpret the Sampo as a sacred fertility statue, such as a guardian of the harvest.[28]

Scholars have been interpreting the nature and origins of the Sampo since the beginning of the nineteenth century. Grimm saw it as a symbol of the morning gleam which continually occurs on the horizon.[29] For Lönnrot and Kaarle Krohn, it was a statue depicting a deity.[30] Under various circumstances, however, Lönnrot did present other interpretations of the Sampo. Justifiably, he considered it ambiguous, as it was depicted in the *Kalevala*: "The Sampo is as yet an unexplained, wondrous object which brought good fortune in providing life's necessities." In addition to this interpretation, Lönnrot also put forth the more abstract idea that the Sampo was a metaphor "for human civilization and culture."[31] It is easy to make a connection between this latter interpretation and the national identity then being sought by Finland: Seen in this light, the Sampo could also have been understood as a metaphor for the emerging Finnish culture.

LIGHT FROM THE SKY AND THE TREE OF LIFE

What was the structure of the world as experienced by the ancient Finns? This question has been pondered by Uno Harva, a pioneer in the Finnish study of comparative religion:

> When the human eye views the earth encompassed by the sky, the idea easily develops that the outer curve of the earth is circular in shape. At the same time, it appears as if the heavens form a mighty dome arching over the earth. The Finns named this dome, visible above the earth, "taivaankansi" (dome of the heavens). Inscribed with bright stars, it was also called "kirjokansi" (the bright dome).[32]

The mythical rune "Forger of The Heavens" (*New Kalevala* 7, 10) is related to a motif which in the *Kalevala* is the heroic feat of the great smith and shaman Ilmarinen. "Can you forge the Sampo, embellish the bright dome?" the Mistress of Pohjola asks him.

The Finns, dwelling in the northern latitudes, have been greatly intrigued by what lies on the other side of the stars. Because there is considerable darkness at those latitudes for much of the year, it is the night sky with its twinkling stars and flashing aurora borealis which is visible to them. A central myth in the ancient poetry relates how the lights of the heavens were freed or how the mythical Tree of Life, the Great Oak, was felled, enabling the sun to shine again and the moon to gleam.

The description of the creation of the world continues in Poem 2 of the *New Kalevala*. Sampsa Pellervoinen is called on to plow and sow the fields and forests. This rune, which is based on an international myth, can be related to the annual rituals of an agrarian society: it is a celebration of summer's victory over winter. The rune about the Great Oak, which in the *Kalevala* is related to plowing and sowing, is one of the oldest and most interesting of the Finnish mythological runes. It includes the internationally known "Tree of the World" or "Tree of Life." Typically, an acorn planted by four maidens gives rise to an immense oak, which conceals the sun and moon and prevents "the clouds from flowing." In order to resolve this primeval crisis, someone is sought to fell it. Many unsuccessful attempts are made until finally a man as tall as a thumb rises from the sea and fells the oak.

Uno Harva, among others, conjectured that "The Great Oak" was a myth about the creation of the Milky Way. Seen from the ground, the Milky Way can be interpreted as a long, felled tree.[33] The Finnish folklorists V. J. Mansikka and Kaarle Krohn interpreted the ancient runes in a Christian light. In "The

"Oh-oh Smith Ilmarinen!
Now you created nonsense!
Gold doesn't shine as a moon,
Silver doesn't shine as a sun!"

In the northern latitudes, the dilemma of the change in seasons is symbolized by the annual disappearance of the sun, moon, and stars. This ancient myth is depicted by S. A. Keinänen. (Finnish National Board of Antiquities)

Great Oak," they saw the "Tree of Life" found in Paradise and Golgotha's Tree of the Cross.[34] However, the many northern Eurasian myths about the Tree of Life greatly predate Christian influences. Correspondences to the poem about the Great Oak are particularly abundant in eastern Asia, and the concept of the "Tree of the World" is one of the most essential elements in northern Eurasian shamanistic rituals. Like the image of the sun, the Saami "päivve," the Tree of the World, is often pictured at the center of shamanic drums.

In Matti Kuusi's opinion, most later versions of the "Great Oak Rune" are based on the "Beer-Froth Oak Rune," in which the function of the rune has been augmented by its use as a drinking song.[35] Poem 20 of the *New Kalevala* includes the creation of barley and beer, which has already been referred to in the first poem of the epic. The central role of barley and beer in ancient runes may also indicate another aspect of runic culture. The runes may not have been sung very often with two singers sitting "hand in hand, fingers entwined with fingers," as many scholars have conjectured.[36] Rather, they were probably sung with a beer stein held in one hand. The myth about barleycorn and the divine origin of beer itself may have provided inspiration for the singing process.

In ancient Finnish religion, the center of the heavens was considered to be the hub of the firmament. According to this concept, the bright dome of the heavens with its rotating stars was supported by the pillar of the world and revolved around the stationary North Star. The North Star, known also as the "Northern Nail," was in fact referred to as the "taivaantappi" (peg of the heavens) or "maailmantappi" (peg of the world). In 1658, the court at Isokyrö, Ostrobothnia, recorded a charm for fire which described how fire was cast on the dome of the heavens: "Where fire is cast, on the hinge of the heavens." Like the Saami, the forefathers of the Finns may have thought that if the hub of the sky gave way, the firmament would come crashing down and set the entire world afire. This would mean the destruction of everything. A Finnish proverb states that a person with a long life lived "as the pole of the world" and "as the pillar of the sky," and kept the world from collapsing. The Sampo poems have also been related to this concept. According to Uno Harva, for example, the theft of the Sampo depicts nothing less than the theft of the sky's pillar, which would result in the destruction of the world and its structures.[37]

Northern cultures typically conceive of the beginning of time as including a period of chaos when life was lived in darkness, without the sun or light, until this was set aright by a particular culture hero. Antti Aarne has interpreted the rune about the rescue of the sun symbolically. In his opinion, it depicted Christ's redemptive work. Martti Haavio later showed that the origins of this rune lay in ancient pre-Christian cosmogony. However, its style and form as found in the Kalevala show the influence of Lönnrot's Christian world view. Perhaps most striking is his concept of a relatively passive but all-powerful god, deus otiosus, under whose watch the actions of various cultural heroes and deities were depicted as taking place. In Lönnrot's New Kalevala, this role is held by Ukko, the supreme god. His influence on the plot of the Kalevala, however, is limited.

THE BEAR: PRIMORDIAL FATHER DESCENDED FROM THE HEAVENS

In Finnish runes, subject matter particularly related to cosmogonic myths is found in the myths about hunting large game. Poem 28 of the Old Kalevala relates how Väinämöinen slays a bear and how the slaying is celebrated as a wedding feast. In the New Kalevala, Poem 46 joins the bear runes with the battle over the Sampo. Louhi, the Mistress of Pohjola, rouses a bear to attack

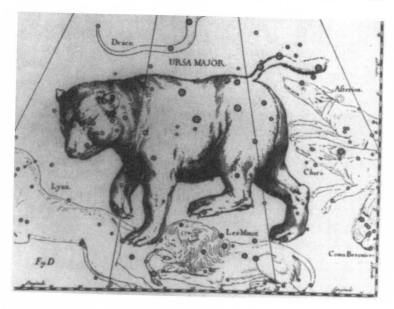

The feast to celebrate the slaying of a bear was actually a marriage ceremony in which the bear, having descended from the heavens, was conveyed back to its celestial origins. Often this ritual had a totemistic connection to a myth about primordial times, when a mythical coupling between the primordial mother and the animal worshipped by the people had taken place. It was from this relationship that the power and efficacy of those particular people was derived. The constellation Otava, the Great Bear (the Big Dipper), from Johannes Hevelius's work *Firmamentum sobiescanium* (1687).

Kalevala's herd. Väinämöinen and Ilmarinen go to slay it. The initial section of the poem describes the slaying of the bear, and this is followed by the wedding feast.

This is, in fact, quite an independent collection of runes, "karhulaulunäytelmä" (the bear song drama), as Lönnrot called it. He published a fifty-eight-verse version of these runes in *Helsingfors Morgonblad* (The Helsinki morning paper).[38] In the *Old Kalevala*, the bear, "king of the forest" and primordial father of the species, is slain, while in the *New Kalevala*, a bear is conjured up as part of a ritual struggle between shamans. In the *New Kalevala*, Lönnrot's poem is a multiverse epic unity composed of dialogue; the slain bear is brought into the main room for its funeral, which is actually a wedding. The bear is the honored guest at these festivities and is then sent on to its original birthplace in the heavens. In the words of the *Old Kalevala*:

The slaying of a bear during the winter of 1903 at Lake Luva in Olonets. (Finnish National Board of Antiquities)

> Bruin wasn't born on straw,
> nor on threshing-house chaff;
> it's there Bruin was born,
> sparse-fur raised,
> at the moon's, by the sun's
> on the Great Bear's shoulders,
> on the seven stars.
> Ukko, golden king,
> a ancient celestial god, that man.[39]

The feast to celebrate the slaying of a bear was an extensive, multiverse cult drama which was preserved in the hunting cultures of eastern and central Finland until the nineteenth century. Even during the twentieth century, it has been possible to record bear-slaying legends, festivals to celebrate the slaying of a bear, and bear-skull pines, on which the skull of a bear has been preserved.[40] From the branches of such a tree, it was believed that the soul of the bear could best attain its celestial home and return to earth. Relating the origins of the bear is an important component of this ancient poetry. The celestial origins of the bear were last sung of in Onega and Ladoga Karelia, as the herds were let out to pasture. The following verses are an example:

Where was Bruin born,
honey-paw shifted 'round?
There Bruin was born,
honey-paw shifted 'round:
at the moon's, at the sun's
on the Great Bear's shoulders.
Let down to the earth from there
in a golden cradle,
in a silver chain.[41]

In Matti Kuusi's opinion, "The Birth of the Bear" was originally the ritual text for the feast to celebrate the slaying of a bear. Only later was it also sung on departure for a bear hunt and in letting herds out to pasture. Central to this feast was ensuring good fortune with game. It is for this reason that bears were placated, and even a slain bear was honored.[42]

"The Birth of the Bear" is a mythical rune for which there are counterparts in prose narratives, myths, and tales throughout the Arctic and sub-Arctic northern Eurasia.[43] The myth of the bear may be related to Stone Age totemistic tradition. The bear is the totem animal of many northern peoples. It is a worshipped animal, a cult object, the symbol of tribe and family. Totemistic myths tell of the marital relationship between the primordial mother and the bear. Thus the bear ritual signifies the transferral of the bear to its kin. Martti Haavio discusses transference of the bear's "emuu" (mother), the primordial bear, to the Great Bear (Big Dipper) constellation, whence it returns again to earth.[44] The Skolt Saami were also familiar with a totemistic myth about the origins of their tribe and this may be the mythical basis for the bear ritual of eastern Finland as well. The fact that the eastern Finnish bear festival is performed as a wedding ceremony is also related to this. A young person from the village is presented to the bear as a bride or a bridegroom. The festival to celebrate the slaying of the bear was, in fact, a wedding ceremony through which the primordial father was born anew, simultaneously bequeathing his power and blessing on his descendants. Thus, the mythical bear was both the guardian of the lives of its animal kin and the primordial father of the tribe or clan which worshipped it as their totem.

In general, the bear was not hunted in White Sea Karelia, at least not for food. This has been interpreted as an indication that the bear was considered totemistic. Many norms of cleansing and taboos focus on this. There are, in fact, concepts related to the bear in old Finnish tradition which indicate that it was considered to be a shaman journeying in the form of the primordial father or bear.[45] Yet in the 1960s, Marina Takalo said that a bear could be a human being. "It looks like a person and sometimes also walks on two feet. A bear was once slain in White Sea Karelia, and there was a money belt under its hide. No doubt it was a person in the form of a bear."[46] This relates to the concept of a shaman wandering as a bear. On the other hand, the boundary between humans and animals, as well as that between humans and gods, is never rigid in tales and myths. Thus, in the conceptual world of the folk, an ecological balance exists between human beings and nature. For them, the bear is not a wild beast but "king of the forest."

MYTHICAL JOURNEYS TO POHJOLA AND THE LAND OF WOMEN

And what of the *Kalevala*'s Pohjola, to which the heroes of the epic journey one after the other for courtship and shamanic knowledge, as well as other purposes, and from which they eventually steal the Sampo? Poem 2 of the *Old Kalevala* relates:

> The wind blew from the northwest,
> The wave drove from the west,
> Bore old Väinämöinen
> To dark Pohjola,
> To the place where men are eaten,
> Heroes drowned.

While editing the *Old Kalevala*, Lönnrot conceived of Pohjola as a mythical place and of "Pohjan akka" (the Old Crone of the North), known also as the Mistress of Pohjola, as a witch similar to the Saami "loihtia" (chanter). In his article "Antiquities," published in *The Bee* in 1836, he presented his view of the geographical location of Pohjola: "Based on this, Luotela—Luode [Northwest Region]—would be to the northwest of Finland; Pimentola [Region of Darkness] would be in the direction of night, opposite the sun; Sariola in the northern area of swamps and marshes, where sedge grass grows; Untamola—Uni [Region of Sleep]—where there was ample sleep during dark winter nights." Lönnrot also believed that in Pohjola, and later in Kalevala as well, there had been numerous buildings or fortresses. Thus he believed that Kivimäki (Stone Hill) signified a stone house on the Pohjola River. Later, based on the rune "Kalevan neito" (Kaleva's maiden), he came to believe there were numerous dwellings in the Kalevala region as well.[47]

Lönnrot believed the heroes of the Kalevala and Pohjola regions were historical people who had battled each other in ancient times. In accordance with his view of the ancient heroic period in Finland's historical past, he believed the *Kalevala* primarily depicted the heroic deeds and journeys of these people. This view also provided a historical background for the Sampo: only when the Sampo was wrested from Pohjola did Kalevala, which was synonymous with Finland for Lönnrot, achieve a better life. This historical view of Kalevala and Pohjola was further clarified in the *New Kalevala*. Lönnrot believed that the people of Pohjola had been "a separate sect of Finns" and supported this viewpoint quite extensively in Section 9 of his preface, where he wrote:

> There is also much support for the idea that Pohjola or the people of Pohja in these runes could be understood to be Lapps. However, it seems more

likely that in Pohjola there lived not Lapps, but a separate sect of Finns. It is true that in repeated clauses (parallelism), Lapland is named in place of Pohja, but that seems merely to have been a derogatory name like "Pimentola" [Region of Darkness], "Untamola" [Region of sleep], "Kylmä kylä," [Cold village], "Miesten syöjä sija" [Place of Man Eaters], etc.

Only in one place (Poem 12, verses 199, 200) is there reference to a strange tongue spoken in Pohjola, but in Lönnrot's opinion, that reference can be explained as "the skill in magic peculiar to Pohjola." In other respects, as well, the entire way of life in Pohjola differed greatly from that in Lapland. In Lönnrot's opinion, both Kalevala and Pohjola were the dwelling places of Finnish groups who could comprehend each other's languages. Initially, Pohjola was more powerful and extracted taxes from Kalevala, until the heroes Väinämöinen, Ilmarinen, and Lemminkäinen brought an end to the tax subjugation. During this period, Lönnrot adapted the growing economic and cultural prosperity of Kalevala into the plot of the epic.

In his search for the location of ancient Pohjola, Lönnrot opened the path to future historical interpretations of the *Kalevala*. However, he was not the first to search for and map the unknown land of the North, "terra Hyperborea incognita." Herodotus (485–425 B.C.), the father of historical writing, had already written of the Hyperboreans, who dwelled in the North beyond the mountains, and were a well-regarded, peaceful people. Their territory, Hyperborea, extended to the sea. In his history, Herodotus referred to an even older source derived from Aristeas of Proconnesus, whose poetic work, the Arimaspeia, related what he had seen, in all likelihood, on his journey to the Far East circa 630 B.C. According to Herodotus: "In his poem, Aristeas claimed to have reached the land of the Issedones ruled by Foiboks (Apollo). He further related that, on the other side of the Issedones, there lived a one-eyed people called the Arimaspians, beyond them the griffons, which guarded gold, and beyond them the Hyperboreans, whose land extended to the sea."[48] Hippocrates (470–364 B.C.), for his part, located the mythical Hyperborea in the North, behind the Rhípai Mountains, which were located beneath Otava or the North Star. As Martti Haavio has shown, Hippocrates is describing the fortification of an unsettled land toward the north: "rhips" was "braided willow or a wall of bullrush, a pile fortification."[49]

The descriptions of Aristeas, Herodotus, and Hippocrates are dated approximately twenty-five hundred years ago, a time when the ethnic map of northern Eurasia differed from what it is today. Aristeas is thought to have traveled the Silk Road, which Herodotus described as beginning at the mouth of the River Don and continuing through the lands of the Sarmatians and Scythians, among others, to the land of the Issedones. H. W. Haussig hypothesized that the Issedones lived in northwestern China. Numerous authors in antiquity described encountering a stormy region in a remote corner of the North, a world related to that of Aristeas. The hole or grotto where the north wind is born is located there. Pliny wrote: "Next to the northern inhabitants (the Scythians), very near the birthplace of the north wind and the cave referred to as its opening, which is called Ges clithron, is said to be where the Arimaspians live." "Ges clithron" is a Greek phrase meaning "the Earth's gate."[50]

The information derived from the ancient authors has presented problems for historians in, for example, delineating the cultures of the Silk Road and the ethnic map of northern Eurasia. In addition to these ancient works, relevant information has been preserved in the folklore of numerous Eurasian peoples. This folklore depicts a mythical place of difficult access in the Far North inhabited by a prosperous people. However, travelers may encounter many perils there. At the farthest edge is the hole or cave of the north wind, which is also referred to as the "world's gate" and was known to Pliny through folklore. It is guarded by mythical animals, often eagles or dragons. The people themselves are one-eyed and gigantic. It is noteworthy that both the earth and the day end at the the boundary of the North. Herodotus and Pliny related that the northern people sleep half the year, an allusion to the Arctic night.[51] Ancient Finnish poetry has also drawn on this international folklore about a journey to the North, and one of the primary themes of the *Kalevala* is based on it.

As the Norwegian folklorist Nils Lid, among others, has shown, the most central traditions of the *Kalevala* are structured around the theme of Pohjola: the journeys of the heroes to the North, their reception and sojourn there, the forging of the Sampo, its concealment deep in Kivimäki (Stone Hill), the theft of the Sampo, and finally the struggle over it.[52] The main figures from Kalevala are men, while those from Pohjola are women. Worthy of note is the Mistress of Pohjola, who rules that region and is characterized as having a "crooked" nose. She sets off in pursuit of the men from Kalevala in the form of a bird bearing soldiers on its wings. And one by one, the *Kalevala* heroes are also enticed to Pohjola to court her extraordinarily beautiful daughter, whose eroticism surpasses that of the daughters of "this land." Although there are also men living in Pohjola, little is said of them except for the old sorcerer who is instrumental in Lemminkäinen's fate. Thus Pohjola is literally "miesten syöjä, urosten upottaja" (eater of men, drowner of heroes).

In the light of this tradition, the chronicle (1073–76) of the medieval scholar Adam von Bremen is of considerable interest. He tells of the Wizzi people, thought to be a reference to the powerful Veps of ancient times. They dwelled between the Land of Women (terra feminarum) and Russia (Ruzzia) and defended themselves with battle lines composed of dogs. "In the Land of Women (terra feminarum) there are no leaders, nor is the Christian God known there; snakes and birds are worshipped there instead." According to Adam von Bremen, the Swedes also ruled broad areas which extended up to the "Land of Women." To the east of this land lived the Veps, the Cheremis, the Scuti people (Scythians), and the Turks, extending as far as Russia. When Adam of Bremen's concept is depicted on a map, terra feminarum could be located somewhere on the Finnish peninsula.[53] Despite attempts at solution, the problem of the Land of Women has remained unsolved to this day. However, it belongs to the intriguing world of mythology rather than that of history.

To the extent that a geographic or historical location can be sought from mythical folklore, the Land of Women is well suited to the description of the ancient Finnish heroes' journeys to Pohjola as the "Gate of the World" or the hole or cave of the north wind depicted above. At issue here is a journey whose goal is "the other side." Supernatural means are used to make this journey to a place of extraordinary dangers, where everything differs basically from how it is here. It was believed that this unknown land was in the northernmost, back corner of the world, where the earth and day end. As knowledge of the world was extended through trade and exploration, as well as wars, the unknown "other side" came to be located further off. The human mind continuously sought new areas to which the age-old myths could be related.

During the Viking Period, there was a decisive change in world view in northern Europe. The Vikings came to know new lands and peoples. At the same time, they gained familiarity with the cultural customs, ideas, and folklore of previously unknown cultures. Ultimately, the Christian religion obscured all else and meant a radical change for these traditions. The world view of the northern peoples was radically altered by Christian contacts. The Crusades changed both the political and cognitive map of the world. This transitional period continued through the Middle Ages. The sagas and charms of this transitional period tell of journeys to the boundaries of the North made by both deities and kings. There are abundant details reminiscent of the journeys to the North made by heroes in Finnish runic poetry. However, these correspondences do not necessarily prove the hypothesis of Kaarle Krohn and others that this material was derived quite recently from Scandinavian sources. It is more likely that Scandinavian saga literature, the Edda as well as the witches' songs, and ancient Finnish poetry are partial manifestations of folklore and mythology which is common, in part, to northern Eurasia. It is characteristic of this folklore that it relates similar experiences from the journeys of various heroes, whether the hero be Odin, Saint Olaf, King Haraldr, Väinämöinen, or Lemminkäinen.

The ancient Scandinavian "fornaldarsogur" collection of legends and numerous runes tell of journeys which have as their goal Trollebotten, the witches' Pohjola, where, for example, the land masses converge at the bottom of a mountain or valley. According to these sagas, many a prince has brought back a young maiden from the Far North who had been the captive of a witch's wife. A magical object which brings good fortune and prosperity has also been sought from Trollebotten.[54] Sometimes the same tales are related to the geographic destinations of Viking journeys, such as Bjarmia. As Martti Haavio[55] has shown, individual and place names do exist in sagas which undoubtedly refer to historical figures and events. In folklore, however, they once again become myths.

In his work *Gesta Danorum* (dating from the tenth century), Saxo Grammaticus tells of Gormr the Old, who was the last of Denmark's pagan kings. With Thorkil, he went to Bjarmaland in search of promised treasure. They came to Geirroðr's camp. Behind the gate lay the remains of a city which

Olaus Magnus was the last Catholic archbishop of Sweden during the sixteenth century. After coming into conflict with King Gustav Vasa, Magnus moved to Rome, where he wrote a book about the northern peoples. In this monumental work, he described what he had learned about the Finns and the Saami, sketching the boundaries of the lands inhabited by the Bjarmians, Finnmark, Scricfinnia, or the land of the "ski-Finns," and also describing the journeys of a Saami sage to "the other realm." Magnus described a northern land where the earth and day end–a subject also central to the *Kalevala*. One after the other, the heroes of the epic–Väinämöinen, Ilmarinen, Lemminkäinen– journey to Pohjola, which is "a village of man eaters, drowner of heroes" with fierce Louhi as its ruler. The object of their journey is Pohjola's fair daughter who, in her beauty and eroticism, surpasses the maidens of this world. The mythical theme of a "northern land" is found throughout the world. It is also one of the central motifs of the *Kalevala*, and the courtship journeys of the heroes and the wedding at Pohjola are centered around it. (Olaus Magnus, *Historia de gentibus septentrionalibus*, 1555)

was guarded by dogs. Between its towers stood spears, and skulls of the dead were placed on them, as in the entrance to Päivölä described in "Lemminkäinen's Poem." While searching for treasure in the realm of the dead, they came on a band of women who, as witches, attacked them. Geirroðr ruled the Kingdom of Death, while his brother, Guðmunðr, was king of Jotunheimr, the land of giants, where good fortune and peace reigned. As Vilhelm Grønbech has shown, in addition to historical knowledge, the sagas also convey the topography of the netherworld.[56] Ancient Finnish folk poems do so as well. The journeying places of the sagas include both Valhalla, the celestial abode of the gods, and Hel, the netherworld of the humans. In Finnish runes, the world mountain known as "Kivimäki" (Stone Hill) or "Kipuvuori" (Pain Mountain) also lies to the north. The tree of the world grows there. This was the cold, desolate, hostile land of the dead, from which it was nevertheless necessary to courageously seek shamanistic knowledge. On the other hand, there were also great possibilities for riches, luck, and treasure, although these were

In the shamanistic world view, balance is achieved through harmony between the microcosm of human beings and the macrocosm of the universe. This sketch is from the perspective of a Saami hut. (Tuula Juurikka)

guarded by supernatural beings, one-eyed giants, dragons, female witches, and eagles.[57]

The *Bosa Saga* relates how the heroes Bosi and Herrauðr traveled to the North with the aim of procuring for themselves the huge eagle Gammr and its wondrously large egg, embellished in gold. In Gandvik they came to the dwelling of a god at the edge of Vinuskog Forest. There they found a picture of the god Jomali, as well as other treasures. These were ruled by the witch Gygr, who owned the vulture brooding the egg. This vulture was killed in the battle which ensued over the egg. The object of the second journey to the North was to demand Hleiðr, a princess imprisoned in a cave. On this journey, there was a third man along as well, the smith Smiðr. They arrived just in time for Hleiðr's wedding, and Smiðr succeeded in carrying off the bride in the musician Bosi's harp. A chase ensued, and in the great battle which resulted, Smiðr made use of the sword which Bosi's stepmother said had been consecrated by the witch wife Buslan. With this witch's sword, Smiðr slew the most dangerous of his opponents, which had simultaneously become a flying dragon. The flying dragon spouted venom over the ship, causing the deaths of many men. The dragon was called Flogdreki, which is similar in form to the Finnish words "lohi" (salmon) and "louhi" (ledge, crag, boulder), and "Louhi, Pohjolan emäntä" (Louhi, the Mistress of Pohjola). Thus, the *Bosa Saga* is similar in numerous respects to the structure of the Sampo cycle.[58]

In Finnish folklore, Pohjola often signifies that most distant place where the world ends and from which it is difficult to escape. The corresponding Saami word, "boasso," also signifies the sacred place in the Saami dwelling where the shaman's drum and hunting equipment were kept. On the northern side of the boasso was a small door which could be used only for religious ceremonies. In Nils Lid's opinion, the function of the boasso in the microcosm corresponds to that of Pohjola in the macrocosm.[59] Let us keep in mind that the central pillar of the Siberian shaman's yurt symbolizes the pillar of the world and that an integral part of the shaman's preparations for his spiritual journey is the symbolic ascent of this symbolic pillar. The shaman's performance in the yurt depicts the spiritual journey he makes while in the cosmos. The shaman's microcosm then, is a depiction of his macrocosm.

The sacred corner in the back of the Saami dwelling, the boasso, would thus depict the expanse of the heavens, where the heavens and the earth join. According to the Arctic people's concept, there was a hole here through which it was possible to travel to the other world just as concretely as smoke rose out of the dwelling and into the air through the smoke hole at the center of the hut. The central pole of the dwelling was the Tree of Life, the basis of the world order.

The hole at the center of the hut, which was at the pinnacle of the structure, symbolized the unity between the various levels of the universe. The shaman with his drum worked beneath the hole which symbolized the central point of the cosmos. Up above him was the North Star, around which the heavens rotated; around him, the human dwelling and parameters of everyday life; beneath him, the world of the dead. The goal of the shaman's spiritual journey was the farthest edge of the heavens. Knud Rasmussen gives the following description of an Eskimo falling into a trance: "When all the helpers had gathered, the session could begin. Thus they departed into the heavens, flew to the place at the edge of the heavens where earth and sky join. From there [the shaman] climbed onto the canopy of the heavens."[60] Related to this is Uno Harva's interpretation of the Sampo which refers to the forging of the world's pillar, the column which keeps the world upright.[61] Setälä also based his interpretation on this, adding that the "kirjokansi" (bright dome) was the sky.[62] The basis for Setälä's interpretation was Harva's concept of the Tree of Life and the World Pillar. Thus the basis of culture was secured by the North Star. There, in mythical Pohjola, which lay in the extreme north where the aurora borealis gleamed, the land ended, as did the day for half the year.

CHAPTER
9

A SHAMANISTIC EPIC

THE FINNISH TRADITION OF SAGES

In 1892, the Italian scholar Domenico Comparetti stated that a hero of the Kalevala runes was more likely to be a shamanistic sage than a swordsman.[1] Comparetti's insight was not new. It had simply been forgotten during the period when the *Kalevala* developed into a national myth. During this period, the epic served the Finnish people as an explanation of their historical past. A century earlier, however, folk poetry had been interpreted primarily from the viewpoint of folk religion. Porthan's student Lencqvist had already described a Finnish sage who had mastered the technique of ecstasy:

> The superstitious assume that each person has his own guardian spirit (Genius familiaris), a kind of protector (rector), as a result of whose influence and with whose aid it is thought that ideas and undertakings succeed. For that reason, a person who is in a fervor and acts like a fanatic is said to be "haldioisa" [imbued with the guardian spirits, in a trance], that is, "haltijan yllyttämä" [possessed by a guardian spirit].[2]

Lencqvist also quoted the formula of the incantation used to invoke the guardian spirit's aid. As early as the seventeenth century, court records about witches told of Finnish sages and of their preparatory charms, which have subsequently also been recorded in various parts of Finland, Karelia, and Ingria. Words of origins are typical of Finnish incantations because it was believed that a person would have power over an animal, a disease, or another person or phenomenon if its origin was chanted in a charm.[3]

In his *Mythologia Fennica* (1785), Ganander had stated his view about the origins of numerous incantations used by sages to achieve a state of trance: "Luontoni nousee, Käypi natuuralleni" (My being rises, goes to my nature). "Luonto" (nature) was a person's self.[4] It was awakened by the sage in the beginning of the healing drama and was put to rest at the end of the ceremony.[5] Another concept central to this is the word "synty" (genesis) which, in addition to origins and narratives related to genesis, also refers to deceased beings which the sage called on for support, using specific words in the form of an incantation to raise them up. Loss of the guardian spirit precipitated a situation in which a person was as if without his or her self. In Ganander's opinion, the existence of the concepts "loveen langeta" (to fall into a trance) and "vaipua ekstaasiin ja vaeltaa ruumiin ulkopuolella Walhallaan" (to fall into ecstasy and wander outside one's body to Valhalla) proved that the Finns had ancient terms in their language for the primary aspects of shamanistic technique.[6]

It was more than half a century before Comparetti's observation found any noteworthy support in Finland. Martti Haavio became one of the primary proponents of this approach. In his book *Väinämöinen* (1950), he said of Väinämöinen: "Now, with the completion of my work, I observe that I have reached conclusions which severely undermine the image created of him based on the *Kalevala*; and even the picture shaped of him by older scholars, based on original folk runes; and even the picture which I myself had previously."[7] In Haavio's opinion, Väinämöinen was a shaman, and the runic poetry about him had been created primarily in Fenno-Scandian seafaring environs during the Viking Period.

> The culture within which the earliest poets who sing about Väinämöinen lived was shamanistic. So it had to be; for only in this way is it possible to situate in time the earliest Väinämöinen runes: "Tuonelassa-käynti" (The journey to Tuonela), "Vipusessa-käynti" (The journey into Vipunen), "Kilpalaulanta-runo" (The singing-match rune). Thus the creators of the Väinämöinen runes lived during a time when the shaman, a sage, a particular kind of witch, played a significant role in religious and community life. It was the shaman who, based on his calling and inclination, primarily mediated between human beings and the spiritual world and who was also considered to have supernatural abilities."[8]

Haavio attributed the background of these to Scandinavian shamanistic epics. This approach has subsequently been shown to be too limited.[9]

Concurring with Haavio, Matti Kuusi observed that "the seeker of words, the traveler to the netherworld, the heroes able to sing another into a swamp, continue the most traditional, inherently Finnish aspect of our spiritual history."[10] Although ideas such as these had already been expressed, the question of shamanism in connection with Finnish epic poetry and ancient Finnish religion in general was still novel in the 1960s. In 1961, for example, the introduction of this topic precipitated a lively debate at the first Nordic Symposium on the History of Religion organized by the Donner Institute in Turku. My report of the seminar proceedings in the review *Kotiseutu* was entitled "Did the Finns practice shamanism?"[11] Since that time, I have grown ever more convinced that the origins of the Finnish tradition of sages lie in northern Eurasian shamanism.

NORTHERN EURASIAN ROOTS OF THE SHAMANISTIC EPIC

The ancient religion of the Finns is inseparable from Arctic shamanism. There is evidence of this, for example, in the noun "noita," which specifically means shaman and is central to the vocabulary of numerous Finno-Ugric peoples. The Ob-Ugric peoples also have a word in common for the shaman's drum, indicating that they have used this instrument. The Baltic Finns use the word "noita" when speaking of a shaman, and a related word is also found among the Saami and the Vogul. In contrast, the Mongol and Turkic peoples who inhabit the areas surrounding the tributaries of the Yenisey River, as well as the Samoyed, use the various forms of the Tungus word "saman" in this connection.[12]

The complex phenomenon of shamanism has been extensively studied within the context of comparative religion. According to Åke Hultkrantz,[13] the central concept of shamanism is the mediation of contacts between this world and the supernatural by a sage, a shaman expert in ecstatic techniques. Leaving aside the interesting question of whether shamanism is a universal phenomenon (Mircea Eliade)[14] or a historical one particular only to certain northern cultures (Vilmos Diószegi),[15] the basis of the Finnish shamanistic epic will be sought in the rich shamanistic tradition of northern Eurasia, which has continued to exist into this century. Recent field work by Soviet ethnographers appears to be shedding additional light on one of the most difficult issues related to Finnish epic.[16]

In Saami culture, as in that of the Finns, shamans were not full-time practitioners, although they were considered to be highly trained specialists in their fields, true sages. A fundamental aspect of Finnish shamanism has been the use of trance techniques by the shaman or "tietäjä" (man of knowledge, sage). The shaman served as the religious leader and was considered an expert in mediating the reciprocal interaction between this world and the other realm. The expression "langeta loveen" (fall into a trance) is specifically used in Finnish with reference to ecstactic experiences characteristic of shamanistic technique.[17]

According to Christfrid Ganander (1785) and Martti Haavio, the word "lovi" (trance) is used synonymously with "Tuoni," the Finnish word for netherworld, and "Jabmeaivo," the Saami word for the same concept. Another more concrete meaning for "lovi" is hole, cavity, cave, or crack.[18] A hole leading from one level of the universe to another is often depicted on shamans' drums. If we consider this hole or "lovi" from the perspective of shamanistic experience, "loveen lankeaminen" (falling into a hole or crack) appears to signify the movement or spiritual journeying of the shaman through this hole into another world where there exists another experiential reality. This perspective is demonstrated, for example, by the trance experiences of Eskimo shamans. Åke Hultkrantz characterized these sessions in the following manner: "An imaginary hole has been opened down into the ground [beneath the shaman], through which the soul's helpmate has disappeared beneath the ground."[19]

The shaman was the fulcrum of life and was called on by the community when there was illness or misfortune. At a shaman's death, it was necessary to find another sage as a replacement. This had to be an individual with "strong blood" and someone who, it was believed, would be competent in this demanding role.

Shamanism in itself is not a religion, but rather an integral part of a particular world view. Shamanistic elements can be found in the written epics of many world religions, as well as in the epics of a number of nonliterate cultures in the North. A shamanistic epic cannot be understood of itself. It must be interpreted with the aid of other information about the culture.

The Soviet ethnographer L. P. Kuzmina stresses that shamanism must be studied from the viewpoint of ideological factors, which she interpreted as careful analysis of its folklore and world view. In general, one prerequisite for the formation of a shamanistic world view is a nonliterate culture. Shamanistic folklore forms part of a ritual order which, in addition to being an ideological unity, is also a functional and structural whole. According to Kuzmina, it was necessary for future shamans to spend a great deal of time familiarizing themselves with the folklore related to their task. Those who were most successful in shamanistic skills were the practitioners with the greatest knowledge of their people's cultural heritage. They attained this knowledge under the guidance of an older shaman.[20]

Some Central Asian peoples consider particular genres of tradition to be sacred, and certain epic poems were specifically part of their esoteric rituals. This was secret knowledge only the sages were permitted to know. Kuzmina considers the genres most typical of shamanistic tradition to be myths, charms, exorcisms, shamans' oaths, songs, and genealogical tales about previous male and female shamans. Shamanistic folklore is part of the totality of a culture's poetic expression. During the shaman's performance, the narration or myth becomes part of the cure for illness, the destruction and restoration of the world order.[21] A particular genre, the shaman's oath, forms part of the shaman's initiation in numerous Siberian cultures. In the presence of the community, the shaman vows to become the guardian of religious customs. Among the Buryats, for example, the oath might have the following content:

> Having performed this initiation rite and having been blessed as a shaman, I vow to be the protector of infants, not to avoid the sick and the poor, not to seek remuneration, not to avoid aliens, not to favor blood relatives, to walk on foot to a sick person and to the poor, even to travel on oxen, not to rejoice in bounteous gifts and not to be angered by small ones. I shall not withhold the truth with regard to a sick person's destiny. . . . Let the father of the high heavens himself know of this vow and let the broad mother-earth be witness to it.[22]

The healing ceremony conducted by a shaman was a totality which included the shaman's implements, the folklore related to that particular circumstance, and a fixed, reciprocal relationship between the shaman, the patient, and the community. Among the implements of the Yakut shaman was this staff, 145 cm. in height, which was set up in front of the yurt where the shamanistic ceremony was taking place. It depicts the path leading to the heavens. The Yakuts believed that the shaman's soul rose upward through the heavens, from one level to the other, in the form of a bird, and rested on the clouds. The picture depicts a journey to the seventh heaven. On the clouds, in each of the heavens, there is a specific religious being encountered by the shaman's soul upon its journey. The knowledge brought back from the heavens was later adapted into the healing drama. (Soviet Academy of Sciences, "Silk Road Exhibition," Finnish Museum of Applied Arts, 1985).

It was also important that shamans govern the mythical tradition about their predecessors as memorized knowledge. Great and gifted shamans may have been able to recall as many as fourteen or fifteen generations of their shaman predecessors. Part of the shaman's role was to be an expert tradition bearer within the community. In this regard, the Finnish word for shaman, "tietäjä" (sage), is particularly apt. In principle, the shaman was the individual who knew everything of significance about the traditions of the community, particularly when dealing with the supernatural.

HISTORICAL TRADITION OF SAAMI SHAMANISM

In Finnish folklore, including both runic poetry and the *Kalevala*, the Saami are presented as a people particularly competent in shamanistic skill. This view is common to the folklore of neighboring peoples as well. The earliest information about Saami shamanism is found in *Historia Norwegiae*, dating from the thirteenth century. In this book, the Saami "noaidde" is described as a sage who practiced a specific technique of ecstasy. With the aid of a drum, the shaman went into a trance during which he or she journeyed to the "other side" on behalf of members of the community or clan. Inspired by drumming and joiku chanting, the shaman's soul then moved from one level of the world to another.

In 1767, E. J. Jessen depicted the shaman's journey to the world beyond in his description of the Saami.[23] When a member of the community fell seriously ill, it was the shaman's duty to prepare for a journey to the netherworld. Thereupon all available men and women of the tribe gathered around him. The sage then seized a drum and began, by joiking, to invoke his spirit helpers. Before long, the others joined in the chanting, which grew more powerful and became increasingly rapid and frenzied. Suddenly the sage would fall into a trance, and his assistant then took up his post beside him, ready to carry out the awakening procedure when it came time for the sage to return. The shaman's journey was directed toward the realm of the dead, from whom he would inquire after the sick person's soul and also request to take it back with him. If someone close to the sick person, such as a relative, wanted to keep the soul in the realm of the dead so that the request could not be met, the shaman was in great peril. The dead could even prevent the shaman's return to the world of the living unless his guardian spirit could foil these plans. But if the dead agreed to return the soul, the patient was saved. The sick person then had to pay the deceased who had stolen the soul the price agreed on, such as a reindeer. Upon awakening from his trance, the shaman would relate the results of his journey to those present and announce whether the patient would recover or be forced to join the dead.

Witchcraft has been considered a specific domain of the Finns. This belief is particularly prevalent in southern and central Europe. For example, the Scotch word "finn" has the meanings Finn, Saami, and powerful sage. Norwe-

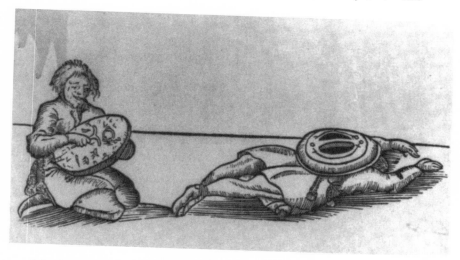

Schefferus's depiction of a sage in a trance (*Lapponia*, 1673). On the left, the sage is drumming and casting lots. A copper ring is made to traverse the surface of the drum, and based on where it stops, predictions are made about the future or decisions are made about the nature of the patient's illness. The shaman is holding a hammer. On the right, the sage is already in a trance as the soul leaves the body to obtain the necessary knowledge. Above him is a drum, the inside of which, "rummun sisin" (the innermost part of the drum), contains information about the shaman and his kin as well as the symbolism and reciprocal relationships pertaining to them. The surface of the drum was the cognitive map of both the shaman and the community. It expressed the concept of a three-level world and the elements of which it was composed.

gian Lappmark or Finnmark has been characterized as the "land of witches." Was it these same people Tacitus was referring to when he wrote about the northern barbarian Fenni people in his history dated A.D. 98?[24]

The roots of the Finnish "tietäjä" (shaman, sage) tradition also lie in shamanism. It has been customary for Finnish sages to go to the cemetery to raise up advice from the dead. In eastern Finland, trance techniques have been used in connection with healing practices up to the present day. Even in this century, a "seula" (grain sieve) has been used to divine "arpa" (fortune) in Karelia and North Ostrobothnia. The seula was used in the same manner as a drum for prophesying the future. A ring or some other object was made to move on the surface of the sieve.[25] When the object stopped, signs were interpreted based upon its location on the surface. The shaman's drum undoubtedly also existed in Finland, although not one has survived. One reason for this is the witch trials held there during the sixteenth and seventeenth centuries. Abundant information exists in trial documents about Finnish shamans who were sentenced to death as "witches" during this period.[26]

The Saami, on the other hand, continued to use the shaman's drum until the eighteenth and nineteenth centuries, when these drums were forcibly collected by missionaries and either sent to museums or burned.[27] Even today, legends are told about Saami who cast these drums into tundras, caves, or deep lakes. Although the drums were destroyed, the Saami culture could not function without shamans. In the 1970s, I still had the opportunity to observe how a community in Norwegian Lapland chose a new sage in order to replace an aging noaidde.

A recurring theme of the *Kalevala* concerns the interaction and competition between Finnish and Saami shamans. As Toivo Itkonen's onomastic studies, among others, have shown, the Saami long dwelled in wilderness areas extending as far south as southern Finland.[28] It is apparent that the Saami and Finns influenced each other in the past. Records of witch trials held during the seventeenth century show that numerous healers and sages traveled to Lapland expressly to attain shamanistic skills. They primarily journeyed to sages in so-called Turja or Norwegian Lapland. Finnish shamanistic epics and legends generally portray Lapland as the home of shamans. There are many similarities between Finnish and Saami shamanistic folklore. Many Finnish charms are specifically shamanistic in nature. They refer to wakening the spirits of the dead and to raising a shaman's helping spirits from beneath the ground–central themes found in Saami shamanic folklore even today.

Historically it is clear that these peoples inhabited and moved about the Finnish peninsula for thousands of years. They had knowledge of and many contacts with each other. Linguists have shown that the words "hämäläinen" (a person from Häme, also known as Tavastia) and "šabmelâš" (the Saami's own name for themselves) have the same meaning.[29] Ancient Häme may indeed have been the region where the Finns and Saami most frequently encountered one another. It is not surprising, therefore, that "Lappalainen" (the name used by the Finns for the Saami) is found quite often in ancient Finnish poetry. The Sampo runes "Hiiden hirven hiihdäntä" (Skiing down the Hiisi elk) and "Lauri Lappalaisen runo" (Lauri Lappalainen's rune), among others, relate how a Saami specifically precipitated a crisis situation, difficulty, or harm. It is the Saami who does something which upsets the world order. Frequently, it is not an everyday event or conflict which causes the crisis, but rather acts of witchcraft.

It is very difficult, however, to identify Lappmark as the historical Pohjola, although this assumption was often made during the nineteenth century. Studies show that the Saami moved about areas noticeably closer to the regions inhabited by the Finns, including the area around the Gulf of Finland and as far as the Gulf of Bothnia. An ancient Lappmark with which the Kalevala folk could have waged war did not exist in reality. In his article "Antiquities," published in *The Bee* in 1836, even Lönnrot stated that these peoples could not have had the resources to carry on great wars.[30] More likely, these ancient conflicts were related to rights of land usage and differing concepts of ownership. The Saami system of livelihood was based on an ancient tradition of herding

Included in Schefferus's *Lapponia* is a copper engraving outlining the activities of a shaman. Above, to the left, a hunter shaman stands in his everyday role, with his wife beside him and arrows in hand. Between them is the drum, which has a direct relationship to the Tree of Life. This Tree of Life is also found in the center of the drum. The shaman rules all four directions of the universe. These are outlined in the square found at the center of the drum. Also at the center is the shaman's opening or hole to the center of the cosmos. The drum depicts the concept of a three-level universe; the heavens are uppermost, in the center is the human sphere, and beneath is the realm of the dead. In the lower right-hand corner of the picture, a bishop is shown riding to the shaman's dwelling. The artist was undoubtedly influenced by the Christian point of view. The shaman is flying, and in the bottom corner on the right, he is drumming in front of his dwelling. At the bottom center is a picture of a worshipper kneeling before a rocky "seita," a cult site common among the Saami. In this drawing, influenced by Christian ideas, the wandering of the shaman's soul is depicted in the guise of the devil. (J. Schefferus, *Lapponia*, 1673)

and the successive use of land typical of a mobile, hunting, fishing, and reindeer-herding economy. The Finnish economy was based on the principle of land ownership or slash-and-burn agriculture which, to a certain extent, was also a fairly mobile use of land requiring that the forests be burned.

As the Finns settled southern Finland, Southwestern Finland, Satakunta, and Ostrobothnia, it became necessary for the Saami to abandon the river valleys they had occupied and to move farther inland. As a consequence of two centuries of industrious settlement from the sixteenth century onward, the wilderness areas of central Finland, Savo, Kainuu, and Karelia were also cleared. The Finns gained productive lands but, as a consequence, the Saami had to move farther and farther north in order to continue their traditional means of livelihood, which required uninhabited wilderness. At the same time, the mythical destination where one had to go to learn Saami witchcraft shifted farther north. Nevertheless, the myth about the shamanic skills of the Saami continued in Scandinavian and Finnish folklore.

ANTERO VIPUNEN: FINNISH PROTO-SHAMAN

In their writings of the 1950s and 1960s, both Martti Haavio and Matti Kuusi related the origins of Finnish shamanistic runes to seafaring culture. In Haavio's opinion, the Väinämöinen runes tell of a shamanistic hunting culture, but above all they tell of a fishing culture which reigned "in these latitudes during those centuries after the birth of Christ when Finnish boats, in search of Baltic herring and salmon, were oriented about the coastal waters of southern Finland."[31] Kuusi has shown that there is temporal stratification in the epic. Initially, he attributed the origins of the runes solely to the cultural tradition prevalent during the Viking Period. He also maintained that a great deal of this poetic material had been reformulated during the Medieval Period after the crusades of the twelfth and thirteenth centuries.[32]

In their later writings, both Haavio and Kuusi reevaluated their positions and concluded that these runes had originated much earlier. Kuusi then held that they even belonged to the deepest level of Finnish folklore.[33] The most important shamanistic runes in the *Kalevala* are "Väinämöisen käynti Tuonelassa" (Väinämöinen's journey to Tuonela), "Vipusessa käynti" (The journey into Vipunen), "Väinämöisen ja Joukahaisen kilpalaulanta" (The singing competition between Väinämöinen and Joukahainen), and "Lemminkäisen matkat Tuonelaan ja Pohjolaan" (Lemminkäinen's journeys to Tuonela and Pohjola). Although it is believed these runes belong to the oldest layer of the *Kalevala*, their motifs may even be thousands of years older than the runes themselves.

In a shamanistic culture, mythical heroes are often prototypes of the first shamans. Among the mythical heroes in the *Kalevala*, shamanistic subject matter has been centered primarily around Väinämöinen's name. It is evident, however, that the main figure in all these runes was not originally called

Väinämöinen. However, Väinämöinen was a favorite of rune singers, and runes earlier sung about others clustered around his name. For example, Kuusi argued that the main figure in "Antero Vipunen's Rune" was originally Lemminkäinen and not Väinämöinen. In White Sea Karelia, Lönnrot heard the following archaic verses sung about a shaman's trance state:

> Lemminkäinen, one bewitched,
> singer of ancient age,
> decaying in his songs,
> rotting in his conjury.[34]

Ganander believed that it was Ilmarinen, the boat builder, who originally journeyed into the belly of Antero Vipunen, the proto-shaman who had died long before and lay rotting.[35] According to the majority of folk singers, however, it was Väinämöinen who lacked the words necessary to construct a boat for his journey to Tuonela, and it was these he went to seek from Vipunen. Lönnrot's *Kalevala* relates that Väinämöinen did not succeed in obtaining the necessary words when he went to seek them from the long-dead shaman. By then, "an aspen grew on his shoulders, a birch all over his brows, an alder at the point of his chin, willow mulch on his beard." As described in the rune, Väinämöinen arrives at Vipunen's grave after a difficult journey and falls through the ancient shaman's mouth into his stomach. There he constructs an anvil from his clothes and begins to pound. This wakens Vipunen. Disturbed from his years of sleep, the ancient sage demands that Väinämöinen leave. As a condition for his departure, Väinämöinen demands the words and leaves once he has received them.[36]

Journeying to the grave of a great sage to seek knowledge was an ancient custom in shamanistic cultures, including the Finnish "tietäjä" tradition. Some scholars have argued that Antero Vipunen is the depiction of a shaman who died after remaining in a trance too long; for some reason, his soul was unable to return to his body.[37]

According to Haavio, proof that later material was added to the Vipunen verses is apparent, for example, in the obstacles the shaman encountered. While searching for Vipunen, Väinämöinen had to traverse "battle-ax blades and needle tips." Corresponding descriptions are frequently found in other sources as well, such as visionary texts of the Catholic Middle Ages.[38] Among the universal themes to which Väinämöinen's journey into Vipunen's belly can easily be compared are folk tales about heroes who fall into the stomachs of various animals and monsters, such as the tale of "Jonah and the Whale." The closest correspondences, however, are found in Saami folk legends.

Just as Antero Vipunen "languished in his charms and lolled in his sorcery," the Saami sorcerers, "Akmeeli" or "Torajainen," long slept in their graves. The hero of the Finnish rune goes to wake the dead proto-shaman of his people: "Hey there, Antero Vipunen, rise from sleeping, from dreaming too much!" The boy or helping shaman in the Saami legend says, "Rise up from the oval of the pike's gut, from the third labyrinth [the bowels or intestines]."[39] The hero

of the rune obtains the necessary words and is freed. However, the peace desired by the proto-shaman is final. Vipunen says: "There's not a man in the
departed . . . my mound of flesh already rotted." Likewise, the Saami shaman
says: "There's not a man in the rotted one." Both the ancient Finnish rune and
the Saami folk legend give a detailed description of the wandering of a shaman's
soul to the land of the deceased in order to encounter a long-dead primordial
shaman of a clan or a people. In the Saami legend, both the reason for the
journey, which is to construct a boat, and the fact that the hero traveled in
the form of a fish to the realm of the dead beneath or beyond the water, allude
to the fact that the goal of the journey was "Jabmeaivo," the Saami realm of
the dead which lay beneath the water.

A primary aspect of shamanistic tradition is the shaman's journey to the other
realm in the form of an animal during a trance state. In Finnish tradition, the
goal of this journey might be the realm of the dead or "Tuonilmainen" (the
upper realm). Ecstatic chanting seems to have been a significant aspect of this
and took the form of "runon laulaminen" (rune singing). In its original function,
rune singing helped the shaman into a trance state. The community also participated. In Saami culture it was the joik which served this function. The shaman's
primary instrument was the drum. Little is known about the dress of either
the Finnish or the Saami shaman, although their regalia clearly included elements related to the journey made by the shaman in animal form, such as a
bear's tooth, a shaman's bag, etc. The shaman's drum served as a cognitive map
to the other realm in much the same manner as the *Book of the Dead*, found
in Egyptian graves, served as a map for the journey to be made by the deceased.[40]

The expert in the use of this cognitive map, as well as ritual technique, was
the shaman, who also instructed a successor in this knowledge. The cyclical
world view of the Saami becomes manifest in the drum, which was probably
read and interpreted from a different direction during each season of the year.
The manner in which it was read also depended on the individual in question
and the circumstances of the crisis which had led to the shamanistic session.
The shaman's drum must be viewed as part of a totality which includes the
drum with all its constituent parts and the world-view system on which it was
based.

The upper face of the drum, which was a leather membrane with drawings
on it, was apparently its collective side. This side was publicly interpreted by
the shaman for an audience. However, the nether side of the drum was more
confidential. The symbolism of a particular clan was drawn on it, as well as esoteric, secret knowledge relating to the owners of the drum.[41] Up to this point,
research has been much more concerned with the collective, outer surface
of the drum, and the nether side has been almost completely ignored. In
Saami culture, for example, the nether side often contains reindeer markings used to designate reindeer as the private property of a particular clan.
These markings provide valuable information about the origins of individual

drums. To date this research has been based primarily on stylistic attributes.

It is indeed possible that, at least for Arctic peoples, shamanism as an institution was related to the totemistic hunting culture of the kin, clan, or tribe. A primary aspect of this world view is the belief in a bond with an animal, the primordial father or mother of the clan. The shaman of a clan or kin battled enemies for the sake of its well-being. The abundant kinship symbols found on drums, as well as information about the great number of them, indicate that shamanism was a kinship institution. As late as the end of the eighteenth century, Thomas von Westen, a Norwegian missionary, was still able to collect tens of drums from the Saami.[42] According to the Soviet ethnographer S. I. Vainstein, there were still as many as seven hundred shamans among the Tuva in central Siberia (pop. approx. 30,000) during the 1930s.[43]

Vladimir Basilov,[44] another Soviet scholar of shamanism, has, in fact, emphasized that the innermost part of the drum, i.e., its "heart," appears to be its nether side. In Siberian folklore, the drum is often identified with an animal, such as an elk or a horse, which is ridden by the shaman on a cosmic journey. For Arctic peoples, the drum typically symbolizes an elk or a reindeer. The concept of the drum as a horse was propagated largely by herding peoples of the Silk Road. In Basilov's opinion, there exist both older and newer elements in the drum symbolism. The fundamental significance of the drum is to provide contact with the shaman's helping spirit. In many cultures, these helping spirits are totem animals such as elk, reindeer, bear, horses, or swans. L. P. Potapov[45] notes the duality of the drum symbolism: on one hand, the drum was the shaman's majestic helping animal; on the other, it was the shaman's very soul, to which the sage's life was joined. The shaman protected this animal and, having raised it up, did everything to keep it alive. Eventually the drum was concealed in the wilderness, lest a competing shaman find and kill the animal it represented (which was considered to be the shaman's soul), thereby causing the shaman's death.

In examining the animal symbolism of the drum, it is important to note the shaman's mythical connection with the primordial father or mother. Among the shaman's helping spirits, one is usually considered to be more powerful than the rest. The Altai Buryats and Yakuts, among others, have considered the primordial shaman to be their mythical forefather. For them, the shaman's journey to the land of the dead is in fact a search for knowledge from a dead forefather who, in Siberian culture, can also take the form of an animal. Matti Kuusi is indeed correct in proposing that the journey into Antero Vipunen's stomach may have been a mythical rune about the first shaman:

> The shaman hero is not a creator of the new, as are the heroes of a creation epic, nor is this hero one who brings back treasure from beyond the seas and conquers women, as in Viking runes. Rather, he brings back ancient words of magic from the land of the dead, for use against the power of the deceased as well as the shamans of foreign peoples."[46]

THE CHANTING COMPETITION:
A SHAMANISTIC STRUGGLE

At the conclusion of the *Old Kalevala* there are a number of runes for which Lönnrot had not yet found an appropriate place in the epic as a whole. Poem 30 describes the singular meeting between Väinämöinen, the "steadfast old" traveler and the garrulous young Joukahainen. When their sledges meet on the road, one of them must yield the way. Neither is willing to do so, and this precipitates a verbal struggle between them which touches on the most basic questions of creation and knowledge.

In this chanting competition, young Joukahainen tests the extent of Väinämöinen's knowledge. He begins by presenting his own knowledge and claims to have been present at the creation of the world. At this point, Väinämöinen accuses him of lying. Joukahainen's aggressive stance eventually angers Väinämöinen so greatly that he chants Joukahainen into a swamp "up to his waist." Thus Väinämöinen is revealed to be a truly powerful shaman, one strong enough to chant his young competitor into complete helplessness. Joukahainen concedes the other's power and begs for mercy: "Stop your sentences, turn back your sacred words." To save himself, Joukahainen promises his sister to Väinämöinen as a wife. In the *Old Kalevala*, the as yet nameless sister prefers to kill herself rather than marry the old man. This episode is followed by Poem 31, "Vellamon neidon onginta" (Angling the Maiden of Vellamo).

In the *New Kalevala*, the competition between Väinämöinen and Joukahainen has been transferred to the opening drama of the epic (Poem 3). From this point on, Lönnrot weaves the plot around Väinämöinen's unsuccessful courtship attempts. In the *New Kalevala*, Joukahainen's sister becomes the maiden Aino, who commits suicide. New dimensions are also added to the encounter between Väinämöinen and Joukahainen. If Väinämöinen is the shamanistic leader of the people of Kalevala (Finland), it is natural for his opponent to be "the thin Lapp boy." Interpreted this way, the duel between Väinämöinen and Joukahainen in Poem 3 is a competition between the shamans of two peoples. In this poem, the esteem and honor accorded the shaman by his people are particularly apparent: the creator of the rune extols Väinämöinen and his power. The entire composition of "Kilpalaulanta" (The competition song) reveals its creator's admiration for "our sage": Joukahainen merely serves as a vehicle to show Väinämöinen's power. Joukahainen is not really able to chant at all during the course of the poem, and his knowledge is depicted as childish. Despite the humiliating manner in which the wedding match between Väinämöinen and Aino has been concluded, Joukahainen's mother expresses her satisfaction on hearing that she will now have "a great man" as her kin.

Martti Haavio and Matti Kuusi have interpreted "The Chanting Competition" as a contest between two shamans.[47] In this rune, Väinämöinen and Joukahainen drive toward each other and their sledges crash. In 1816, Matti

Immoinen, a rune singer living in the Central Scandinavian forests where a great many Finns dwelled, explained this episode to Gottlund as a mythical encounter between two peoples: "No one in the world had come face to face this way before the oldster, ancient Väinämöinen, and the youngster, Joutavoinen [Joukahainen] himself, came face to face on the road."[48] Anna-Leena Siikala has shown that the expression "sledge driving" denotes shamanism among many Siberian peoples.[49] This may in fact belong to the same belief referred to by Vladimir Basilov.[50] In his opinion, a shaman rides his drum physically to encounter his competitor on the celestial journey. G. N. Prokofyev[51] has also made reference to the shaman's ability to animate his drum. During the shaman's preparatory ritual for the trance, he appeared to gather together all the parts of the reindeer including its hair. Animated by symbolic chanting, the drum became the reindeer to be ridden by the shaman to the mythical world. A drum which had not been brought to life could not serve a shaman. A. A. Popov has called attention to the Nganasan reindeer drum and the horse drum of the Yakuts, both of which were brought to life ritualistically by the shaman.[52] In her historical map of Siberian ethnography, E. D. Prokofyeva shows that the Nents, the Voguls, the Nenets, the Evenks, the Yokagirs, the Kets, the Enets, the Nganasan, the Nogas, and the Tofalara are among those Siberian peoples which see the drum as a reindeer ridden by the shaman.[53]

The road on which Väinämöinen and Joukahainen encounter each other may, in fact, denote the Milky Way, which was considered to be the transcendental path of flight to the other realm. The discussion between the shamans also makes reference to the creation of the cosmos. In his rune, Arhippa Perttunen attributed the following words to Joukahainen:

> I know the barrens to be hoed,
> the fish pits dug,
> the heavens starred,
> the pillars of the sky set.

To this Väinämöinen responds:

> Mine are the barrens I've dug,
> the heavens I've starred.
> I was a man, the third,
> setting the pillar of the sky,
> bearing the arc of the sky,
> starring the heavens.[54]

After this competition in knowledge, Väinämöinen chants Joukahainen "up to his waist in a marsh, up to his chest in a meadow, up to his armpits in a heath." These verses, sung by Ontrei Malinen, show that Väinämöinen chanted his competitor into Manala, the cosmic level beneath the ground which was believed to be the abode of the dead. Joukahainen's implements are transformed to become part of the structure which bears the universe, thus establishing the world order: "He chanted Joukahainen's bow into an arch on the water, he chanted Joukavainen's arrow into a speeding hawk high up in the heavens."[55]

This chanting competition is also reminiscent of Scandinavian epic. The supreme deity, Odin, journeys to Jotunheim to see the ancient giant, Vafthrúnir, and to find out whether Odin is omniscient. Their competition to see who has greater knowledge also touches on the origin of the world. Odin eventually reveals that he was a god at the creation of the world. Because he has less wisdom than Odin, Vafthrúnir is destroyed. Based on Dag Strömbäck's studies, Martti Haavio has related the chanting competition between Väinämöinen and Joukahainen to the ancient Scandinavian incantation struggle, the "galdr."[56] Anna-Leena Siikala also concurs with this point of view.[57] And what of the concept of the "runoreki" (rune sledge)? In the rune it is stated that one sledge collides with another during the shamans' encounter. Haavio[58] hypothesized that the word "runo" (rune) is derived from "runoi," meaning shamanic rune singer. In this case, the "runoreki" would be the shaman's means of transport, his drum.

Functional similarities exist between the modes of presentation for the Saami joik and Finnish rune singing. There is a widely known noaidde joik among the northern Saami which describes the journey of a shaman who flies as a bird: beneath him are particular localities such as Kautokeino, Karasjok, and Utsjoki, which this capable shaman is able to see on his aerial journey. Rune singing has also had shamanistic functions. Although both rune singing and the joik have subsequently evolved to fulfill numerous other functions, it is possible to argue that both were used by shamans, although they involved different vocal techniques. The folklorist Lauri Harvilahti[59] has shown that numerous Central Asian peoples are familiar with a special larnyx technique used by the shaman in chanting. It may be concluded that a specific oral code existed which indicated that this was part of a shamanistic session, a particular religious performance per se and not an ordinary singing event.

Presently, no extensive comparative study exists of those phenomenological and etymological connections among the northern Eurasian languages relating to shamanistic phenomena. However, the existence of the same phenomenon in ancient Scandinavian epic, in Finnish and Saami tradition, and also among the Altaic and Uralic peoples indicates its great age. The wide distribution of shamanism in the Arctic area indicates that it is certainly one of the deepest layers of northern Eurasian culture and may have been practiced by these peoples even before they journeyed to their present dwelling places thousands of years ago. If this is true, the connection would date back four or five thousand years, to a time when ancient contacts reigned between the Uralic and Indo-European or Aryan peoples. It is possible, although unlikely, that this does, in fact, indicate a genetic, linguistic, and cultural relatedness extending beyond mere contacts.

Because numerous aspects of shamanism are common to cultures in both Arctic and sub-Arctic environments,[60] it is possible to give it an ecological explanation. From this point of view, shamanism as manifested in northern Eurasia is the cultural response of northern peoples to the conditions created by their severe Arctic and sub-Arctic environments. Scarce natural resources created competitive situations between peoples, clans, and families, typically manifested in shamanism. Interpreted in this light, "The Competition Song" describes such a competitive situation in which the sage, "meidän tietäjä" (our sage), "vaka vanha Väinämöinen" (wise old Väinämöinen), of the Finns is victorious over his rival. Such tradition characteristically served to strengthen feelings of solidarity and common identity among a clan or people.

A UNIVERSE OF THREE LEVELS

The surface of a shaman's drum is divided pictorially into three levels. Celestial deities and other heavenly beings occupy the uppermost level. Humans, animals, and those beings with which man has the most interaction during life on earth are found in the middle level. In the third, beneath the ground, are found various humanlike creatures as well as figures resembling animals. The third level is also the realm of the dead, to which man journeys after death. It is called "Manala" by the Finns and "Jabmeaivo" by the Saami.[61] In their legends, the Saami often tell of double-bottomed lakes called "saivos." The fact that a lake has two bottoms explains why it sometimes yields an abundance of fish and at other times none at all. The "saivo" people live beneath this lake. The world there is actually turned upside down. An ordinary human being can journey to this realm during sleep or supernatural experiences. The shaman is in continuous interaction with this realm.

The upside-down world is part of a broad system of beliefs. In Finnish folk tradition, there are references to groups of humanlike people who reside in the upper realm, the "taivaanääreläiset," dwelling at the edge of the heavens, as well as the "maahiset" (earth spirits, underground peoples), who live in the nether realm. These were considered akin to social groups which led lives basically similar to those of human beings. In Finnish folk beliefs, there is a great deal of lore about the interaction of these beings with the human world. For example, when a cow is lost in the forest, it is said to have gone to the abode of the earth spirits.[62] In Saami tradition, the "staalo," an apparition which appears in many guises, is also found in this supernatural sphere. A staalo is said to appear before people, whistling and accompanied by a dog. It is believed that a Saami man may have a daughter of the earth spirits as a wife or that a Saami girl may have a staalo as a husband.[63] The daughter of earth spirits is more beautiful than daughters of this world. The earth spirits are wealthier than the Finns or the Saami, and under favorable circumstances, it is possible to take possession of their herd by casting a knife over it. A suitor can gain possession of the daughter of earth spirits or a staalo in the same manner. The journey to the upside-down world is also described in fairy tales. For people living in difficult circumstances, this fairy-tale world, with its kings and queens, princesses and princes, signified an imaginary journey to the other realm, after which the real world appeared less difficult than before. In fairy tales, the shoe always fits Cinderella's foot perfectly.

The fundamental world view of the Finns appears to be bipartite, dualistic. From the beginning, it has included a god of creation and his antithesis, good and evil.[64] It is because of this antithesis between creator and anti-creator that not all is good in the world. Evil is not actually man's fault, but rather a reflection of this basic opposition. It is true that the anti-creator was imprisoned by the creator. Hiisi, the Demon, was enchained. In 1698, the Saami shaman Poulsen interpreted his drum in court and stated that the bottommost figure on the drum was Hiisi, the Demon, imprisoned.[65]

The well-known theories about the universe held by Siberian peoples are similar to Saami cosmology. According to these,[66] the universe is divided into three strata, the upper, middle, and nether worlds. These are joined into one by the Tree of Life or the Cosmic River. In the shamanistic cosmogony of the Buryats, the world is divided into three: the celestial, earthly, and nether worlds. Each is ruled by particular deities and spirits. The supreme deity is the Eternal Blue Sky, which is represented by a being in human form. The Evenks and numerous other northeast Asian peoples conceive of the world as unified by cosmic rivers which are, in fact, the shamans' own rivers. The shamans' helping spirits live along the tributaries of these rivers. The people believe that a separate realm of the dead is found at the mouth of each shaman's river. It is to these places that the shamans led members of the clan after death and where the shaman's own helping spirits dwelled. The Buryats, the Altaic people, and the Tuva explain their custom of burying the dead in the ground by saying that people belong to the middle world. Their basic rituals of sustenance and family life are composed of myths about the three-level world, early ancestors, and the creation period. Recalling these through ritual serves to keep intact the good fortune of the community, which is part of the world order. The Chukchi maintain that such tales refer to the events of creation, and in relating them they add the words "and even before."

The status of shaman was often given to the person who knew the myths best. By means of ritual, the shaman brought myths from the golden period of no conflicts into the present. The sum of the community's beliefs, the cognitive map of the clan, was drawn on the surface of the shaman's drum, often by the shaman himself. The shaman, in fact, usually made his own drum. The drawings on it depicted concepts of the universe, deities, and helping spirits. There is a horizontal line at the center of many Hakass drums. An undulating line signifies mountains. Above this is the upper world, beneath it the netherworld. Celestial spirits are drawn in red, those of the netherworld in black. At the center of the Altaic drum, however, there is a being which symbolizes the drum's master. Beneath the figure's hands is a rainbow, and above him the spirits of the upper world. Beneath the rainbow lie the celestial bodies. The drumstick was also a ritual object with its own ruling spirit whose image was often carved on the stick.

A significant aspect of Siberian shamanism is a bond with spirits, which are

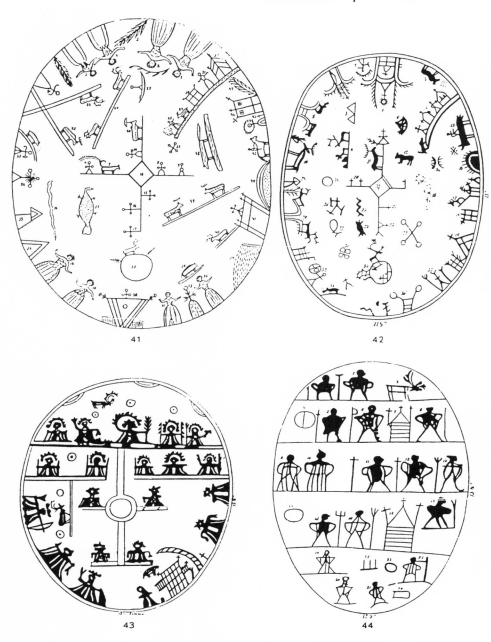

41

42

43

44

The cyclical world view characteristic of shamanism also becomes apparent from shamans' drums. The drum was apparently read from different directions, depending on the season of the year. At the center of the drum are the four points of the compass, with humans and animals drawn on them. When often the shaman's helpers in the form of animals. One of these is often more prominent than the rest and is, in fact, the shaman's soul or ego. Many scholars have interpreted the shaman's falling into a trance as epilepsy or some other illness, whereas the shaman's own people explain such episodes by saying that the spirits carried off the shaman.[67]

Shamanism contains a great many erotic elements. Most Siberian shamans have been men, and it is worth noting that female symbolism and even women's clothing are included in the dress of male shamans. During various parts of the ritual, shamans conduct themselves as women because the spirits require a change in sex. According to the tales told by some Siberian and Central Asian peoples, the shaman has an intimate relationship with a guardian spirit of the opposite sex. Intercourse with the spirit takes place in violent ecstasy, usually attained during the ritual to the accompaniment of drumming.[68] This may also be why abundant erotic symbolism is found not only on the drums but also in rock art, such as that found at Lake Uiku in White Sea Karelia. Runes, drums and even rock art reflect the cyclical world view of northern people, which often includes a totemistic, variable relationship between animals and humans. In this world view, sexuality can be altered within ritual contexts.

SKIING DOWN THE HIISI ELK:
THE SHAMAN'S CELESTIAL JOURNEY

The Soviet ethnographer V. N. Basilov has called attention to the animal symbolism of the shaman's drum and dress. E. D. Prokofyeva has shown that the complex semantic of the drum clarifies the structure of shamanistic beliefs. In Basilov's opinion, the shaman's dress and drum represent an animal. He cites the Evenk of Lake Baikal, whose shamans had both bird and oxen costumes. These represented the shaman's guardian spirits or helpers, which were needed on various journeys. The Selkup shamans also had two kinds of dress: that of a wild reindeer for journeying to the upper realms, and that of the bear for descent to the lower world. The shaman was considered capable of assuming the attributes of all the animals manifested in his dress. It was believed that

---

looking at the drum from different directions, various gods, humans, and other religious subject matter become apparent. It is interesting that the elk is also depicted on the drum as traveling toward the heavens. In a drawing of the heavens found in Rome's Pigorini Museum, there is an elk larger than a large bear which is being shot by a hunter. Apparently, this is the same subject matter as found in the rune, "Skiing Down the Hiisi Elk," and the pictographs. The painted boulder at Hossa was described by one Saami as follows: "From there, the wolverines rise to the heavens." However, in the pictograph, the animals are horned elk and reindeer. (Soviet Academy of Sciences, "Silk Road Exhibition," Finnish Museum of Applied Arts, 1985)

the shaman came to embody a bear, bird, reindeer, or wolf, including all its characteristics. Thus, for example, shamans adorned as migrating birds were believed to have this ability only during certain seasons of the year. The shaman took on these animal forms during rituals in order to make journeys. Basilov has shown that this belief has to do with the shaman's primordial, totemistic relationship to a female animal whose form the shaman took while in a trance state.[69]

Basilov relates that in some cultures the shaman had more than one drum. He believes that the concept of the drum as an animal to be ridden is relatively recent, having evolved approximately five thousand years ago, and is related to that period in human history when the horse was domesticated by cultures on the Silk Road. As a counter-argument, it can be said that animals other than horses have often been used as mounts and the horse is a recent, relatively rare drum symbol which was developed by Yakuts living in the south. For the northern Yakuts the drum symbolized another draft animal, the reindeer.[70]

Recent studies have shown that shamanistic rituals are altered depending on whether the shaman is journeying into the heavens as a bird or a reindeer, or to ancestors living in the netherworld as a bear or a fish.[71] Among the shaman's ritual objects may also have been implements which illustrated rising into the heavens. The Yakut shaman had a cord or pole arrayed with clouds, on which it was believed the shaman rested during his journey to the celestial sphere. When the ritual was over, the Yakuts left the erect pole behind on the taiga. The shaman also had a wooden box for preserving various guardian spirits. The image of a fish or a two-headed plant symbolized a journey to the netherworld, while a two-headed bird represented a celestial journey. These objects belonging to the shaman's ritual repertoire often depicted the cognitive map of the shaman's journey more clearly than the drum. Thus, for example, an image of the bird or animal which ruled a particular level of the heavens was attached to the cloud resting sites on the shaman's pole.

Wherever it is still possible to study shamanistic phenomena as living tradition, northern Eurasian shamanism has proved to be rooted in a broad, multifaceted cosmogonic mythology. Together with folklore, the totality of the shaman's ritual repertoire, including dress, drums, poles, noise-making objects, and images of guardian spirits, has reflected the structure of the universe as seen by the community as a whole. The problem of delineating such a cosmic structure becomes more complicated when concrete evidence about the phenomenon is sparse, as in the case of Finnish shamanism. The question then arises whether conclusions can be drawn about a people's shamanistic concepts of the cosmos based on oral tradition. Keeping in mind the Siberian model presented above, it can be asked whether Finnish epic tradition also included celestial journeys made by shamans and the cosmic dimensions they encountered there.

"Lemminkäisen virsi" (Lemminkäinen's rune) and "Väinämöisen Tuonelan matka" (Väinämöinen's journey to Tuonela) contain numerous instances in which the shaman takes the form of an animal. This is also a familiar theme of traditional Finnish legends, in which shamans generally battle one another as bears. The belief that the shaman changes into a wolf, as well as a tradition regarding werewolves, has also been documented. In the latter case, the shaman changes people into wolves which then bring destruction.

Like the bear, the elk has also served a totemistic function in Finnish folklore. It has in fact been hypothesized that the elk and the bear were the totem animals of two different Stone Age clans in ancient Finland. Although it is rare to find the celestial origins of the elk described in Finnish poetry, the following verses are reminiscent of "Karhun synty" (The birth of the bear):

> Where was the elk born,
> the child of the rock raised?
> There the elk was born
> on the windy waters of the Neva
> in the dense bird cherry groves
> in the close willow thickets
> on the Great Bear's shoulders
> among the stars of the sky.

Among other poems in which the elk has a primary role is the epical rune "Hiiden hirven hiihdäntä" (Skiing down the Hiisi elk). Jouko Hautala[72] has posited that this rune is based on the northern Eurasian version of the Orion myth. It accentuates the hunter's careful preparations for the hunt, such as making skis, and the elk's supernatural speed. In contrast, Martti Haavio and Jalmari Jaakkola are among the scholars who have specifically emphasized the hunter's misfortunes, hypothesizing that the rune was created by western Finns in order to poke fun at the skiing techniques of merchants from abroad.[73] It is highly unlikely, however, that its meaning could be so unidimensional.

In the *Kalevala*, Lönnrot incorporated "Skiing Down the Hiisi Elk" into the tasks Lemminkäinen had to perform when he courted the Maiden of Pohjola. The following verses, which Lönnrot had already included in the *Kantele* (1829), describe a condition stipulated by the Mistress of Pohjola:

> "I'll not give my daughter
> before you ski down the Hiisi elk
> from the end of Hiisi meadow."
> And he skied down the Hiisi elk
> from the end of Hiisi meadow;
> And for this demanded his wife.[74]

The prey is not an ordinary elk, but one created or conjured up by the Demon. It is a creature constructed from various natural materials, the helping animal closest to the shaman. The elk's journey takes it "to the reindeer's far swamps, the Lapp's wood chip strewn fields," or "along Pohjola's fences, beneath Ahti's granaries" to mythical Pohjola or "to the winds of Päivölä." The speed of the elk and Lemminkäinen's chase are well suited for depicting the wanderings of a shaman figure. In the words sung by Ontreini Jyrki of Vuonninen, the elk is attained on its cosmic journey: "Scaling Tapomäki [Tapo Hill], climbing Kirjovuori [Colorful Mountain]," place-names which refer to the topography of mythical Pohjola.[75]

In the version of "Lemminkäinen's Rune" sung by Arhippa Perttunen, the hero travels to Pohjola in the form of a wolf or a weasel,[76] another mythical journey made by a shaman in animal form. Lemminkäinen arrives at the Pohjola festivities and conjures the folk there with a chant. This is another act of shamanism, in this case a shaman's chant. There is, however, one person whom Lemminkäinen leaves unconjured. This is "umpisilmä ukko" (the blind old man), who eventually becomes his murderer. "Karjapaimen märkähattu" (the wet-hatted shepherd) chants Lemminkäinen into the River of Tuonela. In Perttunen's version of the rune, the old man of Ulappala is the murderer.

The shamanistic rune "Skiing Down the Hiisi Elk" is also related to this. Its description of the shaman's pursuit of the mythical elk refers to a shaman's celestial journey. In the rune as sung by Juhana Kainulainen, another of Lemminkäinen's tasks is to hurl down the Hiisi gelding; his third task is to shoot a swan.[77] However, "Tuonelan joutsen" (The swan of Tuonela) is Lönnrot's own creation, as A. R. Niemi has shown. It is also an image which has inspired many artists.[78]

While most of the shamanistic runes in the *Kalevala* emphasize the netherworld, "Skiing Down the Hiisi Elk" and "Lemminkäinen's Journey to Pohjola" relate to the tradition of a shaman whose journey was directed toward the upper world known as "Päivölä." The sacred center of this realm is the sun, Peäivve, which is found at the center of many Saami drums. Occasionally there is a hole drawn inside the sun. In concrete terms, this is the road taken by the shaman to the other realm, referred to as Päivölä by the folk. Later, as the people's concepts of the universe changed, the goal of Lemminkäinen's journey took on more characteristics of the netherworld. Thus Päivölä became the netherworld, the Scandinavian Hel, and Lemminkäinen, the murdered shaman who had skied down the celestial Hiisi elk, was eventually cast into the river which flowed through this region.

In many respects, the shaman's celestial journey in "Lemminkäinen's Rune" is reminiscent of the mythology of Siberian peoples. The Siberian shaman often makes a journey into the heavens to hunt the gigantic elk. It is also possible to conjecture that the Päivölä festivities do not primarily depict the drinking bouts of the gods in the netherworld. Rather, they may describe those celestial feasts to which the shaman Lemminkäinen journeyed. The climax of this rune is erotic. According to the version sung by Simana Kieleväinen in 1872, after having overcome the Hiisi elk, Lemminkäinen says:

> How fitting once to lie here
> with a young maiden
> under the arm of one growing
> on the blue elk's back
> on calves of the reindeer![79]

CHAPTER

10

THE REALM OF THE LIVING AND THE DEAD

INTERACTION BETWEEN THE LIVING AND THE DEAD

Finnish people believed that the boundary between life and death was only a hair's breadth. The kin was a unity, and there was an intimate interaction between the living and dead members. Martti Haavio wrote: "The kin formed a unity, regardless of whether its members were beneath or on the earth."[1] The end of a person's physical life was not seen as an abrupt cutoff signifying the end of contacts between members of the kin. It was simply a gradual transition from this life to the other realm, to the revered community of the dead.

The complex ritual accompanying death consisted of many parts. It was synchronized by the women who organized the wake, washed and shrouded the body, and, in Karelia, sang laments to send the dead clan member off to the realm of the family dead which was known as the "kalmisto" or "kalmisoma" (park or forest place of the dead). This was typically located outside the village, often on an island. A hut of logs known as a "kropnitša" was erected on the grave. Its window faced toward the home of the deceased, who, it was believed, watched the activities of the family after death. Work implements were buried with the dead because it was believed they practiced the same trade in death as in life. In addition, there was an opening in the hut through which the dead one's soul would migrate to the east, to the other realm at the end of the world, in the form of a soul-bird.[2]

Death was accompanied by a strong sense of grief shared by the entire village or community. Even the expectation of death was shared by all. It was important for all the villagers and family members to be present in taking leave of the dead. This leave-taking was, in fact, considered more important than the actual moment of death, when no rituals were performed. The moment of death only marked the beginning of intense activity. The men had to make a coffin without nails, while the women had to wash and shroud the body and equip it for its journey, so that it would be in the grave before the following sunset or at least within three days. In accordance with Christian tradition, these three days symbolized the three days between Good Friday and Easter.[3]

Of the rites of passage which marked the course of a person's life, runes were sung only at the wedding ceremony. Rune singing does not seem to have occurred in conjunction with bestowal of a name or during the burial ceremony. In Orthodox Karelia, women lamenters led both mourning and burials. There is no indication that this ritual also included rune singing. The use of laments was a rare phenomenon in Protestant Finland. The Ingrian Lutherans of Estonia, such as Valpuri Vohta, used laments learned from their Orthodox neighbors in their Lutheran ceremonies before these were replaced by Lutheran burial hymns. In Orthodox Karelia, however, laments remained a crucial part of the burial ritual until the Second World War. Karelian emigrants continued to perform wedding laments until the 1970s. It is still possible to find remembrances such as pirogen left at graves. In Petrozavodsk, as in other Karelian centers within Soviet Karelia, graveside lamenting is quite common. Remembrances are also brought to dead kin at Easter and during other important festivities. The clergyman's role at Orthodox funerals was relatively insignificant. It consisted primarily of reading the words of interment and, in some cases, merely recording the death in church records. Women led the ceremony with laments, thus conveying the deceased into the community of the dead. Lamenting was a way to channel sorrow.[4]

Death was interpreted merely as a transfer to a new abode. The deceased was given food, tools, and his most cherished possessions to take along. In Orthodox Karelia, lamenting was not permitted at a person's deathbed. Only when those preparing the body began work did the first laments rise from the closest female relative of the deceased: "Wash him well, so he need not live unclean in Tuonela!" According to ancient folk belief, the deceased heard what was said to him, although his soul had departed. Obligatory laments were also sung as the body was placed in shrouds and laid out. At this stage, the lamenter represented not herself but the deceased who was bidding farewell to his or her natural surroundings, the landscape and all the people encountered in life. In the home, apologies were addressed to the large communal room known as the "tupa," the steps, the yard, and, along the way, to the fields, the eight points of the compass, the fence, and the jetty.

Leave-taking acquired cosmic dimensions. Man was clearly seen as being part of nature, to which he returned after life's journey. For six weeks after the burial, it was believed the deceased retraced the entire course of his or her life. After this came the "kuusnetäl'iset," or "kuuden viikon murkinat" (the memorial feast after six weeks), when the favorite foods of the deceased were tasted at the graveside and distributed among the poor in his or her memory. It was important for all acquaintances and villagers to participate in the mourning. As they left the grave, people would say: "The final wedding has been celebrated, this one's wedding will no longer be celebrated." Interestingly enough, the funeral was called a wedding ceremony.[5]

People were, in fact, thought to be present at their own funeral. The place of honor among the close relatives, which was known as the "kuolleen paikka" (place of the dead one), remained empty. In addition, the dead were commemorated at a memorial feast held one year later. Thereafter, the deceased was no longer considered to exist as an individual, and was no longer remembered or addressed by his or her own name, but rather as "vainaja" (the deceased). It is worth noting that many older people in Finland when speaking of a dead husband, wife, father, or mother still say: "We lived here with 'vainaja.'" 'Vainaja' is in that photo." The reference here is to a person who is seen as already having taken his or her place in another community, and as belonging to the revered and worshipped category of the dead kin. The deceased could now also partake of those offerings placed at the foot of the tree of the dead. This guardian spirit tree might be a birch or a rowan near the house.

The graveyard was the village of the dead as well as the most important meeting place for the living and dead members of the kin. It was here the dead were appealed to, and it was also here they were remembered on a variety of occasions. This worship of the dead was already described by Mikael Agricola in his list of Karelian deities in the preface to the *Psalter*: "Food was taken to the graves of the dead; it was a place for wailing, weeping, and lamenting."[6] Agricola's information clearly refers to the customs of the Karelian Orthodox.[7]

The days set aside for commemorating the dead were organized according to the Christian calendar, which was influenced in western Finland by the Roman Catholic Church and in eastern Finland by Orthodox tradition. During autumn, there was the day referred to as "vainajien kesä" (summer of the deceased), when the dead were believed to move about. This period coincided with the end of the year according to the Old Calendar. Reverence for the dead involved a complicated set of other interactions, as well. It was aptly described by Uno Harva:

> Those who had gone to Manala played an extremely important role in the beliefs of the ancient Finns. The actual objects of worship were not, however, the dead in general, but the honored dead of a particular family or kin. The continuation of their work and duties, as well as the fulfillment of their wishes, was the sacred duty of their descendants. In former times, all of the social customs of the people were based on this tradition. The dead were appealed to at all stages in the lives of the individual and the kin. The dead were the guardians of morals, the judges of customs, and the maintainers of the societal structure. In this sense, not even God in heaven could compete with those who had gone to Manala.[8]

Christianity naturally meant a radical change from the pre-Christian worship of the dead. Nevertheless, the role of the deceased kin remained one of the most important aspects of Finnish culture. There are many different concepts of life after death stratified in Finnish folk belief which indicate numerous contacts with neighboring peoples throughout Finnish cultural history. The complexity of this tradition has been confusing even for tradition bearers. During her performance, a lamenter might inquire as to the location and direction of the underworld. For instance, the Tver Karelian Oudi asked her mother

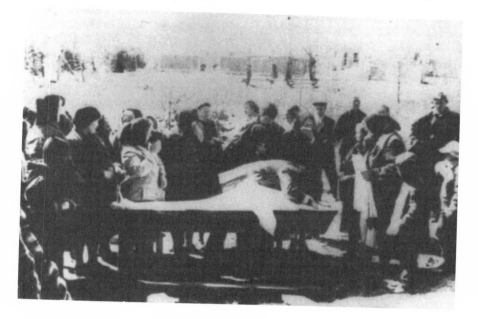

In Soviet Karelia, the Orthodox burial ritual has retained ancient aspects of tradition despite the waning of the Karelian language. The funeral of Marina Takalo's relative Iivana S. Nikitin in Kunnanlahti. The relatives bid farewell to the departed one by one, in a drama synchronized by laments. The lamenter holds the white linen cloth. Not even modern culture has broken old burial traditions. Even in recent years, pirogen have been found on graves in Petrozavodsk. On the sixth week following the death, pirogen are eaten and vodka is sipped at the grave of the deceased, as has been done for hundreds of years. (Photograph collection of Olga Salmi, Kemi)

whether the dead bore her east toward Sunrise Tuonela or west toward Evening Tuonela, or did her mother's spirit remain wandering about the sacred back corner of the common room?[9]

The most ancient concept common to the Finno-Ugric peoples is probably the idea that the soul remains in the graveyard near the body. The river of death, the River of Tuonela, is also mentioned in Finnish folklore in this connection. Both the "Lemminkäinen Rune" and "Väinämöinen's Journey to Tuonela" shed light on how the ancient Finns envisioned the abode of the dead: before it lies a river similar to the River Styx which encircles Hades, the Greek netherworld, which is guarded by the dog Cerberus. Like Hades, the *Kalevala's* Tuonela is also a gloomy region. However, its guardian is a woman, "the daughter of Tuoni, Manala's low maiden."

On the shores of the black River of Tuonela, Väinämöinen called: "Bring a boat, daughter of Tuoni, bring a raft, child of Manala."[10] The myth is the same as that of the Greek Charon on the River Styx. The River of Tuonela can be crossed by boat and also by a bridge, as in an ancient Finnish rune: "Come along Tuonela's road, Manala's bridge." The concept of the River of Tuonela links Finnish tradition to the cultural sphere of Central Asia. It is also found in numerous Byzantine cultures.[11]

Among the Saami, however, another view is encountered. This is the Arctic belief, which is also true of Finnish beliefs, that the kingdom of the dead lies beneath the water or the earth. This is Jabmeaivo, the abode of the dead. Everything in the world of the dead is the reverse of how it is in the world of the living.[12] The Christian concept of hell was actually a very late influence on Finnish tradition. Despite the fact that she was a devout Orthodox Old Believer, Marina Takalo said: "There is no such thing as hell; man cannot have two hells, first here and then again after death."[13]

Runes derived from the Middle Ages also contain depictions of heaven and hell. Eternal darkness reigns in Manala. The following verse from the *Kalevala* indicates a powerful dualism: "There is room there for the sinner, beds for the flawed." Heaven is less frequently depicted than Manala. It is a warm, bright abode of the gods, where they hold their drinking festivities in colorful dress. The Christian faith brought with it an ambivalence toward death. The community of the dead, in its relationship to that of the living, then became divided into two: those who had found peace, and belonged to the revered community of dead ancestors, and those who had not. During the Catholic Middle Ages, the state of Limbo was also spoken of when referring to the fate of unbaptized children and the patriarchs of the Old Testament. They did not attain full glory.

The *Kalevala* is a book more about life than death. Its heroes woo, and they celebrate weddings. Although there are a number of deaths, funeral rites are not described in detail. One reason for this may lie in the runes on which the epic is based. There are, on the whole, no narrative runes in the Finnish tradition about rituals related to death. Laments, rather than rune singing, were the core of Finnish burial poetry. Lyric poetry like that found in the *Kanteletar*, rather than Kalevala epic verse, was preferred as an expression of one's relationship to death. However, concepts of death, life after death, Manala, the heavens, and the River of Tuonela do exist in the *Kalevala* as they do in ancient poetry in general.

THE SHAMANS AT THE RIVER OF TUONELA

In Ganander's *Mythologia*, there is an extensive glossary of terms referring to death. According to it, both "Manala" and "Tuonela" mean realm of the dead. Ganander compared them to Glitnis, the Goths' realm of the dead. He also noted this word's relationship to the "Jabmeaivo" terminology of the Saami, which refers to the netherworld.[14] It is also interesting that, in Ganander's opinion, the expressions "Tuonella käydä," "Tuonelassa vaeltaa" (to go to Tuoni, to wander in Tuonela), like the concept "loveen langeta" (to fall into a "hole," i.e., trance), mean falling into ecstasy or a shaman's journey to Tuonela. According to Ganander, everything lacking on earth existed in Tuonela. There were abundant pleasures, and food such as pork and grain. This is why such items as knives, spears, bows, food, clothing, rings, household items, money, gold, and silver were buried with the dead. It was believed that the deceased took care of their treasures there after death. The kingdom of death was ruled by a female figure known as "Tuonelan morsian" (the Bride of Tuonela), "Tuonen neito" (the Maiden of Tuoni), who lived on "Kipumäki" (Pain Hill) or "Kipuvuori" (Pain Mountain). Ganander compared her to the heroine in the legend of Pandora's box, calling to mind the rune:

> Pain Girl, Maiden of Tuoni,
> goes on gathering pain,
> pain atop the mountain,
> the bright lid in her arms,
> the bright basket in her hand,
> she weeps and cries. [15]

Lönnrot included numerous runes in the *Kalevala* which later twentieth-century scholarship has clearly shown to be based on shamanistic culture. "Väinämöisen Tuonelan-matka" (Väinämöinen's journey to Tuonela), "Vipusen virsi" (Vipunen's rune), and "Lemminkäisen matka Päivölän pitoihin" (Lemminkäinen's journey to the Päivölä festivities) include descriptions of a shaman's experiences while in a trance state. The shaman journeys to Tuonela, where he encounters the dead and other beings as well as numerous dangers. He uses the skills he has learned in order to overcome these situations by, for example, taking the form of a particular helping spirit. In a state of altered consciousness, the shaman has experiences which deviate from the everyday.

The shaman's cognitive map, his views, beliefs, and knowledge, can also be examined from the point of view of mythology. The runes of shamanistic subject matter in the *Kalevala* are often myths about the first shamans such as Antero Vipunen, Väinämöinen, Lemminkäinen, etc., who fell into trance states long ago and journeyed either to the netherworld or to the heavens. The Kalevala runes can be interpreted both as depictions of a particular shaman's mystical experiences and as an instructive description of the experiences a shaman will encounter, including how to proceed under various circumstances. A shaman's falling into a trance can be seen as a ritual by means of which a myth is brought into the present and once again experienced by the community as a whole. Within the context of ritual, religious tradition is brought to life.

The shamanistic heroes of the *Kalevala* are victorious in crossing the borders of the kingdom of death. They each, in turn, cross the River of Tuonela and acquire the information necessary for resolving a crisis. Thus the runes provide some insight into the realm beyond death, where it was believed life continued in basically the same manner as on earth. This is, however, a world in which everything is the opposite of how it is in the world of the living, a place to which an ordinary mortal had no cause to go during life. Particularly instructive in this regard is the rune about Väinämöinen's journey to Tuonela. After returning from there, he warns:

> Many have gone there,
> But few have returned,
> From there in Tuonela's halls,
> From Manala's eternal house.
> No, good fellows,
> Young men, do not,
> Old men, do not,
> Fetch a spike from Tuonela,
> A crowbar from Manala,
> For mending sleighs,
> Building mounts!
> Do not go there.[16]

"Väinämöinen's Journey to Tuonela"[17] gives so detailed a description of a shaman's journey to the realm of the dead that one can read it as a mythological map of the topography of Tuonela. Väinämöinen goes to Tuonela in search of the words needed for the charm to build a boat. He comes to the river of Tuonela, where he is received by "Tuonen tyttö, Manalan matala neiti" (Girl of Tuonela, Manala's low maiden).

Close counterparts to the subject matter of this rune are found in Scandinavian mythology, including Odin's journey to Hel through a river swarming with snakes. In Arctic shamanism, the snake is the creature into which the shaman most commonly metamorphoses during a trance, when the goal of the journey is the realm of the dead. It was believed that the soul of the shaman traveled to Tuonela as a snake. The Mistress of Tuonela weaves an iron net, which is placed in the current to prevent Väinämöinen from leaving. Väinämöinen, however, succeeds in fleeing Tuonela by changing into a snake and swimming through this net. The net symbolizes the obstacles and dangers to which it was believed the shaman became exposed. Although the basis of this rune may be a legend about a shaman's journey to Tuonela in the form of a snake, other versions of the rune, in addition to the one included in the *Kalevala*, show modifications made in the Christian period. Shamanistic Tuonela came to be depicted negatively, like the medieval vision of hell. At the end of the rune, there are also words of warning about the dangers of falling into a trance which are similar to the teachings of Christian missionaries.

TUONELA: HADES OR THE FINNISH KINGDOM OF OSIRIS

In Finnish folk tradition, the topography of the realm of the dead varies greatly, reflecting the various cultural influences the Finns have experienced over the course of their history. In the *Kalevala*, Tuonela is encircled by a river across which the dead are ferried by the Maiden of Tuoni, a depiction similar to that

The River Styx, courtesy of the Finnish-Canadian painter Hilkka Salomaa.

of the realm of the dead found in Greco-Roman mythology. Life in Tuonela is basically similar to that on earth. The dead need food, drink, and clothing. Their activities are similar to those of people living on the earth.[18]

During the 1800s, folk singers performed rather long, unified variants of the "Lemminkäinen Rune" which were almost equal in length to the Sampo cycle. Arhippa Perttunen's version was 296 verses in length,[19] Simana Sissonen's was 306,[20] and Malanie Vuonninen's was 355.[21] These versions include a complex of poetry in which the Lemminkäinen verses are joined to include "Kaukamoisen virsi" (Kaukamoinen's rune), which tells of Kaukamoinen's flight to the island after his act of murder, as well as a rune about the festivities held at Päivölä, to which one person is left uninvited.

As Matti Kuusi has shown, the "Lemminkäinen Rune" has many strata. It is a synthesis of ancient Finnish shamanistic poetry, the later heroic poetry of Viking times, and Russian folk tales.[22] The shamanistic aspect of Lemmin-

käinen's nature has been emphasized by Matti Kuusi. In addition to Lemminkäinen's power as a sage, the descriptions of specific perils he encounters on
his journey to Päivölä have the characteristics of shamanistic poems. However, these tales of peril were influenced by the mystical literature of the
Middle Ages. In Kuusi's opinion, the modified endings of some variants of the
rune, in which the attempt to bring Lemminkäinen back to life is unsuccessful,
are related to shamanistic runes.[23] In 1854, for example, Simana Sissonen sang
the following verses for D. E. Europaeus, in which Lemminkäinen's mother
kneels beside the body of her son, wondering if he will ever become a man
again:

> Will a man yet come of you,
> a new hero function?

To this Lemminkäinen replies:

> There's no man in the one departed
> hero in the one drowned:
> this heart of mine is there
> beside the blue stone
> in the liver-colored belly.
> Already my shoulders sour
> my mound of flesh rots
> in Tuoni's black river
> Manala's eternal stream
> for long was I in darkness
> ages in the cold water
> my nails in a cold stone
> my teeth in a watery snag
> there my shoulders sour
> my mound of flesh rots.[24]

The relationship of this description to the Vipunen verses should also be noted.
The Vipunen verses describe a shaman who, having been in a trance too long,
is unable to waken to life again.

According to Kaarle Krohn, the concept of Päivölä parallels that of
"heaven."[25] Uno Harva also came to the conclusion that Päivölä, Pohjola, and
Hiitola, which find parallel usage in various versions of the "Lemminkäinen
Rune," refer to the "other realm," and not to a geographic location. According
to Harva, the deaths which Lemminkäinen encounters on his journey to Päivölä
also pertain to the other realm. Harva sees the influence of medieval mystical
writing in the depictions of these deaths. According to him, they describe the
folk singers' beliefs about places of torture where the dead are punished or puri-
fied, the fires of purgatory. Harva argues that such detailed, horrific visions
harken back to the Orphic-Pythagorean cabala.[26] In the Kalevala runes, Tuonela, which was originally described quite neutrally, has taken on the dimen-

sions of an "absolutely horrible and dreaded place." Corresponding depictions are also found in Dante's *Divine Comedy.*

In his book *Suomalainen mytologia* (Finnish mythology), Martti Haavio presents the interesting point of view that the origin of the "Lemminkäinen Rune" lies in ancient Egyptian mythology, including the Osiris myth. He deftly establishes this as "the Finnish adaptation of that drama, which was performed during ancient times in temples on the banks of the Nile, the walls of which have long since lain in ruins."[27] Haavio outlines the cultural routes along which this material would have traveled from Egypt to Karelia: Egypt–the Greek Byzantine cultural sphere–the Russian territories from Kiev to Novgorod and northern Russia, mediated by the wandering Russian performers known as the skomorokhi, and finally to Karelia.[28]

The Egyptian text about Prince Khamwesi and his son Si-Osiris includes the so-called Ethiopian Letter, which relates how the Ethiopian Horus goes to practice magic against the Egyptian king. Like Lemminkäinen, Horus is warned about the perils of this journey by his mother: "If you go to Egypt to practice your magic, beware of the Egyptians, so that you can battle against them." Horus responds: "Your words are uncalled for." "If, nevertheless, you still go to Egypt, let us arrange a signal between us. Should things go badly for you, I want to come and save you." Like Lemminkäinen, Horus agrees on a sign between his mother and himself which will enable her to know his fate. When Horus arrives at the court, there is a prolonged struggle between him and the king. Horus uses charms and is badly defeated. At the last moment, his mother, who has surmised her son's fate from the sign arranged between them, arrives to save him.[29]

According to Haavio, if the visions of the three deaths portrayed in the "Lemminkäinen Rune" are omitted from it, the beginning section of the rune clearly relates to the Egyptian text. The three deaths would then be attributed to western origins. As proof for this hypothesis, Haavio compared the subject matter common to the Ethiopian Letter, the "Lemminkäinen Rune," and the Vivilo bylina tale related by the skomorokhi, which includes omens, competitions between sages and the image of heads on stakes.[30] Haavio relates Lemminkäinen's epithets, "lieto" (carefree) and "pillopoika" (wanton fellow), which occur in many variants of the rune, to Russian origins. According to him, "lieto" is derived from the Russian word meaning fun or joyful, and "pillopoika" from the Russian word "spil'man," meaning musician or singer.[31]

There are many points of association with Egyptian mythology in the "Lemminkäinen Rune." In Egypt circa 3000 B.C., there developed a belief in a god who as a king had died on behalf of his subjects and, rising from the dead, had then established an eternal kingdom on the fields of Jalu. There the dead sowed, cultivated, and harvested crops. Upon their arrival in Egypt circa 300 B.C., those Greeks who migrated there adopted this religion and later began sending their deceased to the Elysian Fields rather than to Hades. In Egypt, worship of the dead was related to the belief in the divine kingship of

God: the Pharaoh or the Great House had, as the sole god, taken on a human configuration in order to rule the Egyptian people. As a human, the Pharaoh comprehended the needs of his subjects, and as a god, the wishes of the gods. The first divine Pharaoh was Osiris, who was identified with the flooding of the Nile. This flooding ensured that the earth received the moisture necessary for it to flourish.[32]

The ancient Egyptian myth of Osiris evolved long before the Christian era. Its complete version is preserved in Plutarch's *Ethics*.[33] According to Haavio, a version of the Osiris myth related to the latter part of the Lemminkäinen poem migrated to the region of Finnish rune singing along the route followed by the Ethiopian Letter described above. The following myth describes the establishment of the Divine Kingdom in Egypt: At the beginning of time, there was no other god but Chaos. Chaos was primordial water, and here the father-less, primordial god Atum-Ra gave birth to moisture and air, woman and man through his mouth, and they, in turn, gave birth to the heavens and the earth. From the union of the sky (Atum) and the earth (Ra), the first generation on earth was born. This consisted of two men and two women: Osiris, Seteh, Isis, and Nephtys. They divided fertile Egypt and the arid desert between them. Osiris and Isis, his sibling-spouse, ruled Egypt, and their brother Seteh ruled the desert. Osiris was the world's first cultivator and the creator of Egyptian culture. He used words rather than weapons, and won people over to his side with song and music.

Everything went well until evil entered the picture. Osiris's brother Tyfon (= Seteh) grew jealous of Osiris and slew him, dismembering his body and casting its pieces into the Nile swamp. Destruction had come to power and the world belonged to evil, for its lawful ruler, Osiris, was dead. Together with her sister, Nephtys, the widowed Isis went to search for the remains of Osiris, her husband and brother. His remains were found throughout the known world of that time, in places as distant as Libya and Nubia. Eventually, the siblings massaged Osiris's body back to life. The following lament has been found in the burial chambers of the pyramids: "Isis nears, Nephtys nears, one from the right, the other from the left. They found Osiris, for his brother Seteh had killed him. The women neared, Isis and Nephtys. They had come to embrace their brother, Osiris. Hasten, weep for your brother, Isis! Weep for your brother, Nephtys! Weep for your brother!" In embracing the body, the virgin Isis becomes pregnant and bears Horus, the son of her divine husband. Seteh sets out in pursuit of her; Isis flees into the bulrushes, where she gives birth to Horus. Horus sets out to battle Seteh and, after many episodes, returns victorious to the bier of Osiris, his father. When evil has been vanquished and order restored, Osiris returns to life. Having tasted death, however, he can no longer remain and rule the living. This task goes to his son, Horus. Osiris becomes Pharaoh of the western land, where all the inhabitants are united by the same experience, death.[34]

In addition to their structural similarities, Haavio finds evidence for the relatedness of the latter part of the "Lemminkäinen Rune" and the Osiris myth in many details. He argues, for example, that the figure of Lemminkäinen is related to Osiris through his name, for both names mean "loved one" or "beloved." The plot of the Osiris myth also includes an episode in which Osiris is able to chant all but one over to his side, his jealous brother Seteh. In Egyptian drawings, Seteh is depicted as a doglike creature. In the "Lemminkäinen Rune" as sung by Arhippa Perttunen, Lemminkäinen leaves the blind old man of Ulappala unsung. The same blind old man of Ulappala is also found in the Finnish charm "Koiran synty" (Origin of the dog).[35]

However, some of Haavio's arguments seem a bit far-fetched, and the idea of a historical relationship between these narrative traditions is not fully convincing. Matti Kuusi is skeptical of interpretations of the "Lemminkäinen Rune" based on the theme of resurrection. He argues that in the best variants of the rune, the resurrection of Leminkäinen in fact fails.[36] However, the theme of death and resurrection was not unknown in the world view of the Finnish singers, as the final verses spoken by Lemminkäinen's mother in the "Lemminkäinen Rune," as sung by Jyrki Sissonen of Ilomantsi in 1877, show:

> She looked at, she turned [Lemminkäinen's limbs],
> will a man yet come of that?
> Let's wrap him in fresh hay,
> there anoint him.
> Yes, that one became a man,
> yes, a man came of that one.[37]

FOUR SUICIDES IN THE *KALEVALA*

In addition to reflecting the topography of the Kingdom of the Dead, the Kalevala runes contain depictions of people's attitudes toward death. The *New Kalevala* contains four incidents of suicide. In the *Kalevala*, suicides are seen as the logical consequence of life's circumstances and people's deeds. The Aino runes relate how a young girl commits suicide in order to avoid marriage to an old man. In most versions, the girl's mother sends her to dress in her finest clothes to receive her suitor. The girl does not do as her mother says but hangs her clothes up instead. No one comprehends her despair over the fact that her entire life is about to be negated by marriage to an old man. Even her mother weeps only after she has lost her daughter, and then indeed warns others not to force a daughter to marry against her will.[38] The despair inherent in Aino's death is related to fertility. Aino herself does not vanish into nothingness but returns to full-blooded nature. The tears born of her mother's sorrow give birth to flowing rivers, crags, and trees.

Kullervo and his sister kill themselves because they have broken the incest taboo. In this case, the theme of death is fulfilled as payment for sins. The story of Kullervo does not portray the cyclical nature of life and death as the "Aino Poem" and "Väinämöinen's Judgment" do, for example, and as this dialectic was no doubt actually viewed by the ancient Finns. However, the Kullervo poem adds to the picture by revealing the presence of death in life itself, and not merely afterward.

Inherent in Väinämöinen's departure at the end of the *Kalevala* is the concept of an old man ceding the way to something new which renews life forces. He descends into the whirlpool of a river, and leaves Marjatta's child as the heir to his position. There is a certain element of danger and death always present in Väinämöinen's courtship attempts. He briefly holds in his hand the dead Aino, who has metamorphosed into a fish. After this, he makes further attempts at courtship and must journey to the region of women and death for this purpose. Väinämöinen is unsuccessful in all his attempts. Perhaps the old sage pays for the power of his word and his great ability as a conjurer through his impotence. Perhaps this hero, who was so necessary to the creation, was in fact too far removed from nature. The only woman whom Väinämöinen is finally able to touch concretely is his own mother, symbolized by water, from which he himself began, and to which he ultimately returns at his death. He does not pierce the feminine surface of the water except at his birth and death.

Finnish attitudes toward suicide have changed. The runes reflect a time when Finland was receiving Christian influences as a result of crusades by both the Western and Eastern churches. In the west, the new religion was Roman Catholicism, which decreed suicide a criminal act. As a result of the Reformation at the beginning of the sixteenth century, Sweden-Finland became Protestant. The Protestant attitude toward suicide was more tolerant than that of Catholicism. In the seventeenth century suicide came under the jurisdiction of the ecclesiastical court. Previous to this, suicides and attempted suicides had been considered criminal acts in Sweden-Finland. The attitude of the Eastern Orthodox Church toward suicide has been more lenient than that of the Western Church. [39]

Swedish laws on suicide derived from the fifteenth century decreed that a specific jury was to carry out a study of the mental state of the person who had committed the act. If it was affirmed that the individual had been mentally ill, he or she was quietly buried outside the graveyard. If the suicide was deemed a consciously rational act, the body was burned; this custom was later replaced with burial by an executioner. [40] From the end of the seventeenth century on, the attitude toward suicide or attempted suicide in Finland was the same as that toward violent crime. It was punished by a fine or by penalties mandated by the church. In a law dated 1734, the punishments were made more severe. Attempts at suicide were punished by imprisonment, bread and water sustenance, and whippings or public floggings. When a more tolerant law was adopted by the Finnish Lutheran Church in 1869, people who had committed suicide were granted a quiet burial inside the cemetery. In 1919, a law was passed stating that a suicide should be buried in the same manner as other dead. [41]

Although both state and church law judged suicide and attempts at suicide harshly and as a disgrace, the ordinary folk quietly accepted some suicides as the natural consequence of life's circumstances or as appropriate for certain kinds of guilt.[42] During the czarist period, there even developed a nationalistic idealization of suicide. For example, the poet Kaarlo Kramsu (1855–1895) wrote: "More beautiful than a slave's life is death on the gallows."[43] Here, the emphasis is on the heroic model of suicide, for which there was also support in the folk tradition. It is not actually suicide which is at issue here, but rather voluntary death, which has parallels in Arctic cultures.[44]

CHILD ABANDONMENT AS AN EPICAL MOTIF

Child abandonment is a universal motif in myths. The culture hero is often a child who is thought to have been killed, but is then somehow miraculously saved. This child then often fulfills a predestined fate. Examples of this are Moses, Buddha, Jesus, and Oedipus. In Old Norse epics, this theme occurs in the "Harðar Saga," among others. Matti Kuusi considered the French legend "Saint George and the Dragon" to be one of the models for "Väinämöinen's Judgment."[45] The figure who wishes to do away with the child is usually the infant's father or another symbol of power which it has been prophesied the coming of the child will destroy.

A closer examination of the backgrounds of the rune "Väinämöinen's Judgment" and a number of other Finnish runes, such as the medieval balladlike tale "Marketta and Hannus," shows that they also include the theme of child abandonment or infanticide. In "Väinämöinen's Judgment," a "clergyman" is called on to baptize a child which has been born out of wedlock. He refuses, citing the child's illegitimacy. A trial is held to determine the child's father. The judge is to be Väinämöinen. When no one acknowledges paternity, it is then decreed that the child be taken to a swamp and struck on the head with a cowlstaff. At this point, God's judgment intervenes: the child begins to speak and reveals his father to be Väinämöinen. Following this, the parson Vironkannas performs the baptism. Väinämöinen then steps into his boat and disappears from the cosmos.[46]

References to the abandonment of female children are found in Finnish runes. In the Ingrian rune "Poikako vai Tyttö?" (Boy or girl?), the singer says her mother's heart did not allow the sentence of abandonment to be carried out. These runes, which are found throughout the Balto-Finnic poetry area, imply that abandonment of children as an institution existed in Finland as well as Scandinavia and was declared illegal only with the coming of Christianity. Icelandic sagas and Scandinavian provincial laws show that abandonment of children was among the first issues raised with the advent of Christianity. According to the Nordic sagas, it was usually female children who were abandoned. The sagas do not usually mention that the children were killed violently. Rather, they were left to their own fate. There are also tales describing miracles, such as someone finding a child—as the Pharaoh's daughter found Moses—and keeping it alive.[47]

A saga relates that a son was born to A'sgrim of Telemark as he was about to leave on a Viking journey. He ordered that the boy be abandoned, and instructed a slave to place the child in his grave. Before the child could be picked up, he began to speak, asking to be placed at his mother's breast:

> Take me to my mother!
> I'm cold on the floor.
> Where's a better place for a boy
> than beside his mighty father.
> No need to sharpen the sword
> or to dig pits in the ground. Don't do evil!
> I still want to live among people.[48]

The father was moved by these words. He picked up the child and gave him a name. This act of lifting the child from the floor and the father's placing his hands upon him was referred to as "borit ad foður sínum." According to Nordic legal practice, this was an important ritual of social legitimation. The father demonstrated his acceptance of the child and confirmed its social rights by anointing the infant with water and giving it a name. Thus, baptismal ritual preceded the Christian faith and was referred to as "vattni ausin," the pouring of water. In the saga tradition, Christian baptism is referred to as "skírn," cleansing. In connection with this ritual, the question of whether to allow the child to live or to abandon it became an issue. A child which was not accepted into the clan and did not receive a name was abandoned. However, even in pre-Christian times, the desertion of a baptized child was considered murder. Proof of this is found in the "Harðar Saga," dated 950: "Therefore, the killing of a child after it had been baptized was called murder."[49]

According to ancient Nordic legal tradition, a child's name was its most important criterion for social acceptance. Likewise, a child which had been placed at its mother's breast could not be abandoned. This custom is also considered ancient in origin. According to a pre-Christian Frisian saint legend of the eighth century, if a child was to be drowned, this had to be done before it had suckled. It is interesting that the bestowal of a name and the first feeding were considered equal criteria for determining a child's right to inheritance under Nordic provincial law.[50]

In Icelandic sagas and Norwegian provincial laws, there exists the concept "barna útburðir," which means abandoned children. In Central Ostrobothnia, a murdered child who haunts is also referred to as one who has been "carried out" ("uloskannettu" in Finnish, "utbörding" in Swedish). This is derived from the ancient, complex tradition about murdered children who haunt in order to reveal their parents, to get revenge and ultimately obtain a name which will guarantee them social acceptability.[51]

"The Judgment of Väinämöinen" and other ancient Finnish runes seem to preserve a depiction of a child's baptismal ceremony which dates back to an early stage of Christianization. Before an illegitimate child could be given a name, its father, or an individual who would acknowledge paternity, had to be found. It was possible to resolve the question of paternity by means of legal proceedings, such as the one described in the rune, which Väinämöinen was called on to preside over as a respected figure. If it was not possible to determine a father for the child, the infant was sentenced to abandonment. Refusal to bestow a name can be a forthright death decree in a culture which does not sanction an illegitimate child, a child which lacks the social endorsement conferred on it by a father. However, actual biological fatherhood has not been considered as important in all cultures as the father's social role. It can be succinctly stated that in such cultures, the mother gives the child its biological life, the father bestows its social existence.[52]

This search for a father is described in Finnish runes. A father was needed in order to give the child a name. The name united the child to a clan, which in turn determined the child's place in society here on earth and, ultimately, its status after death as well. In the ancient Finnish social order, kinship was the determining factor in an individual's life. The heroes of the ancient runes always proudly present themselves as the offspring of great kin. Kinship determined a child's right to life, and in general the child's mother complied with this. In acknowledging a child, the father represented the entire clan in addition to himself. Upon bestowal of a name, however, the child became a person, a socially alive human being who could no longer be killed or abandoned. The child could also be confirmed as a member of the kin if the name of a dead ancestor was bestowed on it. In this circumstance, it was believed that the ancestor was reincarnated in the child.[53] Bestowal of a name upon an infant is similar to the initiation rites held by numerous peoples on a child's coming of age and becoming a fully participating sexual and intellectual member of the community.

In this Finnish rune, when the newborn infant opens his mouth, he utters truths which astonish the listeners. The child has achieved the capacity to speak so proficiently that the adults listen to and believe him; he has learned to use the language correctly. The content of the child's speech reveals that he has knowledge of sexuality; whether he tells of Old Väinämöinen's perversities or—as in "Marketta and Hannus"—shows that he is knowledgeable about his own origins. In this poem, the father attempts to kill the child "legally" before he is accepted as a social being by attempting to prevent him from being admitted into the community. But the child saves his own life by demonstrating that he is already a complete human being. The child fulfills two important criteria: he has the capacity to speak the truth and knowledge of sexuality.

It is also of interest that when the father refuses to bestow a name on the child, the boy names his own father. In this way he also gives himself a name, for a child who has a father also has a name. The name is the criterion for paternal inheritance rights. If a newcomer is perceived as belonging to the cycle which transcends life and death—as was the case in ancient Finnish society—and the potential reincarnation of an ancestor whose soul and name it bears, the child's father then also represents its father's father, whose namesake it is and to whom it is indebted for its life. This further legitimates the miracle embodied in this speech by the child of a few days. The father realizes that in judging the child he was, in fact, judging his own father, a fact which shames him and makes him accede.

Therefore, in refusing to give the child a name, the father denies the child 1) its name, 2) the right to remain physically alive, 3) the right to become socially alive, and 4) the right to a proper death and those rituals which would unite the child with its dead ancestors. Thus, the father's refusal threatens to deny all significant human status and social legitimacy to the child. Without a name, the child has no status, soul, power, or abilities. However, once having received a name, it attains status and power and eventually will also become one of the esteemed dead kin who, even beyond death's boundaries, function as guardians of laws with regard to the living.[54]

The relation between death, knowledge, and truth is an interesting one. We have already seen how a child being threatened with death speaks the truth. Death often functions as a revealer of truth. As a measure of truth, it can also be used as a threat. It is often believed that death reveals truths which have remained hidden in life and unifies human knowledge into a greater whole. Thus it is understandable that an effort to preserve this perceived moment of truth in death is also incorporated into initiation rituals in which those words which yield life are taught through a symbolic death. Väinämöinen's threat to slay the child may, in fact, be a threat meant to bring death near, thus showing the child the gateway to life and granting it the key to life, speech.

VÄINÄMÖINEN'S DEATH AS CULTURAL CHANGE

Väinämöinen's departure ends the sequence of events in the *Kalevala*. The fact that this episode is unified at the end of the epic with that about Marjatta's son has provided considerable support for the interpretation that in this rune Lönnrot wished to portray the victory of the Christian religion over paganism, the dawn of a new era and the waning of the old. The finality of Väinämöinen's departure and the possibility of his return remains an open question. Some rune singers, in fact, have believed in Väinämöinen's eventual return.[55]

When the audience in the rune believes the accusations made by Marjatta's son against Väinämöinen, the clergyman christens the child "King of Karelia." The boy is specifically named Väinämöinen in old Väinämöinen's stead. The old man yields to the community's decision, chants himself his last boat, and departs. It is worth noting that the child's words are similar to a decree of fate. The old sage does not struggle against this, but rather departs of his own free will, although somewhat bitterly. Väinämöinen accepts the decision of his own accord. He "feels that his time has come." This corresponds to an archaic natural manner of dealing with one's right to die. The rune is also an adaptation of the model of voluntary suicide found among Arctic peoples which condones killing oneself when one considers oneself of no more use to the community.[56]

In the rune, it appears that Väinämöinen loses his virility at the same time the child achieves his. If bestowal of a name granted life to a child as a social being, then the loss of one's name correspondingly meant social death.˙ This is what happens to Väinämöinen, and the circumstances initially presented in the rune are reversed: In the beginning Väinämöinen had a name and the boy was nameless; at the conclusion, the child has a name and the old sage is without one. With the transference of a name, knowledge is also transferred, and the individual who has yielded it must then step aside. Väinämöinen himself had gotten Antero Vipunen to part with his treasure of knowledge, and following this, the old sage, who was already half-decayed, was able to part from life irrevocably.

Vipunen yielded his knowledge about the origins of the world: the boy, in turn, usurps from Väinämöinen knowledge of a deed Väinämöinen performed before the boy himself existed. In some variants of the rune, the boy claims knowledge of Väinämöinen's birth, which was incestuous in nature. This concurs with the logic of the Kalevala runes, in accordance with which a person who knows the origins of a phenomenon or the circumstance which controls it can decide its fate. In both instances, this knowledge is sexual (birth, conception, origins). In addition, the child tells of Väinämöinen's nonproductive, even perverse sexuality. This immediately casts doubt on Väinämöinen's virility and his powers of creation. Väinämöinen's departure signifies acknowledgment of this accusation, and the change in generations is, in addition to the transference of a name and knowledge, also the transference of virility, sexual productivity, and the responsibilities contained therein.

If we examine this event as a change in epochs that is nevertheless part of an eternal continuity, it can be demonstrated that Lönnrot's *Kalevala* in fact contains three intermediary epochs. The first of these is the true period of no culture which reigned before the birth of Väinämöinen. At this time, the elements of the cosmos were formed. Väinämöinen's birth is followed by the period in which culture is founded and established. Marjatta's son initiates the third epoch which alters Väinämöinen's world. The rune "Väinämöinen's Judgment" in itself telescopes the existence of these three worlds, particularly if we take equal note of those oral variants which were not included in Lönnrot's *Kalevala*. The transition into the final epoch results from a single sign, the power of the boy's act of speech. The boy reminds Väinämöinen of his crimes: his guilt in the death of Aino, the use of a human being as chattel and the worst of crimes, incest. These already indicate Väinämöinen's senility, his unsuitability for the role of a just leader.[57]

Between two epochs, a period of marginality with its own logic ensures the rites of transition which govern the various stages of life, such as birth and life, or life and death. Within such a system of logic, events unacceptable under normal logic, such as virgin birth, are tolerated. During the course of the ritual drama, the world is upside-down, in a state of "anti-structure," as contrasted with the normal structure of the world. Thus under circumstances of marginality, an event such as Väinämöinen's immaculate conception, which would be a crime (incest) under normal conditions, is acceptable. Väinämöinen's two liminal periods are in the womb and in his moment of departure. Väinämöinen's happy and, in itself, ritual beginning, Oedipal desire and its fulfillment, appears as a crime when related by the boy, and Väinämöinen is ashamed. It is the very weight of this transgression which again casts him into a situation of sanctioned marginality between life and death, a realm of logic which tolerates the metamorphosis of these worlds. The circumstances surrounding Marjatta's son parallel those of Väinämöinen, but the rune follows him only until that moment when his period of normal life begins. If the red whortleberry were to be interpreted as communion bread, the image of cyclical determinism would be further strengthened.

The possibility of Väinämöinen's return becomes comprehensible within the context of the cyclical world view of the Finnish folk religion and does not, then, concur with the finality inherent in the Christian religion. Christianity evolved within the context of the Finnish folk religion and eventually displaced it. The possibility remained, however, that the Christian religion might ultimately exhaust itself, at which point the old religion still dormant inside it would once again be able to gather momentum.

If the Freudian death instinct means "to return to the previous state and ultimately to inorganic, absolute rest"[58] and life is merely a series of episodes, circular routes which lead toward non-being, a series of adventure-filled events which nevertheless are determined in that their primary goal is to discover the organism's own manner of death,[59] as Freud's famous postulate states, then Väinämöinen's life and death are in accordance with this logic. He was born of the water, chanted himself superb boats during his lifetime, and always preferred journeys on the water to those on land.

KULLERVO: A TRAGEDY OF GUILT AND DEATH

The story of Kullervo is an utterly gloom-filled tale of death. Lönnrot structured this tragedy to fit into the *Kalevala* as a separate epic in itself, although he interspersed it with other subject matter. It differs from the poems discussed previously in its total pessimism. Discounting Ilmarinen, who appears in the tale as a peripheral character, not one of the figures in it remains alive at the end. Kullervo plays a role in each of approximately ten death dramas which take place within the context of his life. The circumstances of his birth are related to the death of his clan; an attempt is made to kill him even as a child; he is responsible for the death of a small child entrusted to his care; he kills Ilmarinen's wife; he causes his own sister's death; and, in a certain sense, he is responsible for the deaths of the rest of his family. Kullervo even avenges his father's death and slays all of Untamo's band. In the end he is the only one left alive and kills himself. This closes the circle, ending his death-filled life.

Kullervo's life does, in fact, contain more death than life. Even the sole sexual act it contains leads to death. It is also worth noting how three girls respond to Kullervo when he tries to entice them into his sleigh. The first one responds:

"Death to your sleigh, a plague to that fur pelt of yours." Likewise the second one says: "Death to your sledge, of Manala your journey." The girls' responses already predict doom. And when the third girl finally agrees to go on the journey to collect taxes with Kullervo, she turns out to be the very one among the three maidens whom he should not court, for she is his sister. When their kinship is revealed, the girl says that she had already tried to kill herself but was unsuccessful. Only after the fateful event does she succeed. The tale is heavy with fatalism: not even death had cared to have this girl before her encounter with Kullervo. In certain other variants of this incest rune, Kullervo (or, alternatively, Lemminkäinen), after seducing his sister, throws his hands over his loins and curses them as "the doors to the grave." Thus death is seen as residing in misused sexuality. The established balance of things has been disrupted, and the sister's death could not be avoided: it took place at the moment of incest. The unity of incest and death is familiar in international mythology. Often it is based precisely on violence against the complicated but single correct order of the cosmos.[60]

It is decreed that Kullervo's own life be filled with even more death. When he enters his home, his mother sees immediately that he has been touched by death: "What's the matter, my son? What fever on your brow? It's as if you've come from Tuonela, journeyed from Manala!" Now Kullervo is marked by death in others' eyes. In his farewell, as he departs to get revenge, the slaying signifies that he will even more surely be courted by death. Amongst the regenerative words of the *Kalevala*, his is the word of death. Death has already vanquished life, and nothing will make Kullervo turn away from his murderous journey. In the end, as if by chance, Kullervo arrives at the place he was directed to by his dead mother and her dog, the place where he seduced his sister. He notices that the fatal crime has even disfigured nature, for not even grass grows there. In speaking to his sword, Kullervo speaks to death itself, which is symbolized by the impartial and ready sword. The tragedy of death is a tragedy only for the human who suffers it. Death itself is no longer touched by this. For death, guilt and innocence are the same.

> Kullervo, Kalervo's son,
> Unsheathed the sharp sword;
> He looked, he turned,
> He asked, he queried.
> He asked the sword its mind,
> Whether it would like
> To consume guilty flesh,
> To drink flawed blood.
>
> The sword considered the man's mind,
> Pondered the hero's problem.
> Responded in these words:
> "Why wouldn't I gladly consume,
> Consume guilty flesh,

Drink flawed blood?
Even innocent flesh I consume,
Flawless blood I drink.

Kullervo, Kalervo's son,
Blue-stocking, child of the oldster.
The haft shoved deep in the field,
The heft weighed the moor,
Turned the blade toward his breast,
cast himself on the blade.[61]

The story of Kullervo is a Finnish tale of fate which dramatically relates the obvious fact that it is impossible to avoid death, which persecutes all, even early in life. It presents life as tragic and incomprehensible. A person is fated to live a particular life, to do certain deeds without deliberation or substantial reflection. Despite this, he is weighted by guilt for his deeds, and this guilt drives him toward suicide. Like the Oedipus myth, which reveals the paradox of life and death, the Kullervo epic implies at great length that it would have been better not to have been born, or at least to have died as soon as possible. The theory according to which every organism seeks death, and therefore dies in its own way, is called "psychoanalytic tragedy." According to this theory, death, which is already contained in birth, gradually attains greater and greater victory over life–life is, in fact, only the warding off of death, keeping it at bay.[62]

11

THE *KALEVALA* IN FINNISH HISTORY

ON WRITING NATIONAL HISTORY AND MYTHOGRAPHY

What is the role of the *Kalevala* in Finnish history? The answer depends, first of all, on how Finland and its history are defined. A second question concerns the role of the *Kalevala* in the genesis of both Finland and Finnishness. It is the goal of this chapter to clarify the role of the *Kalevala* within that historical process, during the course of which, Finnish self-awareness and identity were formed in the nineteenth century. The role of the *Kalevala* was central to this process. One of its end results was the establishment of the *Kalevala* as the Finnish national epic.

The following is meant to provide a background for this complex series of events by providing a broad outline of both the history of Finland and the Finns. In general usage the word "history" can have three different meanings: It can mean the past, a narrative about the past, and the study of the past.[1] Strictly speaking, however, history is not the same as the entirety of that past. Depending upon the sources, "history" always gives a more or less fragmentary picture of the past which it describes.[2] Finnish history is a narrative which can be written in a longer or shorter temporal sequence. First it is necessary to distinguish between Finland as a country and the Finns as a nation. Within these categories, we should also not forget the histories of the numerous other cultures in Finland.

As a nation, Finland is quite young, whether the beginnings of the state are calculated from the Period of Autonomy starting in 1809 or from December 6, 1917, the date the nation achieved independence. According to Matti Klinge[3] the history of Finland as a state begins in 1809. Finland became a Grand Duchy of Russia and was accorded autonomy along with its own central administration. Throughout the previous historical periods, from the Medieval Era on, Finland had been one of 3–7 provinces of the Kingdom of Sweden. Over the course of centuries, a broader geographical concept of Finland as a country had gradually been established. The concept of Finland, which had initially signified only the southwestern areas of the country (Finland Proper), now included the entire area from Karelia in Russia to the Gulf of Bothnia, and the Gulf of Finland.

As per the introduction to *Kalevala Mythology,* I have considered the relationship between mythology and history. While mythology (ch. 1) is either the study of myths or the collection and synthesis of mythological narratives, mythography is the writing of myths as a part of the "sacred history" of a people. This is particularly true when the "history" concerns the birth of a nation and the rise of national identity, as is the case in Finland.[4] At issue here is "history" which is or has been "sacred" to the people. To study and understand this kind of "history," both "insider" and "outsider" viewpoints are necessary. Although many issues related to the Finnish cultural sphere seem enmeshed in the rug of "historical truth," there is reason to ask, for example: how, where, when, why, and who has written Finnish history and for whom?

The boundary between myth and history is like a line drawn in water. Each could be defined as a narrative. Included in the former are beliefs, rituals, symbols, world views, and conscious as well as unconscious mental structures. According to Claude Lévi-Strauss, "myths think in us."[5] Whereas myths include both oral and written tradition, history has generally been approached as a collection of documented records and texts, based upon written sources. On the other hand, history has usually been accepted "as written," frequently by the victor's pen and based upon sources compiled by representatives of the culture in power. Because history is written at the behest of those in power[6] and from their point of view, the languages and cultures of oppressed minorities have often been ignored, as have those peoples whose traditions are oral, lacking written documented sources. These features are also characteristic of the process by which the oral poetic tradition, beginning with the Karelian singers (ch. 2), was recorded and canonized in the *Kalevala*. The founder of Finno-Ugric studies, M. A. Castrén,[7] considered ethnography a part of cultural history, stating: "All peoples do not have a history in the higher sense of the word, rather, their history is in fact ethnography."

EPOCHS IN FINNISH HISTORY

The history of Finland is not the same as that of the Finnish language or Finnishness as culture. History may be characterized as a narrative which can be written in shorter or longer spans. According to the Dutch cultural historian Johan Huizinga (1872–1945), history is a "spiritual form wherein a culture takes account of its past."[8] Among the founders of the discipline of history in Europe is Leopold von Ranke (1795–1885), a German contemporary of Lönnrot. He was carrying out his archival research at exactly the same time as Lönnrot was conducting his initial fieldwork expedition with rune singers in Savo and Karelia. In 1827, upon departing for a research trip to the archives of Vienna, Venice, Rome, and Florence, Ranke expressed the wish, "as history's Columbus, to discover a past world."[9] Ranke came to the conclusion that "history is constantly being rewritten. Each epoch and its primary orientation makes history its own and transfers its own concepts to this history." According to Ranke, each historical era begins at the same starting point: "Before God all generations are equal, equally entitled, a historian's role must be understood in the same manner."[10]

Ranke's requirement for historical scholarship was that it be written "wie es eigentlich gewesen" (as it actually occurred).[11] Ranke also focused history's search-light upon small nations: "Each of our—meaning the western countries'—govern-ments has a national basis and a national mission."[12] In Finland his ideas were adopted by J. V. Snellman and professor of history Yrjö Koskinen (1830–1903), among oth-ers. Although the concept of a state also exists in their writings, more important than this, as a starting point for the national process of the Finns, was their empha-sis upon the formation of the Finns as a people. Koskinen said that Finland stepped "into the light of history" quite late "because of the country's extremely peripheral location," which was "beside the sea of the Russian peoples."[13]

In the following, Finnish history is scrutinized as an outline composed of ten periods, beginning with the sixteenth century, and the viewpoint is that of the his-tory of a mentality. According to Jacques Le Goff, mentality is that which a person shares with his or her contemporaries.[14] This is in accordance with Huizinga's con-cept that the prevailing spirit of each age aims to direct the spiritual product of the elites.[15] His viewpoint is based upon the idea that each period is marked by genera-tional memory and experience. In addition to being written collectively, history is told, "created," and written in accordance with how individuals in a particular gen-eration remember it: "how the past is re-membered or dis-membered."

It appears that, in intervals of approximately every fifty years, new modes of nationally significant thought have developed in the minds of Finns. This creative process, once begun within a few smaller circles, may last a decade or two. Such ideas and processes may then become an integral part of the nation's written "his-tory" and are revisited and reformulated when necessary, in times of war or other crises.

1. The Evangelical Lutheran Reformation which had occurred in Germany dur-ing the first half of the sixteenth century resulted in the actual joining of "hinterland Finland" to the Kingdom of Sweden and the Swedish culture, now much more powerful than before, during the mid–1550s. Despite the fact that Finland had been part of Sweden since the crusades of the twelfth century, the relationship of the Finns to the Swedish monarchy had remained relatively distant. In Sweden, King Gustavus I Vasa (1496–1560) used the new division of power politics in Eu-rope skillfully to his advantage. The Protestant Reformation had brought with it a new religious division of continental Europe in accordance with the principle and politics of "whose territory, his religion" *(cuius regio, eius religio)*. Now a king or prince could decide for his subjects how they were to worship in his kingdom. Gustavus Vasa had decided to ally himself with the Protestant Reformation in Ger-many for reasons which had more to do with power politics than religion.

Finland played a more important role than previously in the regime's plan to extend its power eastward. Particularly meaningful for Finland's future was the Reformation principle that literature be produced to be read in national languages.[16] It became the task of the Finnish reformer and first Lutheran Bishop in Finland, Mikael Agricola,[17] to create a corpus of Finnish-language church literature. Agricola based this primarily upon the speech patterns and vocabulary of western Finnish dialects. The religious literature translated into Finnish by Agricola formed the basis for the development of Finnish literary language, thus providing the resources necessary for "civilizing" the Finns and Finland.

2. Following the death of Gustavus I Vasa and while an internal struggle was taking place among the Vasa kin over succession, the ambitions of the emerging Swedish power turned southward. Catherine Jagellonica, Polish-born wife of John, Duke of Finland, became the mainstay of the Catholic Counter Reformation in Sweden. Their son, Sigismund (1566–1632), who became king of both countries, ruled Sweden from Poland. John's brother, Duke Charles, however, subsequently overthrew Sigismund and attained the throne as King Charles IX of Sweden (1550–1611). He carried out a significant policy of populating the uninhabited remote regions in his kingdom. For this policy he wisely used new settlers from Karelia and Savo who practiced the expansive burn-beat agricultural economy.[18] The Swedish-Russian boundary was pushed significantly to the east. The boundary of the Treaty of Täyssinä (1595), now drawn for the first time from the Gulf of Finland to the Arctic Sea, was also the religious boundary between the Eastern and Western churches. People from eastern Finland became Sweden's buffers to the west, up to the boundary area between Sweden and Denmark (-Norway). Approximately 40,000 of these so-called Forest Finns moved to the unoccupied forests in central Scandinavia, further extending the Finnish population which had initially settled near Stockholm and in the lake regions of central Sweden during medieval times.[19]

3. The Swedish Kingdom attained its zenith during the 1630s and 1640s. King Gustavus II Adolphus (1594–1632) made extensive conquests in continental Europe. During the reign of Queen Christina, who attained the throne at the age of six years but resigned shortly after her conversion to Roman Catholicism, a Swedish colonial policy was created. New Sweden (Nova Suecia) was founded on American shores at the mouth of the Delaware River in 1638, once again primarily by relocating some of the Forest Finns' Scandinavian settlements.[20] The administration of Finland was systematically organized by Count Per Brahe, who urbanized the coastal regions of the country. In 1640 he founded the Turku Academy (the present-day University of Helsinki). From that time onward, the academic training of the Finns, historically centered in Paris, Prague, Leipzig, Krakow and, during the Reformation in the 1550s, at Wittenberg and later Uppsala, began to take place more and more in Finland.[21]

4. At the close of the seventeenth and the beginning of the eighteenth century, Sweden's position as a great power crumbled as a result of the military campaigns and defeats sustained by King Charles XII. The king was killed during a siege of Frederikstad and, subsequently, thousands of soldiers from the Finnish Carolinian army perished on the Norwegian mountains in a futile Norwegian campaign. As Sweden's power was crumbling in the west, its eastern adversary, Russia, was expanding into Ingria at the eastern end of the Gulf of Finland. Beginning in 1700, Peter the Great, a western European–oriented Russian czar and Charles' vanquisher, constructed St. Petersburg, the capital of Russia. He named the city at the mouth of the Neva River for himself. A powerful new metropolis and an economic and cultural center, St. Petersburg was established in the midst of Finnish-speaking settlements and those of close linguistic relatives, the Ingrians, Votes, and Estonians.[22]

5. During the succeeding period, while Finland continued to remain a battleground for extensive military campaigns between Sweden and Russia, there was

increased education of the Finnish-speaking populace resulting from the Lutheran Church's mission to educate the people during the decades 1730–1750. Supported by Church religious instruction in Finnish, "Finnishness" was bolstered in peripheral areas such as Ostrobothnia, Savo, Karelia, and Ingria. When the Finnish people became able to read religious scriptures in their mother tongue, there emerged a wave of ecstatic religious awakenings. These evolved into socio-religious movements, initially in Southern Finland and in Finland proper and later throughout the country, heightening the self-awareness of the Finnish peasantry. In addition, the status of women rose. Religious revivalism began in rural areas, initiated by women (Liisa Eerikintytär, Anna Rogel), peasant leaders such as Juhana Lustig, Paavo Ruotsalainen, and others "awakened" in Savo.[23]

6. With the advent of the French Enlightenment to Finland, national awareness, led by H. G. Porthan and C. Ganander, progressed during the 1770s–1790s. Their writings and collections of Finnish language and folklore also formed the basis for the *Kalevala* process (ch. 1).

With regard to the evolution of the Finnish mentality, each of the epochs 7–10 listed below and described more extensively in chapters 1–4 of this book uses approximately this same interval of half a century as a benchmark based upon generational memory. Each epoch deserves deeper analysis here because, in this author's opinion, each reflects the multifaceted influence of the *Kalevala* on Finnish history and mythography.

7. Publication of the *Old* (1835) and the *New* (1849) *Kalevala* and initiation of the *Kalevala* process during the decade 1830–1840.

8. Fennomania and Karelianism during the decades of Russian oppression in 1870–90 when the *Kalevala* became the flagship of Finnishness both within Finland and abroad.

9. Following independence in 1917 and during the period between World Wars I and II, Finland experienced the establishment of the national state, along with several national symbols of cultural self-esteem including: The Akateeminen Karjala-Seura (Academic Karelia Society), the Great Finland Movement; and the Kalevala Seura (Kalevala Society), culminating in the grand *Kalevala* jubilee celebration in 1935.

10. Postwar developments in Finland, including an improving economy, urbanization, and industrialization, increased international activism in general and in cultural politics; the *Kalevala* jubilee year, 1985; membership in the European Union in 1996, Helsinki as the City of Culture, 2000, etc.

THE FINNISH LANGUAGE AS A BASIS
FOR CULTURAL IDENTITY

The cultural history of the Finns is a much longer narrative than the relatively brief history of the nation and state beginning in the 1900s. Although Finland has been a multicultural as well as a multilingual country throughout its history, among the most salient characteristics of Finnishness is its unique language.[24] Along with approximately thirty other languages, Finnish belongs to the Uralic language family, the history of which dates back approximately 8,000 years. In light of present-day archaeology, the Finnish peninsula has been populated more than 9,000 years. The most ancient remains of settlement in Finland are, for example, the bog-finds at Suomussalmi and Paltamo in the north, the world's oldest fishing net, found in Antrea, and the Heinola winter sledge in the south, all items dated approximately 7000 B.C.[25]

Although it is not possible to speak with certainty about the languages of the indigenous peoples of Scandinavia and Finland, there may have been proto-Uralic tongues among them alongside other already-dead languages. According to recent theories presented by philologists, archaeologists, and anthropologists,[26] the Finns and the Sami would be the indigenous peoples of Scandinavia. Based upon archaeological finds, the lifestyle of these indigenous peoples seems to have been quite similar to that described in an account of the Fenni given by Tacitus in his *Germania*, 98 A.D. From this point of view, Tacitus may well be describing Lapps (Sami) or proto-Finns.[27] This hypothesis is supported by the linguist Jorma Koivulehto's[28] etymology of the word "suomi." At issue here is the name "zeme" given by the Balts to those who dwelt beyond the Gulf of Finland. According to the Balts, these were speakers of a different language, hunters and fishermen who were "inhabitants of a low-lying, wet land" (suomi). If both the word "sapme," meaning Sami, and the words "häme" and "suomi," denoting the people of Häme (Tavastia) and Suomi (Finland), are of the same root, it is possible, like Koivulehto, to argue that the northern Baltic traders who sold fur and fish were referred to as "zeme" by their Baltic neighbors whether they were Finns, Tavastians, or Sami.

From the point of view of the *Kalevala* phenomenon, it is important to note that folklore is contingent upon the language spoken by the folk. It is possible, in fact, to speak of a "cultural mother tongue."[29] Closely bound to this is the archaic eight-syllable trochaic poetic meter, later known as the Kalevala meter, with its alliteration which was preserved largely by the playing of a unique instrument, the kantele, and the specific singing style which accompanied it (ch. 5).

The folk culture of the Finnish "hinterland" remained vital during the Middle Ages, when ties to Sweden were weak and the language of religion and culture was primarily Latin. By the end of the seventeenth century during the Reformation Period, when Swedish became the language of governance, it became possible to realize within the Kingdom of Sweden the political concept of one religion, one language, one set of laws and customs: *"una religio, una lingua, una lex, iidem mores."*[30] Important to the development of Finnish cultural life was the fundamental principle of the Reformation which held that the people must be able to read God's word themselves. At the same time that the initial basis for Finnish literature was being created, the attitude toward folklore and folk religion, viewed as pagan, became negative, especially during the "period of orthodoxy" in the seventeenth century. The schism between the Finnish upper class of Swedish speakers and the Finnish-speaking "folk" deepened, as the historian Eirik Hornborg notes, "in a manner which today is difficult to comprehend."[31]

Alongside the Finns, Finland's other indigenous people are the Sami (ca. 6,500), whose language, Sami (Lappish), is spoken within the borders of Finland in three different dialects (Northern, Skolt, and Inari Sami) and which attained legal status only in 1995. Based upon its constitution, Finland's second official language has been Swedish which, for historical reasons, has had a particularly powerful role in Finnish governmental, economic, and cultural institutions. From the beginning of the nineteenth century on, Jews and Tatars have existed as religious-cultural minorities in Finland. Their number (ca. 1,000 each) is considerably smaller than that of the Gypsies (6,000–8,000).[32]

From Finland's more than a century-long "period of autonomy" as a Russian Duchy until its independence (1917) and civil war (1918), there were tens of thousands of Russian soldiers in Finland. The influence of the civilian Russian population has been noteworthy in Finnish trade and in the Orthodox Church, the services of which are still held in both Finnish and Russian. The Russians, whose number decreased rapidly after Finnish independence, are, in the 1990s, once again Finland's largest foreign population (ca. 23,000). Approximately fifty languages and peoples are represented by Finland's 80,000–100,000 foreign citizens. Among the religious groups, the number of Moslems in Finland has risen to approximately 21,000 as a result of emigration from Arab lands and the former Yugoslavia.[33]

THE EMERGENCE OF FINNISH IDENTITY UNDER RUSSIAN RULE

From the point of view of the formation of national identity it was significant that, at the beginning of the Period of Autonomy, Czars Alexander I (1801–25) and II (1855–81), in particular, were quite sympathetic to the emergence of Finnish national symbols. At the Diet of Porvoo in 1809, Czar Alexander I proclaimed that the country had been elevated to "membership in the family of nations,"[34] with its own constitution, carried over from the period of Swedish rule, and its own Diet, empowered to act in all matters not reserved for the Czar. When Helsinki became the capital of Finland, it became the country's center of culture and government, where the Senate, the University—with the Czar himself as chancellor—as well as other cultural and economic institutions were located. It appears that the czars wished to develop Finland and Helsinki as an exemplary model and, to a certain extent, Finland became akin to a Russian display window for the West. Significant from the point of view of government, economics, and culture was the fact that Helsinki was located near St. Petersburg, capital of the Russian empire. Had the country's status as part of the Kingdom of Sweden endured, it seems that these reforms would not have been possible. Finland was allowed to evolve independently as part of the Russian Empire because circumstances in the country remained stable. In 1819, however, the Czar found it necessary to cope with pietistic revivalist movements and university student activism which appeared to portend trouble for peaceful integration of the Grand Duchy into the Empire.[35]

From Finland's point of view, these favorable circumstances, of which the *Kalevala* process (chs. 2, 12) was an integral part, continued until the end of the nineteenth century. However, during the nationalistic spirit of pan-Slavism which had arisen during the 1870s in the Russian Empire, the czars began, particularly from the 1890s on, to take steps toward elimination of the Finnish nobility's privileges. Action was taken to bind Finland more closely to Russia economically (the ruble replaced the Finnish mark as the common currency), socially (an obligatory pledge to enter the Russian army), and culturally (the Russian language was utilized in education and administration). This forceful policy of Russification[36] created a backlash which resulted, for example, in the widespread emigration of Finns to America as well as numerous and varied political-nationalistic resistance movements.

KARELIA AND KARELIANISM

One of the cultural nationalistic-romantic movements which emerged at the end of the nineteenth century was Karelianism. It was composed primarily of Finnish intellectuals and university students. In his dissertation on this subject, Hannes Sihvo[37] situates Karelianism within the international context of other ethnic, artistic, provincial, historical, and national romantic movements, such as the Celtic revival in the British Isles, Scandinavian Viking romanticism in Sweden, Brittany romanticism in France, and the Heimat movement in Germany.

The focus of attention for Karelianism is Karelia. The background of the movement includes Karelia's geographically problematic location as a border area between Sweden-Finland and Russia. The importance of the boundary was strengthened by the fact that it coincided with the old religious border between East and West in Europe. Throughout history, as this boundary has vacillated[38] because of differences and power struggles between the Western and Eastern churches, most Karelians, for example, as adherents of the Eastern religion, have fled behind the religious and political boundary. The most remote example of this became Tver Karelia in central Russia.

It is noteworthy that this border becomes manifest in the *Kalevala* process. Most of the runic poetry utilized in the Finnish national epic was written down outside Finland in Russian Karelian villages. The decisive impetus for the genesis of the epic was that, in 1833, Lönnrot went to the so-called Swedish and Russian (Orthodox) villages beyond the old Swedish-Finnish border with Russia in search of singers.

The symbol of the mythical, prehistorical golden *Kalevala* era became the White Sea Karelian area. In 1809, this region had been opened to Finnish scholars who were then able to enter Karelia from the Grand Duchy of Finland as fellow citizens of the Russian Empire. Zachris Topelius the Elder had led the way for folklore collectors to the White Sea District in the 1820s: "There Väinämöinen's voice still chants, there the kantele and the Sampo still play" (ch. 6).

The *Kalevala*'s reinforced status as a national epic had led many scholars and enthusiastic seekers of Finnish identity on journeys directly to White Sea Karelia. Karelia came to be considered a treasure chest of poetry and an idyllic museum of the ancient world. Karelianism was the Finnish national romantic version of the myth of a national golden age, the paradisiacal primal home of the Finnish people. When the national student organizations at the University of Helsinki organized trips to save elements of Karelian culture, the students were simultaneously searching for their own identity in that cultural landscape, considered to be one of the last rudiments of the national golden age.

Karelianism had its peak during the period of most intense Russification at the turn of the nineteenth century. During the 1890s a number of nationalist pilgrims sought inspiration for their art in Karelia. Among them were the authors Eino Leino (1878–1926) and Juhani Aho (1861–1921), the artists Akseli Gallén–Kallela (1865–1931) and Eero Järnefelt (1863–1937), and the composer Jean Sibelius (1865–1957). As a result of their artistic achievements, knowledge of the *Kalevala* increased both in Finland and abroad. These works actually attained international renown more effectively than the epic itself. It is through them that numerous of the *Kalevala* themes, myths, and symbols actually came to be internationally known. The manner in which these artists experienced and interpreted the *Kalevala*, Karelia, and Karelian-Finnish folk art formed the basis for the phenomenon which later became known as Finnish National Romanticism, also called the Finnish Renaissance.

This stylistic trend, characterized by national-romantic symbols, has continued in various forms to the present as an inspiration complementing the *Kalevala* and as a unique introduction to Karelia, its folk art, and the rich ornamentation found at its archaeological sites. One ongoing example of this tradition is Kalevala Koru Limited, owned by the Kalevala Women's Association. Its product designs are based upon prehistoric ornaments found at excavations throughout Finland, not solely in Karelia.[39]

A SYNOPSIS OF THE HISTORY OF INDEPENDENT FINLAND, 1917–1997

The Russian czarist regime ended with the murder of Czar Nicholas and his family during World War I. The unsettled conditions created in Russia by the Bolshevik Revolution led by V. I. Lenin made it possible for Finland to declare its independence on December 6, 1917, initially with the support of Germany. When Lenin's government had validated Finland's sovereignty, a number of western countries were prepared to do likewise.

In 1918 the painful Civil War between the Red and White forces in Finland began, the former supported by some troops of the Russian Army remaining in Finland (only ca. 5,000 out of the ca. 100,000 Russian soldiers in Finland at that time took part in the Civil War) and the White forces, with the help of German and Swedish volunteers as well as Finnish troops, the "jääkärit," trained in Germany. The White Army, led by Gustaf Adolf Mannerheim, formerly an explorer in the Asian Orient and an officer in the Russian Army, won the war. Following this, the newly sovereign nation formed its first constitution as a republic in 1919, in accordance with its old legislative traditions as a part of the Nordic sphere. However, bitter memories of the Civil War, which had taken as many as 40,000 Finnish lives and included executions by both sides, known as the "red and white terror," continued to divide the people for a long time.

Although the genesis of World War II lay elsewhere, the fate of Finland, like that of the Baltic States, had been secretly decided beforehand by the Molotov-Ribbentrop Pact signed by Russia and Germany on August 23, 1939. On November 30, 1939, Stalin announced a war against Finland using Finnish military activity on the Karelian Isthmus as his justification. The Winter War, having lasted 105 days, ended on March 13, 1940. In accordance with the treaty, Finland ceded approximately 10 percent of its territory to the Soviet Union. Once again, most of the Karelian territories had been lost. This was one significant reason why Finland began to wage war against the Soviet Union by siding with Germany between 1941 and 1944.

Without delving into the details of Finland's most recent history,[40] it is possible to state that Finland is the only European country which, having achieved its independence between the two World Wars, was able to maintain this independence during and following World War II. Internationally, the myth of the Winter War, little Finland's (4 million people) struggle against the vast Soviet Union (over 200 million people), is remembered along with Finland's repayment of its war debt to the Soviet Union in 1956, down to the last cent and ahead of schedule. Less attention has been paid to the "War Crimes Trials," as a result of which Risto Ryti, President of Finland during World War II, and ministers central to the government during that period, were sent to jail, or to Finland's refusal to yield its Jewish citizens to the Nazis, etc. For Finland the most difficult phases of World War II included, firstly, the withdrawal of Finnish troops from the war in 1945 as Soviet forces, backed by the armies of the victorious Allies, rolled into Finland and, secondly, the act of dispelling German forces from Finland before a peace treaty could be signed.

From the Finnish viewpoint, the greatest national significance of the difficult Winter War may be that it united the Finns, badly divided by the Civil War of 1918. With his novel *Tuntematon Sotilas* (The Unknown Soldier, 1954), which sold half a million copies, and the trilogy *Täällä Pohjantähden Alla* (Here beneath the North Star, 1959–1962), Väinö Linna (1920–1992), a writer from a working class family in Tampere, interpreted for Finns the traumas of the wartime defeat. He thereby enabled the nation, previously divided by its Civil War, to heal.[41] In his work, Linna creates a portrait of a platoon of Finnish soldiers who have come to the war from differing environs and backgrounds. Linna allows them to speak their own dialects and to share with one another, as well as the readership, the agonizing "why" questions of twentieth-century wars.

After World War II, Finland was a nation changed socially, economically, and culturally. In the effort to pay its war debts, Finland rapidly industrialized and urbanized. The cultures of the provinces were aggregated into one culture. Evacuees from Karelia (over 400,000 people) had to be quickly resettled throughout the country. Although the Karelian Alliance and a remarkable number of emigrant evacuee organizations have remained active throughout the country, the Karelians have been quickly assimilated into Finnish culture. As a consequence, however, the Karelian dialects, as well as many of Karelia's ancient ethnic and folkloric traditions, have faded. Although the majority of the relocated evacuees were already Lutherans or soon adopted the church of the majority, a network of Orthodox congregations also spread throughout the country.[42]

By 1956, the war debt to the USSR had been paid, the nation and Finland began to prosper, too quickly, perhaps. The industrialization and urbanization following World War II led to numerous economic-social problems and to conflicts in values, particularly during the 1960s and 1970s. One indication of cultural rootlessness in the nation was extensive migration from the countryside to cities and emigration from Finland, itself. For example, 400,000 people emigrated to Sweden.

In Finland and the Republic of Karelia in Russia, an effort is being made to support the swiftly deteriorating Karelian culture and language. Since the period of Soviet "glasnost" in the 1980s, the issue of the return of the Karelian Isthmus to Finland has been cautiously raised. However, the discussion has not achieved a great deal of momentum, even among members of the *Karjalan liitto* (the Karelian Alliance) and other Karelian organizations. With Karelian borders now open to travelers, many have revisited their homesteads. They have observed that Karelia has changed greatly since the war and that it would be difficult to return to an area now settled and occupied by Russians, Belarus, Ukrainians, etc. for fifty years. In the politics of Finland's eastern neighbor, Karelia appears to have remained a "battlefield" of sorts where people from various parts of the Soviet Union have been settled, but where little attention has been paid to the development of living conditions in the region.

Another issue is related to the territory of Ingria around St. Petersburg (Leningrad during the Soviet era) and the Ingrian people. Most Ingrians (see map) during World War II fled the war to Finland, and subsequently, via Finland to Sweden. Despite the Soviet Union's promise of amnesty, most of the Ingrians who tried to return to their homes after the war found themselves deported to Siberia. During the 1950s, a significant number of these deportees returned to Soviet Estonia, the St. Petersburg (Leningrad) area, and Petrozavodsk and its surrounding areas in White Sea Karelia. Approximately 20–30,000 returned to each of these three areas. The Ingrian Lutheran Church was revitalized in the 1980s. This had a significant influence on reviving Ingrian religio-cultural identity, as did Finnish-language newspapers such as *Punalippu* (Red Flag) and cultural organizations in Petrozavodsk and St. Petersburg. Ingrians now presented just demands for return of their territory and retribution for the honor which had been taken from them when they were labeled "enemies of the Soviet Nation." Along with revitalization of cultural and religious festivals, these initiatives also called the attention of the Finns to the plight of the Ingrian people. In his 1990 New Year's address, Finland's President Mauno Koivisto accorded them the status of "re-immigrants," and since then approximately 20,000 Ingrian Finns have moved to Finland. One problem for these Ingrians arriving from Estonia, St. Petersburg, and Petrozavodsk has been that, despite family origins, their primary language is either Russian or Estonian. Consequently, at the same time that ancient Ingria's population is declining, there is a population arriving in Finland which has enormous difficulty integrating into Finnish society because of differences in their cultural identity. Therefore, rather than encouraging further migration, Finland has begun to emphasize and support Ingria's own economic and social well-being along with programs to support established manifestations of Ingrian identity in Russia.[43]

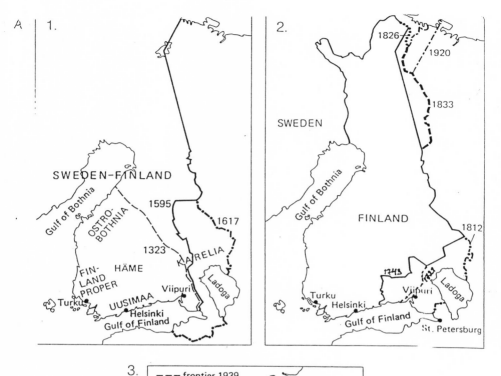

A

1.

SWEDEN-FINLAND

Gulf of Bothnia

OSTRO-
BOTHNIA

1595

1617

1323

KARELIA

HÄME

FIN-
LAND
PROPER

UUSIMAA

Viipuri

Ladoga

Turku

Helsinki

Gulf of Finland

2.

1826

1920

1833

SWEDEN

Gulf of Bothnia

FINLAND

1812

1743

Turku

Helsinki

Viipuri

Ladoga

Gulf of Finland

St. Petersburg

3.

- - - - frontier 1939
———— frontier from
         1944

NORWAY

THE
FRONTIERS
OF
FINLAND
1323–1944

SWEDEN

SOVIET
UNION

Oulu

FINLAND

Vaasa

Turku

Helsinki

Viipuri

CHAPTER

12

KALEVALA MYTHOLOGY AND FINNISH MYTHOGRAPHY

KALEVALA MYTHOLOGY AND MYTHOLOGY ENGENDERED BY THE *KALEVALA*

In their studies of the *Kalevala* over the years, scholars have not been impartial. In addition to specific theories, they have been bound in numerous ways to various historical periods in the development of their nation. During his long lifespan (1802–1884), Professor Lönnrot also became part of the evolutionary process inherent in Finnish national identity, as has been illustrated in this book.

What is the *Kalevala*? Lönnrot himself gave two definitions. One was included in the subtitle of the *Old Kalevala* published in 1835: "Old Karelian Poems from the Ancient Times of the Finnish People." Another is found in Lönnrot's dictionary, where Kalevala is both localized as a specific place—"the dwelling place of the (in Lönnrot's theory mythical gigantic) sons of Kalevala," and, at the conclusion of the entry, defined as the "national epic of the Finnish people." The latter definition, expressed by Lönnrot in 1880 during his old age, had been introduced in the 1830s by such members of the Finnish National Romantic movement as J. L. Runeberg and M. A. Castrén.

Thus, at an early stage, the *Kalevala* became the national property of the Finnish people. In examining its numerous editions and translations, a reader may notice that Elias Lönnrot's name is frequently missing from the cover of the book or the title page. In the book it has been necessary to thoroughly discuss Elias Lönnrot's roles as folklore collector and editor in addition to his role in the entire *Kalevala* process. Whether or not the rights of authorship to the *Kalevala* are Lönnrot's is a relevant issue today when, for example, UNESCO has raised the question of folklore copyright.

For the reader, the situation is further complicated by the fact that he or she must accept the idea of more than one *Kalevala*. By far the best-known version of the epic is the one completed in 1849, which is referred to in this book as the *New Kalevala*. Its length is twice that of the *Old Kalevala* published in 1835. In my opinion, the contents and world view of the *Old* and the *New Kalevala* differ so greatly that, for the sake of clarity, it is necessary to speak of two different books. It is unfortunate that from the point of view of both Finnish and international readership, the concept of One Sole Correct *Kalevala* (i.e., the *New Kalevala,* 1849) has cast its shadow over the *Old Kalevala,* which has a concise plot and could well provide numerous readers a valuable literary experience. A comparison between the *Old* and the *New Kalevala* as detailed in chapter 3 is worthwhile, as this book has attempted to show. The *Old Kalevala,* with its extensive preface, has become difficult to obtain; I have therefore quoted at length from it in this book.

The question of "folklore or fakelore?" has been raised with regard to the *Kalevala* by such noted American folklorists as Richard M. Dorson and Alan Dundes. In its stead, the questions "myth or history?" "sacred or profane history?" "mythology or mythography?" "oral narrative of Holy Scripture?" and "folklore or history?" have been asked in this study. When dealing with these questions, however, it should be remembered that, as a nineteenth-century scholar, Lönnrot had a relationship to these concepts that was completely different from the view held of them by scholars today and from their interpretation in contemporary folkloristics.

The conclusion can be drawn that the *Kalevala* is not a pure folklore collection. Both the *Old* and the *New Kalevala* are the results of conscious choices made by Elias Lönnrot. They contain only a small part of all the epic runes found in Finland. The huge collection *Suomen kansan vanhat runot* (The ancient runes of the Finnish people), published 1908–1948 by the Finnish Literature Society, contains 33 volumes, over 85,000 variants of runic poetry, and more than 1,270,000 lines. It was Lönnrot's role to collect the runes which were still commonly sung in the White Sea Karelian villages during the nineteenth century and to combine them into a unified epic whole. Thus, the *Kalevala* is both a national epic and Lönnrot's epic.

Lönnrot created his *Kalevala* both as a scholar and as a poet. He conscientiously endeavored to be precise and attempted to document everything he himself added. The lines he added and edited constitute only about two percent of the total. The *Kalevala* in its various versions, however, forms quite a new whole. To use an expression suggested by the Finnish literary scholar Kai Laitinen, it is Lönnrot's "collage." Lönnrot had the authority to decide how the poems should be ordered and what kind of structure the epic should ultimately have. In this process, the aesthetic principle superseded the genetic principle, as Väinö Kaukonen has remarked.

THE *KALEVALA* AS THE MYTHOLOGY OF THE FINNS

In assessing the role of mythology in the formation of the *Kalevala,* it is necessary to recognize that Elias Lönnrot's original goal was to compile the material in his notes about the Karelian singers into "a mythological poem, a supplement to Kristfried Ganander's *Mythologia Fennica,*" 1785 (ch. 2). In a manner of speaking, the preface to Ganander's mythology (page 5 in this book) is the fundamental document for the study of Finnish comparative mythology. The reformer Mikael Agricola can be characterized as "the father of the history of religion (and mythology) in Finland" based upon the listing of deities in the preface to his 1551 Finnish translation of the *Psalter* (ch. 1).

While Agricola was laying the foundation for (literary) Finnish by translating the

Psalter, he also published in its preface two lists of deities. Each consisted of twelve deities, one list applied to the Karelians (i.e., the eastern Finns) and the other to the Hämäläinens (western Finns). The text called upon the pagan Finns to relinquish these deities. Although the lists were very heterogeneous, a goal had been achieved. Creation of the twelve-deity olympus had, in a sense, raised the Finns into the ranks of the renowned cultured peoples. The most well-known examples serving as the model for myth come from the Bible (Jacob had twelve sons and Jesus had twelve disciples). This has also been emphasized in the "respectable" classical mythologies of the Greeks, the Romans, the Germanic and Scandinavian peoples. Following Ganander who, in the 1780s, had been among the first to seek ethnographic material to supplement Agricola's work, Lönnrot, half a century later, felt himself to be in the same tradition. He regarded himself as the third Finnish mythologist after Agricola and Ganander (chs. 1–2).

Elias Lönnrot achieved even broader recognition (ch. 4) through his work as collector of the *Kalevala* runes and compiler of the epic. In the time which ensued between publication of the *Old Kalevala* (1835) and the *New* (1849), Lönnrot's role evolved from that of a mythologist to a historical interpreter of the epic, i.e., that of a mythographer of the Finns. In 1849 there was greater awareness and acceptance of the epic in Finland than in 1835 because trends in European politics and attitude had been changed, above all by the French Revolution and romanticism of German origin. The spark for the *New Kalevala* came, not from the Finns themselves, but primarily from Jacob Grimm in his 1845 lecture to the Berlin Academy. Only after Grimm's speech did Lönnrot actually decide to undertake a new edition of the *Kalevala,* to begin that ambitious and painful process, the stages of which are described in chapter 2 of this book.

WRITING FINNISH MYTHOGRAPHY

In describing the role of the *Kalevala* in the development of Finland and Finnish identity, an article about the epic published in the book *Finland* (1997), can be quoted here as representative of an official "consensus" concerning the matter in Finland:

> The second edition of the *Kalevala,* described as new and complete, soon overshadowed its predecessor, which was forgotten. Today, in speaking of the *Kalevala,* it is the second edition that is referred to. It is recognized as one of the great epics of world literature and, translated, in its entirety, into 45 languages, it has aroused interest throughout the world. Although Lönnrot's creation, it is considered to be a poem about distant times that bears comparison to Homer's works. The *Kalevala* is, indeed, a Homeric poem, for the *Iliad* was an important model for Lönnrot, and the *Kalevala,* for its part, has been a direct source of inspiration for other poems, including the Estonian *Kalevipoeg* and Henry Wadsworth Longfellow's "Song of Hiawatha." No other Finnish work of literature has become so well-known outside the country as the *Kalevala,*

and no other Finnish work has had so diverse and profound an influence on national and international culture.

The *Kalevala* continues to inspire the best representatives of Finnish literature, the visual arts and music. Kalevala Day, on the 28th of February, is celebrated as the day of Finnish culture."[1]

What was Lönnrot's own opinion with regard to this issue of the *"Kalevalas"*? As previously described in this book (chs. 1–4), at the beginning of the 1830s Lönnrot viewed the *Old Kalevala* expressly as Finnish mythology. But by 1849 he was prepared to see the *Kalevala* as Finnish pre-history. In his opinion, the Kalevala Period gleamed as the pre-Christian history of Finland. It ended when the Christian history of Finland began. Lönnrot's historical interpretation became readily apparent in his Finnish history published in *The Bee* (Mehiläinen). Its starting point is the end of the Kalevala Period. Lönnrot now had become an author of Finnish mythography, encouraged by the social order provided by the people of his own era.

According to this interpretation, the so-called history of Finland, as part of the Swedish Kingdom united by Catholic Christianity, began with the crusades of the Roman Catholic Church. The first of these took place under the leadership of the English Bishop Henrik and the Swedish king, Erik, in 1155. Another important date in Finland's approximately 600-year history as part of the Kingdom of Sweden is the founding of the Turku diocese in the 1220s.[2] Why Lönnrot focused on that juncture of time is an interesting question. Apparently he wished to find the pre-Christian and pre-historical heroes of the Finns and their golden past, as expressed by the *Kalevala* in the time before the advent of Christianity.

Lönnrot's historical interpretation of the *Kalevala* in *The Bee* adhered to the world view of linear Christianity and western natural science (ch. 4). Accordingly, the world of the *Kalevala* took on a historical configuration in Lönnrot's mind (ch. 8). His starting point was a linear continuum (similar to the biblical Genesis narrative), the creation of the world, and, in the end, Väinämöinen, hero of the *Kalevala* and god of pre-historical paganism (ch. 10), is replaced by the God of Christian religion, the Virgin Mary's son. However, the conflict between Lönnrot's own Christian-based, linear world view and the cyclical world view of the singers described in this book remains apparent. It is also apparent in the *Kalevala* that, although the intricate plot of the epic is linear, individual poems continue to transmit a shamanistic, cyclical (chs. 9–10) concept of man. This is related to nature's eternal cycle in the form of death and immortality, to which humanity and all creation are bound.

In searching for the genesis of Lönnrot's later interpretations, it is necessary to remember contemporary events concerning him and the *Kalevala* in Finland between 1835 and 1849, e.g., Gottlund's criticism, noted in chapter 1, and the fact that Lönnrot's intimate circle was now different. A. J. Sjögren was influential at the St. Petersburg Academy. And in addition M. A. Castrén, for his part, had left Lönnrot during their joint field trip in 1843. While Lönnrot decided to continue his unfinished poetry collection work in Onega,[3] Castrén crossed the Urals in his search for ancient Finnish roots in Siberia. Just as these scholars' research paths diverged geographically, so did their inspired collaboration which had led to a Swedish translation of the *Kalevala* by Castrén in 1841.

Elias Lönnrot's new interpretations may be viewed as an integral part of that process initiated by the *Kalevala*'s new social order in the 1840s. Lönnrot's opinion now reflected his position, alongside J. V. Snellman and J. L. Runeberg, as one of the central architects in the creation of the myths which awakened feelings of Finnishness among their contemporaries. This "triumvirate," who chanced to begin their studies at the Turku Academy in the same year, 1822, began from differing points of departure. They laid the foundation for the Finnish national awakening. Runeberg (1804–1877) became the Finnish national poet although his entire "oeuvre" is written in his mother tongue, Swedish. His poem "Vårt Land" (Our Country) became Finland's national anthem and, based upon his book, *Fänrik Ståls sägner* (Tales of Ensign Stål, 1848, 1960), the war between Sweden (Finland) and Russia (1809–1810) became a sacred heroic tale needed at that time by the Finns in seeking national identity and recognition. Snellman (1806–1881), who had initially completed his thesis on Hegel's philosophy in 1835 and then wrote *Läran om Staten* (The Origin of the State) in 1841, was a statesman. He also founded Lauantaiseura (The Saturday Society, 1830), an organization which influenced the development of Finnish society in diverse ways. As a result of his activities, the Finnish language achieved official status in 1863 and the Finnish mark became the legal currency in 1865.

In terms of historiography, Lönnrot, Runeberg, and Snellman all wrote Finnish mythography and history, each in his own manner and each in his own region of the country. Zacharias Topelius (1818–1898), rector and professor of history at Helsinki University, may have influenced the Finns' concept of history and sense of national identity more than any other individual. His *Maamme-Kirja* (Book of our land, 1875), *Valskarin Kertomukset* (Tales of the surgeon-barber), fairy tale collection, and readings for children, all written in a folksy manner, transmitted self-knowledge and reinforced a deep awareness among the people of the roots they had in common. In music, Fredrik Pacius (1809–1891) had a similar role as composer of both the first Finnish-language opera and the national anthem. Later, the work of Jean Sibelius (1865–1957) in musical composition and Akseli Gallén-Kallela (1865–1931) in the art work displayed in the Finnish Pavilion at the Paris World's Fair, along with the latter's illustrations of the *Kalevala*, were of particular significance in bringing the myth of Finnishness into the international spotlight. The influence of this neo-romantic *Kalevala* art was so powerful that the *Kalevala* came alive more as a result of the national symbols and myths mediated by it than through the book itself.[4]

Thus, in the minds of the Finns, the national process progressed both as part of the nation's "great" and the people's "small" narratives.[5] It sought national heroes, creating through them cult symbols of those who wrote the myths the nation needed. It is significant that the authors of the Finns' great narrative, each in his own region (e.g., Lönnrot at Kainuu in Kajaani in the north and Sammatti in Uusimaa in the south, Runeberg in Swedish-speaking Porvoo, Snellman in Helsinki and at Kuopio in Savo), became, in influence first locally, then regionally, and finally nationally, initiators of the national awakening. At the same time as the *Kalevala* myth was being created, a Finnish *Kalevala* cult with the aging Lönnrot as its natural focus was born. "He was the most approachable of the modern state's founders."[6] At that advanced stage of his life, Lönnrot was still able to initiate the process which led to the *Kalevipoeg* epic in Estonia and he attended song festivals at ceremonies organized throughout Finland, including national *Kalevala* events.

After their deaths, these authors of the national myths themselves became objects of a national cult and mythical symbols who were accorded national memorial days and monuments both in their home regions and in the capital. The first monument to Lönnrot was built in Helsinki in 1902. Snellman's memorial has stood in front of the Finnish Bank since 1923, etc. These memorial sites gradually became "sacred shrines" to which pilgrimages were made, particularly on the young nation's memorial days.

Variable in their magnitude and intensity, the national myth and cult seek focal points from which to renew themselves. During the 1890s "Karelianism," which had attained its zenith at the height of the oppression, was mediated both visually (Gallén-Kallela, Inha, etc.) and musically from the rune-singing areas of Karelia. The great Finnish poet Eino Leino, who was from Kainuu where Lönnrot had crafted the *Kalevala*, became akin to a second Finnish "national" poet. Of interest is the recent revival of the *Kalevala* cult, particularly in Kainuu, where a *Kalevala* opera is being prepared for the 1999 jubilee commemorating the 150th anniversary of publication of the *New Kalevala*.

THE SEARCH FOR NATIONAL POLITICAL MESSAGES IN THE *KALEVALA*

If, in constructing the *Old Kalevala*, Lönnrot was a mythologist in the spirit of Grimm and Ganander (with a view to creating a construct of Finnish mythology), in the *New Kalevala* his is the conscious role of Finnish mythographer in writing the "sacred history" of the Finns. His preface for the *New Kalevala* was revised from this point of view. In Lönnrot's opinion, the epic depicted a war between the inhabitants of Kalevala and Pohjola, the Finns and the Lapps. In spite of the fact that the Lapps do not even have a word for war and, prior to World War II, were not considered suitable for conscription, the war epic was created to fill the need for Finnish national heroism and lacked any narrative tradition to support the idea. Lönnrot constructed a new narrative. Väinämöinen who, in the *New Kalevala*, lost his status as mythical creator to Ilmatar (ch. 7), became the historical hero of the *Kalevala* and the Finns.

The eternal power of "evil" became personified by Joukahainen of the "Competition Song." The "lean Lapp boy" is presented as a "sage" of lesser knowledge within the Lapp context, one of "them." It was Joukahainen who shot Väinämöinen, the great sage who had been borne upon the primordial sea, into the water. As the hero drifts northward, the numerous courtship and war journeys of the *Kalevala* heroes to Pohjola, ruled by the crone witch, Louhi, begin. The plot was rewritten for the *New Kalevala,* modeled on a Viking Period war epic with its climax being the theft of the Sampo. The song wizards of the *Kalevala,* who had previously functioned through the power of their words, now become war heroes. Conquered Pohjola was identified with Lapland and its people with the Lapps. A foundation was then laid for the long period of diminished status in Finland for the Sami. This gave rise to the unfounded claim in Finnish folkloristics that the Sami have no epic at all, and that Fjellner's poetic epic about the sun's son was not genuine.[7]

A number of political visions in Finland during the past century and a half have been based on subject matter taken from the *Kalevala.* From this point of view, the epic has been used for decades to serve various purposes. One of the most crucial national-political elements of the drama in the *Kalevala* is the struggle between the two peoples it depicts. Lönnrot identified his epic above all with the vision of Finnish prehistory formed in his mind during the 1840s. This vision became apparent in the *New Kalevala.* In the introduction to the *Old Kalevala,* written in 1835, Lönnrot was still considering the historical versus the mythical veracity of Kalevala and Pohjola:

> In almost all the runes there are two peoples who do not live together in great harmony. One of these we could name the people of Pohjola and the other the people of Kaleva. According to this poetry, Louhi, who is also known as "Pohjan akka" [The Old Crone of the North], is often mentioned as the leader of the people of Pohjola. There were many heroes among the Kaleva people, the greatest of these being Väinämöinen, Ilmarinen, and Lemminkäinen. With regard to the latter, however, it should be mentioned at this point that the poems do not give exact information as to whether he might be included among the folk of Pohjola as well. Those runes which I have chosen for this book do show that he was often of help to Väinämöinen and sometimes even waged war against Pohjola on his own, courted in Pohjola, and so forth.[8]

The question of the historical versus the mythological basis for the war between the two tribes related in the Sampo narrative does not appear to be central in the runes themselves. However, another opinion is held by the Soviet folklorist E. N. Meletinskii: "As opposed to most heroic-epic monuments, the Karelian-Finnish runes are primarily a depiction of peaceful labor. Relatively speaking, warlike heroism is given less space in them."[9] This was also Lönnrot's interpretation, for the most part, and served to fulfill the social order of his day. At various times, scholars have pondered whether the Sampo cycle is based on a struggle between the Sami and Finnish tribes, or between two Finnish tribes, or whether the entire cycle is a reflection, for example, of the ancient myth about the battle between good and evil.

The historical interpretation of the *Kalevala* and the ancient runes has proved to be a particularly fruitful source for both those people who stressed that the origins of the epic lay in the east and those who stressed its western origins. The question of the historicity of the Finnish heroes in the ancient Kalevala runes was so pervasive an issue for scholars that only after World War II did folklorists who were active in Finnish politics in addition to pursuing their scholarly careers begin to explore the possibility that these heroes may have had other than historical origins.

The 100th anniversary of the *Kalevala* in 1935, eighteen years after Finland became independent, was celebrated as a national event. Several past and future presidents of Finland were present at the festivities, including Kaarlo Juho Staåhlberg, Lauri Kristen Relander, Pehr Evind Svinhufvud, Kyösti Kallio, Gustaf Mannerheim, and Urho Kaleva Kekkonon.

In addition to new trends in the field of comparative religion, this new direction in research was undeniably influenced by the fact that World War II had shattered the concept of Great Finland. This concept had also been supported by numerous folklore scholars. The boundaries of Great Finland coincided with those of the Balto-Finnic rune-singing area. It was this very area which was the objective of Finnish troops during World War II. Earlier in the century, the Finnish national poet Eino Leino had in fact dreamed about the unity of the Finno-Ugric peoples. In 1896, during the period of great Russification and oppression, a poem written by Leino[10] about the Great Oak strongly expressed the dream of the rise to power of the Finnish people and of Finno-Ugric unity, with a new Sampo as the source of strength:

> Beloved is a father's labored field,
> sweet the bread baked by a mother,
> stubborn a stranger's soil,
> bitter a stepmother's cake.

Long our Finland ate barkbread,
begged alms along the roads,
gathered with its tears
too many crumbs from others.
But one day the begging will cease
and the stranger's insult will end,
and Finland will stand tall
and the people will raise their heads:
Already Väino's crop takes root,
and Kaleva's grain grows,
and lack of bread is banished form the land
and the longing for a stranger's crop!

Thus the ramparts of the Finnish state will rise,
So the Finnish Sampo will be readied.
The wave hath taken the Sampo
and borne off the wondrous work of Ilmarinen
and the renown of the Ugric tribes
lies buried 'neath the skirts of night.
But leaning on familiar strength
we discover stars in the night
and with love in our eyes
find bits of Ilmarinen's labor.

The war myth of the *Kalevala* became useful again at Finnish independence, when Karelia had once more been divided. With the victory of the Bolsheviks in the Karelian coup, ending in 1922, 33,500 Karelians fled across the Finnish border along with the White forces.[11] Those who had fought for the Red Army as well as the majority of the original inhabitants remained in Russia in the Karelian Autonomous Republic founded within the Soviet Union. However, the enthusiasm of Finnish students for Karelia was not diminished by this new political reconfiguration. In 1922, approximately 4,000 students took an oath in founding the Academic Karelia Society (AKS) and the University Women's Karelia Society. The fundamental concept here was that of a shared kindred or tribe, in the name of which the national unity of Finns, Ingrians, and Karelians was sought. The liberation of related peoples from the Soviet Union was encouraged and, for example, the role of the Finnish language was reinforced at Helsinki University. The Mäntsälä revolt and President P. E. Svinhufvud's forced exile led the more moderate students to depart the now more radical movement in 1933. At that time, Finland's future long-term president, Urho Kaleva Kekkonen (1956–1981), along with other representatives of the moderate wing, left the movement.

The goal of the Academic Karelia Society was the creation of "Great Finland." The basis for this concept, *"imperium fennicum,"* was the idea, derived from the *Kalevala,* of the Finnish tribe's ancient "home" areas. The wish to join Karelia and Ingria to Great Finland was based upon the image of the ancient "song lands." The poem "Väinölän lapset" (Children of Väinölä) by Arvid Genetz, poet and scholar of Fenno-Ugristics, introduced a map of the ancient poetry areas. Based upon this principle, intense cooperation with the Estonian Republic, which included a small strip of Ingria known as Estonian Ingria, was initiated between the two World Wars. In its politics, the Academic Karelia Society was more liberal than the extreme right-wing party, Isänmaallinen kansanliike (Fatherland National Party, IKL), of the 1930s. Along with the Finnish civil guard, the Academic Karelia Society took an active role in strengthening national defense. In 1939, with a force of 70,000 men, fortification of the Karelian Peninsula was initiated. This was one of the justifications used by Stalin for his attack on the Isthmus of Karelia. The supreme moment for the Society was its twentieth anniversary in 1942 when the movement's black flag flew as a symbol of the reclamation of Äänislinna (Petrozavodsk). The fortification, manned for two years, had, however, led many members of the AKS to conclude that uniting the peoples would no longer be a straightforward task after twenty years of separation and ideological indoctrination there under the Soviets. The Academic Karelia Society was among the movements which, along with the civil guard, had to be dismantled by order of the 1944 Soviet Union–Finland Supervisory Commission, before Finland was permitted to sign the treaty concluding World War II.

THE *KALEVALA*, FINNISH REVIVALISM, AND SPIRITUALITY

The fourth chapter of this book focuses upon the world view of Elias Lönnrot. As a "homo religiosus," he seems to have been a man who thought and behaved according to the "rationale" of his era, in a manner typical of a learned man in an Evangelical Lutheran country, as Finland was during the nineteenth century. While Lönnrot, in his versions of the *Kalevala,* reproduced the mythology of ancient paganism, his own personality was a manifestation of the devout practitioner of moderate Lutheranism as espoused by the Lutheran State Church. Lönnrot's attitude concerning more emotional, radical expressions of Finnish religiosity remained critical and cold. The same is true of his comments about both adherents of the revivalist movements in Lutheran Finland and the Old Believers (Starovery) in Karelia.

It is noteworthy that religious revivalism and national romanticism were simultaneous processes in nineteenth century Finland. Initially, their leaders were not in accord. National romanticism was led by students and teachers at universities and by intellectuals, mainly in urban milieus, many of whom had Swedish as their mother tongue. The first generation revivalist leaders were Finnish peasants, women, and radical clergy such as C. F. Hedberg and H. Rencqvist in Finland. A special case was L. L. Laestadius, a Sami botanist, ethnographer, and minister who, though living in Swedish Lapland, became the founder of the Laestadians, presently the largest revivalist movement in Finland. Before his career as the leader of northern Scandinavian revivalism began in 1844, Laestadius was both mythologist of the Lapps and their mythographer in the same way as Lönnrot was that of the Finns. In his mythology, Laestadius sharply criticized Gottlund and other Finnish scholars for neglect of folk beliefs in their research.[12]

Although differing in their religious views, the leaders of the revivalist movements were staunch opponents of the "moribund" doctrine of the bishops in urban areas. The mythical heroes and the first leaders in both the national and religious folk movements were peasants or illiterate women. A typical example of this process was the evolution, in Finnish minds, of "the two Paavo's," Paavo Ruotsalainen and Saarijärven Paavo (Paavo from Saarijärvi). The latter, a poetic figure created by Runeberg, became identified with the Russification oppression of the late nineteenth and early twentieth centuries. The 1980s opera *The Last Temptations*, composed by Joonas Kokkonen and originally performed by Martti Talvela (1939–1989), the Finnish basso of international operatic fame, has made Paavo Ruotsalainen a symbol of Finnish religiosity. The mythical figure of Saarijärven Paavo portrayed in this opera has become a manifestation of "true" Finnishness.[13]

Within the Evangelical Lutheran Church and the politics of Finland, attitudes toward revivalist movements grew more tolerant as a result of the significant parliamentarian work of the "awakened" members of the Senate, Parliament, and the Church Council of the Lutheran Church. Mauno Rosendahl, a secondary school rector in Oulu and historian of the revivalist movement, together with such well-known Laestadian members of the Parliament as Leonard Typpö, K. A. Lohi, and Wäinö Havas, among others, have all worked to ensure that the significant revivalist movements in Finland have remained within the Lutheran Church.

Typically, several bishops of the Finnish Evangelical Lutheran Church and many elected representatives in the Finnish Parliament have shared revivalist backgrounds. Among the nationalists and revivalists, support for Finnish independence has been strong. During the Civil War of 1918, members of both movements joined the White troops. Between the two World Wars, they strongly supported the Academic Karelia Society. Elias Simojoki became one of the leaders of the AKS.

THE *KALEVALA* AND PARADIGMS FOR THE STUDY
OF FOLKLORE IN FINLAND

When compared to numerous other epics, the *Kalevala* holds a unique position: (1) It was created during the decade 1830–40 as if "on the stage of history." (2) All the literary and oral materials upon which it is based are still in existence and have been well organized in the "most hallowed" section of the folklore and manuscript archives of the Finnish Literature Society. (3) Elias Lönnrot, who collected the majority of the runes upon which the *Kalevala* is based, performed a notable service for future scholarship by carefully preserving all his journals and field trip diaries as well as his entire rune collection. (4) Every episode and detail of the complicated process involved as Lönnrot compiled the various versions of the *Kalevala* is available for study. (5) This clearly indicates that although Lönnrot, in creating the *Kalevala*, stressed his "Homeric" role as a "natural" poet, he was in fact a scholar, a collector of folk tradition, and a folklorist before the discipline itself achieved independent status in Finland and abroad.

Because Lönnrot's fieldwork inspired other collectors, the Folklore Archives of the Finnish Literature Society, founded in 1831, became one of the world's most extensive collections. By the end of the nineteenth century, it had helped form the basis for the study of Finnish and comparative folkloristics as a discipline at the

University of Helsinki. There Julius Krohn became the first Docent and Kaarle Krohn the first Professor of the subject. Although some aspects of the so-called Finnish method may be viewed critically in the light of contemporary scholarship, this method has served to establish an extensive and a remarkably broad range of scholarly material for comparative studies. Critics of the "Finnish Method" seem to have forgotten that, without such extensive archives of folklore materials, it is unlikely that the entire field of comparative folkloristics would ever have come into existence.[14] The geographical-historical method espoused by Julius and Kaarle Krohn, known internationally as the "Finnish method," was based expressly upon their work with fairy tales. Alongside the Krohns, one of the esteemed names in this field is Antti Aarne (1867–1925), who created a typology of folktales.

Regarding contemporary Finnish folkloristics, the question arises: "Why, during recent decades, has Finnish folklore scholarship (the roots of which lie in massive collecting of oral folk poetry and fairy tales from the nineteenth century onwards and in the resulting archives) shown surprisingly little interest in research based upon these vast folklore archives, particularly the runes upon which the *Kalevala* is based?" Until the 1970s, there was much greater research activity regarding runic poetry. Outi Lehtipuro writes, "As late as 1954, one could make the observation that the history of Finnish folklore research is, above all, the history of the study of ancient runes."[15] Following World War II, four primary competitive paradigms have emerged for the study of epic poetry in Finland:

(1) For example, Jouko Hautala's studies, "Lauri Lappalainen's Poem" (1945) and "Skiing Down The Hiisi Elk" (1947) continue, in the method of E. N. Setälä and Väinö Salminen, a "pre-Lordian" analysis of the runes' genesis based upon issues related to singers and their performance, problems concerning morphology as well as astral roots and the world view upon which the runes are based.[16]

(2) Matti Kuusi's dissertation, "The Sampo Epic" (1949), a detailed verse by verse study of the Sampo rune cycle which Kuusi considers the basis for the concept of the Finnish epic, is a classic example of very precise application of the geographical-historical method to the analysis of runic poetry. In Kuusi's numerous writings, summed up in his monumental work *Kirjoittamaton Kirjallisuus. Suomen Kirjallisuus I* (Unwritten literature. Finnish literature 1, 1963), Kuusi has performed cultural-historical and typological analyses of Finnish runes in search of their styles and chronological layers as well as their most ancient religious roots, such as Siberian shamanism, for example.[17]

(3) Martti Haavio's roles brought together those of a poet (pseudonym P. Mustapää), a folklore scholar, and a phenomenologist of religion who sought the mythic roots of the runes in the mythologies of both Scandinavia and Mediterranean antiquity. Fundamental questions asked by Haavio were: when, where, and how had the runes been created, and who were their original singers among the poets of the prehistoric world? Although, for comparative material, Haavio used the heritage of the Lapps, he mapped the environs of the runes' genesis to be the islands of the Baltic Sea; Haavio felt that the religio-phenomenological basis of the myths lay in the distant past, in the religions and classic epics of the Sumerians, Indo-arians, Egyptians, and Greeks.[18]

(4) The verse study approach to the *Kalevala* initiated by A. R. Niemi was con-

tinued by Väinö Kaukonen in his detailed descriptions of the *Kalevala* compilation (1939–1945).[19] Kaukonen was of the opinion that the *New Kalevala* was the fruit of Lönnrot's poetic creative process. Therefore, he concluded, study of the *Kalevala* itself belonged primarily to the field of literature, rather than folkloristics.

Some of the dilemmas of Finnish research on the *Kalevala* lie within the internal history of Finnish research. The *Kalevala* has been relegated largely to the field of literary scholarship, while over the decades another pragmatic division of labor between scholars of "spiritual" and of "material" culture has evolved in the study of Finnish folk culture. Practically speaking, this has meant that, in Finland, "authentic" runic poetry, along with folk narratives and beliefs, is categorized as belonging to the field of folklore, while material tradition, including folk costumes, customs, and buildings, is considered to be within the field of ethnology.

The interaction between oral and literary tradition has not been focused upon effectively. Although, based upon the work of Niemi and Kaukonen, it was known precisely from which poetic variants and texts the *Kalevala* had been compiled, there was less interest in what became of the rune traditions after the poems, formerly orally transmitted and sung, had been canonized as the national epic. It may be concluded that the issue of the "inauthenticity" of the *Kalevala* has fettered the study of folklore and mythology in Finland.[20]

While recent Finnish folkloristics has largely turned away from its previous focus upon genres such as runes, fairy tales, proverbs, folk legends, and materials found in archives and has focused upon newer research data and trends, the study of epic has been of more interest to scholars with an interdisciplinary orientation combining folkloristics and comparative religion, a field established at Finnish universities during the 1970s. Since his dissertation, "Krankheitsprojektile" (1958), Lauri Honko[21] has mapped the religious background of runes, charms, and laments, using new methods of study for international comparative epic. Anna-Leena Siikala has written about Siberian (1978) and Finnish shamanism (1992) and charms, as well as the relationship of the Finnish runes to Scandinavian tradition.[22] The significance of the genre of incantations and charms in the *Kalevala*, first noted by the Italian folklorist Domenico Comparetti in 1892, has been rediscovered.[23] The basis of comparison has now become Siberian shamanism and, at present, also the study of the little-known Sami epic.[24]

THE MYTH OF THE LAST RUNE SINGERS

The rune singers, from whom the runes were recorded by Lönnrot and others, and the corpus of the epic itself, comprise a story of their own (chs. 2–4, 6). In the spirit of romanticism and in accordance with the myth of the Homeric rune singer, the singers were initially considered interpreters of "the people's soul." Singing sages were individuals to whom people came almost like pilgrims to sacred shrines, the mythical sites of the sages, and in whose proximity feelings of deep inspiration akin to the ecstatic trance were experienced (ch. 6). When the *Kalevala* became recognized as a national epic, as Lönnrot was elevated to a position of national hero, its singers were mythologized as well. Even Lönnrot himself, believing that he had come upon the last masters of the ancient epic rune tradition, wrote about the decline of rune singing. In the preface to the *New Kalevala,* Lönnrot delineated the core of the rune singing area and excluded, for example, northernmost White Sea Karelia and Lappland. Because Lönnrot himself had authoritatively stated that there was no reason to seek ancient runes in those areas of the extreme north, the folklore collectors' journeys ended at Lake Kuittijärvi and the runes of the northernmost Karelian and Sami regions remained entirely uncollected until the 1940s when the linguist Pertti Virtaranta began extensive field research. He came upon emigrant singers who had fled through Finland to Sweden as refugees from that area during the unsettled interim period between the two World Wars.[25]

In the 1960s it surprised this author to discover competent oral singers like Marina Takalo (1890–1970) "beyond the boundary of the rune areas." Unable to read or write, Marina Takalo had fled to Finland in 1922 because of the Karelian revolt. During the course of our fieldwork in the decade 1960–70, her individual life history and the background of her vast knowledge were gradually revealed. It was of key significance that she, like most singers from northernmost Viena as described by Lönnrot and other tradition collectors, belonged to the exclusive Old Believer sect. In chapter 6 we have demonstrated that, because of the conservative world view of the Old Believers living in this area, runes were preserved there generations after they had been otherwise lost and forgotten. This fact remained unnoticed by the early rune collectors, who were deeply moved by nationalist sentiment. In their opinion, the Old Believer religion had been instrumental in corrupting the original rune culture of the Golden Era of Bjarmia, the mythical territory of the White Sea Karelians. As becomes apparent from the travel journals of Lönnrot, Castrén, and other rune collectors of this period, they considered the Old Believer religion alien to genuine Karelianism and a Russian element to be rejected.[26]

Visions of the imminent "death" of rune singing and of the "last rune singers" expressed by Lönnrot and his successors appear to have blinded Finnish scholars to important ethnographic fieldwork regarding rune singing and singers for some time. *Viimeiset Runonlaulajat* (The Last Rune Singers, 1954) was Haavio's inspiring tribute to the Finnish epic and lyric rune experts he called "the last singers and poets."[27] In his book *Väinämöinen* (1950), Haavio seeks the prototypical rune singer and locates him or her on Gothland and other remote islands in the Baltic Sea. Kuusi too was interested in the foremost singers both as individuals and as kin. For example, based upon genealogical research, Kuusi maintains in *Sampo-Eepos* (The sampo epic, 1949) that, for example, the tar trade and migration brought numerous of the singing kin (the Perttunen family, among others) to White Sea Karelia from the seaside parishes along the Gulf of Bothnia. The creative techniques of the singers from Ingria (Lauri Harvilahti) and White Sea Karelia (Katja Hyry) have been scrutinized[28] in the same manner as have the repertoire and oral transmission techniques of the multifaceted tradition bearer Marina Takalo in *Marina Takalon Uskonto* (Marina Takalo's religion, 1970) and *Oral Repertoire and World View* (1978). It is important to note that many of these singers are women. Although, in terms of genre analysis, the boundaries between runes, charms, and laments are quite clear in people's minds, these are like lines drawn in water (Aili Nenola), reflecting the importance of oral poetry in human life history and world view.[29] When, in the summer of 1996, this author asked Stepanie Kemova (b. 1912), Marina Takalo's illiterate daughter and also a rune singer and sage (ch. 6), about laments, she said: "Why kindle them? My whole life has been a lament."

THE *KALEVALA* AND THE DILEMMA OF FINNISH IDENTITY

The *Kalevala* was both the product of Lönnrot's work as a scholar and a poet and a National Romantic adaptation. It became a national epic because the Finnish people needed and were, in fact, directly seeking a basis for their emerging feelings of national identity. The epic thus struck a responsive chord with the people and their time, providing a foundation for Finnish identity and the rise of national feelings. Whether a Finnish people, conscious of their own uniqueness, would have come into existence without the *Kalevala* can justifiably be asked. The epic provided the impetus for the rise of Finnish identity, the Finnish language, culture, arts, scholarship, and national feelings.

Finnish identity was based upon the notion of the *Kalevala* as the national epic. During periods of Russification and oppression, the Karelian forests became the object of national veneration. Pilgrimages by Sibelius, Gallén-Kallela, Inha, Järnefelt, Aho, Leino, etc., to the last Karelian singers were inspired by Greek models. Arhippa Perttunen's son, Miihkali, was not among the best of the singers but, as a blind man, he became symbolic of the last Karelian Homeric singer and the focus of pilgrimages in the spirit of Karelianism.

The Kalevala process which had begun in the 1830s was both conscious and unconscious. A dramatic transformation had taken place in the minds of the Finnish people. The Finnish language had finally attained official status at the University. Finnish emigration to America had begun in the 1860s and had led to yet another phase in the identification of Finnishness with *Kalevala* symbols as a manifestation of the self-esteem which continues even today among the American and Canadian Finns.[30]

While encouraging feelings of Finnish identity and self-esteem, the *Kalevala* process united the inhabitants of Finland but discouraged the other cultures there, in particular the Sami. In his preface to the *New Kalevala,* Lönnrot delineated the borders of the rune areas and negated the possibility of a Lapp epic. In his opinion, the basic plot of the *Kalevala* was historical, based upon an imagined war between "us" (the Finns) and "them" in the North, i.e., the Lapps. The poor Lapp boy Joukahainen became demonized as the manifestation of evil powers. All evil entered golden Eden when his marksmanship felled Old Väinämöinen into the primordial sea.

As Finnish history unfolded after the Civil War in 1918, both the Whites and Reds needed mythographers of their own. Most of the Finnish folklorists belonged to the right wing. Some of them were founding members of the Academic Karelia Society whose goals included conquering and incorporating the so-called rune areas into Finland. Typically enough, however, Otto Wille Kuusinen, a member of the Soviet politburo with a long career in the Finnish Communist Party, was also an active folklore scholar and compiled his own version of the *Kalevala*.[31] Since Kuusinen became the symbol of Marxist-oriented Karelianism beyond the Finnish border to the east, it is natural to find a statue of him in front of the University of Petrozavodsk.

There exist a whole set of questions whose answers might further clarify the significance of the *Kalevala* in the evolution of Finnishness and Finnish history. However, because the epic forms an integral, "self-evident" part of Finnish identity, it has not been customary to ask or even to ponder these issues in Finland. It may be assumed, based upon national and regional sources, that the Finns have sanctioned a number of assertions concerning the *Kalevala* and, unaware, simultaneously become entangled by their nationalistic point of view.

Among these is the special position of the *New Kalevala* as the "Only Correct" epic in comparison with the other *Kalevala*s. The situation is worthy of note. Although February 28 is celebrated as Kalevala Day and the Day of Finnish Culture in honor of the day the *Old Kalevala* was completed, the work is not, nor has it been for generations, available in Finnish, even during the *(Old) Kalevala*'s International Festival Year. When the 150th jubilee of the *Kalevala* was celebrated throughout the world in 1985, the *Old Kalevala* (1835), the true hero of the day, was not available at the festivities. It is interesting that, initially, Lönnrot was not of this opinion, nor did he consider the *(New) Kalevala* to be a final version as it later came to be viewed by the Finns. In compiling the *New Kalevala* at the end of the 1840s, Lönnrot noted that additional field notes had multiplied to such an extent that seven different *Kalevala*s could be compiled of them.[32] In his mind, this creative process seemed ongoing. Thus the *Kanteletar*, completed in 1840, actually yielded 2,000 verses back to the *New Kalevala* and Lönnrot's ever-increasing collection of charms saw the light of print in 1839.

Examples of editions of the *Kalevala* published after Lönnrot included numerous abbreviated versions for schools and study circles. By dint of his brilliant intuitive imagination, the folklorist Martti Haavio created skillful reconstructions of both the Finnish epic (*Kirjokansi* [Bright lid] *pro Kalevala*) and the lyric poetry (*Laulupuu* [Song tree] *pro Kanteletar*). *Kansanruno-Kalevala* (Folkpoetry-Kalevala, 1976), edited by Matti Kuusi, is an interesting attempt by the Finnish folklorist who, during his long career, penetrated most deeply into the world of the ancient runes to help guide school children and other readers to the "genuine" rune variants upon which the *Kalevala* is based and, thereby, to the world which lay behind the *Kalevala*.[33]

Given this set of issues and special circumstances in Finland, the *Kalevala*'s status, canonized in 1849 as "its final poetic form," was that of a "book" comparable to the Bible, the *Niebelungenlied,* the *Edda,* and Homer. It was relatively easy to establish the *Kalevala*'s place alongside the Bible, the church's book of homilies, and the hymnal on bookshelves in the homes and institutions of the Finnish people, who greatly value books and literary culture. It was also quite natural that, when a Finn emigrated to Sweden, America, or Russia, he or she often took a copy of the *Kalevala* along with other religious works to put on a bookshelf place of honor.[34]

Although the background of the *Kalevala* is known and the entry of each verse into the *Kalevala* has been recorded (by A. R. Niemi, Väinö Kaukonen), a comprehensive ideological comparison of the *Old* and the *New Kalevala* has not been emphasized. To the Finns it has been self-evident that the *New Kalevala* is the final, true version, and that all others are embryonic stages in its development. Therefore, this is the version of the *Kalevala* which usually has been precisely translated into approximately 45 languages to date and for which Finnish artists have composed and illustrated.[35] Finnish school children have been required to read the *New Kalevala* or an abbreviated version of it to the point of saturation. This has been the unquestioned course of events despite the fact that the *New Kalevala* is almost twice the length of the *Old Kalevala*. Because of the huge amount of additional material it contains, the plot of the *New Kalevala* may seem much less exciting, coherent, and informative than its predecessor. In this author's opinion, at least as an experiment, Finnish school children should experience the succinct *Old Kalevala*, true to the White Sea rune singers' style, alongside the *New Kalevala* with its myriad of occasionally tedious details.

In contemporary Finland, attitudes toward the *Kalevala* are somewhat ambivalent. On one hand, the epic is viewed as a well-known masterpiece of Finnish literature which has appeared in numerous versions and editions. On the other hand, the *Kalevala* itself does not seem to belong to that body of work popularly read and beloved by the Finns. The Finns consider it to be their classic epical work and, although few of them actually have much familiarity with its contents or have read it from cover to cover with great enthusiasm or love, its value is acknowledged by the public. A notable Finnish cultural and political figure, Edwin Linkomies, expressed this attitude on the occasion of the Kalevala anniversary in 1947:

> How many Finns actually have a living interest in the *Kalevala*? How many pick it up now and then and really read it out of pleasure and not merely because of a certain feeling of national obligation? I believe that there are relatively few such people, at most one in a hundred in that group which considers the *Kalevala* to be even a passably tolerable way to satisfy their enjoyment of reading. However, the *Kalevala* is spoken of often. Festivities are organized in its honor, but by and large there is no desire to delve into it or to draw from it such worth as is usually sought from good literature. . . . What is the reason for this? It cannot be a lack of exhortation and propaganda, because for decades there has existed the rallying call: Familiarize yourselves with the *Kalevala*, for ours is the fortunate circumstance that our people have created an epic poem such as this.[36]

In Linkomies's opinion, the age of twelve to fourteen, which is when Finnish children are required to read the *Kalevala* in secondary school, is too early:

> The beauty of the *Kalevala* and the appreciation of its poetic content require a mature mind. . . . Only at a fully mature age can a mind be stirred to absorb its contents. If there is a desire to make the *Kalevala* a contemporary work for the Finnish people, then, in my opinion, means must be found to persuade adult citizens to read it and to really delve into it.

The *Kalevala* has become a part of Finnish history. At the same time, it is a national myth which has even become the basis of ritual behavior expressed in annually repeated festivals. The first Kalevala Festival was held by the Savo-Karelian

The relationship of the *Kalevala* to national identity is particularly apparent among descendants of Finnish immigrants living abroad. In the United States, members of the Knights and Ladies of Kalevala gathered before their emblem in this photograph taken in July 1985 to celebrate the third annual summer Finnfest in Hannock, Michigan. The three-day festivities were attended by 3,000 to 5,000 American Finns, and the central theme of the gathering was the meaning of the *Kalevala*. The slogan "There's a lot of Finn in me" appeared on numerous posters. (Juha Pentikäinen)

fraternity at the University of Helsinki in 1864, and the first major Kalevala celebration was organized in honor of the fiftieth anniversary of the epic in 1885.[37] The annual Kalevala Day celebrations were officially initiated in 1909. Kalevala Day, celebrated on February 28, has given generations of Finns the opportunity to recall their roots and to return to the sacred origins of national feeling, the golden era of Finnish antiquity. The Kalevala Festival provides everyone the substance and structure for an experience, the depth of which depends on the participant, the time, and the place.

The *Kalevala* is perhaps most highly esteemed by Finnish emigrants, who see it as revealing the sacred history of their forefathers. Given below is a description by a third-generation Finn, living in the United States, of what the *Kalevala* means to her. Her grandparents had moved from Finland. Although her parents spoke Finnish, her generation no longer did. Nevertheless, like many third- and fourth-generation Finnish Americans, she became interested in Finnish culture, folk poetry, and the *Kalevala*. The following is her introduction to an essay on the *Kalevala* as a work of literature:

> The *Kalevala* is a work which, in my childhood, I heard to be the Finnish national epic and which was never questioned. Of course I never read the *Kalevala*. My parents had read it long ago in Finnish literature courses at church, but they had never read or lent it to us or referred to its main characters or tales. It was enough for us to know that this was an epic about Finland. Finland was not one of those small countries without culture, of which no one had heard. Finland had a rich tradition, about which it could be proud. Later, my grown-up brother and I read the *Kalevala*, which our parents had bought for our cultural enrichment. We became familiar with the tales related to the titles of Sibelius's pieces. By that age, both he and I knew that the *Kalevala*, strictly defined, was not a folk epic and that the folklorists did not consider it to be authentic folklore. Despite this, we were nevertheless interested in the work because it represented a great deal to us of that which we understood to be Finnish as we ourselves understood Finnishness. For us, it has been no less than a symbol of national identity.[38]

THE *KALEVALA* AS SACRED SCRIPTURE

The *Kalevala* process has generally been viewed as part of Finnish national history, but until recently the epic has not been compared extensively to the sacred texts created by other peoples and religions. In bolstering Finnish identity, the *New Kalevala* achieved the status of a national epic in Finnish minds during the mid-nineteenth century. It was usually canonized "as a communally and culturally shared scripture,"[39] a sacred "book" comparable to the Torah and the Vedic texts. Common to these texts was that their original sources lay in oral song and that they had survived in their cultures as sacred texts primarily due to the national-religious feelings they have engendered, the symbols they have transmitted.

A unique characteristic of the *Kalevala* is that it is a long narrative. To a certain extent this kind of epic tradition lives on in Finnish literature, where there is a tendency to write books in series, such as Mika Waltari's *Valtakunnan Salaisuus* (Secret of the state), Eeva Joenpelto's *Lohja* series, Antti Tuuri's *Pohjanmaa* (Northland), Erno and Arto Paasilinna's Petsamo books. Väinö Linna's *Täällä Pohjantähden Alla* (Here beneath the North Star) was published as a trilogy. Kalle Päätalo's *Koillismaa* (Northeastern land) is a long regional and personal narrative about the life experiences of a Finnish man which has continued, still uncompleted, since World War II. Samuli Paulaharju, Finland's most assiduous folklore collector, was an author in whose works the folk speak. In White Sea Karelia it also has been customary to write long narratives (Antti Timonen, etc.).

In numerous aspects, toward the end of the nineteenth century, for the Finns the *Kalevala* had become a book comparable to the Bible, esteemed for its nationalistic worth, although many Finns hadn't read the epic. Finnishness may thus be

Emil Petäjä is a Finnish-American author who in his novels has adapted Kalevala myths into the present. *The Stolen Sun* is an adaptation of the lost orbs of the heavens, also described in the *Kalevala*.

characterized primarily as "belief in a book." For the Finns the *Kalevala* (ch. 2) was an epic like the *Niebelungenlied,* the *Edda,* the songs of the Ossian, or Homer. In its time, the epic had been edited with religious zeal like Milton's classical *Paradise Lost.*[40] This leads to issues related to the phenomenology of religion.

FINNISHNESS AS CIVIL VS. NATIONAL RELIGION

Although the word "uskonto" (religion) came into the Finnish language only in the nineteenth century and it does not have exactly the same meaning as the Latin "religio" and the religious terminology derived from it in European languages,[41] the following is an attempt to review the concepts "national" vs. "civil" religion in accordance with Finnish circumstances. Recently, within American sociology of religion, the concept of civil religion,[42] introduced by Robert Bellah in 1967, has been used to describe religious beliefs, rituals, and symbols which influence people on a very general level. The term was first used during the Enlightenment by the French philosopher Jean-Jacques Rousseau in 1762.[43] His "religion civile" was not bound to any established religion, and therefore had the potential of being acceptable to everyone; "it should teach people to love their own nation and state accordingly."

Bellah wrote about civil religion in America, meaning specific elements of religion generally shared by every American regardless of the specific religion he or she might espouse. According to Catherine L. Albanese,[44] there has been a creed, ethical (code), and ritual dimension (cultus) in American civil religion throughout history. In presidential and other political speeches, America has been called the "Promised Land"; its divine mandate was bequeathed by God in his Union with the Nation (the USA), its primary values being Democracy and Freedom of Religion to be granted to all humankind (hence, the active foreign policy and international war by the U.S. against communism). There are special national mythical heroes (George Washington, Abraham Lincoln, John F. Kennedy, Martin Luther King, etc.), memorial sites (e.g., veteran cemeteries), days in the National Calendar to be commemorated annually (e.g., Thanksgiving Day, Labor Day, Memorial Day).

The deficiency in the debate concerning American sociology of religion is that it did not distinguish between concepts of national vs. civil religion. In discussion of the *Kalevala* process, this division is essential. From this point of view, Finnishness may be described as a kind of contemporary unification of the "national" and "civil" religion of the Finns. The former used to be related to Finnish nationalism with the *Kalevala* as its sacred scripture, the latter with the role of Lutheran Christianity as the religion of the majority (today ca. 86%) in Finland.[45] In addition to being central to Finnish history, the *Kalevala* was central to Finnish mythology and its writing, or mythography. A key role in this is held by Finnish spirituality, to be dealt with as a representation of Finnishness. When considering this phenomenon, crucial problems include when and to what extent its forms may be described as a manifestation of the national vs. civil religion of the Finns.

Narratives about the Winter War, payment of the war debt, Sibelius' music, the Finnish sauna, and symbols of "sisu" (strength, power, energy) such as Paavo Nurmi, the Flying Finn, in addition to being well-known abroad, are also part of the Finnish national cult at home. The primary hero of this cult is the Finnish commander during both World Wars, Marshall C. G. E. Mannerheim, a White general whose statue, astride his horse, stands in the center of Helsinki. In the Finnish calendar there are many calendar days related to the wars when pilgrimages are made to Mannerheim's grave and to the graves of heroes in the National Cemetery at Hietaniemi in Helsinki. These are the centers of the Finnish national cult of the dead, where those lost in wars are remembered. This "cult of the fallen" is observed yearly at hundreds of soldiers' graves throughout the country on occasions such as Independence Day, at Christmas, and on Memorial Day. Based upon the ideal "a brother doesn't desert a brother," the Finnish soldiers did their utmost to see the body of every man felled in war to a soldier's grave. War veterans continue the same tradition today, bringing spruce wreaths and wearing their veteran insignia at the funeral services of veterans. In Finland, after World War II, the widespread tradition of lighting candles in cemeteries on Christmas Eve got its start from the dead hero cult. It is customary to sing oral and written poetry based upon the *Kalevala* at these annual ceremonies. Many messages contained therein are concealed in the "silent language" of Finnishness as encapsulated in Martti Haavio's verse:

> Yksi pieni kansanlaulu,
> Ei sanoja ollenkaan.

> (A brief folk song,
> No words at all.)

Appendix A.

CHRONOLOGY OF ELIAS LÖNNROT'S LIFE

1802	Born in Sammatti, the son of a tenant farmer
1822	Begins his studies at the Turku Academy
1827	Earns M.A. degree and becomes a Doctorate of Philosophy candidate at the Turku Academy
1828	Embarks on his first rune-collecting journey
1829	*Kantele* folio is partially completed
1831	Second rune-collecting journey
1832	Third rune-collecting journey
	Earns Doctor of Medicine degree at the University of Helsinki
	Appointed assistant to the district physician in Oulu
1833	Appointed district physician in Kajaani
	The Collection of Poems about Väinäminen is completed
	Fourth rune-collecting journey; meets Ontrei Malinen and Vaassila Kieleväinen
1834	Fifth rune-collecting journey
1835	Publication of the *Old Kalevala*
	Sixth rune-collecting journey
1836–37	Seventh rune-collecting journey
1838	Eighth rune-collecting journey
1839	Publication of *The Finnish Farmer's Family Doctor*
	Ninth rune-collecting journey
1841–42	Tenth rune-collecting journey
1844–45	Eleventh rune-collecting journey
1848	Holds first series of lectures in the Finnish language at the University of Helsinki
1849	Marries Maria Piponius
	Publication of the *New Kalevala*
1853	Becomes Professor of Finnish Language and Literature at the University of Helsinki
1862	Retires from his professorship to Sammatti
1867	Part One of the *Finnish-Swedish Dictionary* is published
1880	Part Two of the *Finnish-Swedish Dictionary* is published
1883	Interim *Hymnal* is published
1884	Dies in Sammatti

Appendix B.

CHRONOLOGY OF FINNISH HISTORY

Previous to Lönnrot's Time

B.C.

7000–3000	Pre-Ceramic Suomusjärvi culture
3000–1800	Comb Ceramic culture
	–earthenware vessels decorated with comblike motifs
4000–400	–pictographs with elk, bear, boat, and anthropomorphic motifs
1900–1600	Cord Ceramic culture
	–dominant among new inhabitants of southwestern Finland
	–herding and agriculture
	–contacts over the Gulf of Bothnia
1600–1300	Kiukainen culture
	–results from merging of Comb Ceramic
	–and Battle Ax cultures
	–centered on the coast
1300–500	Bronze Age
	–Scandinavian cultural orientation
	–bronze artifacts from eastern Europe
500–	Iron Age

A.D.

600	–increase in farming settlement
	–trade with Estonia
600–800	Meroving Period
	–development of an autonomous Finnish culture (e.g., spreading of Finnish burial customs)
	–extensive trade to the east and west
800–1050	Viking Period
	–increased contacts with western Europe
	–initial Christian influences in northern Europe
	–Christian mission begins from both west and east
	–settlements become more populous and spread inland from the coastal region
1155–57	First Crusade to Finland
	–Christian influences first become apparent (e.g., shift to Christian burial customs)
1216	Pope places Finland under Swedish jurisdiction
1323	Peace Treaty of Pähkinäsaari marks the initial division of Finland, at this time between Russia and Sweden
1527	Swedish King Gustavus Vasa stays the power of the Western Church Reformation begins, led in Finland primarily by Mikael Agricola in conjunction with the Reformation, situation of Finnish language begins to improve
1551	Agricola's *Preface to the Psalter*

1550s	Settlement spreads toward eastern and northern Finland and extends into central Scandinavia (slash-and-burn agriculture)
1600s	Orthodox Period, Evangelical Lutheran Church
1638	New Sweden Colony founded in Delaware (the majority of the settlers are Forest Finns)
1640	Governor-General of Finland, Peter Brahe, establishes Turku Academy
1642	Finnish-language Bible is published −growth of literature in the Finnish language
1700s	The Enlightenment begins
1770s	−period of religious revivalism
1770–1790	Gustavian Period −Porthan Period: scholarship on Finnish topics at the Turku Academy
1785	Publication of C. Ganander's *Mythologia Fennica*

From Lönnrot's Time Onward

1808	"Finnish War" breaks out between Sweden and Russia
1809	Finland becomes an autonomous Grand Duchy of Russia
1810–1820s	Period of Turku Romanticism
1812	Helsinki replaces Turku as the capital, but Turku remains the cultural center
1817	Gottlund puts forth the concept of unifying Finnish runes into one epic
1819	Schröter edits his collection *Finnische Runen*
1827	The Turku Fire and consequent (1828) removal of the Academy to Helsinki −The Helsinki Romantics
1831	Finnish Literature Society is founded to support the collection and preservation of folklore
1835	The *Old Kalevala* is published −Runeberg's positive critique of the *Old Kalevala* in the *Helsingfors Morgonblad*
1839	Arwidsson asserts that the *Kalevala* is Lönnrot's creation
1840	The *Kanteletar* is published
1841	Castrén's Swedish translation of the *Kalevala* is published
1845	A French prose translation of the *Kalevala* is published −Grimm's lecture about the *Kalevala* at the Berlin Academy of Science
1849	The *New Kalevala* is published
1852	The *Kalevala* is translated into German
1863	A manifesto for the equality of the Finnish language is initiated by J. V. Snellman −years of language feud and Fennomania follow; Finnish intelligentsia struggles to establish a Finnish culture under the pressures of Swedish language and Russian political dominance
1860s	Emigration to America begins; over 400,000 Finns move overseas by World War I
1885	Celebration of fiftieth anniversary year of the *Kalevala*; the first general, extensive *Kalevala* Festival
1892	Sibelius composes his *Kullervo Symphony*, heralding the nationalistic and *Kalevala* Period in Finnish musical composition
1895–1900	Sibelius composes his "Lemminkäinen Suite"
1900	Gallén-Kallela's *Kalevala* frescoes are exhibited at the Paris World's Fair
1909	Annual *Kalevala* Day commemoration is initiated

1917	The Russian Revolution
	–Finland becomes independent
1918	The Finnish Civil War
	–the Swedish-language Åbo Academy is founded in Turku
1921	Compulsory education law is passed
1922	The Finnish-language Turku University is established at Turku
1930s	The Rise of Finnish nationalism
	–struggle between the Finnish and Swedish languages
1935	The 100th-year celebration of the *Kalevala*
1939–1945	The Winter War and the Continuation War between Finland and the Soviet Union
	–Finland cedes the Karelian Isthmus, the Salla territory, and Petsamo to the Soviet Union
1946	Resettlement of evacuees
	–payment of reparations to the Soviet Union, followed by rapid industrialization and economic growth
1952	The Helsinki Olympics
1956–1981	Urho Kekkonen is president of Finland
1960s-70s	Urbanization intensifies
	–extensive migration to Sweden
	–a network of new universities is established throughout the country and a state system of higher education is created
1975	European Conference on Security and Cooperation in Helsinki
1978	*Kalevala* Day is designated an official flag day and is renamed Finnish Culture Day
1985	The 150th anniversary of the *Kalevala* is celebrated around the world

Appendix C.

GLOSSARY

Ahti:	Guardian spirit of the water.
Aino:	Joukahainen's sister, whom he promises to Väinämöinen as a wife. Rather than marry an old man, she drowns herself in a lake and becomes a fish.
Boasso:	The sacred back corner in the north of a Saami dwelling where the shaman's drum is kept. Above it is a hole through which the shaman's spirit is believed to travel to the other realm.
Hiisi:	A sacred forest; a guardian spirit of the forest, mountains, or water; a powerful giant; the Demon.
Hiitola:	Hiisi's abode, place of the evil spirit.
Iku-Tiera:	Ancient Tiera, a culture hero; Väinämöinen and Ilmarinen's helper in some versions of the Sampo cycle.
Ilmarinen:	One of the three major heroes of the *Kalevala*; the Kaleva people's smith; god of the sky, weather, and fire.
Ilmatar:	Daughter of the sky; Väinämöinen's mother, the creator of the universe in the *New Kalevala*.

Jabmeaivo:	The netherworld of the Saami, depicted on shamans' drums as the nethermost part of a three-level world.
Joiku:	Archaic Saami singing tradition.
Joukahainen:	A shamanic hero of the *Kalevala*; Aino's brother.
Juksakka:	Goddess of hunting in Saami culture.
Kaamos:	Sunless midwinter period in the north.
Kaleva:	A giant; forefather of the Kaleva people.
Kalevala:	Home of Kaleva; land of the Kaleva people; Finnish national epic.
Kalma:	Graveyard being; death; ruler of the dead.
Kalmisto (also Kalmisoma):	Abode of the dead; a graveyard located in a park or a forest outside the village, often on an island.
Kantele:	A traditional Finnish stringed instrument which frequently has five strings; cf. harp, lute, guitar.
Kaukamoinen:	A man who longs for distant lands; another name for Lemminkäinen in the *Kalevala*.
Kihavanskoinen (also written Kihovauhkoinen):	Prophesier of the end of the world, he is mentioned in the preface of the *Old Kalevala* as one of the Kaleva band along with Väinämöinen, Joukahainen, Lemminkäinen, etc.
Kivimäki:	A mythical hillock made of stone; also Pain Mountain, the gloom-filled land of the dead to which shamans journeyed to attain knowledge; in the *Kalevala* it is the place in Pohjola where the Sampo and the lights of the heavens are concealed after being stolen by the Old Crone of Pohjola.
Kropnitša:	A small log construction built on graves in Orthodox Karelia; it includes a window facing toward the home of the deceased through which it was believed the deceased could watch the activities of his or her kin; the kropnitša also included implements used by the deceased and an opening through which the soul-bird could depart.
Kullervo:	One of the *Kalevala* heroes whose tragic tale Lönnrot included as a miniature epic in the *Kalevala*. A much more expanded version of theKullervo tale is presented in the *New Kalevala* than in the *Old*.
Kuusnetäl'iset:	A commemorative ceremony for the deceased held six weeks after death; the final wedding celebrated for a particular individual, after which it was believed that the soul of the deceased departed to join the dead kin.
Lemminkäinen:	One of the central heroes of the *Kalevala*; a shaman; Lönnrot presented him as a light-hearted, wandering hero who died during his adventures but was brought to life again by his mother.
Lempi:	Love, cherished one; in Lönnrot's opinion, the name of Lemminkäinen's father.
Lempo:	The devil.
Liekkiö:	The soul of a murdered child or a concealed embryo which was believed to haunt and to weep at night in the place where it had died.
Louhi:	The Mistress of Pohjola, the Old Crone of the North; the ruler of the Pohjola folk.
Lovi:	A hole, an opening in the ground, a pit; the "loveen lankeaminen" (falling into a pit) of a shaman means a journey through a hole into the other world, Tuoni, Jabmeaivo.
Luonto:	Nature.

Luontola:	One of the places where Lemminkäinen encountered perils during his journey.
Luotela:	A region in the northwest; another name for Pohjola.
Maahiset:	A group of supernatural beings who were believed to reside inside the earth and live a humanlike existence in an upside-down world.
Manala:	The dwelling of Mana, ruler of the world of the dead; the abode of the dead; the netherworld (see Tuonela).
Marjatta:	The mother of the infant boy who judges Väinämöinen at the conclusion of the *Kalevala*; the Finnish name for the Virgin Mary.
Mielikki:	Daughter-in-law of Tapio, the forest deity.
Naisten Pohjola:	Cf. Terra feminarum; Pohjola was a land reigned over by women; the kingdom of the dead to which heroes ventured to attain knowledge.
Noaidde:	A shaman, a Saami sage who used the technique of ecstasy.
Noita:	A shaman, also a female witch.
Otava:	The Bear Constellation (the Big Dipper); the Great Bear.
Pimentola:	A shadowy, dark place, the home of darkness; another name for Pohjola.
Pohjola:	The dwelling place of the people of Pohjola; a dark, cold region; the realm of death.
Päivölä:	Originally the upper realm which had the sun (päivä) as its center.
Saivo:	In Saami tradition, a sparkling lake with a double bottom; beneath this double bottom lay the netherworld of the Saami.
Sampo:	A central element in the *Kalevala*; the interpretation of its meaning has been a source of great controversy; possibly a symbol of culture, a source of wealth, the basis of world order.
Sariola:	Another name for Pohjola; according to Lönnrot's interpretation, a swamp where sedge grows, typical of northern Finland.
Staalo:	An evil being in Saami culture which was believed to appear as an anthropomorphic figure in the form of a whistling dog; a Saami girl could be married to a staalo.
Taivaanääreläiset:	Tiny, humanlike beings which lived at the boundary of the earth and the firmament.
Tapio:	Forest deity or guardian spirit.
Tuonela:	The netherworld, abode of the dead; also the grave (see Manala).
Tuoni:	The ruler of death; death; the abode of the dead.
Ukko:	God of thunder (Ukkonen); the highest of the pre-Christian Finnish deities.
Untamola:	Home of Untamo, the ruler of sleep and dreams; Kalervo's brother.
Vipunen:	Antero Vipunen, a primordial sage even older than Väinämöinen; proto-shaman of the Kaleva people.
Väinämöinen:	Ilmatar's son, who was revered as a deity in the *New Kalevala* by the ancient Finns because of his knowledge and wisdom; a shaman and culture hero; primary hero of the *Kalevala*.
Väinölä:	Väinämöinen's home.

Appendix D.

INDIVIDUALS SIGNIFICANT TO STUDY OF THE *KALEVALA*

(Sources: *Facta 2001*, Porvoo 1981. HAAVIO, MARTTI *Viimeiset Runonlaulajat* (The last rune singers), Porvoo 1948. HAUTALA, JOUKO *Suomalainen kansanrunouden tutkimus* (Finnish folklore research), Turku 1954. KUUSI, MATTI & ANTTONEN PERTTI *Kalevala-lipas* (Guide to the *Kalevala*), Pieksämäki 1985. *Otavan suuri ensyklopedia* (The large Otava encyclopedia), Keuruu 1978.

MIKAEL AGRICOLA (ca. 1510–1557). Religious reformer of Finland and the father of Finnish literature. Of peasant origins, he studied languages and theology at Wittenberg under the guidance of Luther and Melanchthon. He created the basis for the Finnish literary language. The list of pagan deities included in his preface to the *Psalter* is an important source for the study of Finnish religious history.

AUGUST ENGELBRACHT AHLQVIST (1826–1889). Professor of Finnish language and literature, a poet who wrote under the name "Oksanen." He collected runes for the *New Kalevala* and clarified aspects of the epic's vocabulary and meter.

JUHANI AHO (1861–1921). Author. He journeyed to Karelia with his wife and Eero Järnefelt in 1892. The journey inspired him to write *Lastuja* (Chips). Other works include the novels *Panu, Juha*, and *Kevät ja takatalvi* (Spring and winter again).

MATTHIAS AKIANDER (1802–1871). Teacher, historian, professor of Russian, scholar of Finnish religious revivalism. Active in the Finnish Literature Society. He made arrangements for printing Lönnrot's works.

AUGUST ANNIST (1889–1972). Estonian folklorist and literary scholar. Translated the *Kalevala* into Estonian in 1939 and 1959.

AARNE ANTTILA (1892–1952). Literary scholar who wrote a comprehensive biography of Lönnrot.

ADOLF IVAR ARWIDSSON (1791–1858). A Romantic who played a major role in awakening the national consciousness. Having studied at Uppsala, he was in part responsible for the atmosphere in Turku when Lönnrot, Runeberg, and Snellman arrived there in 1822. The charms collected by Arwidsson and E. A. Crohns were available to Lönnrot.

ELIEL ASPELIN-HAAPKYLÄ (1847–1917). Art historian. His sole folkloristic study *Kalevalan tutkimuksia I* (Studies in the *Kalevala* I), is significant. As a proponent of Tylor's theory of animism, he interpreted the Sampo as the sun.

REINHOLD von BECKER (1788–1858). On the faculty of Turku University; editor of *Turun Wiikko-Sanomat* (The Turku weekly). He published a noteworthy article about Väinämöinen. Under von Becker's direction, Lönnrot wrote his dissertation *De Väinämöine*.

A. A. BORENIUS (1846–1931). Collector and publisher of folklore. It was based on his ideas that Julius and Kaarle Krohn developed their "Finnish" historical-geographic method.

ADAM von BREMEN (previous to 1045–ca. 1085). German historian and writer. His primary work, "Decriptio insularum aquilonis," is one of the oldest sources describing circumstances in the Nordic region, such as the spread of Christianity, for example.

JOHAN FREDRIK CAJAN (1815–1887). Clergyman. Met Lönnrot in 1835. He became interested in Finnish history and collecting folklore. Cajan aided Lönnrot in editing *The Bee*, and traveled with him in Kainuu and White Sea Karelia.

ZACHARIUS CAJANDER (1818–1895). Agronomist and author. He became so interested in the Finnish national consciousness as a youth that he taught his fellow students Finnish and gave accounts of the *Kalevala*

MATHIAS ALEXANDER CASTRÉN (1813–1852). The first Professor of Finnish Language at Helsinki University. Founder of the study of Finno-Ugric languages and culture. Lönnrot's travel companion. Castrén was the first to translate the *Old Kalevala* into Swedish (1841). He criticized the repetitive nature of the *New Kalevala*.

FABIAN COLLAN (1817–1851). Poet. Lönnrot's devoted friend and salon critic of the *New Kalevala*. He interpreted the *Kalevala* from a mythological point of view.

DOMENICO COMPARETTI (1837–1927). Italian senator who was the first to raise the subject of ancient Finnish folklore internationally. In his opinion, Finnish folklore was based on shamanism.

FREDRIK CYGNAEUS (1807–1881). Among the most renowned orators and scholars of aesthetics during his time. His "Det tragiska elementet i Kalevala" (1853) was the first noteworthy essay about the *Kalevala* as a work of art.

OTTO DONNER (1835–1909). Finnish scholar of religion and a proponent of the nature-mythological school. Published a study of the Sampo.

ROBERT VILHELM EKMAN (1808–1873). The most prominent artist of his time. From the 1850s on he painted pioneering works on themes related to the *Kalevala*. For example, he illustrated *Kalevala kerrottuna nuorisolle* (The Kalevala for young people).

PEKKA ERVAST (1875–1934). Theosophist and writer. He was a member of the Theosophist movement and the Anthroposophical Society when the Ruusuristi (Rosicrucian) organization was founded in 1920. In his opinion, the *Kalevala* was one of the mystical texts and gave information about ancient knowledge and counsel on seeking truth.

D.E.D. EUROPAEUS (1820–1884). Lifelong student. A man of vast ideas, and an avid collector of folklore who discovered poetry areas to the south, such as the rich Ingrian tradition. He traveled to Kajaani in 1845 as Lönnrot's assistant. The Kullervo sequence of the *New Kalevala* is based on his collection.

JACOB FELLMAN (1795–1875). Clergyman. Scholar of Lapland. Published religious texts in the Saami language. He was an avid collector of antiquities and information about the history and ancient religion of Lapland. This was published by his son under the title *Poimintoja J. Fellmanin muistiinpanoista Lapissa* (Excerpts from J. Fellman's notes in Lapland) (1906).

GALLÉN-CALLELA (1865–1931). Artist who devoted almost his entire oeuvre to art based on the *Kalevala*. He illustrated the Werner Söderström edition of the *Kalevala*, which is the most renowned publication of the epic.

CHRISTFRID GANANDER (1741–1790). Chaplain at Rantsila; Finnish mythologist. Collector of folklore, lexicographer. His works include *Nytt Finskt Lexicon* and *Mythologia Fennica*, a basic source for the study of ancient Finnish poetry. The latter contains an alphabetical listing of names gathered from the ancient runes as well as information about Finnish and Saami mythology, history, and archeology.

CARL AXEL GOTTLUND (1796–1875). Collected extensive amounts of folklore. Discovered the "Forest Finns" in Scandinavia. Gottlund first put forth the concept of "an epic of Finnish runes" in 1817. Lönnrot's ardent opponent, he severely criticized the *Kalevala*, which overshadowed his *Otava*.

JACOB GRIMM (1785–1863). German philologist and renowned scholar of mythology. On March 13, 1845, he gave a presentation at the Berlin Academy of Sciences which brought international fame to the *Kalevala*. His basic interpretation was mythological.

VILHELM GRØNBECH (1873–1948). Danish scholar of religion. Among the subjects on which he published was the ancient religion of the Scandinavians.

PAAVO HAAVIKKO (1931-). An author whose works include rejuvenation of folkloristic themes such as *Kaksikymmentä ja yksi* (Twenty and one) (1974), *Kullervon tarina* (Kullervo's tale) (1982), and the film *Rauta-aika* (The Age of Iron).

MARTTI HAAVIO (1899–1973). Ethnologist and scholar of religion, well-known poet under the name P. Mustapää. He interpreted the *Kalevala* as a shamanistic epic, Väinämöinen as a shaman-hero, and the Sampo as the Tree of Life. Haavio edited

Pienois-Kalevala (The miniature *Kalevala*) for schools. He was director of the Folklore Archive.

MATHIAS HALLENIUS (1697/1699–1748). Linguist. In his dissertation "De Borea Fennica" (1932), he presented a considerable number of Gothic words which have Finnish correspondences in form and meaning.

ALBERT HÄMÄLAINEN (1881–1949). Folklorist who concentrated on mythology and magic in his scholarship. He authored a study of the psychology of charms entitled *Ihmisruumiin substanssi suomalais-ugrilaisten kansojen taikuudessa* (The substance of human body in the magic of Finno-Ugric peoples) (1920).

UNO (HOLMBERG) HARVA (1882–1949). Professor of sociology at Turku Unversity, particularly renowned for his scholarship in religion. He interpreted the Sampo to be the "pillar of the world." His work *Suomalaisten muinaisusko* (The ancient religion of the Finns) (1948) is a classic study of folk religion.

JOUKO HAUTALA (1910–1983). Scholar of Finnish folklore and religion. He wrote extensively about the history and methodology of folkloristics.

G.W.F. HEGEL (1744–1831). German philosopher. Lectures on Hegel's philosophy were already being given in Turku in 1820, and his views predominated there until the 1860s.

J. G. HERDER (1744–1803). German National Romantic who wrote the pioneering work of his time about the folklore of various peoples, entitled *Stimmen der Völker in Lieder* (1778). Herder's ideas inspired Sjögren and Poppius, among others, to collect folklore.

LAURI HONKO (1932–). Professor of Folkloristics and Comparative Religion at the University of Turku. Has done extensive studies on the methodology of folklore research, Finnish epics, ritual poetry, folk belief, and folk medicine.

JALMARI JAAKKOLA (1885–1964). Professor of Finnish History at Helsinki University. Called attention to folklore in his studies of the Medieval Period in Finland. He was a proponent of the historical interpretation of the *Kalevala*, which was emphasized in his work *Suomen varhaishistoria* (Early Finnish history).

E. J. JESSEN (1833–1921). Danish linguist and scholar of the ancient history of the Nordic peoples.

JUHANA KAINULAINEN (1788–1847). The first notable rune singer encountered by Lönnrot. On his 1828 journey to Ilomantsi in North Karelia, Lönnrot collected fifty-seven runes from him.

K. F. KARJALAINEN (1871–1919). Linguist. Published the study *Jugralaisten uskonto* (The religions of the Finno-Ugric peoples), which is the most extensive work in the series Suomen suvun uskonnot (Religions of the Finnic peoples).

MARTISKA KARJALAINEN (1768–1839). White Sea Karelian rune singer. Lönnrot collected approximately eighteen hundred verses from him during his rune-collecting journey in 1843.

VÄINÖ KAUKONEN (1911–). Literary scholar who has studied the *Kalevala* from an aesthetic viewpoint. Has done extensive studies of the method and subject matter used by Lönnrot in the *Old* and the *New Kalevala*.

KAARLE NIKLAS KECKMAN (1793–1838). Worked as a university librarian and lecturer in the Finnish language. The Finnish Literature Society was founded in his home. As the secretary of this organization, he was instrumental in the publication of Topelius's and Lönnrot's primary works.

SIGRID AUGUST KEINÄNEN (1841–1914). Painter. Won the Savo-Karelian Student Association art competition in 1891. He painted a number of works on *Kalevala* themes.

VAASSILA KIELEVÄINEN (1760–1840). Rune singer from Vuonninen in White Sea Karelia whom Lönnrot met in 1833. Although his memory was no longer acute, the one song he related to Lönnrot proved to be the catalyst for Lönnrot's compilation of runes about Väinämöinen into a single whole.

ALEKSIS KIVI (1834–1872). Author. Among his works is a play on a *Kalevala* theme entitled *Kullervo*.

JULIUS KROHN (1835–1888). Scholar of Finnish folklore and literature. A poet under the name Suonio. Founder of the study of Finnish folkloristics. Krohn was of German origins. He published *Tutkimus Kalevalasta* (A study of the *Kalevala*) (1883–1885) and *Kantelettaren tutkimuksia* (Studies of the *Kanteletar*) (pub. 1900–1902). He also edited *Kullervon runot* (The Kullervo poems) (1882).

KAARLE KROHN (1863–1933). Folklore scholar. Docent in Finnish and comparative folklore and the first Professor of Folkloristics at Helsinki University. Krohn encouraged and strengthened the historical-geographic approach. He studied fairy tales, Kalevala runes, and mythology. He founded the international "Folklore Fellows" Society and began publication of the series Folklore Fellows Communications.

MATELI KUIVALATAR (1771–1846). Singer and creator of runes from Ilomantsi whose skill in singing was praised by Lönnrot in his preface to the *Kanteletar*.

MATTI KUUSI (1914–1998). Professor of Finnish and Comparative Folkloristics at Helsinki University. He developed a typological method of analysis which he used in his dissertation "Sampo-eepos" (The Sampo epic). He has written numerous works on *Kalevala* topics and about Finnish folklore.

TOIVO VILHO LEHTISALO (1887–1962). Linguist who concentrated on the Samoyed language and ethnology.

ANNI LEHTONEN (b. 1866; was still alive in White Sea Karelia in 1941). The great-granddaughter of Ontrei Malinen, whose extensive repertoire of ritual poetry was studied by Samuli Paulaharju.

EINO LEINO (1878–1926). Poet from Kainuu. Advocate of the new National Romanticism; one of the greatest Karelianists. He was inspired by ancient poetry and the *Kalevala* at an early age.

ERIK LENCQVIST (1719–1808). Clergyman, author, docent. One of the most active members in the Aurora Society. He prepared manuscripts on mythological themes which were used by his son, Christian, for his thesis under Porthan. This dissertation is a presentation of Finnish mythology using folk traditions as a source.

JORMA LEPPÄAHO (1907–). Archeologist. In his writings he has called attention to archeological factors in dating runes and charms.

NILS LID (1890–1958). Norwegian scholar of ancient Nordic religion. He has argued that the source of the Finnish runes was in the "fornaldar" sagas. His primary works include "Kring Kalevala-miljöet" (In the *Kalevala* atmosphere) (1943) and *Kalevalan Pohjola* (The *Kalevala*'s Pohjola) (1949).

OLAUS MAGNUS (1490–1558). The last Catholic bishop of Sweden. He wrote the famed illustrated work *Historia de gentibus septentrionalibus* (1555). The maps in this work are among the primary sources for study of Nordic religious and cultural history during late medieval times. It includes descriptions of Finnish magic and charms as well as important sources for Finnish mythology.

ONTREI MALINEN (1780–1855). One of the foremost singers in the village of Vuonninen in White Sea Karelia. He sang for Lönnrot in 1833. The framework of the *Proto-Kalevala* is primarily derived from the Sampo cycle.

J. V. MANSIKKA (1884–1947). Folklorist and Slavist. Used the historical-geographic method. His primary works are *Über russische Zauberformen* and *Die Religionen der Ostslaven*.

OSKAR MERIKANTO (1868–1924). Composer. He composed the first Finnish opera based on *Kalevala* themes, *Pohjan neito*" (Maid of the North).

A. R. NIEMI (1896–1931). Professor of folklore. He studied the history of rune collecting and the initial stages of compilation of the *Kalevala*.

AXEL OLRIK (1864–1917). Danish folklorist. Worked with Kaarle Krohn to found the international Folklore Fellows (FF) in 1907. He was a proponent of the historical-geographic method along with A. Aarne.

HEIKKI PAASONEN (1865–1919). Linguist. Specialist in Mordvin culture and language. He was to write the section on Mordvin religion in the series Religions of the Finno-Ugric Peoples but died before the completion of his work.

LARIN PARASKE (1833–1904). A renowned rune singer who became symbolic of female singers from the southern regions.

SAMULI PAULAHARJU (1878–1944). Teacher, author, and, along with his wife, an avid collector of Finnish folklore. He collected over thirty thousand items of folklore from Karelia, Ostrobothnia, and Lapland. His literary work has great ethnographic significance.

ARHIPPA PERTTUNEN (1769–1840). Singer from Latvajärvi referred to as the "king of White Sea Karelia," whom Lönnrot met in 1834. Blind Arhippaini Miihkali (1815–1899) was his son.

RIETRIKKI POLEN (1823–1884). Lönnrot's student. Collected Ladoga Karelian runes which served as a basis for the New Kalevala.

ABRAHAM POPPIUS (1793–1866). From Juva. He became a folklore enthusiast along with A. J. Sjögren and C. A. Gottlund. His collection served as a source for Lönnrot.

HENRIK GABRIEL PORTHAN (1739–1804). Professor at the Turku Academy and a historian. In 1766–78 he published his study of Finnish runes De Poesi Fennica. Along with Ganander, Porthan collected Finnish proverbs and planned for an extensive Finnish dictionary. He was a scholar of Finnish dialects.

MARI REMSU (b. 1893; has lived in Sweden since 1948). White Sea Karelian rune singer, storyteller, and lamenter.

HENRIK RENQVIST (1789–1866). Clergyman at Liperi in Karelia. Leader in religious revivalism. Proponent of knee-praying, consecration, and daily penitence. He wrote, translated, and published literature. He was a pioneer in missionary work and the temperance movement.

JOHAN LUDVIG RUNEBERG (1804–1877). National poet of Finland. He was among the first to realize the significance of the Kalevala. He translated sections of the Kalevala and the Kanteletar into Swedish.

PAAVO RUOTSALAINEN (1777–1852). Leader in the North Savo revivalist movement, which stressed personal unity with Christ and surrender of oneself to His mercy.

ELIEL SAARINEN (1873–1950). Among the foremost Finnish architects. In collaboration with Gesellius and Lindgren he organized a Finnish pavilion on Kalevala themes for the Paris World's Fair in 1900.

VÄINÖ SALMINEN (1880–1947). Professor of Finnish Folklore. Made numerous collection trips. Salminen criticized the historical-geographic method. He studied runes in the context of daily use.

SAXO GRAMMATICUS (d. ca. 1220). A Danish historian whose history is a primary source for the study of Nordic mythology. E. N. Setälä presented numerous correspondences between the Danish Amleth tale told by Grammaticus, Shakespeare's Hamlet, and the Finnish "Kullervo Cycle."

EUGENE SCHAUMAN (1875–1904). Political activist. On the National Board of Education, assistant treasurer. He mortally wounded N. I. Bobrikov (1839–1904), the Russian Governor-General of Finland, and thereafter shot himself.

JOHANNES SCHEFFERUS (1621–1679). Professor at the University of Uppsala. He wrote, in Latin, Lapponia, a description of Lapland, its inhabitants, and their customs. This pioneering work in the religious history of the Saami was based on western Saami sources.

H. R. SCHRÖTER (1770–1831). German doctor of medicine. He went to Sweden, where he became acquainted with Finnish and heard about Finnish runes. In 1819 he published his work Finnische Runen. Lönnrot wanted to reprint the runes Schröter had published.

E. N. SETÄLÄ (1864–1935). Linguist and politician, Councillor of State. Proponent of the mythical interpretation of ancient Finnish poetry. Studied the origins of the Sampo. He criticized the historical-geographic method.

JEAN SIBELIUS (1865–1957). Renowned Finnish composer who grew enthusiastic about Karelianism in 1890. He traveled to Karelia in 1892. His compositions on *Kalevala* themes include *Kullervo, Lemminkäinen-sarja* (The Lemminkäinen suite) and *Pohjolan tytär* (Daughter of Pohjola).

SIMANA SISSONEN (1786–1848). Finnish-Karelian rune singer who sang for Europaeus in 1845 and Ahlqvist in 1846. The repertoire of the Sissonens was akin to that of the Perttunens of White Sea Karelia. This similarity influenced the shaping of the *New Kalevala*.

ANTTI JUHANA SJÖGREN (1794–1855). Scholar of the Finnish language, folklorist, and historian who became an Academician at St. Petersburg. Made field trips to White Sea Karelia, Kazan, and the Perm region to collect linguistic and cultural material.

JOHAN VILHELM SNELLMAN (1806–1881). Philosopher of Finnish nationalism, national activist, and supporter of the national literature. He admired Lönnrot more than the *Kalevala*, which he considered to have worth as a reflection of the past.

LOUIS SPARRE (1863–1964). Italian-Swedish count and artist. Traveled to Karelia with Gallén-Kallela, and later with Emil Wickström. He was very influential in Finnish cultural life.

RUDOLF STEINER (1861–1925). Austrian philosopher and educator. Founded the Anthroposophical Society in 1912.

MARINA TAKALO (1890–1970). White Sea Karelian rune singer from Oulanka. Based on her varied and extensive repertoire and life history, Juha Pentikäinen wrote the works *Marina Takalon uskonto* (Marina Takalo's religion) (1971) and *Oral Repertoire and World View* (1978).

JOHAN JACOB TENGSTRÖM (1787–1858). Philosopher and historian. Nationalist. Urged the study of the Finnish language and the collection of folklore. A founder of the Finnish Literature Society. A teacher at whose home Lönnrot, Runeberg, and Snellman gathered.

ZACHRIS TOPELIUS the Elder (1781–1831). District physician in Ostrobothnia who collected runes from White Sea Karelian peddlers. His major work was the five-volume *Suomen kansan vanhoja runoja ynnä myös nykyisempiä lauluja* (Ancient poems of the Finnish people as well as more recent songs), which was one of Lönnrot's most important models and sources for the *Kalevala*.

ZACHRIS TOPELIUS the Younger (1818–1898). Son of the above. One of the most famous Finnish authors of fairy tales. Published the work *Boken om Vårt Land* (A book of our land) (1875).

JOHAN AGAPETUS TÖRNGREN (1772–1859). Professor of medicine. Lönnrot came to his home to tutor his adopted son in 1842. Törngren supported Lönnrot's scholarly aspirations. His wife, Eva Agata (1782–1849), inspired Lönnrot to collect folklore. Their daughter Anna, who died at the age of twenty-one, was a close friend of Lönnrot's during his youth.

EMIL WICKSTRÖM (1864–1942). Sculptor. Worked with *Kalevala* themes, particularly in creating fountains.

PERTTI VIRTARANTA (1918–1997). Linguist. Professor of Finnish at the University of Helsinki 1959-1981. Has studied Finnish dialects and the Karelian language. Editor-in-chief of *Karjalankielen sanakirja* (Dictionary of the Karelian language) since 1955. Avid collector of folklore, focusing in particular on White Sea and Tver Karelian culture.

VALPURI VOHTA (b.1887–). Estonian Ingrian tradition bearer from Kallivieri.

A. O. VÄISÄNEN (1890–1969). Ethnomusicologist. Specialized in Finno-Ugric music. Collected folk music, runes, and an extensive collection of laments.

Notes

I. A MYTHOLOGICAL VIEW OF THE *KALEVALA*

The peotry in this volume has been translated from the original by Rítva Poom.
1. Grimm 1845, 17.
2. Anttila 1931–1935 I, 238–241; Kaukonen 1979, 88–112.
3. *Old Kalevala*, Preface i–v, lxiii.
4. Krohn, J. 1885, Preface.
5. Niemi 1898; Kaukonen 1939–1945.
6. Kaukonen 1979, 72, 176–185.
7. See, for example, Hautala 1954, 174–197.
8. Ibid., 118.
9. *Old Kalevala*, Preface xiii.
10. Porthan 1983.
11. Becker 1820.
12. Ganander 1960.
13. Lencqvist 1982.
14. Topelius 1822–1831.
15. Porthan 1983, 37.
16. Ibid., 88.
17. Lencqvist 1982, 45.
18. Hautala 1960, vii–viii; Sarajas 1956, 286; Tarkiainen 1941, 9.
19. Ganander 1960, Preface.
20. Ibid.
21. Ibid.
22. *Old Kalevala*, Preface iii.
23. See "Muinelmia": *Mehiläinen* January 1836.
24. Lönnrot's letter to Keckman 14.3.1834. Lönnrotiana Collection, Archives of the Finnish Literature Society.
25. Borenius & Krohn 1891–1895 II, 176.
26. See chapter VII in this book.
27. Lencqvist 1982, 76.
28. *Old Kalevala*, Preface xvii.
29. Harva 1948, 3.
30. For example, Haavio 1959, 5–7.
31. Pirinen 1973; Sarajas 1956, 10–14.
32. Sarajas 1956, 38.
33. Hallenius 1732, 5. Cf. Sarajas 1956, 152.
34. Lencqvist 1982, 46.
35. *Old Kalevala*, Preface xv.
36. Castrén 1852–1870 I, 79.
37. Lönnrot 1880.
38. Saarinen 1984.
39. Castrén 1852–1870 I, 79.
40. See, for example, Lönnrot's interpretation of the "Päivänpäästö Runo" (The release of the sun), *Old Kalevala*, Preface v–vi.
41. Krohn, J. 1885.
42. Haavio 1931, 55–57.
43. Hautala 1954, 174–197.
44. Krohn, K. 1914, 8–9.

45. Ibid., iii–iv, 7–10.
46. Ibid., 8.
47. Anttonen 1987.
48. Haavio 1967, 12.
49. *Old Kalevala*, Preface xiii.
50. See, for example, Manninen 1977.

II. THE GENESIS OF THE *KALEVALA*

1. *Old Kalevala*, Preface iv.
2. Gottlund 1847, 95.
3. Ibid.
4. See Heikinheimo 1960, 7.
5. *Old Kalevala*, Preface iv.
6. Annist 1944, 11.
7. Branch 1966, 260–266.
8. Cf. Niemi 1898, 28.
9. Ibid.
10. Tengström 1817–1818, 126.
11. Schröter 1819.
12. Anttila 1931–1935 I, 170, 210.
13. Niemi 1898, 81.
14. Kaukonen 1979, 34.
15. Lönnrot's correspondence in the Lönnrotiana Collection of the Finnish Literature Society.
16. Borenius & Krohn 1891–1895 I–III.
17. *Elias Lönnrotin matkat* 180–181.
18. Borenius & Krohn 1891–1895 I–III. In his dissertation (1898), A. R. Niemi examines the structure and contents of *Runokokous Väinämöisestä* in great detail.
19. Kaukonen 1979, 55.
20. Borenius & Krohn 1891–1895 II, 179.
21. See Kaukonen 1979, 15.
22. *Old Kalevala*, Preface i.
23. *Old Kalevala*, Preface lxiii.
24. Kaukonen 1979, 26.
25. Grimm 1845.
26. Ibid., 18.
27. Anttila 1931–1935 I, 248, 249.
28. Cf. Kunze 1952, 63.
29. Grimm 1845.
30. Ibid., 44–47.
31. Kunze 1952.
32. Grimm 1845, 17. Lönnrot also became interested in Indian epics to such an extent that the "Creation Rune" of the *New Kalevala* clearly reflects Indian origins.
33. Borenius & Krohn 1891–1895 II, 179.
34. Cf. Anttila 1931–1935 I, 239.
35. Sarajas 1984, 39–41.
36. Collan 1838.
37. *Old Kalevala*, Preface xiv–xvi.
38. Castrén 1841.
39. See Anttila 1931–1935 I, 241.
40. Gottlund 1847, 94–95.

41. Gottlund 1840, Preface.
42. Cf. Anttila 1931–1935 I, 243.
43. Gottlund 1847, 95.
44. Ibid.
45. Anttila 1931–1935 II, 4–5.
46. Ibid., 63–65; Hautala 1954, 128, 160; Haavio 1931, 33–36.
47. Anttila 1931–1935 II.
48. Kaukonen 1979, 162.
49. Anttila 1931–1935 II, 63.
50. Ibid., 78.

III. THE STRUCTURE OF THE *KALEVALA*

1. *Old Kalevala*, Preface iv.
2. Borenius & Krohn 1891–1895 III, 2–3.
3. Annist 1944, 182–187.
4. "Forest Finns" were the descendants of the Finns who, during the sixteenth, seventeenth, and eighteenth centuries, migrated from Savo to the forest areas in central Scandinavia located at the present border between Norway and Sweden. In the 1630s–1660s a group of them also sailed to Delaware to settle the colony of New Sweden in America. Of the several hundred colonists in this settlement, a great number were "Forest Finns."
5. SKVR VII,5:10.
6. Gottlund 1872, 32.
7. SKVR I,1:79.
8. SKVR I,1:54.
9. Borenius 1904, 449
10. Kuusi 1949; Haavio 1952, 280–194; Krohn, K., 1914.
11. Kuusi 1949.
12. Haavio 1952, 288–294.
13. Kuusi 1949.
14. SKVR I,1:79a.
15. SKVR I,1:54.
16. Kuusi 1963, 67–69; Kuusi 1959.
17. SKVR I,1:54.
18. Setälä 1932.
19. *New Kalevala*, Poems 7–10, 18–25.
20. Kuusi 1949.
21. SKVR I,1:54.
22. *New Kalevala*, Poems 39–43.
23. *Mehiläinen*, May 1836.
24. Bosley 1985.
25. Borenius & Krohn 1891–1895 I, vi.
26. Ibid. III, 1.
27. *New Kalevala*, Preface chapter 2.
28. Kuusi 1963, 253.
29. Haavio 1967, 232–235.
30. Ibid., 236.
31. *Old Kalevala*, Preface xvi.
32. *Mehiläinen*, May 1836.
33. Ibid.
34. Borenius & Krohn 1891–1895 III, 5.

35. For variants of the poem, see Kuusi 1980, 141–146.
36. *New Kalevala*, Poem 35.
37. Ibid., Poem 36.
38. Cygnaeus 1853.
39. Achté, Lönnqvist 1972, 293–294.
40. See Tawaststjerna 1965, 269–270.
41. Ibid., 249–250.
42. Hirn 1939, 231.
43. Tawaststjerna 1965, 265–286.
44. Freud 1961, 337.
45. *New Kalevala*, Poem 5.
46. Pentikäinen 1983.
47. Sarmela 1981.
48. Borenius & Krohn 1891–1895 III, 2.
49. Anttila 1931–1935 II, 93.
50. For example, Kuusi 1963, 222.
51. Krohn, K. 1903.
52. Among others, M. A. Castrén (1852–1870 IV, 163) was of this opinion.
53. *Old Kalevala*, Preface xvii–xviii.
54. The sage who led the ancient wedding ceremony and protected the newlyweds from harm by charms.
55. The woman who came with the bridegroom to look after the bride and take her to her new home. She was usually the bridegroom's sister or the "patvaska's" wife.
56. Castrén 1852–1870 IV, 163; see Anttila 1931–1935 II, 71.
57. Comparetti 1892, 22.
58. Ibid. 25.
59. *Old Kalevala*, Preface xli.
60. Anttila 1931–1935 II, 71.

IV. ELIAS LÖNNROT

1. Anttila 1931–1935 I, 35, 46–148; Kaukonen 1979, 20–24. Cf. Honko 1984.
2. Anttila 1931–1935 I, 70–84, 150; Kaukonen 1979, 23, 25–27.
3. Anttila 1931–1935 I, 171–173; Kaukonen 1979, 41.
4. Anttila 1931–1935 I, 176.
5. Ibid. II, 265.
6. Ibid., 295–298.
7. Ibid. I, 264–265, 373–374.
8. *Old Kalevala*, Preface lxii.
9. Anttila 1931–1935 II, 362–363.
10. Sihvo 1984, 101.
11. Anttila 1931–1935 I, 324–333: Wilenius 1984, 96–99.
12. Sihvo 1984.
13. Ibid., 104.
14. Anttila 1931–1935 II, 317: Sihvo 1984, 101.
15. *Elias Lönnrots svenska skrifter*, 51–60.
16. Ibid., 60–79.
17. *Mehiläinen* November 1837.
18. Wilenius 1984, 99.
19. *Kanteletar*, Preface li–lii.
20. Castrén 1852–1870 I, 89.

21. *Mehiläinen* January 1836.
22. Lönnrot's letter to the National Board of Health 5.5.1835.
23. Lönnrot 1839, 15.
24. *Mehiläinen* November 1837.
25. *Mehiläinen* August 1836.
26. "Heränneet" means the awakened; "korttiläiset" is the name given to the revivalist sect led by Paavo Ruotsalainen and refers to a particular dark dress used by the revivalists called "körtti" (derived from "skjörta," meaning shirt in Swedish).
27. Takala 1929, 115–118, 121–135; A. Haavio 1965, 39–55.
28. *Murtorinne* 1986, 63–76.
29. Anttila 1931–1935 II, 243–245. The Evangelical movement, the "evankeliset," was a branch of Ruotsalainen's revivalism. It originated in the 1840s in Southwestern Finland under the leadership of Fredrick Gabriel Hedberg (1811–1893), a Lutheran minister.
30. Haavio 1965, 15, 18–20; Raittila 1977, 138–149.

V. THE SOURCES OF ANCIENT FINNISH RUNES

1. Kuusi 1963, 16–30.
2. Ibid.
3. *Old Kalevala*, Preface iv–v.
4. Kuusi 1963.
5. Niemi 1898; Kaukonen 1939–1945.
6. Kuusi 1980.
7. Kuusi 1963, 26.
8. Ibid.
9. Ibid.
10. Kaukonen 1982.
11. Kuusi 1963, 130.
12. Kuusi 1980, 21–23.
13. See Hajdú 1975, 11–52; Korhonen 1981.
14. Hajdú 1975; Lehtinen 1986.
15. Fodor 1975.
16. Jutikala 1981, 31; Terho Itkonen 1981, 16.
17. Taivalsaari 1985.
18. Jutikala 1981, 35.
19. Meinander 1981, 8–9.
20. Ibid.
21. Korhonen 1981, 13.
22. Ibid.; Taivalsaari 1985.
23. Haavio 1952.
24. Kuusi 1981, 26.
25. Kuusi 1963. "Baltic influence" here is a reference to the contacts of the Proto-Finns with the peoples then occupying the Baltic area, who probably spoke Proto-Slavic languages.
26. Lehtinen 1986.
27. See Pekkanen 1986.
28. Smirnov 1986.
29. Hirviluoto 1986, 73.
30. Meinander 1981.
31. Ryabinin 1986.
32. Ibid., 218.

33. Leppäaho & Vilkuna 1937.
34. A paper by Meinander entitled "The Ancient Runes and Reality: The Historical Basis of the Ancient Finnish Runes" presented at a seminar in Helsinki February 16–17, 1985.
35. Valonen 1984.
36. Ibid. When studying the ancient art found on the boulders, it is necessary to make a distinction between "petroglyphs," carvings made by hammer, ax, or knife, and "pictographs," paintings made with red clay color, for example. At times both techniques were used in making images on the same cliff.
37. See Hautala 1954, 392–394.
38. Sarvas 1969, 8–9.

VI. THE CONTRIBUTION OF THE RUNE SINGERS

1. Becker 1820.
2. Fellman 1906, 498.
3. *New Kalevala*, Preface chapter 4.
4. *Elias Lönnrotin matkat* I, 3–116.
5. Anttila 1931–1935, 139; Kaukonen 1979, 29–32.
6. *Elias Lönnrotin matkat* I, 181.
7. Haavio 1948, 19–20, 23–31.
8. *Elias Lönnrotin matkat* I, 181.
9. Runeberg to Grot.
10. For example, Niemi 1904; Haavio 1948.
11. *Elias Lönnrotin matkat* I, 222–223.
12. Haavio 1948, 274.
13. *Elias Lönnrotin matkat* I, 221–222.
14. Haavio 1948, 98.
15. Ibid., 91.
16. Interview tapes of Remsu, Vohta, and Takalo in the archives of the Finnish Literature Society, the Turku University Center for Cultural Studies, and the Department of Comparative Religion at Helsinki University.
17. Haavio 1931, 75–87; Haavio 1948, 23–31, 271–300.
18. Pentikäinen 1978.
19. Anttila 1931–1935 II, 62.
20. See note 16.
21. *P. Mustapään kootut runot.*
22. SKVR I,1:88b.
23. *Mehiläinen* March 1836.
24. Ibid.
25. Haavio 1950, 54.
26. Olrik 1965, 131.
27. Dundes 1976, 78–79.
28. Lévi-Strauss 1969, 11–12.
29. Propp 1968, 112.
30. Lord 1964.
31. Pentikäinen 1978, 263–264.
32. Ibid.
33. *New Kalevala*, Preface chapter 5.
34. Cf. Niemi 1898, 248–249.
35. *Old Kalevala*, Preface xxiv–xxv.
36. Ibid., i–ii.

37. Borenius & Krohn 1891–1895 III, 407.
38. Kaukonen 1979, 140.
39. *New Kalevala*, Preface chapter 8.
40. Ibid., chapter 6.
41. Kaukonen 1984, 10–11.
42. Haavio 1967, 246–248.
43. Honko 1985.
44. *Elias Lönnrotin matkat* I, 270.
45. Ibid., 267–268.
46. Ibid., 151, 153.
47. Castrén 1852–1870 I, 169–170.
48. Surakka 1938, 67.
49. See, e.g., Hauptman 1963.
50. Härkönen 1932, 256.
51. Pentikäinen 1978, 100–104.
52. Ibid.
53. Kuzmina 1983.
54. Morris 1969, 1983.
55. *Elias Lönnrotin matkat* I, 267–268.
56. Pentikäinen 1978, 329–330.
57. Ibid., 247.

VII. COSMIC DRAMA

1. SKVR 1,1:79a.
2. SKVR I,1:79.
3. See Borenius & Krohn 1891–1895 I, 31–71.
4. *New Kalevala*, Poem 1.
5. Pentikäinen 1978, 296.
6. Ibid., 296–297.
7. Fellman 1906, 498.
8. *Mehiläinen* December 1839.
9. Ibid.
10. *Satapathabrāhmana* XI:1,6,1–3.
11. *Rgveda* X 129.
12. *Mehiläinen* December 1839.
13. Ibid.
14. *Atharvaveda* XIX 53.
15. *Mehiläinen* December 1839.
16. Kuusi 1959.
17. Kuusi 1963, 67–70.
18. See Kuusi, Bosley, & Branch 1977, 83–92.
19. Kuusi 1959.
20. Krohn, J. 1885 I, 390.
21. Krohn, K. 1903, 190–213.
22. Haavio 1950, 79–81.
23. Kuusi 1959, 72.
24. Haavio 1955, 7–46.
25. SKVR I,1:689.
26. SKVR I,1:695a.
27. SKVR I,1:688.
28. SKVR I,1:688, 1.

29. SKVR I,1:692.
30. See Kuusi, Bosley, & Branch 1977, 279–282.
31. *Old Kalevala*, Poem 32.
32. See note 34.
33. Pentikäinen 1968, 86–93.
34. *Elias Lönnrotin matkat* I, 197.
35. Fromm 1980, 27.
36. Ibid.
37. Ervast 1916, 18–19.
38. Ibid., 19–20.
39. Ibid., 133.
40. Ibid., 417.
41. See the "*Kalevala* Drama" 1985.

VIII. THE WORLD VIEW OF THE *KALEVALA*

1. See Eliade 1965.
2. Honko 1984.
3. *Old Kalevala*, Preface viii–ix.
4. Lönnrot 1958.
5. See Kuusi & Anttonen 1985, 84.
6. *Old Kalevala*, Preface xi–xii.
7. *Mehiläinen* 1839–1840.
8. Ibid.
9. Ibid.
10. Ibid.
11. For a recent historical attempt to locate Kalevala and Pohjola, see Klinge 1983.
12. See Wilson 1976.
13. *Old Kalevala*, Preface xi–xii. Kihavanskoinen is the name of an eschatological prophet in Finnish folk legends. Liekkiö is the name of a Tavastian deity on Agricola's list, which is actually a dead-child being known in northern Satakunta. This being is conceived of as haunting the place where it was murdered and hidden by its mother. Pentikäinen 1968.
14. *Old Kalevala*, Preface xiv–xv.
15. Ibid., xv–xvi.
16. Borenius & Krohn 1891–1895 III, 323.
17. One of the early proponents of this theory was E. Lencqvist (1982).
18. *Mehiläinen* January 1836.
19. Ibid.
20. Ibid.
21. Ibid.
22. Kuusi 1963, 147–165.
23. Ibid. 59.
24. This aspect of the Sampo's meaning is also apparent in contemporary Finnish culture. For example, Sampo is the name of an insurance company.
25. Kuusi 1980, 223.
26. SKVR I,1:88b.
27. SKVR I,1:79.
28. Kuusi 1963, 226–227.
29. Grimm 1845, 29.
30. *Mehiläinen* January 1839.
31. Cf. Kaukonen 1983, 88, 91.

32. Harva 1948, 42.
33. Ibid., 70–73.
34. See Haavio 1941.
35. Kuusi 1963, 79.
36. See, for example, Porthan 1983, 80.
37. Harva 1948, 42–47.
38. *Elias Lönnrots svenska skrifter* I, 60–79.
39. The "Great Bear" in this poem refers to the Big Dipper, also known as Otava.
40. Haavio 1967, 15–41; Paulson 1965.
41. SKVR VII, 5:3931.
42. Kuusi 1963, 41–51.
43. Haavio 1967, 26–38.
44. Ibid., 26–30.
45. Ibid., 15–41.
46. Pentikäinen 1978, 223–224.
47. *Mehiläinen* January 1836.
48. Herodotus IV:13.
49. Haavio 1965 176.
50. See Pekkanen 1986.
51. Ibid.
52. Lid 1949, 105.
53. Adam von Bremen 1917, 247–248.
54. Lid 1949, 107.
55. Haavio 1965.
56. Grønbech 1909–1912 II, 916.
57. For example, Harva 1948, 42–73.
58. Lid 1949, 108–109.
59. Ibid., 114.
60. Ibid., 117.
61. Harva 1948, 47.
62. Harva 1925, 1945; Setälä 1932.

IX. A SHAMANISTIC EPIC

1. Comparetti 1892, 211–212.
2. Lencqvist 1982, 73–74.
3. Haavio 1967, 342–344.
4. For a definition of self, to which "the ego is related as part to whole," see Jung, *Aspects of the Feminine,* p. 148, par. 315, "The Psychological Aspects of the Kore."
5. "Active imagination," a technique of intrapsychic contrasexual dialogue which resembles descent into the fountainhead of the psyche. A link between "active imagination" and psychological aspects of shamanism is posited by Kaarina Kailo in her doctoral dissertation currently being prepared for the Centre for Comparative Literature at the University of Toronto.
6. Ganander 1960, 8, 51.
7. Haavio 1950, 5.
8. Ibid., 309.
9. Ibid.
10. Kuusi 1963.
11. Pentikäinen 1962.
12. Haavio 1967, 283–341; Janhunen 1986, 109; Karjalainen 1918, 555; Hajdu 1968.

13. Hultkrantz 1978.
14. See Eliade 1964.
15. See Diószegi 1978.
16. See, for example, Lehtinen 1986; Diószegi & Hoppal 1978.
17. Haavio 1967, 290–293.
18. Ibid.
19. Hultkrantz 1962, 394.
20. Kuzmina 1986, 1–3.
21. Ibid., 4.
22. Ibid., 7–8.
23. Jessen 1767, 30–32.
24. See Kuusi 1963, 6–7.
25. Manker 1968.
26. Haavio 1967, 323.
27. See Pentikäinen 1987.
28. T. I. Itkonen 1948.
29. Meinander l981, 7; Terho Itkonen 1981, 19.
30. *Mehiläinen* January 1836.
31. Haavio 1950, 310.
32. Kuusi 1963, 251–260.
33. Kuusi 1963.
34. SKVR I,1:398.
35. Ganander 1960.
36. *New Kalevala*, Poem 17.
37. Haavio 1950, 153–157; Kuusi 1963, 146, 164–169.
38. Haavio 1952, 261–268.
39. I. Itkonen 1963, 559–560.
40. Salonen & Holthoer 1982, 160–175.
41. Karjalainen 1918, 561.
42. Friis 1871, 19.
43. Vainstein 1984, 353.
44. Basilov 1986.
45. Potapov 1978.
46. Kuusi 1963, 259.
47. Haavio 1950, 102; Kuusi 1963, 254–259.
48. SKVR VI,I:26.
49. Siikala 1986, 225.
50. Basilov 1986, 45–48.
51. Cf. Basilov 1986, 40.
52. Cf. ibid., 41.
53. Cf. ibid.
54. SKVR I,1:170.
55. SKVR I,1:185a.
56. Haavio 1950, 90–93.
57. Siikala 1986, 226.
58. Haavio 1967, 319–321.
59. Harvilahti 1986.
60. Hultkrantz 1978.
61. Nielsen 1934.
62. See, for example, Harva 1948, 263–319.
63. See Turi 1910, 200–206.
64. See Haavio 1967, 341.
65. T. I. Itkonen 1948, 341–343.

66. For example, Siikala 1978.
67. See Merkur 1985, 10–40.
68. See Eliade 1964.
69. Basilov 1986.
70. Ibid., 45–46.
71. See, for example, ibid.
72. Hautala 1947.
73. Haavio 1952, 243–245.
74. Cf. Hautala 1947, 7.
75. SKVR I,2:872.
76. SKVR I,2:758.
77. SKVR VII,1:823
78. Niemi 1898, 242.
79. SKVR I,2:858.

X. THE REALM OF THE LIVING AND THE DEAD

1. Cf. Pentikäinen 1987, 207.
2. For example, Harva 1948, 488–511.
3. See, for example, Pentikäinen 1984, 209–211.
4. See Pentikäinen 1978, 204–208, 249–259.
5. Paulaharju 1924, 136.
6. Agricola 1931.
7. Pirinen 1973.
8. Harva 1948, 511–512.
9. Honko 1963, 107–116.
10. *New Kalevala*, Poem 16.
11. See Kuusi 1980, 226.
12. See Harva 1925.
13. Pentikäinen 1980, 235.
14. Ganander 1960, 55.
15. Ibid., 94.
16. *New Kalevala*, Poem 16.
17. Ibid.
18. Harva 1948, 489.
19. SKVR VII,1:259.
20. SKVR I,1:835.
21. SKVR I,2:811.
22. Kuusi 1963, 259.
23. Ibid., 253–254.
24. SKVR VII,1:835.
25. Krohn, K., 1903, 587.
26. Harva 1945, 222.
27. Haavio 1967, 264.
28. Ibid., 249.
29. Ibid., 238–249.
30. Ibid.
31. Ibid., 244–245.
32. Salonen & Holthoer 1982, 193–196.
33. Haavio 1967, 249–251.
34. Ibid.; Salonen & Holthoer 1982, 186–192.
35. Haavio 1967, 249–264.

36. Kuusi 1963, 322.
37. SKVR VII,1:840.
38. See Achté, Pentikäinen, & Utriainen 1987, 135.
39. Ibid., 130.
40. Ibid.
41. Elo 1931.
42. Relative to international statistics for suicide rates, the frequency of suicide in Finland has been surprisingly high compared to that in neighboring cultures such as Norway, for example. In 1987 more than 1.400 suicides were committed in Finland, where the population is under 5 million. The suicide statistics for Finland and Norway in 1985 were, respectively, 0.25% and 0.14%. Both suicides and attempted suicides are much more frequent among Finnish men than women. Suicide is, in fact, the most common cause of death among men aged 25–45. The attitude toward suicide is ambivalent; it appears to be both approved of in a certain manner and also severely sanctioned. (Statistics from Jouko Lönnqvist of the Helsinki Psychiatric Clinic.)
43. Kupiainen 1959.
44. Pentikäinen 1983.
45. Kuusi 1963.
46. See Kuusi 1980, 114–115, 136, 236.
47. Pentikäinen 1968, 68–71.
48. þórsteins þáttr Tjaldstǽings 1904, 431–432.
49. Haŕar saga ok Holmverja 1945, 11–14.
50. Pentikäinen 1968, 68–73.
51. Ibid.
52. See Achté, Pentikäinen, & Utriainen 1987.
53. Ibid.
54. Ibid., 132.
55. For example, SKVR I,1:692 (sung by Ohvo Homani from Vuonninen).
56. Pentikäinen 1983.
57. See Kuusi 1980, 114–115.
58. Laplanche & Pontalis 1967, 376.
59. Ibid., 108.
60. See Berglund 1975.
61. *New Kalevala*, Poem 36.
62. Lacan 1978, 259–274.

XI. THE KALEVALA IN FINNISH HISTORY

1. Cf. Setälä 1988, 139; Brockelman 1992; Heikkinen 1996, 9ff.; Sjöblom 1997, 130.
2. Jenkins 1991, 5–26. Heikkinen 1996, 68ff. Sjöblom 1997, 129–159.
3. Klinge 1997, 141–151. More details in: Klinge 1996, 11ff.
4. Heikkinen 1996, 18ff.
5. Lévi-Strauss 1963, 31–54, 206–231.
6. Pentikäinen 1997a, 27–34.
7. Castrén 1857, 8. Pentikäinen 1997b, 224–236.
8. Huizinga 1936. Heikkinen 1996, 16ff.
9. von Ranke 1949, 123–126. Heikkinen 1996, 21–22.
10. von Ranke 1890, 569–571; 1971, 54–63. Heikkinen 1996, 18–19. Sjöblom 1997, 129–130.
11. von Ranke 1971, 93–95. Heikkinen 1996, 30–33.
12. von Ranke 1971, 93–95. Heikkinen 1996, 31–32.
13. Snellman 1842. Koskinen 1869, 1879 (1933, 1960). Heikkinen 1996, 31–33.

14. Le Goff 1980. Heikkinen 1996, 53–54. Sjöblom 1997, 142–144.
15. Huizinga 1936. Heikkinen 1996, 53–54.
16. Klinge 1997, 142.
17. Nuorteva 1997, 150–166.
18. Nuorteva 1997, 191ff.
19. Revera 1995. Pentikäinen 1995.
20. The articles of the volume *New Sweden in America* 1995.
21. Nuorteva 1997, 20–100, 353–447.
22. Klinge 1997, 143.
23. Nuorteva 1997b, 257–259.
24. More details about the basic elements of Finnishness, variety of Finnish culture as well as recent phases of Finnish history are introduced in two recent publications: *Cultural Minorities in Finland. An Overview towards Cultural Policy,* ed. Juha Pentikäinen and Marja Hiltunen (1995), and *Finland. A Cultural Encyclopedia,* ed. Olli Alho, Hildi Hawkins, and Päivi Vallisaari (1997). The former is a collection of the contributions written by scholars and representatives of respective minorities for the Publications of the Finnish National Commission for UNESCO No. 66. The latter includes 300 articles, intended mainly for an international readership, published in the volume to honor Finland's 80th year of independence by the Finnish Literature Society.
25. Lehtosalo-Hilander 1997, 250–252.
26. E.g., Sammallahti 1993. Carpelán 1994. Savontaus et al. 1995.
27. Tacitus (1952), 72–73.
28. Koivulehto 1993, 101–105.
29. About shamanism as cultural mother tongue, Pentikäinen 1998.
30. Jutikkala 1961, 122.
31. Hornborg 1965, 185. Cf. also Wilson 1976.
32. *Cultural Minorities in Finland* 1995, 101–172.
33. Ibid. 173–226. Recent information in the articles by Horn 1997 and M. Pentikäinen 1997.
34. Jutikkala 1961, 187. Klinge 1997, 141ff.
35. Klinge 1997, 144.
36. Jutikkala 1961, 227.
37. Sihvo 1973; 1997, 173–174. Cf. Wilson 1996.
38. About the problematical concept of Karelia and Karelians in Hyry 1994; 1995, 84–100.
39. Sihvo 1997, 173–174. Lehtosalo-Hilander 1997, 168. Wilson 1996.
40. Klinge 1997, 141ff.
41. Klinge 1997, 141ff. Laaksonen 1997, 188–189.
42. Hyry 1995, 84–100.
43. *Cultural Minorities in Finland* 1995, 173–199.

XII. KALEVALA MYTHOLOGY AND FINNISH MYTHOGRAPHY

1. Laaksonen 1997, 168.
2. Klinge 1997, 141ff.
3. Pentikäinen 1997b.
4. About the role of the *Kalevala,* the importance of meeting with Larin Paraske, the Ingrian rune singer, and Karelian pilgrimage experiences for the composition work by Jean Sibelius, see Wilson 1996, 143–160.
5. About the distinction between the "great" and the "small" traditions, see Redfield 1960.
6. Laaksonen 1997, 195.
7. Pentikäinen 1997a, 30–32.
8. *Old Kalevala,* Preface vi–vii.
9. Meletinskii 1963.

10. Leino 1896.

11. About the role of the Karelian rebellion in Marina Takalo's life history, see Pentikäinen 1978, 58–76. Hyry 1994; 1995, 84–100.

12. Pentikäinen 1997c, 238–263.

13. Siltala 1992. Nuorteva 1997, 257–259.

14. E.g., Hautala 1969. Pentikäinen 1971. Lehtipuro 1974. Holbek 1992. Virtanen 1993.

15. Lehtipuro 1974, 10.

16. Hautala 1945, 1947. Lehtipuro 1974, 15–18.

17. Kuusi 1949, 1963, 1972. Lehtipuro 1974, 12–14.

18. Haavio 1949, 1950, 1955, 1965, 1967.

19. Niemi 1898, Kaukonen 1939–1945.

20. In accordance with this trend, Mythology is introduced in *Finland, A Cultural Encyclopedia*, 1997, p. 219: "An important source is nonetheless the oral tradition which appeared chiefly in poetic metre and which began to be collected in the time of A. J. Sjögren (1794–1855) and Elias Lönnrot. The epic which Lönnrot compiled from these poems doubtless reflects the ancient Finnish world view, but as a secondary source it does not qualify as a source for religious studies nature."

21. Honko 1958, 1974, 1996.

22. Siikala 1978, 1986, 1992.

23. Comparetti 1892.

24. Pentikäinen 1997a, 1998.

25. Virtaranta 1958.

26. Pentikäinen 1978, 1999.

27. Haavio 1948, 1949.

28. Harvilahti 1992, Hyry 1994.

29. Nenola-Kallio 1992.

30. E.g., Wargelin-Brown 1980; Kortes-Erkkila 1994.

31. Kuusinen 1949. Cf. also the critique by Kuusi 1972.

32. Laaksonen 1997, 167.

33. Kuusi 1976.

34. Wargelin-Brown 1980.

35. Cf. the list of the most significant translations in Laaksonen 1997, 167.

36. Linkomies became a professor of literature at the University of Helsinki in 1923. He was rector of the university from 1956 to 1962 and chancellor from 1962 to 1963. From 1933 to 1945 he was a member of the Finnish Parliament, and from 1939 to 1943 he served as its vice-chairman. In March 1943, Linkomies formed a government which had as its aim to disengage Finland from the war. This objective was not realized, and the government was dissolved in August 1944. As a result of the postwar trials, Linkomies was sentenced to prison for four years and six months in 1946. This quotation is part of a speech he gave at the Helsinki municipal prison in 1947.

37. Mäkelä-Henriksson 1959.

38. Wargelin-Brown 1980.

39. Holdrege 1996, 2–19.

40. Robert A. Erickson's work "The Language of the Heart 1600–1750" brings a new point of view to Milton, focusing upon the significance of the King James (1642) English-language translation of the Bible as a basis for world view in medicine as well as religion. 41. Pentikäinen 1995, 2–11.

42. Bellah 1967, 1970, 1974. Ketola, Pesonen & Sjöblom 1997.

43. Ketola, Pesonen & Sjöblom 1997, 106ff.

44. Albanese 1992, 446.

45. Recent statistics in *Cultural Minorities in Finland* 1995.

Bibliography

ACHTÉ, K., & LÖNNQVIST, J. "Cultural Aspects of Suicide in Finland." *Psychiatria Fennica* 3, 1972.

ACHTÉ, K., PENTIKÄINEN, J., & UTRIAINEN, T. "Kalevalan itsemurhhista." *Kotiseutu* 3, 1987.

ADAM VON BREMEN. Hamburgische Kirchengeschichte. Dritte Auflage, herausgegeben von Bernhard Schmeidler.—Scriptores rerum germanicarum in usum scolarum ex Monumentis Germaniae historicis separatim editi. Hannover & Leipzig 1917.

AGRICOLA, MIKAEL. *Davidin Psalttari—Mikael Agricolan kootut teokset III.* Porvoo 1931 (1551).

ALBANESE, CATHERINE L. *America—Religions and Religion.* Belmont 1992.

ANDERSEN, H. C. *Den lille Havfrue.* Eventyr 3H. København 1837.

ANNIST, AUGUST. *Kalevala taideteoksena.* Porvoo 1944.

ANTTILA, AARNE. *Elias Lönnrot. Elämä ja toiminta I-II.* Helsinki 1931–1935.

ANTTONEN, VEIKKO. *Uno Harva ja suomalainen uskontotiede.* Jyväskylä 1987.

ATHANASSAKIS, APOSTOLOS N. *Hesiod, Theogony, Works and Days.* Baltimore 1983.

———. Introduction, *Essays on Hesiod I,* Ramus, vd. 21, No. 1, pp. 1–10. 1992.

———. "Glimpses of Modern Ethnography in Hesiod: Soul and Space." *The Ancient World,* 1996, vol. 37, 2.

———. "The Cosmography of the Nether World in the *Odyssey*: Then and Now." In: Proceedings: Center for Odyssean Studies. Ithaca 1996 (b), vol. 8.

Atharvaveda. *Sacred Books of the East.* Vol. XLII. Delhi et al. 1964.

BASILOV, V. N. "The Shaman Drum among the Peoples of Northern Europe and Siberia: Evolution of Symbolism." *Traces of the Central Asian Culture in the North* (ed. Lehtinen, I.). Helsinki 1986.

von BECKER, REINHOLD. "Väinämöisestä." *Turun Viikko-Sanomat* 10, 11, 20, 1820.

BELLAH, ROBERT N. *Beyond Belief.* New York 1970.

———. "American Civil Religion in the 1970's." In: Russel E. Richey & Donald G. Jones (eds.), *American Civil Religion.* New York 1974.

BERGLUND, AXEL-IVAR. *Zulu Thought-Patterns and Symbolism.* Uppsala 1975.

BHATTACHARYYA, NARENDRA NATH. *History of Indian Cosmological Ideas.* New Delhi: Munshiram Manoharlal 1971.

BORENIUS, A. "Kertomus runonkeräyksistä Venäjän Karjalassa v. 1871." *Runonkerääjiemme matkakertomuksia 1830–luvulta 1880–luvelle* (ed. Niemi, A. R.). Helsinki 1904.

BÖRENIUS, A., & KROHN, J. *Kalevalan esityöt* I-III. Helsinki 1891–1895.

BOSLEY, KEITH. *Wanton Loverboy.* Kalevala Cantos 11–15. Pieksämäki 1985.

BRANCH, M. A. "Kaksi A. J. Sjögrenin omaelämänkerrallista teosta." Virittäjä 1966.

BROCKELMAN, PAUL. *The Inside Story: A Narrative Approach to Religious Understanding and Truth.* New York 1992.

CARPELÁN, CHRISTIAN. "Katsaus saamelaistumisen vaiheisiin." *Johdatus saamentutkimukseen,* toim. Kulonen, U.-M., Pentikäinen, J., Seurujärvi-Kari, I. Pieksämäki 1994.

CASTRÉN, M. A. *Kalevala* (Swedish translation). Helsinki 1841.

———. *Nordiska resor och forskningar* I-VI. Helsingfors 1852–1870.

COLLAN, FABIAN. "Väinämöinen och Ilmarinen, näst Ukko Fornfinnarnas högsta gudar." *Helsingfors Morgonblad* 1838.

COMPARETTI, DOMENICO. *Der Kalewala oder die Traditionelle Poesia der Finnen.* Halle 1892.

Cultural Minorities in Finland: An Overview towards Cultural Policy (ed. Pentikäinen, Juha,

& Marja Hiltunen). Publications of the Finnish National Commission for UNESCO No. 66. Helsinki 1995.

CYGNAEUS, F. *Det tragiska elementet i Kalevala.* Helsingfors 1853.

DIÓSZEGI, VILMOS. "Pre-Islamic Shamanism of the Barba Turks and Some Ethnographical Conclusions." *Shamanism in Siberia* (ed. Diószegi, V. & Hoppal, M.). Budapest 1978

DIÓSZEGI, V., & HOPPAL, M. *Shamanism in Siberia.* Budapest 1978.

DUNDES, ALAN. "Structuralism and Folklore: Folk Narrative Research." *Some Papers Presented at the VI Congress of the International Society for Folk Narrative Research* (ed. Juurikka, T., & Pentikäinen, J.). Pieksämäki 1976.

ELIADE, MIRCEA. *Shamanism: Archaic Technique of Ecstasy.* New York 1964.

———. *The Myth of the Eternal Return.* Princeton 1965.

Elias Lönnrotin matkat I-II. Helsinki 1902.

Elias Lönnrots svenska skrifter. Helsingfors 1908–1911.

EIO, O. E. "Über Selbstmorde und Selbstmörder in Finland." *Deutsche Zschr Med* 17, 1931.

ERICKSON, ROBERT A. *The Language of the Heart 1600–1750.* Philadephia 1997.

ERVAST, PEKKA. *Kalevalan avain.* Jyväskylä 1968 (1916).

FELLMAN, JACOB. *Antickningar under min vistelse i Lappmarken I-IV.* Helsingfors 1906.

Finland: A Cultural Encyclopedia. Finnish Literature Society (ed. Alho, Olli, Hildi Hawkins, & Päivi Vallisaami. Vammala 1997.

FODOR, ISTVAN. "Suomalais-urgrilaisen arkeologian pääongelmia." *Suomalais-ugrilaiset* (ed. Hajdú, P.). Pieksämäki 1975.

FREUD, SIGMUND. *Unien tulkinta.* Jyväskylä 1961.

FRIIS, J. *Lappisk Mythologi, Eventyr og Folkesagn.* Christiana 1871.

FROMM, HANS. "Kalevalan reseption historiaa." *Sananjalka* 22, 1980.

GANANDER, CHRISTFRID. *Nytt Finskt Lexicon I, II, III.* Porvoo 1937, 1938, 1940 (1786, 1787).

———. *Mythologia Fennica.* Turku 1960 (1789).

GANZ, TIMOTHY. *Early Greek Myth* I, II. Baltimore 1993.

GOTTLUND, C. A. *Runola.* Helsingfors 1840.

———. "Läsning för Finnar." *Suomi* 1847.

———. *Den finska Sampo-myten närmare uttydd och förklarad.* Helsingfors 1872.

GRIMM, JACOB. "Über das finnische epos." *Zeitschrift für die Wissenschaft der Sprache.* 1845

GRØNBECH, V. *Vor Folket i Oldtiden.* København 1909–1912.

GUTHRIE, W. K. C. *Orpheus and Greek Religion.* Princeton 1993.

HAAVIO, ARI. *Suomen uskonnolliset liikkeet.* Porvoo 1965.

HAAVIO, MARTTI. *Kansanrunouden keruu ja tutkimus.* Helsinki 1931.

———. "Iso Tammi." *Kalevalaseuran vuosikirja* 20–21, 1941.

———. *Viimeiset runonlaulajat.* Porvoo 1948.

———. *Kansanrunouden sepittäjät ja esittäjät.* Helsinki 1949.

———. *Väinämöinen.* Porvoo 1950.

———. *Kirjokansi.* Porvoo 1952.

———. *Laulupuu.* Porvoo 1952.

———. *Kansanrunojen maailmanselitys.* Porvoo 1955.

———. *Karjalan jumalat.* Porvoo 1959.

———. *Bjarmian vallan kukoistus ja tuho. Historiaa ja runoutta.* Porvoo & Helsinki 1965.

———. *Suomalainen mytologia.* Porvoo 1967.

HAJDÚ, PÉTER. "Sukulaisuuden kielellistä taustaa." *Suomalais-ugrilaiset* (ed. Hajdú, P.). Pieksämäki 1975.

———. "The Classification of Samoyed Shamans." *Popular Beliefs and Folklore Traditions in Siberia* (ed. Diószegi, V.). Budapest 1968.

HALLENIUS, MATHIAS. *De Borea-Fennica.* Aboae 1732.

Hafar saga ok Holmverja. Reykjavik 1945.

HÄRKÖNEN, IIVO (ed.). *Karjalan kirja.* Porvoo 1932.

HARVA, UNO. "Vasen käsi ja vastapäivään." *Valvoja-Aika* 1925. Helsinki.

———. "Lemminkäisen matka Päivölän pitoihin." *Virittäjä* 1945.

———. *Suomalaisten muinaisusko.* Porvoo 1948.

HARVILAHTI, LAURI. "Overtone Singing and Shamanism." *Traces of the Central Asian Culture in the North* (ed. Lehtinen, I.). Helsinki 1986.

———. *Kertovan runon keinot.* Helsinki 1992.

HAUPTMAN, PETER. "Altrussischer Glaube. Der Kampf des Prototopen Avvakum gegen die Kirchenreformen des 17. Jahrhunderts." *Kirche im Osten: Studien zur osteuropäischen Kirchengeschichte und Kirchenkunde in Verbindung mit dem Ostkircheninstitut,* hrsg. von Robert Stuppernich 4. Göttingen 1963.

HAUTALA, JUOKO. *Hiiden hirven hiihdäntä.* Helsinki 1947.

———. *Suomalainen kansanrunoudentutkimus.* Turku 1954.

———. "Christfrid Ganander ja hänen Mythologia Fennicansa." Foreword to Ganander 1960.

———. *Lauri Lappalaisen runo. Vertaileva kansanrunoudentutkimus.* Suomalaisen Kirjallisuuden Seuran Toimituksia 227. Helsinki 1945.

———. *Finnish Folklore Research 1828–1918.* Helsinki 1969.

HEIKINHEIMO, ILMARI. "Gottlund ja Lönnrot." *Kalevalaseuran vuosikirja* 40, 1960.

HEIKKINEN, ANTERO. *Menneisyyttä rakentamassa.* Helsinki 1996.

HERODOTUS. *Historiateos 1–2.* Antiikin klassikot. Helsinki 1964.

HIRN, YRJÖ. *Matkamiehiä ja tietäjiä.* Helsinki 1939.

HIRVILUOTO, ANNA-LIISA. "Finland's Cultural Ties with the Kama Region in the Late Iron Age Especially in the Light of Pottery Findings." *Traces of the Central Asian Culture in the North* (ed. Lehtinen, I.). Helsinki 1986.

HOLBEK, BENGT. "On the Comparative Method in Folklore Research." NIF Papers 3. Turku 1992.

HOLDREGE, BARBARA A. *Veda and Torah: Transcending the Textuality of Scripture.* Albany, N.Y. 1996

HONKO, LAURI. "Itkuvirsirunous." *Suomen kirjallisuus I. Kirjoittamaton kirjallisuus* (ed. Kuusi, M.). Keuruu 1963.

———. *Krankheitsprojektile. Untersuchung über eine urtümliche Krankheitserklärung.* Folklore Fellows Communications No. 178. Helsinki 1959.

———. "Balto-Finnic Lament Poetry." *Studia Fennica* 17. Forssa 1974.

———. "Lönnrot: Homeros vai Vergilius?" *Kalevalaseuran vuosikirja* 64, 1984.

———. "Epic and Identity." *Epic along the Silk Road.* A UNESCO workshop in Turku, Finland (ed. Honko, Lauri). *Oral Tradition* vol. 11: 1. Columbus, Ohio 1996.

HORN, FRANK. "Suomen venäläiset." In: J. Pentikäinen & M. Hiltunen, *Suomalaiset kulttuurivähemmistöt.* Suomen UNESCO-toimikunnan julkaisuja 73. Helsinki 1997.

HORNBORG, EIRIK. *Suomen historia.* Porvoo-Helsinki 1965.

HUIZINGA, JOHAN. *In the Shadow of Tomorrow.* New York 1936.

HULTKRANTZ, ÅKE. "Die Religionen der Amerikanischen Arktis." *Die Religionen der Menscheit* (hrsg. von C. M. Schröder). Stuttgart 1962.

———. "Ecological and Phenomenological Aspects of Shamanism." *Studies in Lapp Shamanism* (ed. Bäckman, L., & Hultkrantz, Å.). Stockholm 1978.

HYRY, KATJA. "The Karelians in Finland." In: *Cultural Minorities in Finland* 1995.

———. Rajakansan historia ja historian kokijat: vienankarjalaisten vaiheet 1900–luvulla. Uskontotieteen lisensiaatintutkimus. Helsingin yliopisto. Helsinki 1994.

ITKONEN, ERKKI. "Lappalainen kansanrunous." *Suomen kirjallisuus I. Kirjoittamaton kirjallisuus* (ed. Kuusi, M.). Keuruu 1963.

ITKONEN, TERNO. "Kielemme kantasuomalaiset juuret." *Suomen kansan juuret.* Yleisradion julkaisusarja 73. Lahti 1981.

ITKONEN, T. I. *Suomen lappalaiset vuoteen 1945.* Porvoo 1948.

JANHUNEN, JUHA. "Siberian Shamanistic Terminology." *Traces of the Central Asian Culture in the North* (ed. Lehtinen, I.). Helsinki 1986.

JENKINS, KEITH. *Re-thinking History.* London 1991.

JESSEN, E. J. *Afhandling om de Norske Finners og Lappers Religion, med en Techning af en Rune-Bomme.* Kjøbenhavn 1767.

JUNG, C. G. "The Psychological Aspects of the Kore." *Aspects of the Feminine* (trans. Hull, R. F. C.). Princeton 1982.

JUTIKKALA, EINO. *A History of Finland.* New York 1961.

————. "Yhteenveto kansamme varhaisista vaiheista." *Suomen kansan juuret.* Yleisradion julkaisusarja 73. Lahti 1981.

Kalevalan draama. Kalevan näyttämö ry:n juhlajulkaisu (ed. Kuusela, M.). Hämeenlinna 1985.

Kanteletar. Helsinki 1840.

KARJALAINEN, K. F. *Jugralaisten uskonto.* Suomen suvun uskonnot III. Porvoo 1918.

KAUKONEN, VÄINÖ. *Vanhan Kalevalan kokoonpano I-II.* Helsinki 1939–1945.

————. *Lönnrot ja Kalevala.* Pieksämäki 1979.

————. "Kansanrunous ja perinne." *Virittäjä* 3, 1982.

————. "Sampo runouden symbolina ja myyttinä." *Virittäjä* 1, 1983.

————. *Kansanrunon kaukokarjalaa ja Kalevalan synty.* Porvoo 1984.

KETOLA, KIMMO, PESONEN, HEIKKI, & SJÖBLOM, TOM. *Uskonto ja moderni yhteiskunta. Uskontososiologian keskustelunaiheita.* Ketola, Kimmo, et al., Näköaloja uskontoon. Helsinki 1997.

KLINGE, MATTI. *Muinaisuutemme merivallat.* Keuruu 1983.

————. *Finlands historia 3: Kejsartiden.* Helsingfors 1996.

————. "History." *Finland: A Cultural Encyclopedia.* Helsinki 1997.

KOIVULEHTO, JORMA. "Suomi." Virittäjä 1993.

KORHONEN, MIKKO. "Suomalaisten tausta historiallis-vertailevan kielitieteen valossa." *Suomen kansan juuret.* Yleisradion julkaisusarja 73. Lahti 1981.

KROHN, JULIUS. *Suomen suvun pakanallinen jumalanpalvelus I.* Helsinki 1894.

————. *Suomalaisen kirjallisuuden historia I.* Kalevala. Helsinki 1885.

KROHN, KAARLE. *Kalevalan runojen historia.* Helsinki 1903.

————. *Suomalaisten runojen uskonto.* Helsinki 1914.

————. *Kalevalan kertomarunojen opas.* Helsinki 1932.

KUNZE, ERICH. "Kalevalan vaikutus Jacob Grimmiin." *Kalevalaseuran vuosikirja* 32 1952.

KUPIAINEN, UNTO. *Suomen kirjallisuuden vaiheet.* Helsinki 1959.

KORTES-ERKKILA, HELMI. *Relevance of the Kalevala (A Finnish Epic): Comments, Quotes and Quips.* Vancouver, Wash. 1994.

KOSKINEN, YRJÖ. *Suomen kansan historia.* Helsinki 1933.

————. *Johtavat aatteet ihmiskunnan historiassa.* Helsinki 1960.

KUUSI, MATTI. *Sampo-eepos.* Helsinki 1949.

————. "Suomalaisen luomisrunon jääteitä. *Kalevalaseuran vuosikirja* 39, 1959.

————. "Otto Wille Kuusisen marxilais-kalevalainen eskatologia." *Katsauksia.* Suomalainen Suomi 1972.

————. *Kansanruno-Kalevala.* Helsinki 1976.

————. *Kalevalaista kertomarunoutta.* Jyväskylä 1980.

————. "Esihistoriallisen muistitiedon perintö historialisessa Suomessa." *Suomen kansan juuret.* Yleisradion julkaisusarja 73. Lahti 1981.

————. *Le discours direct comme critère de datation de la poésie épique ancienne.* Budapest 1992.

————. (ed.). *Suomen kirjallisuus I. Kirjoittamaton kirjallisuus.* Keuruu 1963.

KUUSI, MATTI, & ANTTONEN, PERTTI. *Kalevala-lipas.* Pieksämäki 1985.

KUUSI, M., BOSLEY, K., & BRANCH, M. A. (eds.). *Finnish Folk Poetry: Epic.* Helsinki 1977.

KUUSINEN, OTTO VILLE. *Kalevalan alkulause.* 1949.

KUZMINA, L. P. "Old Believers in Russia." A paper presented at the Eleventh Congress of Anthropological and Ethnological Sciences, Vancouver, B.C., Canada 1983.
———. "Generic Diversity of the Shamanic Folklore among the Peoples of Siberia." *Traces of the Central Asian Culture in the North* (ed. Lehtinen, I.). Helsinki 1986.
LAAKSONEN, PEKKA. "Kalevala; Linna, Väinö; Lönnrot, Elias." *Finland: A Cultural Encyclopedia.* Helsinki 1997.
LACAN, J. *Le Séminaire, Livre II.* Paris 1978.
LAPLANCHE, J., & PONTALIS, J. B. *Vocabulaire de la Psychanalyse.* Paris 1967.
LE GOFF, JACQUES. *Time, Work and Culture in the Middle Ages.* Chicago 1980.
LEHTINEN, ILDIKO (ed.). *Traces of the Central Asian Culture in the North.* Helsinki 1986.
LEHTIPURO, OUTI. "Trends in Finnish Folkloristics." *Studia Fennica* 18. Forssa 1974.
LEHTOSALO-HILANDER, PIRKKO. "Prehistory; The Kalevala Koru." *Finland: A Cultural Encyclopedia.* Helsinki 1997.
LEINO, EINO. *Tarina suuresta tammesta ym. runoja.* Porvoo 1896.
LENCQVIST, CHRISTIAN ERICI. "Vanhojen suomalaisten teoreettisesta ja käytännöllisestä taikauskosta." *Henrik Gabriel Porthanin valitut teokset.* Jyväskylä 1982 (1782).
LÉOUZON LE DUC, L. A. *Kalevala* (French translation of the *Old Kalevala*). Paris 1845.
LEPPÄAHO, JORMA, & VILKUNA, KUSTAA. "Muinaisrunojemme sotisopa." *Kalevaleseuran vuosikirja* 17, 1937.
LÉVI-STRAUSS, CLAUDE. *Structural Anthropology 1.* Harmondsworth 1963.
———. *The Raw and the Cooked.* New York 1969.
LID, NILS. "Kalevalan Pohjola." *Kalevalaseuran vuosikirja* 29, 1949.
LINKOMIES, EDWIN. Speech given while in the Helsinki municipal prison, 1947.
LÖNNROT, ELIAS. *Suomalaisen talonpojan kotilääkäri.* Helsinki 1839.
———. *Suomalais-Ruotsalainen Sanakirja. Finskt-Svenskt lexikon I-II.* Povoo 1958, 1980.
———. *Suomen kansan muinaisia loitsurunoja.* Helsinki 1880.
LORD, ALBERT B. *The Singer of Tales.* Cambridge, Mass. 1964.
MÄKELÄ-HENRIKSSON, EEVA. "Kalevalanpäivän vieton varhaisvaiheita." *Kalevalaseuran vuosikirja* 39, 1959.
MANKER, ERNST. "Seite Cult and Drum Magic of the Lapps." *Popular Beliefs and Folklore Tradition in Siberia* (ed. Diószegi, V.). Budapest 1968.
MANNINEN, JUHA. Maailmankuvat maailman ja sen muutoksen heijastajina." *Maailmankuvan muutos tutkimuskohteena* (ed. Kuusi, M., Alapuro, R., & Klinge, M.). Keuruu 1977.
Mehiläinen. Oulu 1836–1840.
MEINANDER, CARL-FREDRIK. "Suomalaiset Koillis-Euroopan väestön osana." *Suomen kansan juuret.* Yleisradion julkaisusarja 73. Lahti 1981.
———. Speech at the seminar "Muinaisrunot ja todellisuus-Suomen vanhojen runojen historallinen tausta" organized by "Historian ystäväin liitto" and "Suomen arkeologinen seura," in Säätytalo, Helsinki 16.–17.2.1985 (not in print).
MELETINSKII, E. N. *Proiskhozhdenie geroitseskogo eposa.* Moskva 1963.
MERKUR, DANIEL. *Becoming Half Hidden: Shamanism and Initiation among the Inuit.* Stockholm 1985.
MORRIS, RICHARD A. "Accommodations on a Religious Rite and the Role of Informal Dispensations among Russian Old Believers." A paper presented at the Eleventh International Congress of Anthropological and Ethnological Sciences. Vancouver, B.C., Canada 1983.
———. "Three Russian Groups in Oregon: A Comparison of Boundaries in a Pluralistic Environment." Ph.D. thesis, University of Oregon, 1969.
MURTORINNE, EINO. *Suomalainen teologia autonomian kautena.* Helsinki 1986.
NAGY, GREGORY. *The Best of the Achaeans.* Baltimore 1979.
———. *Homeric Questions* (VTP 1996).

NENOLA-KALLIO, AILI. *Studies in Ingrian Laments.* Folklore Fellows Communications No. 234. Helsinki 1992.
New Kalevala (= *Kalevala*). Helsinki 1849.
New Sweden in America (ed. Hoffecker, Carol E.; Waldron, Richard; Williams, Lorraine E.; & Benson, Barbara E.) Cranbury, N.J.-London 1995.
NIELSEN, KONRAD. *Lappisk Ordbok II.* Oslo 1934.
NIEMI, A. R. *Kalevalan kokoonpano l. runokokous Väinämöisestä.* Helsinki 1898.
——— (ed.). *Runonkerääjiemme matkakertomuksia 1830–luvulta 1880–luvelle.* Helsinki 1904.
NUORTEVA, JUSSI. *Suomalaisten ulkomainen opinkäynti ennen Turun Akatemian perustamista 1640.* Suomen Kirkkohistoriallisen Seuran Toimituksia 177. Helsinki 1997.
———. "Revivalist Movements." *Finland: A Cultural Encyclopedia.* Helsinki 1997(b).
Old Kalevala (= *Kalewala taikka Vanhoja Karjalan Runoja Suomen Kansan muinaisista ajoista*). Helsinki 1835.
OLRIK, AXEL. "Epic Laws of Folk Narrative." *The Study of Folklore* (ed. Dundes, A.). Englewood Cliffs, N.J. 1965.
PARRY, A. (ed.). *The Making of the Homeric Verse.* Oxford 1971.
PAULAHARJU, SAMULI. *Syntymä, Lapsuus, Kuolema.* Kalevalaseuran julkaisuja 2. Porvoo 1924.
PAULSON, IVAR. "Karhunkallon riitistä Kalevalassa ja arktisissa kansanuskonnoissa." *Kalevalaseuran vuosikirja* 45, 1965.
PEKKANEN, TUOMO. "The First References to the Silk Road in Classical Literature." *Traces of the Central Asian Culture in the North* (ed. Lehtinen, I.). Helsinki 1986.
PENTIKÄINEN, JUHA. "Ovatko suomalaiset harjoittaneet shamanismia?" *Kotiseutu* 1962.
———. *The Nordic Dead-Child Tradition: Nordic Dead-Child Beings, A Study in Comparative Religion.* FFC 202. Helsinki 1968.
———. "Julius and Kaarle Krohn." *Biographica. Nordic Folklorists of the Past.* Studies in honour of Jouko Hautala 27.6.1970. Arv 25–27. Uppsala 1971.
———. Oral Repertoire and World View. FFC 219. Helsinki 1978.
———. "Yksilö perinteentutkimuksen kohteena." *Perinteentutkimuksen perusteita* (ed. Lehtipuro, O.). Porvoo 1980.
———. Suomalaisen kansanperinteen ihmiskuva ja käsitys luonnosta. Helsingin yliopiston uskontotieteen jaoston toimitteita 3. 1984.
———. "Voluntary Death and Single Battle: Suicidal Behavior and Arctic World Views." *Suicide Research.* Proceedings of the Symposium on Suicide Research by the Yrjö Jansson Foundation 1982 (ed. Achté, K., Nieminen, K., & Vikkula, J.). Helsinki 1983.
———. "The Shamanic Drum as Cognitive Map." *Mythology and Cosmic Order* (ed. Gothoni, R., & Pentikäinen, J.). Studia Fennica 32. Pieksämäki 1987.
———. "The Forest Finns and Transmitters of Finnish Culture from Savo via Central Scandinavia to Delaware." *New Sweden in America* (ed. Hoffecker, Carol E., et al.). Cranbury, N.J.-London 1995.
———. *Die Mythologie der Saamen.* Ethnologische Beiträge zur Circumpolarforschung Band 3. Berlin 1997(a).
———. "Castrénilainen 'pohjoisen etnografian' paradigma." *Kaukaa haettua* (ed. Anna Maria Viljanen ja Minna Lahti). Vammala 1997(b).
———. "Lars Levi Laestadius som samisk mytolog och mytograf." *Fragmenter i Lappska Mytologien af Lars Levi Laestadius.* NIF Publications 37. Åbo 1997(c).
———. *Shamanism and Culture.* 2nd, revised edition. Jyväskylä 1998.
———. "Being an Old Believer: Identity, World View and Folklore." *Starovery (Old Believers): Studies on Old Ritualism in Eastern Christianity.* London 1998(b).
PENTIKÄINEN, MARJA. "Inkeriläiset, Pakolaiset ja turvapaikanhakijat." In: J. Pentikäinen

& M. Hiltunen, *Suomalaiset kulttuurivähemmistöt*. Suomen UNESCO-toimikunnan julkaisuja 73. Helsinki 1997.

PIRINEN, KAUKO. "Agricolan psalttarin esipuhe tunnustusten välisessä polemiikissa." *Kalevalaseuran vuosikirja* 53, 1973.

P. *Mustapään kootut runot*. Porvoo 1957.

PORTHAN, HENRIK GABRIEL. *Suomalaisesta runoudesta* (De Poesi Fennica). Vaasa 1983 (1766, 1768, 1778).

———. *Valitut teokset*. Jyväskylä 1982.

POTAPOV, L. P. "The Shaman Drum as a Source of Ethnographical History." *Shamanism in Siberia* (ed. Diószegi, V., & Hoppal, M.). Budapest 1978.

PROPP, VLADIMIR. *Morphology of the Folktale*. Austin, Tex. 1968.

RAITTILA, PEKKA. "Herätysliikkeet 1900–luvalla." *Kirkko suomalaisessa yhteiskunnassa* (ed. Heikkilä, M., & Murtorinne, E.). Hämeenlinna 1977.

RANKE, LEOPOLD VON. *Zur eigenenen Lebensgeschichte*. Hrsg. von Alfred Dove. Leipzig 1890.

———. *Das Briefwerk*. Hrsg. von W. P. Fuchs. Hamburg 1949.

———. *Über die Epochen der neueren Geschichte. Aus Werk und Nachlass 2*. Hrsg. von W. P. Fuchs und T. Scheider. München 1971.

REDFIELD, ROBERT. *The Little Community and Peasant Society and Culture*. Chicago-London 1960.

REVERA, MARGARETA. "The Making of a Civilized Nation: Nation-Building, Aristocratic Culture and Social Change." *New Sweden in America* (ed. Hoffecker, Carol E., et al.). Cranbury, N.J.-London 1995.

Rgveda X. *A Vedic Reader for Students*. Delhi 1972.

RUNEBERG, J. L. "Förord till: Nionde Runen i Kalevala." *Helsingfors Morgonblad* 1835, n:o 91.

———. *Efterlämnade Skrifter I–III*. Helsingfors 1878, 1876.

RYABININ, Y. A. "Cultural Links of Finno-Ugric Tribes in Medieval Times (Based on Archeological Data)." *Traces of the Central Asian Culture in the North* (ed. Lehtinen, I.). Helsinki 1986.

SAARINEN, SIRKKA. "Fennougristiikka ei-eurooppalaisten kansojen tutkimuksena." *Wallinista Wideriin* (ed. Melasuo, T.). Tampere 1984.

SALONEN, A., & HOLTHOER, R. *Egypti ja sen kulttuuri*. Keuruu 1982.

SAMMALLAHTI, PEKKA. "Suomalaisten ja saamelaisten juuret." Kieliposti 1993.

SAMUELS, ANDREW, et al. (eds.). *A Critical Dictionary of Jungian Analysis*. Routledge & Kegan Paul, London 1986.

SARAJAS, ANNAMARI. *Suomen kansanrunouden tuntemus 1500–1700 lukujen kirjallisuudessa*. Porvoo 1956.

———. "Snellman ja Kalevala." *Kalevalaseuran vuosikirja* 64, 1984.

SARMELA, MATTI. "Suomalaiset häät." *Pohjolan häät* (ed. Sarmela, M.). Vaasa 1981.

SARVAS, PEKKA. "Die Felsmalerei von Astuvansalmi." *Suomen museo* 1969.

Satapathabrāhmana XI. *Sacred Books of the East*. Vol. XLIV. Delhi 1963.

SAVONTAUS, MARJA-LIISA, et al. "The genetic relationship between the Finns and the Saamis." In: Heikki Leskinen, et al. (eds.), *Congressus Octavus Internationalis Fenno-Ugristarum*, Jyväskylä 10.–15.8.1995.

SAXO GRAMMATICUS. *Saxonis Grammatici Gesta Danorum* (hrsg. von Alfred Holder). Darmstadt 1886.

SCHRÖTER, H. R. *Finnische Runen*. Upsala 1819.

SETÄLÄ, E. N. *Sammon arvoitus*. Helsinki 1932.

SETÄLÄ, PÄIVI. "Moni/nainen historiaan." *Naishistorian sanoma*. In: P. Setälä & H. Kurki, *Akanvirtaan*. Helsinki 1988.

SIHVO, HANNES. *Karjala-kuva*. Suomalaisen Kirjallisuuden Seuran Toimituksia No. 314. Helsinki 1973.

————. "Virsiseppä Lönnrot." *Kalevalaseuran vuosikirja* 64, 1984.
————. "Karelia and the Karelians; Karelianism." *Finland: A Cultural Encyclopedia.* Helsinki 1997.
SIIKALA, ANNA-LEENA. *The Rite Technique of the Siberian Shaman.* FFC 220. Helsinki 1978.
————. "Shamanistic Themes in Finnish Poetry." *Traces of the Central Asian Culture in the North* (ed. Lehtinen, I.). Helsinki 1986.
————. *Suomalainen šamanismi.* Helsinki 1992.
SILTALA, JUHA. *Suomalainen ahdistus.* Keuruu 1992.
SJÖBLOM, TOM. *Menneisyyden malleja.* In: Ketola, K., et al., *Näköaloja uskontoon.* Helsinki 1997.
SJÖGREN, A. J. *Anteckningar om Församligarne i Kemi-Lappmarke.* Helsingfors 1828.
SKVR = *Suomen kansan vanhat runot I–XIV.* Helsinki 1908–1948.
SMIRNOV, K. A. "The Finns in Eastern Europe in the First Millennium B.C." *Traces of the Central Asian Culture in the North* (ed. Lehtinen, I.). Helsinki 1986.
SNELLMAN, J. V. *Läran om staten.* Helsingfors 1942.
SURAKKA, MARTTA. *Itäkarjalan luostarit. Karjalan historiaa.* Jyväskylä 1938.
TACITUS. *Germania.* Helsinki 1952.
TAIVALSAARI, EERO. "Sukulaisia tapaamassa Komissa." *Suomen kuvalehti* 1985.
TAKALA, LAURI. *Suomen evankelisen liikkeen historia 1.* Helsinki 1929.
TARKIAINEN, VILJO. "Kristfrid Ganander, Porthanin työtoveri." *Virittäjä* n:o 1, 1941.
TAWASTSTJERNA, ERIK. *Jean Sibelius I.* Helsinki 1965.
TENGSTRÖM, J. J. "Om några hinder för Finlands litteratur och cultur." *Aura* 1817–1818.
TOPELIUS, ZACHRIS. *Suomen kansan vanhoja runoja ynnä myös nykyisempiä lauluja I–IV.* Turku ja Helsinki 1822–1831.
TURI, JOHAN. *Muittalus samid birra.* København 1910.
þórsteins þáttr Tjaldstæings.-Fjörutíu íslendi-gafættir. Reykjavik 1904.
VAINSTEIN, S. I. "Shamanism in Tuva at the Turn of the Twentieth Century." *Shamanism in Eurasia* (ed. Hoppal, M.). Göttingen 1984.
————. "Origin of Reindeer-Herding in Eurasia." *Traces of the Central Asian Culture in the North* (ed. Lehtinen, I.). Helsinki 1986.
VÄISÄNEN, A. O. "Vienan-Karjalan kylissä. Piirteitä keräysmatkalta kesällä 1915." Article, SKS.
VALONEN, NIILO. "Ancient Folk Poetry in Eastern Karelian Petroglyphs." *Ethnologia Fennica* 1982–1983. Vammala 1984.
VIRTANEN, LEEA. "Is the Comparative Method Out of Date?" *Telling Reality: Folklore Studies in Memory of Bengt Holbek.* NIF Publications 26. Copenhagen-Turku 1993.
VIRTARANTA, PERTTI. *Vienan kansa muistelee.* Porvoo 1958.
WARGELIN-BROWN, MARIANNE. "American-Finnish Folklore." A paper presented in Prof. Pentikäinen's course "Finnish and Scandinavian Folklore," University of Minnesota, 1980.
WILENIUS, REIJO. "Lönnrot ja uskonto 1830–luvulla." *Kalevalaseuran vuosikirja* 64, 1984.
WILSON, WILLIAM A. *Folklore and Nationalism in Modern Finland.* Bloomington, Ind. 1976.
————. "Sibelius, the Kalevala, and Karelianism." *The Sibelius Companion* (ed. Goss, Glenda Dawn). Westport, Conn.-London 1996.

Index

JUHA H. PENTIKÄINEN, Professor of Comparative Religion at the University of Helsinki, has published numerous articles and twenty books. He has won two major folklore prizes, the Chicago Folklore Prize (1978) for *Oral Repertoire and World View* and the Pitre Folklore Prize (1990) for the first edition of *Kalevala Mythology*.

RITVA POOM writes about Finnish and Estonian culture. Her translations of Finnish and Estonian literature and ethnography have appeared in *Literary Review, Scandinavian Review, Drama Review,* and *Ethnologia Fennica*. Her translation *Fog Horses* received an award from the Columbia University Translation Center. She is the translator of *Estonian Short Stories* and the recipient of fellowships from the National Endowment for the Humanities and the National Endowment for the Arts.